TWIXT THE COMMONS

THE DEVELOPMENT OF A SOUTH LONDON SUBURB

TIMOTHY WALKER

First published in 2010 by
Timothy Walker

A CIP Catalogue of this book is available from
the British Library

ISBN: 978-0-9567163-0-9

CHANDLER
BOOK DESIGN

Typeset in Sabon 10½ by
www.chandlerbookdesign.co.uk

Printed in Great Britain by
Ashford Colour Press Ltd.

CONTENTS

Acknowledgements   vii

List of Illustrations   xi

List of Maps   xiv

Chapters		page
1	Introduction	1
2	Early Development – Merchants and Bankers	23
3	The suburbs come to South West London slowly	65
4	The suburbs come quickly	83
5	South Battersea – the housing starts	119
6	South Battersea – filled with terrace housing	139
7	The Dents and Old Park estates	177
8	How it happened	235
9	Old Park Avenue	261
10	The Houses – interior and exterior	295
11	The early twentieth century 1914-1945	335
12	Modern Times	361
13	Conclusions	399
Bibliography		403
Index		409

DEDICATION

For Anna, Sophie, Beth and Polly

ACKNOWLEDGEMENTS

Many people have helped me in the writing and production of this book; they have improved the book enormously but any omissions or inaccuracies are mine alone.

Peter Jefferson-Smith read an early draft and his knowledge of Clapham's history helped me fill in some gaps and correct a number of misunderstandings. Colin Thom generously shared his draft of a chapter on 'Twixt the Commons' for the Battersea volume of The Survey of London and we exchanged a number of sources. I benefitted greatly from the advice of two genuine historians, John Hardman and Roger Knight. Ian Rodger read the book not once but twice in great detail and I am very grateful indeed for his editing. It has made the book much more readable; all the errors remaining are mine.

Many organizations provided access to their Archives. Staff at the Wandsworth Historical Library were unfailingly helpful, as were those at the Lambeth Minet Library. Philip Gale and staff at the Church Commissioners Record Centre helped me locate the deeds of the Old Park Avenue Houses owned by the Church Commissioners and the Lambeth Palace Library provided a wonderful place to study them. I am also very grateful to Ruth MacLeod of the Wandsworth Historical Library for allowing me to have a copy of one map taken to the Lambeth Palace Library for reproduction and to staff there for agreeing to do so. I also owe thanks to staff at the London Metropolitan Archive and the National Archives.

A number of people kindly shared the results of their own research. Graham Fuller gave me helpful information on Erskine Clarke from his eagerly awaited biography. Ken and Suzanne Smith gave me information about her ancestor, John Coles, and Nick Dent about his ancestor, Robert Dent. Many people shared their memories of the area which often went back more than seventy years. I am particularly grateful to Derek Bird, Mary Hynds and Pat Williams (née Hynds) and to Josie Miller who sadly died earlier this year. I should also like to thank St Luke's Church Parochial Church Council for their kind permission to use extracts from the St Luke's parish magazine and to reproduce pictures from it and elsewhere.

I am also very grateful indeed for the cooperation of copyright holders listed below in granting permission to print relevant extracts from published works. Whilst every effort has been made to trace and make contact with copyright owners I regret that this has not always been possible.

Mike by PG Wodehouse : by permission of Sir Edward Cazalet and the Trustees of the P G Wodehouse Estate

The Life of Graham Greene by Norman Sherry, published by Jonathan Cape. Reprinted by permission of The Random House Group Ltd.

Things Can Only Get Better by John O'Farrell, published by Doubleday. Reprinted by permission of The Random House Group Ltd.

Extracts from *Charles Booth Handbooks* reproduced by permission of the London School of Economics

Present Indicative and *This Happy Breed* by Noel Coward © Methuen Drama, An imprint of A&C Black Publishers Ltd.

Falling Angels by John Walsh. Reprinted by permission of Harper Collins Publishers Ltd.© 1999 John Walsh

Excerpts by Stephen Potter from *Steps to Immaturity* (© Stephen Potter, 1959) are reproduced by permission of PFD (www.pfd.co.uk) on behalf of the Estate of Stephen Potter.

Extracts from *Marianne Thornton* by E M Forster are by permission of The Society of Authors as the literary representatives of the E M Forster Estate and the Provost and Scholars of King's College, Cambridge,

I am also grateful to copyright holders for permission to reproduce a number of images as below and to Alyson Wilson of the Clapham Society for providing a digital copy of illustration 36.

Maps 1, 3, 7 reproduced by permission of Ordnance Survey on behalf of HMSO. © Crown Copyright 2010. All rights reserved Licence Number100050009

Map 4 London Borough of Lambeth, Archives Department

Map 5 The London Topographical Society

Map 9 Wandsworth Historical Library

Maps 13, 14, 15, 16, 19 Reproduced by permission of the Church Commissioners.

Map 20 reproduced by permission of the City of London, London Metropolitan Archives

Illustrations	Copyright holder
3,31,56	Ron Elam
4,5,27,37	London Borough of Lambeth, Archives Department
9	City of London, London Metropolitan Archives
26, 46, 47, 49, 71, 75	St Luke's Parochial Church Council
36	Wandsworth Museum
72	London Transport Museum
73	RIBA Library Drawings Collection

All other illustrations are from the author's own collection including the author's own photographs.

I am, of course, particularly grateful to my family for putting up with an author in the family. They too have read various drafts and improved them, but equally importantly they have allowed me the time to write and borne with me as I have tried to explain what I am trying to achieve. It is not their fault if I have not been successful.

LIST OF ILLUSTRATIONS

CHAPTER 2

1	Battersea Bridge 1846 by Greaves	33
2	Old Clapham church in 1750 by William Prior	35
3	John Thornton's house as part of Notre Dame convent	38
4	Battersea Rise House	39
5	Broomfield Lodge (later Broomwood House)	41
6	View from Mr Akerman's house. Clapham Common 1790	51
7	View of Clapham Common in 1790	51
8	Spring well, Clapham Common 1820	51
9	Undertakers regaling themselves at Death's door	60

CHAPTER 3

10	Cubitt's houses: Victoria House, 84 Kings Avenue	73
11	Cubitt's houses: 126 Atkins Road	73
12	Barges at Battersea. Edmund Cook 1828	77
13	Launch of Luisa Shelbourne, Battersea 1864	77
14	Battersea Agricultural Show 1861	78
15	Pneumatic parcel handling 1861	79
16	207 Balham High Road	80

CHAPTER 4

17	Clapham High Street	102
18	Clapham Common underground station c 1904	104
19	Horse drawn cab Balham High Road 1899	113
20	Balham High Road c 1907	114
21	Balham High Road c 1911	114
22	Opening of Electric trams to Totterdown 1903	115

CHAPTER 5

23	Bolingbroke Arms pub	127
24	Stonell's Road	127

CHAPTER 6

25	Servants' door, Wakehurst Road	145
26	John Erskine Clarke	147
27	The Shrubbery	150
28	St Mark's School gable	155
29	St Mark's church	155
30	St Mark's School letter change	155
31	Bolingbroke House/hospital	164
32	Bolingbroke Hospital ward	166
33	Examples of 196-22 Broomwood Road	170
34	Hillier Road change of housing from gault to red brick	172
35	John Burns - Colossus	175

CHAPTER 7

36	Bolingbroke Grove House	179
37	Old Park, 1830	184
38	Nightingale Pub	188
39	Old Park sale advertisement, 1866	193
40	69-79 Nightingale Lane, T E Colcutt 1879	200
41	Post card Nightingale Lane	204
42	Post card Nightingale Lane	205
43	Post card Nightingale Lane	205
44a-d	E R Robson houses	210
45	Bill of sale for ground rents	218
46	Iron church	223
47	Iron Church	224
48	St Luke's church, c1904	226
49	St Luke's church, hall and vicarage	227

CHAPTER 8

50	Site of Arding and Hobbs store	236
51	New building of Arding and Hobbs store	237
52	Cycling in Battersea Park 1895	245
53	90 Alfriston Road	249

CHAPTER 9

54	1 Old Park Avenue built by Saker	268
55	30, 32 Old Park Avenue	271
56	View of Old Park Avenue c 1910	279
57	View of Old Park Avenue 2009	279

CHAPTER 10

58	Floor plans	299
59	Barge boarding in Honeywell Road	300
60	Belleville School	305
61	Sunflower from Old Park Avenue	307
62	Roof Crest in Old Park Avenue	308
63	Floor plan for Kettle Houses	309
64	Auction sale of 26 Old Park Avenue	314
65	Railings in Old Park Avenue	315
66	Hall floor tiles	318
67	Overdoor	320
68	Red marble fire place	325
69	Ceiling rose	328
70a	Claw and ball cornice	328
70b	Dentate cornice	328
70c	Plain cornice	328
71	Advertisement for electrician	331

CHAPTER 11

72	Clapham South tube station, 1926	344
73	Sign for Nightingale Lane tube station	344
74	Dainty advert	353
75	Dainty Shop front	354

LIST OF MAPS

CHAPTER 1

| Map 1 | Street map of area | 2 |

CHAPTER 2

Map 2	John Rocque's map of Surrey, 1745(detail)	23
Map 3	Parishes and postcodes	24
Map 4	Smith's map of houses round Clapham Common, 1800	52
Map 5	Thomas Milne's land use map 1800	57

CHAPTER 5

| Map 6 | Stanford map, 1862 | 120 |
| Map 7 | Twixt the Commons street map | 123 |

CHAPTER 6

| Map 8 | Roads and land boundaries | 143 |
| Map 9 | Sale of Battersea Rise House, 1907 | 173 |

CHAPTER 7

Map 10	Boundaries from 1836 Tithe map	179
Map 11	John Cary's map, 1790 (detail)	183
Map 12	Sale of Old Park, 1876	196
Map 13	Sale of Dent's estate, 1868	206
Map 14	Residual Dent's estate, 1872	208
Map 15	Original plans for land in mortgage, 1882	212
Map 16	Sale of ground rents, 1893	215

CHAPTER 8

| Map 17 | Charles Booth Poverty map 1900 | 250 |
| Map 18 | Roads and boundaries | 259 |

CHAPTER 9

| Map 19 | Location of the mound | 272 |

CHAPTER 11

| Map 20 | Second World War bombs | 356 |

CHAPTER 1

INTRODUCTION

'The Victorian suburb must not only be one of the most obvious but also one of the darkest corners of English social history.'

So wrote Jim Dyos[1] in his book on Camberwell some forty years ago. This book tries to shed some light on the subject for a small area of south west London only slightly further from the centre than Camberwell. It covers two, interconnected, subjects. The first deals with the local history, that is to say the inhabitants, the roads, the houses and the builders. This is necessarily detailed but it has enough colour to be of interest to the general reader as well as those who live in the area. The second subject is the underlying rationale for people moving in and out of the southern London suburbs and the reasons why the present houses were designed as they are. This reflects the interplay of large numbers of builders, investors and customers, in turn influenced by a variety of social and economic factors and displaying the usual cycles of economics and fashion. This second theme provides the context for the more detailed study and is illustrated by it. In turn the history of almost three hundred years of part of south west London is an example of how the capital as a whole was developed.

My own journey

Kate Tiller argued that local historians should always be prepared to use their work to shed light on wider concerns, claiming:

'Local history should understand itself, and be understood by other historians, as part of the same intellectual history as general history, and as bringing unique value to that general history.'[2]

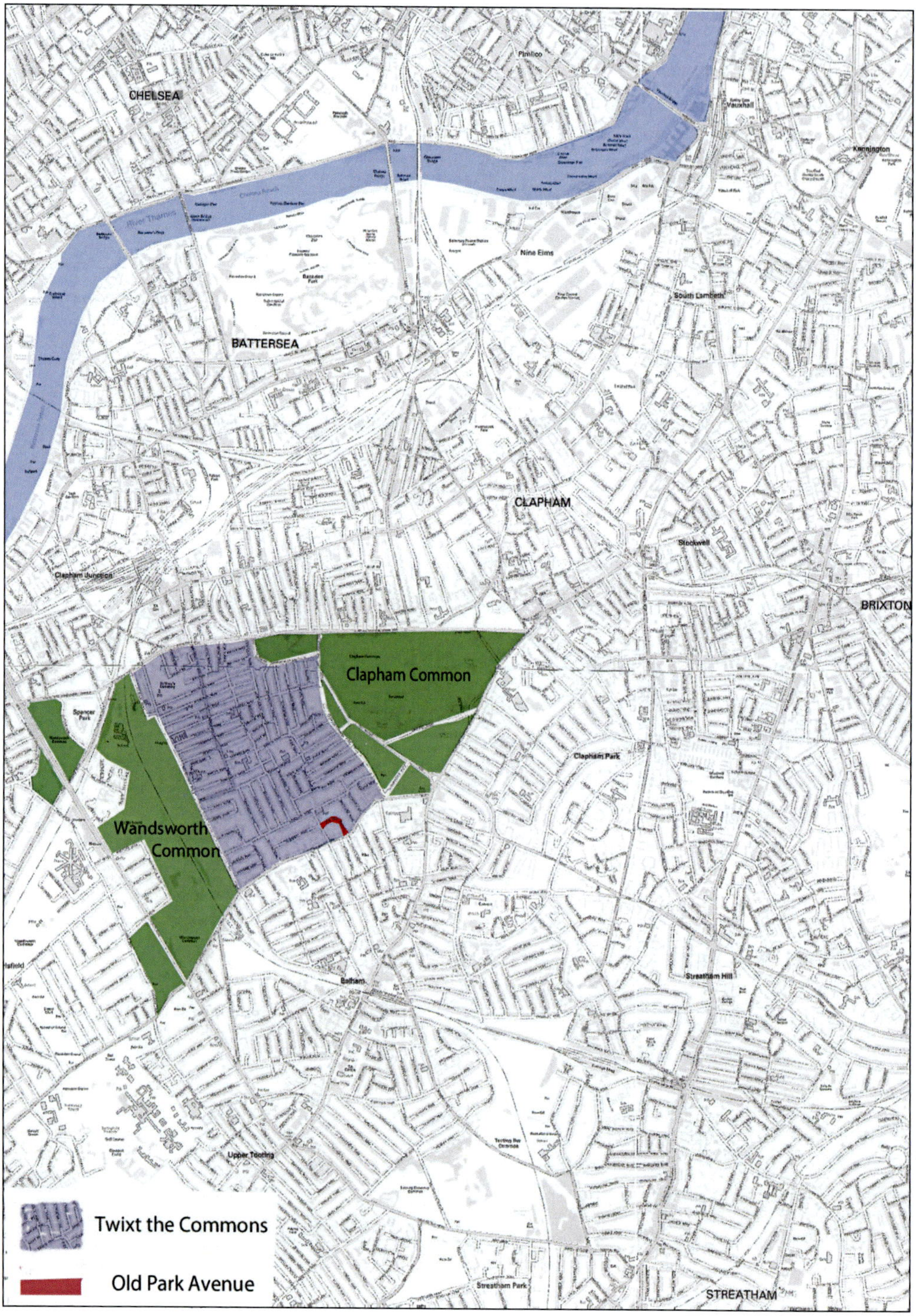

Map 1: Street map of area

This is the challenge that I set myself, but the idea of shedding light on changing populations and the cycle of wealth, decline and wealth again, was not quite where I started. The book began from a long standing desire to understand the specific history of the house I have lived in for the last twenty five years. It is located in Old Park Avenue, part of a neighbourhood in south west London lying between Wandsworth and Clapham Commons which reached its present urban form in the last quarter of the nineteenth century and the first few years of the twentieth century. This area has variously been called Clapham, Battersea, Balham, New Wandsworth, and just plain Wandsworth, but in the last 20 years its position between the two commons has resulted in estate agents coining a new name for it, 'Twixt the Commons'. Map 1 shows how it relates to the neighbouring parts of South London.

The house is very similar to the 29 others in the street, built by two different builders during 1890-1901, so my interest extended naturally to the history of the whole street. The advantage of concentrating on a single street with a small number of houses of relatively few designs is that the data can be collected fairly easily, individual names can be tracked, relationships between neighbours recognised, deeds compared, and a fairly complete picture obtained. A good picture can also be pieced together of the original internal layout and fittings from what is left in a number of the houses.

Old Park Avenue is similar to many other Victorian streets of semi-detached houses in South London. It was developed in the same ways, requiring the demolition of an eighteenth century house, and has gone through the same transition as much of Victorian housing, starting with single family occupation, moving gradually into multi-occupation from the early 1930s. As elsewhere, bombs dropped on the road in the Second World War, in this case destroying two houses, and property was bought – and later sold – by the local authority as its political complexion changed. Finally the street went through the same metamorphosis as many other parts of London and changed back, largely to single family occupation, after the gentrification that began, in Old Park Avenue at least, in the mid 1970s.

No apology is needed for being interested in the history of either one's own home or street and this is becoming increasingly common. Julie Myerson[3] produced both a book and radio serial about 'all the people who had ever lived in her house' – also in Clapham – and at least one estate agent now has an in-house historian who will do the necessary work for a purchaser. Their fliers promoting their properties give advice on how to do one's own research. The Financial Times weekend supplement 'House and Home'[4] even had a front page spread on this service.

As I became more familiar with how my immediate surroundings had been developed, I realised that their development could only be understood in the context of a larger geographical area. But how large should that larger area be? The whole of London is too large although there will be many necessary references to London as a whole, even if only for comparison, London remains the backdrop rather than the main subject. For reasons that I hope will become clear, I decided that it made sense to focus the most detailed study on the area between the two commons, or 'Twixt the Commons'.

This does not avoid entirely the need to look at a somewhat wider geographic area. This extension is necessary because what now seem well characterised neighbourhoods did not exist in the middle of the nineteenth century or were defined very differently. There have been frequent changes to the administrative boundaries. Map 1 shows the boundaries of 'Twixt the Commons' set in a current street map of inner south west London. The surrounding area includes the western part of the historical parish of Clapham, the southern part of Battersea, and the small part of the parish of Streatham which included Balham.

I also learnt that Victorian development was not random and could only be understood by looking at what had happened in the two centuries before the street was built. The former mediaeval parish boundaries do still have an influence, as do several other factors, such as the patterns of land ownership that prevailed two or three hundred years ago, the timing of the sale of particular land for development, and even the shape or size of the individual fields, the location of the main roads to the coast, and the path of the streams that used to wander into the Thames. Many of the place names have long antecedents or refer to previous owners or occupiers. The architectural historian, John Summerson, identified the potential interest here[5], referring to the 'planless sprawl' of the suburbs.

'But it is also something which really happened and is really there and was made by real people and for which there are brutish, involuntary but still human reasons if you can discover them. If the study of modern man and his environment is worth anything they are worth discovering.'

By the end of the nineteenth century, according to the architectural historian Stefan Muthesius[6], the vast majority of Englishmen, including the middle and lower classes, lived in neatly ordered and at least moderately ornamented terraced houses. A historian of London housing recently summarised it in much the same way[7].

'When the first World War began in 1914, London's ordinary housing stock, like that for most cities, was dominated by small private houses for rent by the better paid working class and middle class, erected by speculative builders on cheap land and sold in the private property market as an investment.'

All this encourages the desire to understand how it all happened and to answer a number of questions. Who built and who financed this development? Why are the 'original features' as they are? Who moved into the rows of terrace and semi detached houses? How did they fare in the twentieth century? In short, how did large areas of London get to look like they do now?

I naturally looked to see what other research had been done. While there has been a considerable amount written on housing development both at the London and borough level, the content tends to be either statistical and difficult to relate to smaller geographical areas or anecdotal supported by carefully collected pictures. Most work which has been carried out on even part of this lengthy process has concentrated on the Georgian or early Victorian years. Others have studied gentrification, often to prove a political point. Apart from Dyos' pioneering book on Camberwell almost fifty years ago, virtually the only systematic attempt to understand the development of a London Victorian suburb is Gillian Tindall's book on Kentish Town,[8] and that too was written thirty years ago when gentrification was just beginning. To my knowledge no one has tried to cover the whole period together, including the late twentieth century, for a distinct geographical area as opposed to a statistical exercise for all London. Nor is it usual to combine local demographic and economic material with an analysis of the interior and exterior design which itself contains information on the people for whom the houses were built. This book attempts to do so.

One possible reason for the relative lack of analytic books of this kind is the attitude to local history. Local history was for a long time looked down on by 'professional' historians who wrote about the State, battles, the constitution and politics and the people deemed to influence such matters. It was regarded, often correctly in practice, as no more than an antiquarian collection of fact, anecdote, or even local myth justified by repetition rather than evidence, and without any analysis or context. Later in the twentieth century, it became accepted, at least in principle, that local history could serve to illustrate the themes of national history, particularly in economic history, and more recently there has been interest in its contribution to social history. Even so, as Gillian Tindall remarked in the introduction to her book[9], there was a tendency to suppose that local history was only worth investigating in depth about places which were in some predetermined sense 'interesting', which meant 'historical' with 'old' buildings still standing. She contrasted the large number of books written on Hampstead with the few on Kentish Town.

The story – early suburbs

'London what are your suburbs but licensed Stewes?'

Although Clapham and Battersea go back to Saxon times and probably earlier, they were country villages and no part of London. Indeed, there were few if any suburbs then and the word had a rather different meaning. It comes from Cicero's 'suburbium' through Old French and first appears in English in Wyclif in the early 1380s, defined by the Oxford English Dictionary as the residential parts belonging to a town or city that lie immediately outside and adjacent to its walls and boundaries. The subsidiary meaning of a place of inferior, debased and especially licentious habits of life gives a clear idea of how these places were viewed. Chaucer[10] had his canon's yeoman living in the suburbs 'lurking in corners and blind alleys where robbers and thieves instinctively huddle secretly and fearfully together'. 'Suburban' became a term of abuse and a suburb sinner was another phrase for prostitute. The quotation at the head of this section is from Nashe's analysis [11] of the vices of contemporary society at the end of the sixteenth century. The word 'stewe' meant brothel, a reference to Southwark whose brothels had been licensed by the Bishop of Winchester in the early fifteenth century until closed, at least officially, by Henry VIII in the middle of that century.

In 1550 the City Guilds had received charters extending to the suburbs their powers to control their crafts, but they were unable to put these into practice on any consistent basis. As a result, craft and manufacturing grew quicker there than anywhere else. By 1580, the suburbs were a source of pressure on food supply as well as a breeding ground for plague. Elizabeth issued the first royal proclamation forbidding the building of houses or tenements within three miles of the City gates where none had stood before and similar proclamations followed at regular intervals under both James I and Charles I. Enforcement was patchy, to say the least, and in any case both Stuart kings found selling permissions to illicit dwellings a useful source of extra-parliamentary revenue. Expansion continued accordingly and as late as under the Commonwealth, Parliament tried the same, passing a law that fined an owner of a new house, out-house or other building, a year's rent but only if built on a new foundation or with less than four acres of adjacent land.

It is instructive at the same time to compare the geographical extent of the suburbs. Southwark was always the most obvious, but Fleet Street was still described as a suburb in 1439. The seventeenth century saw this extended to Houndsditch, Covent Garden and Hackney [12] and gradually the term 'suburban' became a term of commendation rather than the reverse. The Oxford English Dictionary gives positive references as early as 1661 such as 'The rich had stately monuments on the sides of the publick ways in their own suburban fields'. By the middle of the eighteenth century it was possible to express the hope that 'the air of your agreeable suburbane North-End will restore you' and in 1781 Cowper, the evangelical poet supported by Clapham bankers, wrote in 'Retirement'.

'Suburban villas, highway-side retreats
That dread th'encroachment of our growing streets'

What had changed? A study of Clapham and its neighbouring parishes helps to answer this question.

The story - how the suburbs developed

In all cases and at all times it must be remembered that suburbs, the smaller individual neighbourhoods, sometimes even individual roads, were keen to differentiate themselves to retain – or even improve - their relative desirability. The ability to create and manage these differences was key to whether an area was able to achieve and maintain status, as described by Dyos and Reeder[13].

'The middle class suburb was an ecological marvel
...... it offered an arena for the manipulation of social
distinctions to those most adept at turning them into
shapes on the ground; it kept the threat of rapid social
change beyond the horizon of those least able to accept
its negative as well as positive advantages.'

As is still the case, the choice of where to live helped to define who you were. Many guides gave advice on the most appropriate locations and helped the supplicant find 'respectability', summed up by Dyos[14].

'Suburban respectability was largely a matter of the
right address and possession of it was the source of an
indefinable satisfaction that did not evaporate until the
social structure of the suburb was unbalanced by the
emigration of its top people and the immigration of a
different breed of people from the inner suburbs'.

South West London began the eighteenth century largely as countryside with the population engaged in agricultural pursuits. Soon it began to be recognised as a very desirable place to live and was colonised first by the wealthy and then the not so wealthy but still affluent, supported of course by those needed to provide the services required by big houses. Greater affluence was always an important element in the change but there were others too, notably: a move away from living over work, whether voluntary or forced; the availability of regular, safe, and affordable transport; the availability of land and finance for its development and the desire for a 'safe' investment. At the same time, people sought a better and healthier environment – salubriousness was a strong selling point which Clapham's clean air and water provided. Finally, the desire for a change in living style should not be underestimated, sometimes for more time spent with the family and sometimes less.

The balance between these different motivations varied from time to time, not least reflecting how much it was a genuine choice and how much forced by circumstances. We can distinguish five waves of changing population. The first saw rich bankers and merchants move from living 'over the shop' in the City, initially to weekend houses and then moving their wives and families out of central London entirely. Clapham was the fashionable suburb par excellence in the second part of the eighteenth century, and probably the richest in London with up to six governors of the Bank of England living around the Common and the Clapham Sect centred on Henry Thornton's house on Battersea Rise.

The second wave involved the less wealthy, but still comfortably off, moving to the areas freed up by the rich moving either further away or back to the middle of London. But Clapham was still a force to be reckoned with, and even by the third quarter of the nineteenth century, its intellectual societies were interesting enough to entice Tennyson, Browning and Huxley from London.

In the second half of the nineteenth century the forces for change began to bear on larger less well-off groups. Population pressures in central London were exacerbated by redevelopment to make better economic use of the land; jobs changed; transport improved. Those with less money were enabled - or forced - to move out to what were still thought of as London's suburbs. This third wave saw the large scale movement of clerks and artisans into rows of terraced or semi-detached houses built on land formerly occupied by large villas with gardens. This takes us to the end of Victoria's reign and the start of the twentieth century. By then the area had already started to decline in attractiveness. The term 'man on the Clapham omnibus' (coined by a judge building on a phrase of the nineteenth century editor of the Economist, Walter Bagehot) was used as an example of extreme normality; later Clapham was cited as an example of lack of taste[15].

It was perhaps no coincidence therefore that H M Bateman, the great cartoonist of suburbia, was brought up and lived in Clapham and Balham, living for some time in a house just round the corner from mine and built by the same builder. By this time the word 'suburban' had gone full cycle and was again a term of abuse, although of a rather different kind to the fifteenth century. This is captured by the Edwardian commentator, T W H Crosland[16].

> 'To the superior mind, in fact, 'suburban' is a sort of label which may properly be applied to pretty well everything on the earth that is ill-conditioned, undesirable and unholy. If a man or a woman have a fault of taste, of inclination, of temperament, of breeding, or even of manner, the superior mind proceeds, on little wings of haste to pronounce that fault 'suburban'.

The last two major changes in suburban living in London had no single cause but a coming together of a variety of different factors. What was still a fashionable and affluent suburb until the middle of the nineteenth century, and in some places for longer, declined still further in the first sixty years of the twentieth century. Why live in an old unmodernised Victorian house when the delights of new housing in the next circle of suburbs were available? The large houses were no longer suitable for smaller, often nuclear, families, and the small houses did not attract. It declined into bedsit land, multi-occupancy bringing with it a relatively high proportion of immigrants both before and after the Second World War. The fourth wave is therefore the movement after the First World War to the outer suburbs with continuing decline until the end of the 1960s; Peter Sellers' vignette of Balham as the 'Gateway to the South' is still remembered fifty years later.

And then the wheel turned again. Leases fell due and ground rents were bought up, even before their formal end ninety nine years after the houses were built. Rehabilitation became more fashionable than demolition and new build. The middle class sought to benefit from investment in their own housing. The costs of commuting out of

London rose in relation to inner city housing, all the more so if sitting tenants could be made to leave. Families where the wife wanted – and expected – to work had differing needs. Combined together these caused the fifth and so far final wave, younger professional families being more attracted to living closer in to the centre of London, This helped to fuel the process sometimes known as gentrification which continues to the present day, when the house prices are such that only the rich can afford them and, although there are still pockets of relative poverty, the area is more consistently affluent than it has ever been and with about 20,000 inhabitants.

For many generations the communities were based on the old ecclesiastical parish boundaries with the Parochial Church Council, the only form of local government, often being chaired by the Vicar or the Churchwardens. Even apart from providing the boundaries and the local government, the established church, and from the middle of the nineteenth century churches of all denominations, continued to play an important role in the community. Of course, this could only be a surprise to someone living in the twenty first century. Charles Booth's study of life and labour in London in 1900 devoted no fewer than five volumes to the role of the various churches in society, analysing what kind of person attended the various denominations. The importance of the Church of England was captured by a church historian in 1964[17].

> '[The Church of England] mattered in the ordinary course of life to a degree now to many people incredible; it lay inescapably across the workaday paths of the lawyer, the politician, the magistrate, the farmer and the labourer; it could scarcely be avoided by the man of property, the ratepayer, the lover, the father, and the corpse.'

Both Battersea and Clapham knocked down their mediaeval churches and built new larger ones towards the end of the eighteenth century, not an era greatly known for church building. The grouping round Henry Thornton and William Wilberforce, later known as Clapham Sect, was based at Holy Trinity, Clapham Common, and had great influence both locally and nationally. Charles Spurgeon, the great Baptist preacher, lived in the area and in the last quarter of the nineteenth century, the Vicar of Battersea, Canon John Erskine Clarke played an important role, building 11 churches in Battersea as well as schools, hospitals, and dispensaries, and being involved in many local issues including the naming of roads. He too had a national role, having started the first parish magazine when he was Vicar of Derby and editing two successful boys' magazines for many years. The churches he built still play an important part in the community and two of them may have larger congregations now that they did at the start of the twentieth century.

The houses

> 'Truly the state of London houses and London house-building at this time, who shall express how detestable it is, how frightful!'

> '.... the genuinely and decisively valuable feature of the English house is its absolute practicability. Whatever it is, it is a house in which people want to live.'

These two quotations give two pictures of London's housing. The first, from Thomas Carlyle[18] in 1867, is typical of the period, and the unattractiveness of the suburban townscape was accepted by arbiters of taste. In 1878 Charles Eastlake commented in his influential 'Hints on Household Taste'[19].

> 'Most of us are obliged to accept the outward appearance of our abode as we find it. In London it is as a rule irretrievably ugly, and any attempt to alter its character would be met not only by a remonstrance on the part of our landlords, but by a universal objection shared by all of us, and founded on an inherent disinclination to differ conspicuously from our neighbours.'

(Note also Eastlake's implicit acknowledgement of the almost universality then of private renting rather than owner occupation.)

Hermann Muthesius, the German architect posted by his government in 1896 to the embassy in London to investigate British housing, was equally dismissive[20].

'Like the suburbs of the great English industrial centres, the inner suburbs of London, most particularly lying to the east and south, are covered by endless expanses of small houses all exactly alike. The deadening uniformity that we noted in the terraced houses of the city reaches its peak in the suburbs and anyone approaching London above the roofs of these little houses has only to glance at this sea of dwellings to feel something of the misery that seems to prevail there. The commercially-minded ruthlessness of the developer reigns triumphant...... The streets have been laid out with dull-witted indifference.'

But despite his evident distaste, Muthesius recognised that the houses met a need very successfully.

'And yet these little houses fulfil their purpose. Here they have at least a measure of independence and quiet, they are nearer to the soil and in a home that is easily reached from the street, they cultivate their gardens and, best of all, know that they are masters in their own houses. The basic form of these houses is immutably fixed, as a mass produced article, and in every respect they are built so cheaply that, in return for a low rent, the lessee or owner lives in a relatively comfortable and sound house which would not be available to him in any other way.... Who knows how long the houses will stand...'

The second quotation at the head of this section is also from Muthesius[21]. It emphasises that although the townscape was thought unattractive by many of those looking from outside, the houses were liked by those who lived in them at the time. For this reason it is important to look at the nature of the houses, their layout and decoration, and to match these up with who built and lived in them. This is relatively untouched territory. Much has been written on the eighteenth century suburbs of London, or more accurately on those with many houses remaining from the eighteenth century or even before, but Victorian suburbs have received less attention. This is probably because until relatively recently Victorian housing, particularly en masse, continued to be thought unattractive and was not lived in by those likely to investigate their history. Summerson[22], writing on Victorian Architecture dismissed such building with 'The enormous increment of suburbia will not be our concern at all.'

Whatever their aesthetic merits, these houses provided homes for London's rapidly growing population in the second half of the nineteenth century when England was at the peak of its power. Lack of suitable housing was a major problem and population growth continued to outstrip provision of new housing. There was little innovation in the mechanics of house building and the costs of housing space rose in real terms for most of the nineteenth century. As a result, housing absorbed enormous amounts of capital - and labour - and, as now, played an important part in economic development. It was all financed speculatively by the private sector, mostly by small investors, meeting a range of defined and usually satisfied markets. Further, there was little in the way of controls. Attempts to stop building by the most local of the authorities involved were routinely overruled, and a unified streetscape was dependent on a developer using a single builder or, rarely in South Battersea, imposing the same plan on a number of builders. Land ownership was generally fragmented and there were few attempts to impose, let alone maintain, standards for any sustained period. This contrasts with the firm (and continuing) controls of the Alleyn's estate in Dulwich, only a couple of miles away, which enables the author of The Book of Herne Hill[23] to comment,

> 'The management of the estates ensured that the Dulwich and Herne Hill remained far more pleasant that any of South London's suburbs and did not later have to be cleared of slums.'

In the event only one street between Wandsworth and Clapham Commons was subject to slum clearance, which suggests that a range of other factors may have influenced whether or not houses became a slum. Indeed we shall see that for many years the houses were thought to be desirable.

Muthesius' view quoted above is paralleled by some German friends visiting London in the last few years. At first they could not understand why anyone would want to own, let alone live in, one of a row of apparently identical houses. Yet having visited a few in the road, they recognised that individuality is expressed not in the exterior arrangements but in the internal. Indeed our friends commented that they had not realised that there could be so much variety in internal arrangements in what had looked to them to be identical houses. This might lead us to review the received wisdom about the Victorian suburb as does the chronicler of the growth of Victorian London, Donald Olsen[24].

> 'Even the much maligned speculative building of the Victorians, when painted, cleaned, fitted with bathrooms and central heating, and manageably compact kitchens, provides as satisfactory a domestic environment as anything our architects and planners can construct for us afresh.'

It is worth mentioning one cautionary point. There are substantial differences between North and South London and not just because some believe that the South is essentially less fashionable than the North. Much of South London was developed in the last quarter of the nineteenth century while the corresponding North London suburbs were more likely to have been built in the first half of Victoria's reign, say by 1870. Because of this we cannot assume the reasons for people moving are the same. The houses also often have different interior design and arrangements; relatively few houses in South London have a basement and there are usually three rather than two rooms on a floor.

A note on Sources

Making the local history come alive also requires detailed information about who lived in the houses and this comes from a variety of sources. This section explains how these can be used to get as full a picture as possible of the inhabitants. It gives confidence in the results but can be skipped by those less interested in the detail.

The most detailed source is the various census records, starting in 1841 and repeated every ten years, with each successive census asking yet more information. Until recently the last census whose results were published was 1901, but the 1911 Census recently became available. This can be backed up by electoral registers which recorded those with the right to vote, and Rate Books which recorded those liable for the local Rates, usually (but not always) the owner of the freehold or the holder of a long lease. The rate books go back the furthest, certainly to the middle of the eighteenth century and the rateable value also gives some idea of the size of the piece of land. None of these records is perfect; electoral registers exclude those not entitled to vote such as women and most servants (for much of the period), and, of course, children. The Census will miss those abroad or staying elsewhere, while rate books do not necessarily record the occupier as opposed to the freeholder or possessor of a long lease.

These main sources are supplemented by a number of more specific records such as deeds, wills, local newspapers, street directories, parish magazines, and by a range of maps, of which one of the most important is the 1836 Tithe map which recorded the pattern of land ownership in that year. The Inland Revenue record of property for land tax purposes (IR58) gives detailed information for the period 1910 until 1920 when the relevant tax was discontinued. Birth, marriage and death certificates also give additional information, particularly about family relationships, and telephone directories become relevant early in the twentieth century. Sources such as these have allowed a considerable amount of information to be extracted about those who lived 'Twixt the Commons' which has informed the detailed chapters later in the book. A major help has been the ability to search databases by computer made possible by a number of organizations, including Ancestry.co.uk and Findmypast.com.

Unfortunately, the information gets less complete and sketchier as one moves on from the published 1901 and 1911 Censuses towards the present day. Although the census at a detailed level is not yet available after 1911, there is some information about the occupiers from other sources. While the right to vote, and hence a place in the electoral roll, was extended in 1918 to all men over 21, with a proviso of six months residence, the only women then included were those over 30 whose property entitled them to vote in local government elections, or the wives of husbands so entitled. It was only in 1928 that the vote was extended to all women over 21. The electoral roll can also be cross-checked against the rate book (which contains details of the house-owner), postal directories or even telephone directories as the phones began to be taken up in greater numbers. These all suffer from a bias against children and those who moved frequently as well as those who did not want to pay for an entry in a directory. There is also likely to be a bias in the searching, in that it is easier in practice to find people who already lived in the area or who were born and stayed in the UK.

This means that it is hard to work out the family or other structure of a group of people living at the same house, and virtually impossible to identify servants as opposed to lodgers. Not everyone gave all the information to the tax collector. Not everyone is included and children are particularly difficult to trace. Many of them depend on handwriting, often copied more than once with the inevitable mistakes. Often the clerk recording the names was disinclined to record an uncommon name, for example Milln was variously recorded as Milne, Milner, Miller, as well as the correct spelling. Ailsa was recorded as Alice. Even before Sydney Presburg changed his name to Presbury, both the census and the rate books recorded his name as one and sometimes the other as the relatively unusual 'g' was transmuted into a 'y'.

Generally it is necessary to examine a variety of sources and combine them to help complete the picture. This becomes like a crossword puzzle and here it becomes possible to use the 1901 previous censuses and more recently that of 1911, to piece together a picture of the family. This is particularly easy when there are unusual names, or combination of names or occupations, in the family (eg Burton Ravenscroft, The Rev Nicholas Kelynack, Thurza Saul, Phyllis Gotto). There is only one person in the census for any years with a name such as Cornelius James Wernham, Bennett Greasley Saywell, or Winstanley Gifford Stratford, but this is not necessarily conclusive of having found the right person without some further corroborating evidence, particularly if the name only appears in a single census some long time in advance of the appearance in some reference to Old Park Avenue. The combination of censuses and marriage or birth certificates can often be used to work out relationships such as brother or mother in law living with a family or to confirm which names belong to parents and which to children. For example one can use the fact that children appear on the electoral roll once they reach 21 to guess their date of birth and confirm by finding the birth certificate. Death registers which also give age at death can also help confirm the links between the different references to the same person.

The censuses up to and including 1911 allowed considerable information about date and place of births and occupation which has formed the basis for the detailed analysis of the people who lived in the roads between the commons in the latter half of the nineteenth century. For Old Park Avenue, where I wanted more detail, it also proved possible, with much work and computer searching, to trace virtually everybody who was recorded as living in the road during the first forty or fifty years of its existence and to establish something about their age and relationships. Some further reassurance of the validity of these methods is given by the results of the 1911 Census. These only became available relatively recently, and confirmed the information that had already been produced about the inhabitants of the road with only one change – the names of some servants who were 'house sitting' during the occupants' absence. Two examples of how these sources can be made to work are given in an Appendix to this chapter.

Structure of the book

'Suburbia has many aspects and to take one suburb and scrutinize it, take it apart and minutely describe its components, is to learn – and to teach – about suburbia itself. To explain one part is to unlock the whole.'

Summerson's words, written almost forty years ago[25], set out the basic premise of this book, that a study of a small local area of London's housing can shed light on wider issues and that the area around my particular street allows such illumination. An appreciation of this part of the city's history is the key to understanding its present and perhaps its future.

Answering these questions provides the elements of the structure of the book. I start by describing the development of inner south west London– essentially Clapham, part of Battersea and Balham, and then concentrate on smaller and smaller areas. After the wider south west London, the focus closes in on what used to be called South Battersea, although in the nineteenth century many tried to avoid the appellation of Battersea by calling it 'New Wandsworth'. Part of it is, or has been called, Clapham, and some of it is now in Balham, although this is another label sometimes avoided by those who live there. Its latest name, certainly in estate agent speak, is 'Twixt the Commons' since it lies between Clapham and Wandsworth Commons. The next tighter focus is to consider the development on two adjacent estates located between the commons, Dent's and Old Park, both of which were owned by different parts of the Dent family. This naturally moves on to the history of Old Park Avenue, built after the demolition of the eighteenth century house, Old Park.

This is followed by an analysis of the detailed interior and exterior design of the houses, described by Helen Long[26] as another previously neglected area. This analysis explains why English housing of the time was so different from that in continental Europe and helps to understand the clientele whom the developers and builders were aiming to attract. Victorian suburban design was well behind the latest thinking, although the Arts and Crafts movement had some impact on exterior design, largely through the associated Queen Anne style, and a number of Edwardian houses in the area have significant Art Nouveau features. Two final chapters cover the twentieth century and up to the present day.

The book quotes contemporary sources to understand how the area was viewed by those who lived there, or might be contemplating living there, and how that view changed over time. These sources come from the large numbers of histories produced in the nineteenth century, the guides to Victorian suburbs which, although sometimes reading like estate agent speak, still contain some clear views about the relative attractiveness of areas. The large number of guides to household taste and manners help explain what lay behind the exterior and interior design of the houses. Charles Booth, or his researchers, investigated the life of Londoners by walking and commenting on the streets of Battersea, having interviewed policemen as well as local priests and ministers. Local newspapers also add background as do parish magazines; the title deeds of the houses often record many different transactions over long periods of time and other local material, including the prospectus for auction sales, adds further colour. There is no direct South London counterpart for Mr Pooter in George Grossmith's classic of nineteenth century literature about suburban clerks, Diary of a Nobody, but a number of novels have been set in the area. Autobiographies and biographies also record the lives and impressions of those who lived there.

The road also has its own humorist, Stephen Potter, the inventor of the concepts of Gamesmanship and Oneupmanship, who was born there in 1900 and whose autobiography gives a picture of what Old Park Avenue was like to live in at the start of the last century.

Oral history is also an important input about the last seventy years and the combination of gentrification and Wandsworth politics have stimulated a number of recent sociological studies of 'Twixt the Commons' which have reached conclusions of varying value, such as the following, 'The common good in Battersea is established through market based commonalities of interest based upon households acting atomistically'[27].

Overall, I am trying to meet the two aims of covering both local history and illustrating the great changes that created London's south western suburbs. This is at least a first step in shedding light on this 'darkest corner' of English social history and confirming Summerson's assertion that it is indeed worth discovering the reasons for the 'planless suburbs' being as they are.

(Endnotes)

1   H J Dyos. 1961 Victorian Suburb p11
2   Kate Tiller. 1998 English Local History: The State of the Art p6
3   Julie Myerson. 2004 Home
4   Financial Times. 16 June 2007
5   In Foreword to H J Dyos. Ibid p 9
6   S Muthesius. 1982 The English Terraced House p 11
7   Colin Thom. 2005 Researching London's Houses
8   Gillian Tindall. 1977 The Fields Beneath
9   Gilliam Tindall. Ibid p 15
10 Geoffrey Chaucer. 1386 Canon Yeoman's Prologue l 104
11 Thomas Nashe. 1593 Christ's Teares over Jerusalem
12 Oxford English Dictionary
13 Dyos and Reeder. in Dyos and Wolff Ibid 1973 p 369
14 H J Dyos. Ibid p 23
15 T W H Crosland 1905 The Suburbans
16 T W H Crosland. Ibid p 8
17 G F A Bell. 1964 Temporal Pillars p 9
18 Thomas Carlyle. 1867 'Shooting Niagara: and after?' Macmillan's Magazine, xvi 332
19 Charles Eastlake. 1878 Hints on Household Taste Fourth Edition p 41
20 H Muthesius. 1904 The English House p 146 in English edition of 1979
21 H Muthesius. Ibid p 146
22 John Summerson. 1973 'London the Artifact' in The Victorian City ed Dyos and Wolff p 311
23 Patricia M Jenkins. 2003 The Book of Herne Hill p7
24 Donald J Olsen. 1976 The Growth of Victorian London p 332
25 Foreword to H J Dyos. Ibid p 9
26 Helen Long. 1993 The Edwardian House p 2
27 Butler and Robson. 2001 Urban Studies 38 p 2151

Appendix: Using the census

Charles H Garland moved into 21 Old Park Avenue in 1905/6 and Jennie Garland joins the electoral roll in 1918. The Rate Book for 1910 shows that the house was owned by a Miss Jennie Ohlson, although by 1911 the owner was listed as Charles Garland. Checking the marriage lists shows that Charles Garland married Jennie Ohlson in 1905. She had been living with her father, a gold jeweller, at 5 The Chase, in Clapham in 1901, while Charles had been living with his widowed mother and siblings in 39 Broadhinton Road. The Inland Revenue records in the tax return IR58 show that the house was sold at the end of 1904 (for £555) ie when the Garlands moved in, and records a number of transactions subsequently, although it is not possible to tie them unambiguously with the various changes of occupation. The birth of a child, Charles Ohlson L Garland in 1909, suggests that we do indeed have the right identification comes from with final confirmation in the 1911 Census.

The second case involves the Bodger family. Frank Bodger appears for the first time on the electoral register for 4 Old Park Avenue in 1911. He is also in the Rate Book for the same address in 1911 and in the IR58 as owner at the inspection in 1912. He is identified as a juror from 1922 until 1929, the last time a Bodger appears. The Rate Book for 1925 also lists him as owner. All this is consistent. In 1918 he is joined as an elector by Alice Bodger and by two others, William and Thurza Saul. Bodger is not a very common name and by searching the 1901 Census one finds a Frank Bodger, born in 1871, married to an Alice Bodger, born in 1870, living at 49 Rathbone Place, Marylebone. Happening to look at the rest of that census page, one sees that a William and Thurza Saul were living next door at 47 Rathbone Place, and checking the marriage lists, one finds that a Frank Bodger married an Alice Saul in 1899. This suggests that this is the Frank and Alice Bodger who lived at 4 Old Park Avenue, and that they were joined after a few years by Alice's parents; the 1911 Census confirms this interpretation. We also find from earlier censuses that Frank's elder brother, Alfred, lived in nearby Salcott Road with his in-laws in 1891 so this is probably the way that Frank got to know the area.

William Saul no longer appears on the electoral roll after

1918, and one finds the death of a William Saul of the right age is indeed registered in Wandsworth in 1918. Alice Bodger no longer appears on the electoral roll in 1926 and her name is in the death register for Wandsworth in the third quarter of 1925. A somewhat improbably named Violet Lurina Bodger appears on the electoral roll in 1927. Although there are no children of that name, we find that Frank Bodger married a Violet Lurina Warren in the second half of 1926. The phone books then show that the Bodgers moved to West Wickham in 1930, when they leave the Old Park Avenue electoral roll, and lived there until 1941 when they both died. Thurza appears not to have moved with them to West Wickham and died in Hastings in 1936 aged 90.

So there is clearly enough evidence to be sure that we have got the right Bodgers. We can also work out their occupations. Frank's father, William, was a draper living in Holborn and elder brother Alfred was a commercial traveller in 1891 and a drapery traveller in 1901. Frank was a drapers' assistant in the 1891 census – when he was 20 and living with his other elder brother Arthur who doubled up as a hotel manager and secretary to a hospital. All this suggests that the occupation given for him in the 1901 census of 'buyer, own account' was in fact that of drapery buyer. There were a number of other people in Old Park Avenue working in the drapery trade at the same time and it is interesting to speculate on whether they had any commercial connection. One also wonders whether running a business of this kind from home would have been in conflict with the restrictive covenants that purported to prevent the houses from being used for business.

CHAPTER 2

EARLY DEVELOPMENT – MERCHANTS AND BANKERS

Geography: defining the area

In the Middle Ages there had been a number of small villages in what is now south west London. By the seventeenth century there were still very few houses around the two mediaeval churches of Battersea and Clapham, and the rest of the land was in agricultural use. These two parishes, St Mary and Holy Trinity respectively, provided what local government there was until the mid nineteenth century. They did not cover Balham, being part of the parish of Streatham until 1855 when it became a parish on its own.

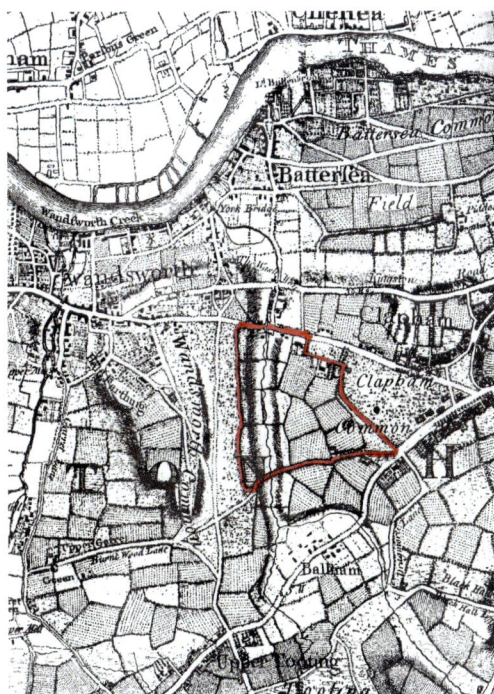

Map2: John Rocque's map of Surrey, 1745 (detail)

Map 1 shows how the area considered in this book fits into south west London as a whole. Its boundaries are Clapham Common West Side on the east, Battersea Rise on the north, Bolingbroke Grove (and Wandsworth Common) on the west and Nightingale Lane on the south. The two commons are separated by a valley where the Falcon River used to run on its way to the Thames. The four roads are shown in John Rocque's map of Surrey published in 1745 (Map 2) but they go back much further in time. This is only the first example of how the detailed geography of this part of London reflects, even to the smallest of bends, the various roads and estates which existed long ago. For a long time, the area was described as South Battersea and it is only in the last twenty years that estate agents have renamed it 'Twixt the Commons'.

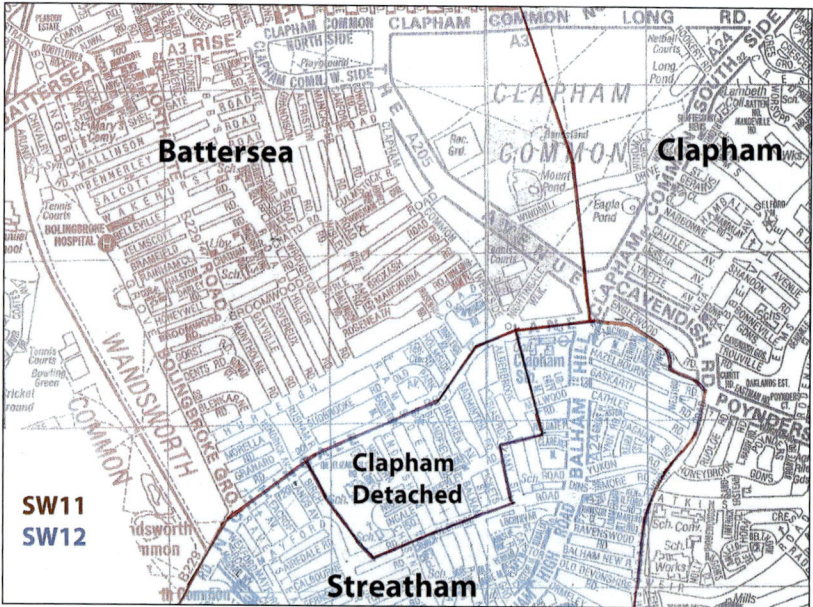

Map 3: Parishes and postcodes

While the boundaries of the area are clear and have remained unchanged for many hundreds of years, its name and the administrative unit in which it falls have been much less constant. The names Battersea, Clapham and indeed Balham, were used in many different ways at different times and often for overlapping or even the same areas. The most important members of the 'Clapham

Sect' lived in the parish of Battersea; part of the parish of Clapham was entirely separate from, and unconnected to, the rest (hence called 'detached') and located south of Nightingale Lane in what now seems more naturally part of Balham. These shifting boundaries are shown in Map 3.

Sometimes the names were chosen in order to mislead; it is alleged by Railway Magazine that the railway station Clapham Junction, which is manifestly in Battersea, was so named in the 1860s as a cynical marketing ploy. Bradshaw used to include a footnote in its timetable to warn travellers that it was 1½ miles from Clapham. It is perhaps significant that the current estate agents' appellation of 'Twixt the Commons' makes no explicit reference to any of the established geographical areas, perhaps to avoid any reference to 'South Battersea'.

There have been numerous changes to administrative boundaries since the middle of the nineteenth century, reflecting fluctuating populations and changes to local authorities. Battersea escaped Wandsworth to become a metropolitan borough in its own right in 1888 and was merged back into Wandsworth in 1963 when the Greater London Council (GLC) was created. Balham was split up at the same time, some parts remaining in Wandsworth and some going to join Streatham in Lambeth. The excellent book 'The Buildings of Clapham'[1] includes South Battersea and part of Balham in its coverage, even though they were not part of the original parish of Clapham, on the grounds that the authors 'think present residents consider that they live in Clapham.' For the similar, but opposite, reason, they exclude most of the detached part of the Clapham parish.

The westernmost part of Clapham Common had always been claimed by Battersea but this was challenged either in principle or in practice by Clapham residents. This led to many boundary disputes in times gone by and even now the story may be told differently by the two sides. The boundary had, at least since the fifteenth century, been marked by a ditch that ran from the southern corner of Wix Lane to the corner of the South Side of the Common and Nightingale Lane. Over time, this ditch became less obvious and the Clapham farmers allowed their cattle to graze on both sides of it. In 1716, Battersea residents erected a long bank and ditch to prevent their Clapham counterparts from grazing their cattle on the Battersea part of the common. The ditch was promptly filled up and the rampart levelled, not least because Battersea had taken the opportunity to move it six feet further towards Clapham than the old one. A subsequent action by Battersea for trespass failed but its parishioners continued to include the extra land when they beat the bounds of the parish on Ascension Day each year. The boundary is still set out by cast iron boundary markers, placed at intervals along the Common.[i]

Old Park Avenue is named after the Georgian house, Old Park, built on a substantial estate developed for terrace housing during 1870-1901 The house itself was only knocked down in 1890 and Old Park Avenue constructed on what was left of its grounds. The road lies in the southern part of the original parish of St Mary's, Battersea, putting it on the Nightingale Lane edge of South Battersea or 'Twixt the Commons'. The south of the borough was developed later than the north, which had always been more intensively built on, catering for the less well paid working class. The difference was always important and an advertisement of an auction in Battersea in The Times in 1790 made clear that the house to be sold was 'in the preferable part of Battersea'.

The variation of geographical label described above applies equally to Old Park Avenue. What was the Old Park Estate, always clearly in the parish of Battersea, was described at the time of its creation as being in Clapham and is now part of the Balham ward of the Battersea parliamentary constituency. Unlike the majority of 'Twixt the Commons', it is in the post code SW12. This is because the boundary between SW11 and SW12 is the more northerly Thurleigh Road, rather than Nightingale Lane, the original boundary between Battersea and the detached part of Clapham, and subsequently between Battersea and Balham/Streatham.

The confusion of names alone suggests that a proper understanding of the development of South Battersea requires a consideration of all three related areas, Clapham, Battersea and Balham. This is all the

---

[i] It may be that it was the setting of this boundary that caused part of Clapham parish to be detached. There are some earlier maps that show the boundary between Clapham and Battersea running along the west side of the common, and then down the centre of Nightingale Lane and round the 'detached' part to connect it securely to the whole.

more so because substantial building development did not begin there until well into the second half of the nineteenth century by which time many of the underlying patterns had been set. This chapter describes the limited number of houses that were built before the end of the eighteenth century and the people who lived in them.

Early Development

The early history of Clapham is set out in Michael Green's book 'Historic Clapham'.[2] The name stems from the Anglo Saxon, the earliest reference being to Cloppaham in the late ninth century. Anglo Saxon records also demonstrate the existence of an estate, or part of an estate, which corresponds exactly to South Battersea or 'Twixt the Commons'. It was called Hildeburna, after the former name of the Falcon Brook.

The Manor of Clapham (but no church) appears in the Domesday Book when it was held by Geoffrey de Mandeville. The church, the precursor to the present Holy Trinity, seems to have been built towards the end of the twelfth century and then acquired by Merton Abbey. Having got the church, the Abbey wanted to make something of it. Green suggests that the Abbey contrived to change the pilgrimage route from the west to Canterbury from its traditional route along what is now Lavender Hill and Wandsworth Road to run along what is now Northside Wandsworth Common, Battersea Rise and Northside Clapham Common. Pilgrims would thereby have to pass their Clapham Church where penances could be obtained in return for gifts and indulgences could be purchased

Before the mid seventeenth century, this part of London had very few inhabitants. Henry Atkins, the physician to James I, bought the Manor of Clapham for £6000 in 1616[3] and by 1638 the village of Clapham only had 46 ratepayers. The first house on the north side of Clapham Common was built in the 1660s by Denis Gauden and was described by Samuel Pepys[4] in his diary in 1663.

'Resolved to go to Clapham to Mr Gauden's. When I came there, the first thing was to show me the house, which is almost built. I find it very regular and finely contrived, and the garden and offices almost as convenient and as full of good variety as ever I saw in my life.'

Denis Gauden was one of the principal victuallers to the Navy, becoming the chief victualling officer in 1660 under the title of Surveyor General. He was knighted in 1667 just before his tenure was renewed in 1668. The house was called 'Clapham Place' and it appears that Gauden used the large (430 acre) agricultural estate that accompanied the house as a major source of the victualling he supplied to the Navy. However his career came to an end when he was arrested for debt in 1677, largely because Charles II owed him the enormous sum of £310,695, admittedly down from some £425,000 twelve years earlier. Pepys' former clerk, William Hewer, bought a lease on the house in 1678 but allowed Sir Denis to remain there until his death in 1688. Hewer then bought the estate and Samuel Pepys moved in towards the end of the century and died there in 1703. John Evelyn[5] records that Pepys lived in Clapham in 'a very noble house and sweate place where he enjoyed the fruit of his labour in great prosperity.'

Battersea, like Clapham and Balham, was still largely agricultural, although there had been some industrial development at Nine Elms. There were certainly fewer houses than in Clapham although the Lord of the Manor, Sir Walter St John, lived in Battersea Manor House on the bank of the Thames, from 1656 till his death in 1704 at 87 years old. By the mid seventeenth century the north of Battersea was increasingly used for market gardening, which according to Fuller's Worthies in 1660,[6] 'hath crept out of Holland into Kent and Surrey'. The first asparagus grown in England was grown in Battersea and this may well be the reason for the unusual name of 'The Asparagus' for the present pub on the corner of Falcon Road and Battersea Park Road.

The development of this part of London, as for much elsewhere, demonstrated the gradual changes set out in the Introduction. Large agricultural estates were divided into smaller estates – at least in relative terms - containing substantial houses with many servants. This was followed by much more intensive development later in the nineteenth century as those owners in turn sold up, usually taking the benefit from the increase in land prices and either moving further out or returning to central London.

Eighteenth Century

Being about four to five miles from the centre of London (whether City or West End) Clapham, Battersea and Balham in the early eighteenth century were part of the relatively undeveloped South of London. Nevertheless, transport was beginning to improve and the first stagecoach travelling between Clapham and the City (Gracechurch Street) was established in 1690 and was one of the earliest regular suburban coaches. Further change was on its way with the General Post Office instituting regular mail deliveries within a 10 mile radius of the City in 1710.[ii] By the 1720s, Clapham was already becoming established as a desirable place to have a house, if not to live permanently. The Thorntons, a merchant and banking family from Hull with strong connections to the Baltic trade, were already established in Clapham before 1720 when John Thornton was born at his father Robert's house there. Robert Thornton was the first in a number of Thornton philanthropists. He is reported to have raised the money to pay the debt incurred by the local doctor in giving drugs to paupers without charge.[7] We shall hear much more of them because John, who became an avowed evangelical, was related closely to the two founders of the Clapham Sect, being the father of Henry Thornton and uncle by marriage to William Wilberforce.

Defoe[8] also mentions Clapham in his second letter describing his travels in Britain in 1724-7. He gives the view 'from the little rising hills around Clapham' as an example of the beauty of the countryside, so it was:

> 'impossible to view these countries from any rising ground and not be ravish'd at the delightful prospect ....with an innumerable number of fine buildings in Clapham ....giving a fair prospect of the whole city of London itself; the most glorious sight without exception that the whole world at present can show since the sacking of Rome in the European, and the burning the Temple of Jerusalem in the Asian part of the world.'

[ii] This became necessary because the restrictions on suburban building were not being enforced. The most recent attempt had been the 1657 Act designed to prohibit suburban building within10 miles of the City.

In 1728 the History of Surrey[9] described Clapham as 'A pleasant village situate upon rising ground, full of good houses inhabited by rich gentlemen, and great merchants, of whom the family of Atkins is one of the most famous.' and also commented favourably on Gauden's house, Clapham Place, although misplacing it in Battersea.

> '[Battersea] is beautiful with diverse handsome houses and particularly Sir Dennis Gauden built a fine house upon the Heath or Common for his brother Dr John Gauden Bishop of Exeter. It hath of late been purchased by one Mr Hewer, who has so exceedingly improved it by planting trees around it, that it is much altered for the better.'

The position of Clapham must have been liked by the Pepys family, because about 1718 one of Samuel's nephews and executor, John Jackson built a house in the grounds of Gauden House; his house, The Cedars, was demolished in 1860.

Nevertheless, there was still a need for improvements before Clapham reached its heyday towards the end of the eighteenth and start of the nineteenth century. No doubt like elsewhere there were problems with highwaymen, but the chief issue was the Common itself. It must have been singularly unattractive and Green[10] gives a very telling analysis of the land. He points out that the common itself, based on Lynch Hill Gravel, had lost its original overlying alluvial soil and was acid and infertile. It was undrained and there are no traces of conventional prehistoric field systems. Until the eighteenth century, the commonest flora on the Common were thorn bushes and brambles. Green refers to the 'desolate pools and bogs of Clapham Common' lit from time to time by marsh fire caused by self igniting gases from decaying plants. A spot near what is now Clapham South Underground Station was called 'Grendel's bog' in the tenth century.

So it is hardly surprising that Daniel Lysons, a Putney curate, described Clapham Common in the first part of the eighteenth century as 'little better than a morass, and the roads almost impassable'.[11] Brayley's history of Surrey written in 1850 (but no doubt drawing on Lysons) described the common land as 'an almost impassable marsh'[12]. In 1761, a book [13] claiming to be 'An account of whatever is most remarkable for grandeur, elegance, curiosity of use, in the city and the country thirty miles around it.' could dismiss Clapham in eleven words as 'a village three miles from London, on the road to Richmond.'

Nevertheless, the Common was drained, chiefly due to the energy of Christopher Baldwin, who lived on its west side at The Grange. He had begun a programme of planting and draining the Common and, while this was partly funded by other residents, he made a major contribution himself. Baldwin described the area to one of his potential purchasers as[14] 'the most beautiful, the most healthy and highly improved spot of land, not only round the metropolis, but perhaps in the kingdom.' He did, however, profit from the exercise since Lysons[15] reports him having sold 14 acres near his house in the 1780s for £5,000.[iii] One of Henry Thornton's biographers put it.[16]

> 'The Great Common, until 1760 a tangled wilderness, now looked a vast and pleasant stretch of land. Paths had been laid and drains installed. But this was still the country. The parish paid a shilling bounty for every polecat killed and four pence for hedgehogs.'

84 hedgehogs and 19 polecats were killed at public expense between 1718 and 1732.[17]

The land in South Battersea, and much else besides, remained in the hands of the Lord of the Battersea Manor. Walter St John's son, Henry who became Viscount St John and Baron of Battersea, was as long lived as his father and remained in Battersea Manor House until his death in 1742 at 90. In turn that gave his son, Viscount Bolingbroke and Queen Anne's Secretary of State, the opportunity to retire to Battersea, having, it is said, 'long wished to spend the evening of his days there and to breathe his last in the house of his ancestors.'[18] He achieved this, dying in December 1751, eighteen months after his wife. He left no children and the manor was bequeathed to his nephew, Frederick, whose infant daughter, Charlotte, was the last of the St John family buried at Battersea in 1762. Frederick always needed money and, having sold the right

---

[iii] It seems likely that this was the 15 acres that Baldwin sold to Henry Cavendish in 1785. There were continued arguments between them about the need for fencing and over the handling of a nearby strip of land.

to present the vicar of Battersea for £420, he moved on to more substantial disposals by obtaining an Act of Parliament under which he sold the manorial property to trustees of John, Lord, and later Earl, Spencer for £30,000[19]. This was the end of the St John family's direct connection with Battersea, but they are remembered by the number of roads named after Bolingbroke or St John and, after the other branch of the family who had become Viscount Grandison.

In 1750 Battersea still retained over four hundred acres of open fields[20], and it was not until Westminster Bridge (1750) and Blackfriars Bridge (1769) had been built that Clapham became linked to working London in a major way with the laying out of Westminster Bridge Road and Kennington Road. The Battersea ferry, which generated an average £42 annual income in the late 1760s, provided a north/south link but the natural transport links remained east/west. Battersea Bridge, built by Earl Spencer and friends after securing an Act of Parliament in 1766, opened in 1771, and then provided some more direct links with Chelsea and the West End.

This bridge had a particularly chequered history. Earl Spencer had originally intended to build a fine stone bridge but his optimism about local residents investing was ill-founded and he was only able to raise about a fifth of would have been needed.[21] As a result, he commissioned a wooden bridge which turned out not to be a commercial success. It was only 24 feet wide, ruling out its use by larger vehicles, and the difficulty for boats in navigating beneath it caused many accidents. Concern for the safety of the bridge caused it to be the first Thames bridge to be lit, by oil lights in 1799, and then in 1824 by gas lights. From 1825, when the mediaeval bridge at Kingston was demolished, it was the last wooden bridge across the Thames, which gave it a considerable attraction, especially to artists. Many painted it, including Turner and Whistler, but perhaps the picture which shows it the best is that by Greaves. (Ill 1)

From 1763 Earl Spencer began to dispose of an extensive acreage of agricultural land, on either lease or freehold, to prosperous businessmen, bankers and City gentlemen. The fields to the south and west of Battersea were transformed into (relatively at least) modest landed estates and the existing farmhouses redeveloped. A number of substantial houses were built and South Battersea as well as Clapham was becoming a place where distinguished well off people could live with equanimity. Henry Venn, one of the first evangelicals and who became curate of Clapham in 1754 wrote.[22]

> 'As soon as we were married we lived at Clapham in Surrey, a favourite village where many London merchants having acquired fortunes, chose their country seats, desiring in general only to enjoy themselves.'

1: Battersea Bridge, 1846 by Greaves

Venn appears to have been responsible for converting John Thornton to evangelicalism but the quotation above suggests why he did not find many of the local population supportive. Six years later, possibly at Thornton's instigation, he was tempted by another evangelical, the Earl of Dartmouth, to accept the living at Huddersfield even though that was much less well paid. He left claiming to be 'disappointed and disheartened at the obstinate rejection of the gospel by the rich.'[23]

New churches

This initial breaking up of the agricultural estates brought a much greater number of occupiers of status to the area and with them the need for support from servants, retailers and a variety of tradesmen as well as the consequent housing for them. One effect of this was to create a desire for bigger or at least better built churches and, even though the eighteenth century was not known for its church building, two new (or rather replacement) churches were built within a mile of each other at Battersea and Clapham within two years.

The first was Holy Trinity on a new site on Clapham Common, where the vestry had applied in 1768 to the Lady of the Clapham Manor, Mrs Penelope Pitt, the last member of the Atkins family, for permission to build a new church.[iv] These arrangements were finally ratified by Act of Parliament in 1774 and the church, designed to accommodate 860 people, was opened on 10 June 1776 having cost £11,000, with John Thornton a major donor. His generosity allowed the pews to be built of foreign oak – at increased expense – so that English oak could be kept to build ships. The building of this church also reflected the increased population, as explained in the Act's preamble[24].

> 'The Parish Church of Clapham in the County of Surry is a very ancient fabrick and inconveniently situated at the Extremity of the said parish and by length of Time become very ruinous; and the Number of inhabitants within the said parish is so greatly increased that if the said church was in a Condition to be repaired it would not be large enough to contain them for the purposes of Divine Worship'

Although attractive to twenty first century eyes, this was not so for the Victorians. The Suburban Homes of London described Holy Trinity in 1871[25] as 'about as ugly a specimen of ecclesiastical structure as can be found....and a monument of what monstrosities

---

[iv] She donated some of the common land for the church; unfortunately it appears to have been a piece of waste and boggy ground which E F Smith claimed caused problems for the foundations for much of the nineteenth century.

in the way of architectural art our grandfathers were capable of.'
At least the Victorians appear consistent since Edward Walford
writing in 1897 in 'Old and New London - the Southern Suburbs'[26]
describes Holy Trinity as:

> 'the Parish Church built on the north west of the
> common, a dull heavy building, a sort of a cross between
> the London parish church of Queen Anne's time and the
> 'chapel of ease' of last century. It dates from 1776. Yet
> Macaulay was fond of it to the last.'

And it would seem that this was a common view, because E
M Forster, writing in 1956[27] (but himself born in 1879), describes
Holy Trinity as 'Too ponderous to be quaint, it is now a depressing
object'. This can be compared with a description of it at the end
of the 18th century[28] as 'a handsome and regular built edifice of
the Tuscan order, neatly built with grey stock bricks, and decently
ornamented both within and without.' The old twelfth century
church on Rectory Grove (Ill 2), which had been the subject of long
neglect both by Merton Abbey and afterwards[29], was knocked down

2: Old Clapham church in 1750, by William Prior

leaving memorials, not least of the Atkins family, the long standing lords of the manor of Clapham.

One of the less well known gravestones is quoted by Brayley[30].

'From Duns secure, if Creditors could come
For me a Debtor may be found at home.
By Death awaited, and in Gaol have laid.
The first and last, the only debt he paid.'

The other church that was rebuilt was St Mary's, Battersea. It was also a church of some social standing and Edmund and William Burke attended a wedding at the old church in 1757. However there was pressure to have a new church and particularly to enlarge the graveyard. Selling part of the vestry's land on Penge Common to pay for rebuilding was first suggested in 1769, and anxious surveys of the building were done, hoping to prove it was irreparable. The vestry there also concluded that an Act of Parliament was necessary to help them to raise the money and this was passed in 1774, the same year as for Holy Trinity. The preamble to the Act was much the same.

'Whereas the Parish Church and Steeple of Battersea in the County of Surrey is in a very ruinous condition insomuch that the Parishioners cannot assemble therein for the Performance of Divine Service without danger; that the said Church and Steeple have been examined by skilful surveyors who have declared the same to be incapable of being repaired and that there is a necessity of rebuilding the same; that the present Churchyard is much too small for the purpose of burying the dead and the Right Honourable John Earl Spencer has given certain houses and grounds for the purposes of enlarging the said Churchyard; and the Inhabitants of the said Parish are not capable of raising a sum of money sufficient to rebuild the said Church and Steeple without the aid of an Act of Parliament.'

The Act empowered land to be enclosed to build the church and also created Trustees who could levy a rate to pay for the church, to borrow against those future revenues, and to let up to 30 pews.

A limit to the borrowing was set at £5,000. In this case no real attempt was made to have a larger church, the new one having its walls only one foot outside the old walls. The costs were estimated at £4,400, but as is the nature of these things turned out to be £6,200, including the £190/9/10 it had cost to secure the Act of Parliament. The first service in the new church was held on 16 November 1777. William Blake married Catherine Butcher, the daughter of a Battersea market gardener, at the new church on 18 August 1782. Most of the Clapham Sect attended the wedding there of James Stephen and Sarah Clarke in 1800. J M W Turner painted many of his cloud scenes from the vestry oriel window.

Who lived in the houses?
The Clapham Sect and others.

Henry Hoare, of the banking family, had a house built on Clapham Common by Flitcroft in 1755, although he only moved in on a permanent basis shortly before his death in 1785. His house was called 'The Wilderness', which may well say something about Clapham at that time. Others living in the area included William Willis of the bank Willis Percival, a number of directors of Child's Bank, Thomas Martin of Martin's Bank, members of the Barclays family and many more. It was claimed that in 1765, no fewer than five past Governors of the Bank of England had a house in Clapham. [v]

One of the most successful Clapham businessmen was Robert Thornton's son John who probably became the largest landowner in Clapham itself[31] and was described in his obituary as 'the greatest merchant of Europe except Mr Hope of Amsterdam'[32]. John Thornton gave enormous amounts of money to evangelical causes, including buying the right to put clergy of his choice into a variety of parishes. He was also a major donor to Dartmouth College in the USA. It is not surprising therefore that William Cowper writing to his memory emphasised qualities others than purely commercial[33].

---

[v] The Governors were then appointed for a single two year term.

*'Thee, therefore, of commercial fame, but more
Famed for thy probity from shore to shore
Thee, Thornton! Worthy on some page to shine,
As honest and more eloquent than mine,
I mourn.'*

3: John Thornton's house as part of Notre Dame convent

His house (Ill 3) was singled out by James Edwards in his book describing the houses on the road to Brighton[34].

*'The next is a large brick house, the seat of John Thornton
esq. On the top of this house Mr Thornton has a study;
a large square room, higher than the common roof, and
is covered with lead. The paddock at the back of the
house consists of a varied lawn, well scattered with single
trees, and some clumps, and so enclosed with wood as
to be perfectly rural, though so near London. A gravel
walk runs round the whole, and encompasses several
meadows, to the extent of about two miles. It is in most
cases shaded thickly with wood, and on one side very well
broken with venerable oaks etc. Almost in front of the*

house, it leads to a gothic bench that is light and pleasing. At each end it terminates in a beautiful shrubbery that joins the house. A small river runs through it, gently bounding by rising hillocks and smooth green slopes, very well varied and spotted with shrubs and trees in a judicious manner. The bends of the water are natural, and the union with the lawn and wood well imagined. To the right it seems lost in the retiring grove. The rock work grotto is (the lantern excepted) extremely well executed, but in a style too wild for a gentle stream, and a smooth shaven lawn, spotted with shrubs; it requires a romantic situation, on the banks of a rapid stream tumbling over broken fragments.'

The house was inherited by his eldest son, Samuel, and the second son, Robert, lived next door and made his gardens the most beautiful and extensive in Clapham, with a Grecian summer house of exquisite proportions where Queen Charlotte and her daughters once came to take refreshment. It still stands, rather sadly, in Worsopp Drive.

His youngest son, Henry, bought another early eighteenth century house nearby in 1792 which he renamed Battersea Rise House (Ill 4).

4: Battersea Rise House

It was first known as Clapham House and had many distinguished occupants; the businessman Isaak Ackerman lived there in the mid 1760s and played a major part in the rebuilding of St Mary's Battersea. Subsequent occupants included William 'single speech' Hamilton, an MP renowned – apparently erroneously – for having given only one speech in the House of Commons, and the banker Sir John Lubbock, the occupant from 1787. Henry extended the Queen Anne house substantially, finishing with 34 bedrooms. It was there that his daughter Marianne, E M Forster's great aunt, was born.

Despite Forster's description, following Lysons and others, of the west side of Clapham Common being then 'a wild and marshy tract' he wrote about the area at that time[35].

> *'The Clapham area had become civilised, there was no longer danger from highwaymen, the merchants and politicians who were beginning to settle there could leave their families in safety when they drove the four or five miles up to Westminster, or the City.'*[vi]

Henry Thornton then built two houses either side of his own residence, the first house being occupied by Charles Grant, Chairman of the East India Company from 1805. He named it Glenelg, after his estate in Scotland, and lived there for eight years before he moved back to town, living in Russell Square. The other house, designed by J T Groves and called Broomfield Lodge, was occupied by Edward James Eliot, the brother in law of William Pitt.

At that time, William Wilberforce, from another Hull merchant family, often stayed with his aunt Hannah who lived with her brother John Thornton after she was widowed. Wilberforce then moved in with his cousin Henry Thornton, but after Eliot's death and Henry Thornton's marriage, he succeeded Eliot as tenant of Broomfield Lodge, later Broomfield House, and renamed by a later owner Broomwood House (Ill 5).

[vi] Even so, there were still examples of highwaymen on Clapham Common. Sir Thomas Hankey and his wife Sarah, were victims in 1751; Captain Freeman shot and killed a highwayman in 1761, and there continued to be isolated examples of such attacks until at least 1801.

5: Broomfield Lodge (later Broomwood House)

These two men formed the focus for the group of Anglican Evangelicals now known as the Clapham Sect. Wilberforce, Thornton and their friends took their Christian responsibilities very seriously and gave both their money and time generously. They worshipped in the new church of Holy Trinity where Henry Venn's son, John, was the dynamic rector.[vii] The evangelical group in Clapham were undoubtedly influential, with the abolition of the slave trade only one of their achievements. They also started the Bible Society and the Church Missionary Society. Many have argued that their influence extended both upwards to the aristocracy and downwards to the various levels of the middle class so that their mindset and priorities effectively set the tone for the forthcoming Victorian age. However they were, perhaps, less successful in influencing the higher reaches of the church, as recorded by one church historian[36]:

[vii] John Thornton had purchased the right to choose the vicar (a tradeable piece of real property called the advowson) and Henry followed the instruction in his will to appoint Venn to succeed after the death in 1792 of the absentee vicar, Rev Sir John Stonehouse, who had taken the income of £500 pa but remained on his own estate at Radley.

'.... it was hoped in the drawing rooms of Clapham that the expansive force of Evangelicalism would carry it into the higher orders of the church as rapidly as it was carrying it through the middling and lower orders. It was not unreasonable to have entertained such great expectations in 1800; but by 1820 it was clear that the campaign was not working out quite to plan.'

It is sometimes assumed that the term 'Clapham Sect' was coined by Sydney Smith but, although he did make references to Wilberforce as 'the leader of the church of Clapham', this seems to be incorrect.[37] There were certainly other references to Wilberforce as 'the head, indeed the founder, of a powerful religious sect'[38] but the originator of the term appears to be Sir James Stephen in an article in the Edinburgh Review in 1844[39]. He uses the term explicitly in the opening paragraph and also refers later to 'that confederacy, which, when pent up within the narrow confines of Clapham, jocose men invidiously call a Sect.'

There is no definitive list of members of the Clapham Sect. Some of those closely associated with the group did not live in Clapham although they visited regularly. Others from later generations are still associated with it. A tablet was placed on the south wall of Holy Trinity church in 1919 with the following list of names chosen by descendants of the Venns and Thorntons.

Charles Grant	*Chairman of directors of East India Company and MP*
Zachary Macaulay	*Governor and later Secretary of Sierra Leone*
Granville Sharp	*anti-slavery campaigner*
John Shore, Lord Teignmouth	*Governor General of India*
James Stephen	*Master in Chancery and MP*
Henry Thornton	*Banker and MP*
John Thornton	*Merchant*

Henry Venn	*Curate of Clapham*
John Venn	*Rector of Clapham*
William Wilberforce	*MP and campaigner against slave trade*

But others who could easily have been included are:

Thomas Babington	*MP and philanthropist*
Claudius Buchanan	*Chaplain to East India Company*
Thomas Clarkson	*Anti-slavery campaigner*
William Dealtry	*Rector of Clapham*
Edward James Eliot	*MP*
Thomas Gisbourne	*clergyman and author*
Isaac Milner	*President of Queens' College Cambridge*
Hannah More	*writer and philanthropist*
Charles Simeon	*Anglican Minister, promoter of missions*
William Smith	*MP, nonconformist*

Henry Thornton's biographer wrote of them[40] 'They were earnest because their religion had convinced them of the reality of sin, the awfulness of death and the eternity of hell.' Thackeray put it much the same way when he described Sophia Hobson's house in "The Newcombes"[41], clearly modelled on Battersea Rise House.

> *'It was a serious paradise. The lodge-keeper was serious, and a clerk at a neighbouring chapel. The head gardener was a Scotch Calvinist, of the strictest order, only occupying himself with the melons and pines provisionally, and until the end of the world.'*

It is not surprising that Wilberforce ranked 'the reformation of manners' as highly among his purposes as the suppression of the slave trade. He persuaded King George III to issue a Proclamation against Vice and Immorality, formed a Society to follow up the proclamation, and in 1801 supported a Society for the Suppression of Vice, which Sydney Smith immediately retitled 'The Society for the Suppression of Vice amongst those with less than £500 a year'.

It should not be thought that they were liberal in the modern sense. Making money was important and their God was nothing if not a rule-maker. Simon Schama put it[42]:

> *'what stirred the Clapham Sect was commerce and Christianity, sustained in mutual nourishment.... God was not love. He was Truth and the Law. He was owed submission.'*

They also expected people to know their place. The French Revolution had frightened them. The Society for Bettering the Conditions of the Poor, of which Wilberforce was one of the founders, had as one of its objectives'... teaching [the poor] the true value of those gradations of rank and condition which our Creator has thought fit to establish.'[43] Henry Thornton believed firmly that God Himself had sanctioned class distinction. His book of Family Prayers, which ran to many editions after his death, prayed God to give to the poor contentment with their lot and to the rich a spirit of compassion and benevolence.

Others knowing their place also moderated the need for education. Certainly neither Henry nor his great friend Hannah More believed in too much education for the working classes other than instruction in how to fulfil their duties; he told the poor women of Clapham 'It is not necessary that you should read books which you have nothing to do with, or that you should comprehend affairs of state.'[44] She described her teaching programme to the Bishop of Bath and Wells along much the same lines.

> *'My plan of instruction is extremely simple and limited. They learn, on weekdays, such coarse works as may fit them for servants. I allow no writing for the poor. My object is not to make fanatics but to train up the lower classes in habits of industry and piety.'*

As we shall see, the evangelical movement was one of a number of important factors in causing rich merchants and bankers to move out of London to the suburbs. Henry Thornton's substantial extension of his house together with building two more houses in his grounds suggests that he may well always have had in mind the idea of using them to create and sustain a community of likeminded people in Clapham.

Why did people move to Clapham?

Clapham's attractions had been recognized since early in the eighteenth century when Defoe and others were reporting substantial gentlemen's houses in Clapham. The environment was changing with the improvement in the Common and it was recognised that the air was 'salubrious', particularly in comparison with the City. Access was getting better as the roads were improving with the new bridges and roads connecting Kennington with the West End and the City and the threat of highwaymen was decreasing. The great landowners of the area such as Lord Spencer and the Atkins family were prepared, even keen, to make land available for sale. John Thornton made sure his sons had land for houses in the area. All this demonstrates that the opportunity for housing was there, but why was it taken? Why did a significant proportion of the wealthiest bankers and merchants decide to move out of central London, away from what had always been regarded as the place for the elite to live?

A combination of factors drove them, including work, lifestyle and their view of relations with their families. One or two hundred years previously, a few very rich merchants and bankers had bought themselves landed estates, acquired a title, and settled down to the life of the aristocrat living off the rents from land. Such income required relatively little attention and insofar as an office might have been required, the aristocrat's country home provided the natural focus for the management of the estate. They liked to own the freehold and took steps to make sure that it remained in the family by preventing spendthrift sons from disposing of it. However Stone has argued that this change of lifestyle was rare after the sixteenth century.[45]

By the eighteenth century, few bankers and merchants wanted to 'retire' from business, not least because by the end of the century the British were taking full advantage of Napoleon having ruined the Dutch commercial and financial positions. Businesses with strong overseas interests could not be left for months at a time; their capital was constantly at risk and the owners needed to keep in touch with the progress of their various deals and investments and to meet their colleagues at the various coffee houses. Remaining an active – and profitable – banker or merchant meant remaining in easy touch with the City. They normally lived 'over the shop', often with apprentices in the house, and with constant coming and going of business colleagues and tradesmen, surrounded by a noisy variety of both poor and wealthy and with the streets drained only by a ditch running down the middle.

It was hardly surprising that there was increasing dissatisfaction with the environment in the City. After all, a visitor in 1765 said of the most fashionable street in London[46].

> 'In the most beautiful part of the Strand... I have during my whole stay in London, seen the middle of the street constantly foul with a dirty puddle to the height of three or four inches; a puddle whose splashings cover those whose walk on foot, fill coaches where their windows happen not to be up, and bedaub all the lower parts of such houses as are exposed to it'

The merchant elite could have moved to the fashionable squares now being built by aristocratic landlords in places such as Covent Garden or Bloomsbury and which were proving attractive to peers and to the landed gentry coming to London for the Season. Instead they began to purchase land a few miles away from London, in easy reach of their office. Soames Jenyns[47], no fan of those not members of the landed gentry, described the merchants in 1767.

> 'The merchant vies all the while with the first of our nobility in his houses, at table, furniture and equipage, the shop-keeper who used to be well contented with one dish of meat, one fire, one maid, has two or three times as many of each, his wife has her tea, her card parties and her dressing room and his 'prentice has climbed from the kitchen fire to the front boxes at the playhouse.'

At first these were country homes and used for weekends. Then wives and children moved out more or less permanently while the men kept a place to sleep in London during the week. Eventually, the London house was converted into a full time office, possibly with some rooms rented to junior members of staff. The banker Henry Hoare used his villa on Clapham Common 'that he might be enabled, with greater convenience, to attend to his business in London without having to sleep within its smoky atmosphere.'[48] These 'villas' were rarely on the scale of a country house, nor was that desired, although Soames Jenyns[49] commented that tradesmen's wives who felt suffocated by the smoke in London must have their villas at Clapham.

The bankers and merchants had relatively little land and did not let it for income to any great extent. This distinction was first described in 1698 by Roger North[50] in what Stone suggests may be one of the first uses of the word 'villa' to describe anything other than a house of the classical period.

'The country model, and that of a suburban villa, are different. The former partakes of the nature of a court, as a lord of a manor doth of regality, and should, like the court, have great rooms to contain numbers.... A villa is quasy a lodge, for the sake of a garden, to retire to enjoy and sleep, without pretence of entertainment of many persons.'

A hundred years later, the distinction was described by a London architect in more detail[51].

'Villas may be considered under three different descriptions: first as the occasional and temporary retreats of the nobility and persons of fortune from what may be called their own town residence, and must, of course, be in the vicinity of the metropolis: secondly as the country houses of wealthy citizens and persons in official stations, which also cannot be far removed from the capital; and thirdly, the smaller kind of provincial edifices, considered either as hunting seats or the habitations of country gentlemen of moderate fortune. Elegance, compactness and convenience are the

characteristics of such buildings… in contradistinction
to the magnificence and extensive range of the country
seats of our nobility and opulent gentry'

A further consequence of this distinction was that there was little emotional commitment by the families to the villas in Clapham. Often they rented or took short leases. People moved from one house to another. They, or certainly their children, had no hesitation about selling the houses when they decided to move, whether into or out of London. A history of London and Middlesex published in 1883[52] showed only three families that had been settled in the county for more than 200 years. This was very different from the aristocracy who were much more likely to extend or rebuild their family house on the same site.

But there may have been a more fundamental reason for moving in, or out, than merely seeking a better physical environment. Family structures and relationships were changing[53]. There was a greater sense of personal and familial autonomy, particularly among the successful merchant classes. Greater privacy was wanted; life expectancy increased so it was more worthwhile to invest in long lasting emotional relationships within a nuclear family. Robert Fishman[54] argues that the overriding reason for the move to the eighteenth century suburbs was the desire for a change in the way that the family functioned, largely driven by Evangelical Christianity. The city was inherently an evil place, providing temptation for men and certainly not appropriate for women or children. William Cowper[55], the evangelical poet supported financially and otherwise by the Thornton family, expressed their conviction in graphic terms. 'God made the country, and man made the town'[viii] His poem Retirement was even clearer.

'The tide of life, swift always in its course
May run in cities with a brisker force,
But nowhere with a current so serene
Or half so clear as in the rural scene.'

[viii] There is a later addition – 'The Devil ran up the suburbs.' – added by T H Hughes and E A G Lamborn in Towns and Town Planning, Ancient and Modern. Oxford 1923 p 35

It was no doubt for this reason that Wilberforce resigned from his five London clubs after his conversion.

The changing view of the role of women was also important. Wilberforce viewed women as men's 'medium of intercourse with the heavenly world' and saw their role as[56]:

> *'That when the husband should return to his family, worn and harassed by worldly cares or professional labours, the wife habitually preserving a warmer and more unimpaired spirit of devotion, than is perhaps consistent with being immersed in the bustle of life, might revive his languid piety.'*

This was a fundamental change from Daniel Defoe's assertion only fifty years before of the need for there to be close cooperation between husband and wife in a business to ensure continuity in case of the husband's death. Defoe had criticised the merchant who 'is foolishly vain of making his wife a gentlewoman by excluding her from the counting house'[57]. Wilberforce on the other hand wholly endorsed his friend Hannah More's comment 'I have often heard it regretted that ladies have no stated employment, no profession. It is a mistake, Charity is the calling of a lady; the care of the poor is her profession.'[58] It was in a suburb such as Clapham that the role of women in the rich evangelical families could properly be developed and maintained.

It is possible to overstate the importance of the Clapham Sect itself in attracting bankers and others to Clapham. For the reasons set out earlier, bankers and rich merchants had been moving to Clapham since the early eighteenth century. The lifestyle would have been attractive to those who were not themselves passionate evangelicals and this would have been increased by having so many of their peers nearby. Even at the height of the Clapham Sect's influence, probably no more than a dozen active members lived in Clapham, and although they may well have been attracted by their close friends and colleagues, and encouraged by the life style promoted by Henry Thornton, they and their families only amounted to about 15% of the gentry population.

Round the Common in 1800

Clapham had certainly changed during the eighteenth century. Its population had increased from 600 in 1664, to 1,625 in 1774, and some 3,000 in the early 1790s and would almost double again over the next twenty years. By this time there were about 240 houses in the parish of Clapham, 23 large houses in South Battersea with some smaller dwellings concentrated around the junction of Battersea Rise and the Falcon brook. At least eleven stage coaches a day ran to London from Clapham, including to both City and West End. The corresponding increase in building is reflected in the steady increase in the total rateable value of Clapham property, and the even faster increase in the sums raised for the Poor Rate![59]

POOR RATE

Year	Rateable value (£)	Poor rate collected
1700	2830	47
1753	4207	316
1775	7024	966
1784		1,187

Clapham's growing wealth is also illustrated by the sum of almost £2,177 collected as an alternative to Rates for the Loyalty Loan and sent to the Government on 13 March 1798 to help pay for the prevention of invasion by Napoleon.

Two views of the Common around this time are shown in Ill 6 and 7, while Ill 8 shows the Spring Well that provided water until 1825. The many fine houses built around Clapham in the eighteenth century are illustrated in Map 4 of 1800 which shows the perambulation of the Common with 'the Gentlemen's seats and the names of their occupiers'.

6: View from Mr Akerman's house, Clapham Common 1790

7: View of Clapham Common 1790

8: Spring Well, Clapham Common 1820

from Tooting

to Wandsworth

Bradley Esq.
Bristol Esq.
L.Singleton Esq.
M.Harrison
Mrs.Bellamy
R.Dent Esq.r
A.Home Esq.r
Goodie Esq.
Fletcher Esq.
Cleodenn Esq.
C.Baldwin Esq.
Bromfield House
W.Wilberforce Esq.r
Wedderburn Esq.r
Ponder Esq.r
C.Graham Esq.r
Britan Esq.r
G.H.Wollaston
Whitaker Esq.
Miss Vassalls
H.Thornton Esq.
C.Grant Esq.
T.Astle Esq.
Alderman Esq.r
to Wandsworth

Grant Allen Es.
Cotton Esq.
Mrs Samler
Rt Hon.H.Cavendish
to Streatham
Wm Esdaile Esq
Mrs Snell
Anty.Brough Esq.
Bond Esq.
Crew Esq.
Mrs Akins
Wiltshire Esq.
Mrs Davis
Lady Tibbs
Mrs Chevers
Miss Horseman
Mrs S.Smith
Metcalf Esq.
Foster Reynolds Esq.
R.Thornton Esq.
Mellor Esq.
Kenyon Esq.
J.Yerbury Esq.
J.Castle Esq.
S.Thornton Esq.
to Stockwell
J.March Esq.

Goldsm..
Railton Es
Chevers Esq
Francis sq.
Davenport Esq.
Poinder Esq.
Harford Esq.
Brant Esq.
Mrs Mathews
Latham Esq.
Casslin Esq.
Mrs Waldoe
Warner Esq.
Myers Esq.
Maitland
Farrer Esq.
Rothwell Esq.
Birkhurst Esq.
Waters Esq.
Scholey Esq.
to Battersea Rise
Miss Horne's
J.Brigden Esq.
G.Hibbert Esq.
Mrs Barclay
R.Barclay Esq.
Dr Gardner

Battersea Rise

Clapham Common

Winstanley Esq.
Windmill Inn
M.S.

Clapham

Plough Inn

to Battersea

to South Lambeth

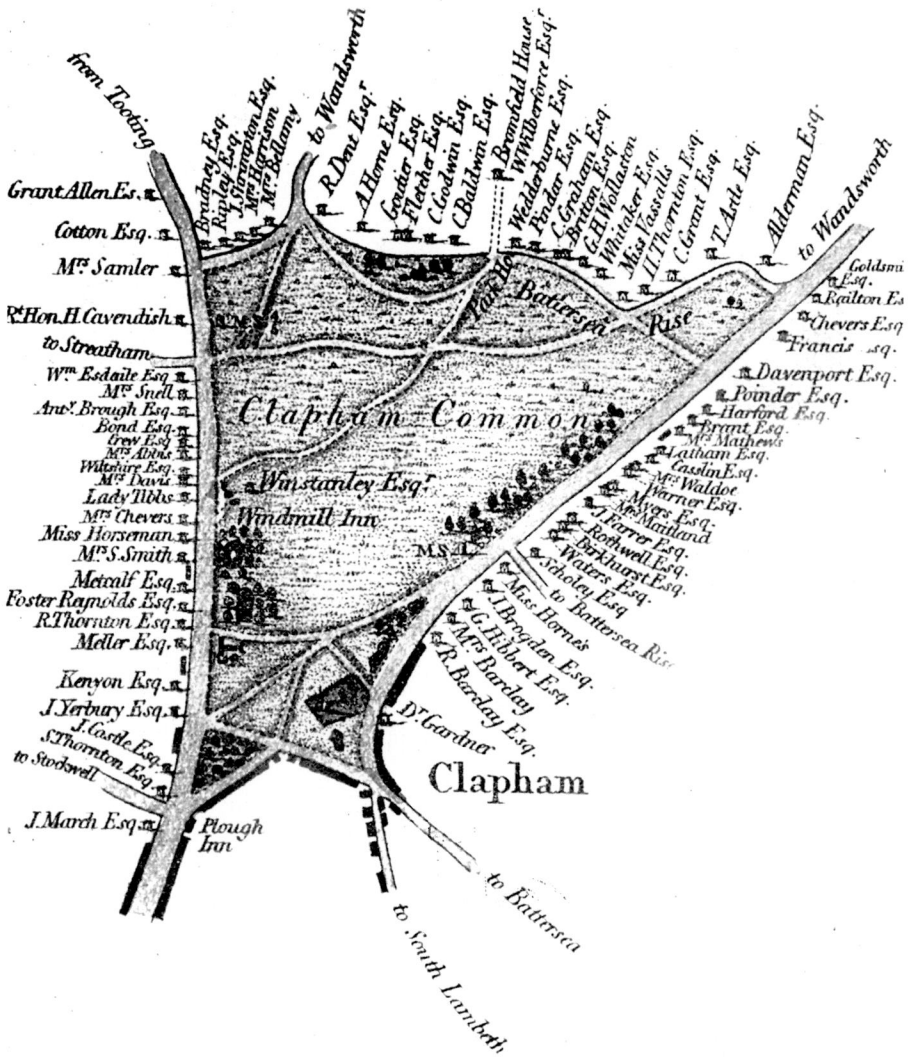

Map 4: Smith's map of houses round Clapham Common 1800

This marks some 75 houses, compared to only 31 on a comparable map published in 1790, It is instructive that even this level of building, leading Olsen[60] to describe Clapham as 'the most famous of all Georgian suburbs', stimulated a Clapham child to observe 'If they go on building at such a rate, London will be next door to us.'[61] It is unlikely that the amount of building in 1787 would have provoked that response in a twenty first century

Londoner. There were 14 houses along the west side of Clapham Common in 1800, by 1907 the number was 87, already more than all the houses round the common in 1800, and when building stopped there were 122.

Map 4 shows all but one or two of the houses occupied, and includes some, such as the houses of Wilberforce and Henry Thornton which were some way from the edge of the Common. Virtually all of these houses were occupied by bankers or merchants, including from Barclays, Hoares and Childs Banks. They probably included a substantial proportion of the 24 Aldermen and 200 Common Councillors of the City and provided considerable opportunities for networking in Clapham itself. It is noticeable that there are very few aristocrats.

The map also includes on the south side of the Common the residence of the great scientist and only genuine aristocrat around the Common, Henry Cavendish. The house had been built some time before 1730 and Cavendish rented it in 1785 until his death. James Edwards describes it as 'a tolerable good house, built with red brick' but went on to explain that 'In a paddock at the back is a mast of a ship, erected for the purposes of making philosophical experiments.' A biographer put it rather differently[62].

> 'He lived in a commodious villa in Clapham. Most of the rooms were well stocked with apparatus for his experimental work, and on the lawn there was a large wooden stage from which Cavendish was able to ascend a large tree, from the top of which he made some of his observations for his astronomical and meteorological researches.'

Cavendish died in the house in February 1810. Fearing he was dying, his servant had rushed to fetch the surgeon, Sir Everard Home. Home reported that Cavendish blamed his servant for summoning the surgeon, adding that at his age (he was then 79), any prolongation of life would only prolong his miseries. He died early the next morning. Subsequently the builder, Thomas Cubitt, lived there before moving to Lincoln House, Clapham Park. The house was finally knocked down in 1907 to allow the building of

Cavendish Parade and the start of Cavendish Road, a name thought more elegant than the original name of Dragmire.

The houses on the west side of the Common included many that would be demolished for later Victorian development, but some still remain, for instance the ones that are now 81-84 West Side or Frankfort House, a pair of coach houses/stables, Leanach Lodge and Western Lodge, all of which were built in 1796-8. Clapham North Side had also seen some fine houses built, many of which also remain, for example The Elms built in 1754, lived in by the banker Robert Barclay from his marriage in 1784 until his death in 1816, and Gilmore House built by Isaak Ackerman in 1763 and formerly one of a pair called 'The Sisters'.

Some idea of how these houses were viewed by their contemporaries can be gauged from The Times, where they were regularly advertised. One house was described in loving estate agent detail in 1790.

> 'A desirable household dwelling house, double coach house, stabling for six horses, and every requisite attached and detached office, Pleasure ground, Fishpond. Hot-house, Green-house, Melon-ground, Kitchen Garden fully stocked, together with two fields of rich Pasture Land adjoining, pleasantly situated on the South Side of Clapham Common, and is a suitable residence for a genteel family. The House comprises three Servants Rooms, six Bed Chambers, a Dressing Room, genteel Drawing Room, and two Parlours.

Another advertised the next year gave some indication of the attraction of such houses, 'These premises are beautifully situate on the Extremity of Clapham Common, commanding circuitous Prospects of great extent and Richness and in a most complete and elegant State'. Large freehold plots were advertised in the Times on 30 April 1803 in glowing terms, with an interesting reference to the views, which recalls the point made by Defoe earlier.

> 'Valuable and very eligible FREEHOLD ESTATES, situated in many parts of the admired and wealthy village of Clapham, in the county of Surry, consisting

*of several and substantially built Dwelling-Houses,
occupied by the most respectable Merchants, Gentlemen
and others; part thereof on short leases at ground
rents, with valuable Reversions, sundry Shops and
other Premises, well fitted for trade; and several Plots
of Freehold Land from 2 to 7 acres each, of which
early possession may be had, most admirably fitted for
building upon, having full command of view over the
River Thames to the Villages of Highgate, Hampstead,
Harrow and rich surrounding country. This property
being at so easy distance from the metropolis, and in a
neighbourhood justly preferred to most other environs
of London, renders it of a material advantage to the
purchasers. At the expiration of the existing Leases, the
annual value is estimated to be at least £2000.'*

The 1800 map also shows five houses on the part of Nightingale
Lane overlooking the Common, one of which, built in 1782 and
formerly called Hollywood, is identified as the residence of Mrs
Harrison, It was subsequently the home of her son, Benjamin
Harrison, treasurer of Guy's Hospital and a great supporter of the
Clapham Sect. It still remains and is now a private school. The last
of these is shown as occupied by John Bellamy, a wine merchant and
Housekeeper to the House of Commons. He had bought the house
in 1794 from the descendants of William Hewer and it was his land
that comprised the 'detached' part of the Clapham parish.

Along the eastern perimeter of Battersea West Common (now
Wandsworth Common), five new houses had been built although
we do not have the dates for all of them. They all had pleasure
grounds containing landscaped gardens and walks. Initially called
(for obvious reasons) Five Houses Lane, the road was later renamed
Bolingbroke Grove, after Henry St John, Viscount Bolingbroke. We
shall deal with these houses and their occupants later in the chapter
on the Dents and Old Park estates.

Balham was less developed than either Clapham or Battersea and
was still virtually all country with the few existing houses very much
tied to the various farms. One was called rather unattractively 'Great
Bleak Hall Farm', after its location on the bleak and blustery western

side of Brixton Hill, while the oldest was probably Hyde Farm which had been built in the early seventeenth century and allegedly contained a concealed secret staircase to the roof. In 1761 its house and 62 acres of land provided a rent of £55 per annum[63] and was later leased (but not lived in) by Sam Thornton, one of the Thornton family. Hyde Farm was not demolished until 1896 when the estate was auctioned by Emmanuel College, Cambridge, the owner of the freehold since 1587. This sale made clear that the land was to be cleared for building purposes and thirty years later old inhabitants still spoke of the difficulty in pulling down its massive oak beams.[64]

Eighteenth century development in Balham was connected to the main road either being directly on it or on the estates near it, whose older farm houses were knocked down and rebuilt for rich merchants. Balham Hill is the immediate extension of the South Side of Clapham Common and in turn becomes the Balham High Road. House building started in Balham Hill in the 1770s. The building was more mixed than the Georgian mansions erected along the south side of Clapham Common But there were nonetheless some fine houses. Alfred House, a large property built in 1782, became a boarding school first for young ladies and by 1841 for young gentlemen. Balham House, lying back from the Balham Hill with ornamental gardens and walks, was built in 1787 for John Whitteridge, a London silk mercer.[ix]

Further down, on the Balham High Road, and confusingly with the same name as the house higher up the hill, another Balham House was being developed. The existing seventeenth century timber house, in fifteen acres of grounds, had fallen into disrepair and was rebuilt in brick. This then attracted George Wolff, a timber merchant and Consul General to the Court of Denmark. He moved there in the 1780s and bought the property in 1794. Wolff was a friend of John Wesley who was a frequent visitor describing the Wolffs as a 'lively family'[65]. Wesley also slept there on his way back from preaching in Leatherhead what proved to be his last sermon.[66] Russell House, next door to Balham House on a ten acre estate, first appeared in 1547.

[ix] Its last resident James Madden Holt MP preferred greater ostentation and spent £30,000 to replace it with a baronial mansion in 1880, itself pulled down to make way for the Duchess Theatre in 1898.

It was also modernised in the late eighteenth century and stood until demolished in 1901 for a block of shops and flats. By 1803 there were 325 people living in Balham, with 106 families in 60 buildings, two thirds of which were on or near Balham Hill with the shops and traders principally on the east side.

A map by Thomas Milne, published in 1800 but with the fieldwork carried out in the 1790s, sums up very well the character of the area at the end of the eighteenth century. This shows the land use in London and an extract is shown at Map 5.

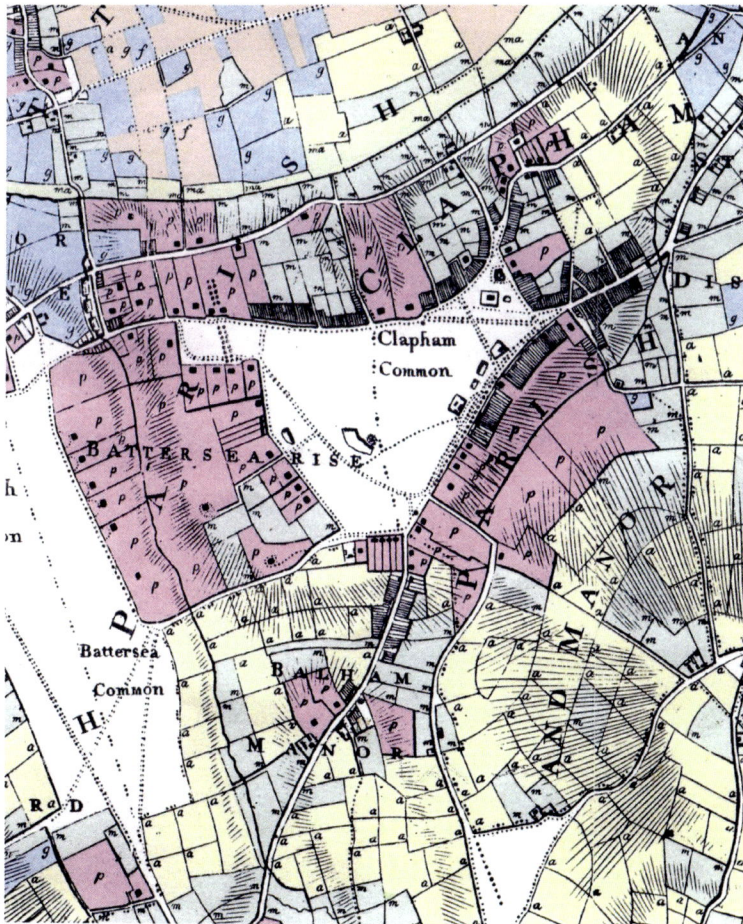

paddocks/little parks p
arable a
enclosed meadow/pasture m
enclosed market garden g

Map 5: Thomas Milne's land use map 1800

Virtually all of Battersea and Clapham is given as pasture, with some arable land in Balham and both market gardening and meadows towards the river. The area was still famous for its asparagus, sold in 'Battersea bunches' and the Spirit of the Times wrote in 1802[67].

> 'Gardeners in shoals from Battersea shall run
> To raise their kindlier hot-beds in the sun'

It is not surprising that the 1801 census described the majority of the Battersea residents as engaged in agriculture activity or in small enterprises along the Thames, often themselves related to agriculture.

The country nature can be illustrated by the two pubs on Lavender Hill which was of course the main road from London to Portsmouth. The original Plough Inn on St John's Hill was built in 1701 but replaced in the 1880s, with the most recent one having been demolished in 2008. John Pilditch, the Battersea District Surveyor, described the old pub in a speech given to the Bolingbroke Ratepayers Association in 1895[68].

> 'The old building was surrounded with garden ground
> well stocked with trees, etc, and had all the appearance
> of an old fashioned country roadside inn. At the side
> of the house was a spacious covered building, open at
> the front, and provided with seats and tables, in which
> country wayfarers and weary travellers would rest and
> take refreshments. In front of the doorway was the
> remains or trunk of an old tree which was used as a lamp
> post. It is said that Dick Turpin used to fasten his horse
> to this tree when he rested for refreshments. Poultry used
> to roam about in front of the building, giving it in all
> respects a country appearance'

He also remembered the former Falcon Inn, whose sign commemorates the falcon in the crest of the St John coat of arms, and is located at the junction of Falcon Road and St John's Hill.[69]

> 'It stood back from the roadway some distance and not in
> the position of the present house which was erected on an
> advanced line since 1882. In the olden times the old house
> was essentially a country house standing in the midst of

country and surrounded by green fields and trees. Falcon Road and St John's Hill being at that time in all respect country roads. I am unable to give the date when the old house was erected but I find that it was offered for sale by a Mr Smith at Garroway's Coffee house on 23 March, 1803, as the freehold estate of the late John Sewell. At that time the house was in the possession of a man named Robert Death, a peculiar name for a publican and it was largely used by undertakers and mourners on their return from attending funerals, and there is a famous picture of the house in existence, entitled 'Undertakers regaling themselves at Death's Door.'

This story is told in more detail by Robert Chambers in his 'Book of Days'[70].

'In the last quarter of the eighteenth century, there flourished at the corner of the lane leading from Wandsworth Road to Battersea Bridge a tavern yclept The Falcon kept by one Robert Death – a man whose figure is said to have ill comported with his name, seeing that it displayed the highest appearance of jollity and good condition. A merry-hearted artist, named John Nixon, passing this house one day, found an undertaker's company regaling themselves at 'Death's door'. Having just discharged their duty to a rich nabob in a neighbouring churchyard, they had... found an opportunity for refreshing exhausted nature; and well did they ply the joyful work before them. The artist, tickled at a festivity among such characters in such a place, sketched them on the spot. This sketch was soon after published, accompanied by a cantata from another hand of no great merit, in which the foreman of the company, Mr Sable, is represented as singing as follows, to the tune of 'I've kissed and I've prattled with fifty fair maids':

Dukes, lords, have I buried, and squires of fame'
And people of every degree;
But of all the fine jobs that ere came my way,

9: Undertakers regaling themselves at Death's door

A funeral like this for me.
This, this is the job
That fills the fob;
Oh! The burying a Nabob for me!
Unfeather the hearse, put the pall in the bag,
Give the horses some oats and some hay;
Drink our next merry meeting and quackery's increase,
With three times three and hurra!'

Ill 9 shows a print from Nixon's original drawing in 1801.

This was not the only poem written about Robert Death and the following makes even more play upon his name[71].

'O stop not here, ye Scottish wights,
For purl nor ale not gin:
For if you stop, who e'er alights
By Death is taken in.

When having eat and drank your fill
Should ye, O hapless case,
Neglect to pay your landlord's bill
Death stares you in the face.

With grief sincere I pity those
Who've drawn themselves this scrape in
Since from this dreadful gripe heaven knows
Alas! there's no escaping.

This one advice, my friends, pursue
Whilst you have life and breath –
Ne'er pledge your Host, for if you do
You'll surely drink to Death.'

In the next chapters, we will see how much these country scenes changed in the nineteenth century.

(Endnotes)

1   The Buildings of Clapham. 2000 The Clapham Society
2   Michael Green. 2008 Historic Clapham
3   Gillian Clegg. 1998 Clapham Past p 15
4   Samuel Pepys. Diaries 1663
5   John Evelyn. Diaries 1700
6   Quoted in J G Taylor. 1925 Our Lady of Batersey
7   J W Grover. 1886 Old Clapham , p105
8   Daniel Defoe. 1724-7 A tour thro' the whole island of Great Britain
9   History of Surrey. 1728
10 Michael Green. Ibid p 17,79
11 Lysons. 1792 History of Battersea
12 Edward Brayley. 1850 History of Surrey Vol III
13 London and its Environs 1761 printed by R and J Dodbury
14 Quoted in Christa Jungnickel and Russell McCormmach. 1999 Cavendish p325
15 Lysons. Ibid
16 Standish Meacham. 1964 Henry Thornton of Clapham p 32
17 J W Grover. Ibid p 14
18 Lysons. Ibid
19 J G Taylor. Ibid
20 Keith Bailey. 1980 Battersea New Town p 5
21 Brian Cookson. 2006 Crossing the River p117
22 Quoted on Ancestry.com web site
23 Quoted in Gillian Clegg. Ibid p 43
24 Quoted by E F Smith. 1976 Clapham p 7
25 W S Clarke. 1881 Suburban Homes of London
26 Edward Walford. 1897 Old and New London – the Southern Suburbs
27 E M Forster. 1956 Marianne Thornton p32
28 James Edwards. 1801 Companion from London to Brighthelmston. Part II p 8
29 Michael Green. Ibid p 107
30 Edward Brayley. Ibid
31 Milton M Klein. 2004 An Amazing Grace p 25
32 The Gentleman's Magazine 1790, quoted in Peter Thorold 1999 The London Rich p 233
33 William Cowper. 1790 To the Memory of the late John Thornton Esq
34 James Edwards. Ibid p 11
35 E M Forster. Ibid p 4
36 G F A Best. 1964 Temporal Pillars p 243
37 Ernest Howse. 1953 Saints in Politics Appendix
38 Lord Brougham .1839 Historical Sketches of Statesmen who flourished in the time of George III p 346
39 Sir James Stephen. 1944 Edinburgh Review LXXX July-October p 269
40 Standish Meacham. 1964 Ibid p 2
41 W M Thackeray. 1853 The Newcombes p18
42 Simon Schama. 2005 Rough Crossings p 356
43 J Baker. 1819 Life of Sir Thomas Bernard Bt p 6
44 Quoted in Standish Meacham. 1964 Ibid p140
45 Lawrence Stone. 1986 An Open Elite ? chapter 1
46 Pierre Jean Crosley. 1772 A Tour to London trans Thomas Nugent p 1.109

47 Soames Jenyns. 1762 Essays
48 J H M Burgess. 1929 Chronicles of Clapham Appendix C VII
49 Quoted in Lewis Mumford. 1938 The Culture of Cities p 211
50 Roger North. 1698 Lives of the Norths
51 Charles Middleton. 1793 quoted in Stone Ibid p 287
52 W J Loftie. quoted in Peter Thorold 1999. The London Rich p 186
53 Lawrence Stone. 1977 The Family, Sex and Marriage
54 Robert Fishman. 1987 Bourgeois Utopias p 33
55 William Cowper, from The Sofa, in The Task
56 William Wilberforce. 1797 A practical View of the Prevailing Religious System of
    Professed Christians in the higher and Middle Classes of this Country, Contrasted
    with Real Christianity .p 366
57 Daniel Defoe. 1727 The Complete English Tradesman quoted in Robert Fishman Ibid
58 Hannah More. 1809 Coelebs in Search of a Wife 1.239
59 R J Lister. 1930 Clapham in the Eighteenth Century p 10
60 Donald J Olsen. 1976 The Growth of Victorian London p 190
61 Henry Kett. 1787 quoted by Olsen Ibid p 41
62 A J Berry. 1960 Henry Cavendish p 14
63 R J Lister. Ibid p 25
64 J Harvey Bloom. 1926 Bygone Balham and Tooting Bec
65 Graham Gower. 1996 Balham A brief history p 18
66 Arthur Porritt. 1930 A Home of Fellowship p 9
67 Quoted in Edward Walford. 1878 Old and New London
68 John Pilditch. 1895 The Progress of Battersea
69 John Pilditch. Ibid
70 Robert Chambers. The Book of Days quoted by Edward Walford. Ibid
71 Mr Pilgrim. 1785 European Magazine November

CHAPTER 3

THE SUBURBS COME TO SOUTH WEST LONDON - SLOWLY

The transformation of South West London to terrace housing took virtually a century and started slowly. This saw the very rich leaving the near suburbs, allowing the next waves of what Roy Porter[1] called 'the most sensational transformation of the century'.

> *'First the plutocrats, then the professionals and lesser businessmen, and finally the shopkeepers quit Cheapside and Clerkenwell for suburbs like Primrose Hill and Herne Hill, or later Muswell Hill and Beulah Hill, while, pushed and shoved by central overcrowding, the poor wormed themselves into erstwhile middleclass strongholds, precipitating neighbourhood depreciation.'*

It is no coincidence of course that all the suburbs mentioned by Porter here are hills and hence with better air, even if much of the development was not always on the high ground; Clapham itself being on relatively high ground - the 220 acre Common itself is 66 feet above sea level - qualified in the same way and we come across many references to the 'salubrity' of its air.

This change was paralleled, and indeed made possible by, continued changes in the land ownership from large agricultural estates with absentee landowners to comfortable estates with their own important residences but still with either gentleman sized farms or landscaped grounds, to the selling for development first of the grounds of the large houses, often for substantial villas, and finally for demolition and wholesale development for pairs of semis or terrace housing.

We see this pattern in the Clapham Sect. Most of them had maintained at least a pied à terre in the centre of London and many began to move their main residence back to London in the first decade of the century. Proximity to parliament and other London activities was increasingly important but, in Wilberforce's case, ill health also persuaded him to abandon moving between two houses. He sold both his Clapham house and his smaller one in London to purchase a house on the present site of the Albert Hall in three acres of gardens. Lord Teignmouth, who had lived since 1802 in what had been John Thornton's house moved back into the centre of London. James Stephen, who became an MP in 1808, moved back too, and Charles Grant did so a little later.

Broomfield House was bought by the banker William Henry Hoare for £8,400 and he lived there until his death in 1819. Both he and his wife, Louisa, were committed evangelicals and he supported both the Church Missionary Society and the African Institute, established for the purpose of 'instructing and civilising Africa'. When Hoare died, John Deacon, another banker and future partner of Henry Sykes Thornton in Williams Deacons Bank, bought the house for £8,000.[2] But despite all this change, Henry Thornton still wrote in his diary for November 6 1814, 'God grant that Clapham may more and more become the theatre on which elevated piety is exhibited without affectation and without extravagance.'

Despite the quickening pace of suburban development, for the first half of the nineteenth century it was certainly possible to regard Battersea, Clapham and Balham as being countrified, if not part of the country. The local gentry - and Disraeli - came to the fields and marshes to shoot live pigeons (purchased at 15/- a dozen), starlings (4/- a dozen), and sparrows (2/- a dozen) and the 1836 Tithe map still shows a pigeon shoot. Afterwards they repaired to mix with the working class folk at temporary drinking booths scattered along the river bank and in the notoriously bawdy Red House Tavern painted by Paul Sandby and often patronised by Charles Dickens who featured it in Sketches by Boz. However these country scenes did not last much longer, with the estate owners beginning to sell off at least part of their land for development, sometimes for large houses or, in some cases, selling out entirely to developers.

Although most of the original members of the Clapham Sect had moved back to London, Clapham retained its association with the earnest and evangelical and was satirised accordingly[3].

> '*Indeed, Clapham has long been regarded as a suburb whose residents are chiefly distinguished by social prosperity and ardent attachment to Evangelical opinion and hence it is sneeringly spoken of by Tom Ingoldsby as 'that sanctified ville*"

The last reference is to the Lay of St Odile, one of the popular and mildly satirical Ingoldsby Legends written by Richard Barham.

> '*Since not even Clapham, that sanctified ville,
> Can produce enough saints to save every Odile.*'[4]

Thackeray himself wrote of Clapham 'Of all the pretty suburbs that still adorn our Metropolis there are few that exceed in charm of Clapham Common.'[5] That did not stop him satirising the Clapham Sect in 'The Newcomes' published in 1853 which gives a amusing, if somewhat one sided, version of the role of the heiress Sophie Hobson[6].

> '*Her mansion at Clapham was long the resort of the most favoured among the religious world. The most eloquent expounders, the most gifted missionaries, the most interesting converts from foreign islands, were to be found at her sumptuous table spread with the produce of her magnificent gardens. [She had] to attend to the interests of the enslaved negro; to awaken the benighted Hottentot to a sense of the truth; to convert Jews, Turks, Infidels, and Papists; to arouse the indifferent and often blasphemous mariner; to guide the washerwoman in the right way; to head all the public charities of her sect, and do a thousand secret kindnesses that none knew of; to answer myriads of letters, pension endless ministers, and supply their teeming wives with continuous baby-linen; to hear preachers daily bawling for hours, and listen untired on her knees after along day's labour, while florid rhapsodists belaboured cushions above her with wearisome benedictions; all these things had this woman to do.*'

But although some of Clapham's inhabitants may have moved back to London proper, the greater flow was still in an outwards direction, stimulated both by growing wealth and the desire to live in what was still seen as the country, enabled at least for the comfortably off by better transport into the centre of London. These changes were captured in a piece of doggerel written in 1813 by Horace and James Smith and entitled 'The Spread of London'[7].

> *The builder's plank, the mason's hod*
> *Wide and more wide extending still*
> *Usurp the violated sod*
> *From Lambeth Marsh to Balham Hill.*
>
> *Pert poplars, yew trees, water tubs*
> *No more at Clapham met the eye*
> *But velvet lawns, acacian shrubs*
> *With perfume greet the passer by.*

The first residential estate in Clapham was laid out the mid 1820s as a family investment by Francis Child, comprising what is now Crescent Grove, built on the site of Edward Polhill's eighteenth century villa. The estate once had its own stabling, water supply and mill house, and was responsible for its 'watching and lighting' all managed by a trust set up in 1830 although varied since, and so resembles in some ways the present walled communities! The owners agreed to preserve the look and tone of the estate and to maintain the essential appearance of the houses unaltered. The estate still retains control over its own roads, and according to Hermione Hobhouse[8], was the last small private estate in London to do so. It also retains some 'dog railings' designed to keep stray dogs off the door step and which survived the removal of the railings around the square for salvage in the Second World War.

The improvement in how Clapham was regarded can be judged by comparing the following descriptions of the village.

> *'Clapham is a greatly improved, improving and highly respectable village. Clapham and its immediate neighbourhood abound with beautiful seats, villas etc, principally inhabited by London merchants and opulent gentlemen. The salubrity of the air, its beautiful situation and its contiguity with London, render it a highly eligible place of residence.'*[9]

'The pleasant village of Clapham is situated on the skirts of a common, containing about 200 acres, which has of late years been much improved, chiefly by draining and the judicious planting of trees, as to have the appearance of a park. It is surrounded by villas belonging to some of the most opulent merchants in the City of London.'[10]

'The village has for many years been considered one of the most respectable and pleasant among the many delightful ones that environ the metropolis; the road to it from London, especially that part called 'Clapham Rise' has on either side large and elegant mansions, with lawns and gardens in front, in a continuous line to the common, which occupies a space of many acres, surrounded by noble residences and tasteful villas; the area itself, being intersected by carriage drives, and planted with trees and shrubs, presents the appearance of a handsome part; indeed the whole of the vicinage of Clapham bears the stamp of wealth, taste, and comfort which, joined to salubrity of air, and the views commanded from that part of the parish towards Brixton, render it particularly attractive as a place of permanent residence or temporary retirement.'[11]

The Times carried regular advertisements promoting the delights of houses in Clapham. Here are four taken from the edition of May 18, 1836.

To be Let, Unfurnished, In Nightingale Lane, Clapham Common, a delightfully situate HOUSE for 2,3 or more years, with coach house, stables, garden field and lawn.

To be let, for 5 or 6 weeks, a FURNISHED HOUSE on Clapham Common. It is commodious, delightfully situate, and adapted for the reception of a large family; possession may be had about the middle of June. Terms 6 guineas a week.

Clapham, to be let, an excellent FAMILY HOUSE, in good repair, with coach house, stable, pleasure ground and paddock in Larkhall Lane.

Clapham Common To be LET on LEASE with immediate possession, a desirable FAMILY HOUSE, fitted with every convenience, with coach house and 3-stall stable, small productive garden and abundant supply of good water.

During the first part of the nineteenth century the increase in population created a demand for local shops and traders. As a result, The Pavement, which had probably been started at the beginning of the seventeenth century and at that stage was largely residential, continued its transformation to a commercial shopping street with shop fronts built out into the front garden. Pigot[12] goes on to describe the shopping in glowing terms.

'As a trading village it is by no means conspicuous, it being confined to that necessary for the accommodation of the numerous opulent residents; the most prominent brand is that of brewing, for which there are several opulent establishments; and the house of public accommodation will be found by the stranger to partake of that respectability so apparent throughout this village.'

By the late 1830s a number of the mansions built by the wealthy merchants were also beginning to find their ways into other uses, particularly private schools. Clapham Rise, now Clapham Road, was a favourite place for girls' schools, or to use the term of the time, 'seminaries for young ladies' referred to in another of the Ingoldsby Legends 'The Babes in the Wood'[13] .

'And Jane, since, when girls have 'the dumps'
Fortune hunters in score to entrap 'em rise,
We'll send to those worthy old frumps,
The two Misses Tickler of Clapham Rise.'

It was from one of these schools in Clapham – Mrs Fenning's School – that Harriet Westbrook eloped with Shelley in 1811.

Clapham Common was also used as a suitable place to conduct duels as late as 1827. Sir Charles Forbes challenged a young surgeon, Hale Thompson, to a duel following a dispute about Forbes allegedly making public some disputes over treatment with George Guthrie, his partner in the Royal Westminster Infirmary for Diseases of the Eye. They faced each other with pistols on Clapham Common on 29 December 1827. Each man fired three times without inflicting injury, and the seconds then declared the duel at an end, against the combatants' wishes.[14]

Cubitt comes to Clapham

The first major development in Clapham was carried out by Thomas Cubitt, the builder and developer of Pimlico. He already had a number of contacts with Clapham since many of the members of his investing syndicates lived there. He purchased a lease from the Atkins family on 230 acres of farmland from the Bleak Hall Farm estate in 1825 which led to his development of Clapham Park. Unlike his other developments, he planned an estate of detached villas with large grounds and very few of them were built on a speculative basis. Although only half an hour by carriage from the City, it was still regarded as rural, not least by the gas company, and the inhabitants had to petition for ten years before gas lighting was eventually installed in 1854, long after the rest of the parish.

Cubitt's approach was to prepare the main roads and then lay out the land in substantial plots on which the individual owners could build their own houses within the general framework of his scheme. But he must have liked the area because the next year he also purchased a large mansion standing in its own grounds between Bleak Hall Farm and the Common which had belonged to a member of the Bridgeman family, and set about rebuilding it. In the meantime, he moved into Cavendish House, the former residence of Henry Cavendish.

Cubitt's rebuilt house was a substantial one, in 22 acres of grounds, and was kept up to date with modern facilities, being refurbished as soon as 1841, 15 years after the original purchase and rebuilding. Hermione Hobhouse[15] describes it as having on the left a 60 foot suite of study, dining room and boudoir and on the right dining room, library and smoking room, elaborate services with a servants' wing and their own sleeping accommodation. The main house had six first-floor bedrooms (but only one bathroom) and eight smaller bedrooms on the second floor. Outside, there was a large vinery, an extensive fruit garden, stabling for six or seven horses, four coach houses and standings for a small herd of cows. Cubitt lived there until 1851 when he moved out to Denbies near Dorking and next to Polesden Lacey, which he had also built twenty five years earlier. Clapham Park had some success to start with, and it was described in 1850:[16]

> 'This park may be described as a new locality, deriving again from the creative genius of Mr Thomas Cubitt, the well known eminent architect and builder. The situation to the South east of Clapham on the rising ground between that village and Brixton, renders it more airy than the former; while it is less exposed to the wind than the latter – Clapham Park has already become a favourite place of residence for families of respectability and affluence.'

Nevertheless, it was not as successful as Cubitt hoped and he himself said,[17] 'I can assure you that had all my speculations been similar in their result to the Clapham Park one I should have been ruined very many years ago.'

Clapham Park was one of the few estates in the neighbourhood of London where restriction and limitation as to building were in force, giving a certain exclusivity. A local guide claimed in 1893[18] that it was one of the most favoured of residential quarters in South London even though 'the rage for exclusiveness on the part of the possessors of great wealth may have caused a few of the richer families to seek retirement further afield.' The result was that some plots were still undeveloped at the start of the First World War even though Besant wrote[19] 'All the houses in these roads are of the highest class of the Victorian house of the suburbs standing in large grounds, an idea of which can be gained from 'Woodlands' on the corner of Park Hill, which is to let and stands on 11 acres.'

Few of the resulting large villas still exist, as they were far too large for modern households, although the street pattern endures. Cubitt's houses remain at 84 Kings Avenue (Ill 10), at 24 and 58 Thornton Road, and 126 Atkins Road. (Ill 11).

Typically they were large houses arranged on lower ground and two upper floors with adjoining coach houses and stabling. Artisans'

10: Cubitt's houses: Victoria House, 84 Kings Avenue

11: Cubitt's houses: 126 Atkins Road

cottages followed, starting in 1850. Cubitt's own house, Lincoln House, was demolished in 1905 making way for Rodenhurst Road and the houses on the west side of Clarence Avenue to be built on its extensive grounds. Ironically, the present day Clapham Park Estate of local authority housing built partly on Cubitt's original estate is now one of the most deprived in London.

Cubitt also extended his interest in the Bleak Hall farm estate to the nearby Friday Grove and Hyde Farm. The purchase of Friday Grove in 1841 allowed Cubitt to lay out the south west side of Atkins Road. He helped his cash flow by selling some of the land to a successful Reigate architect and builder, James Thomas Knowles senior, who built himself a lavish house in the Italianate style. This house was completed in 1846 and Knowles named it Friday Grove House. It was the second largest house in Clapham Park after Cubitt's own, and Knowles had purchased some adjoining land to guarantee his privacy. When the house was auctioned in 1876, there were descriptions of the spreading lawns and the garden extending 400 feet to the south with shrubbery walks and trees including, chestnuts, rhododendrons, lilac, Portugal laurel, weeping lime, laburnum, may trees and a filbert grove. Hardly surprising then that the sale catalogue said[20]:

> 'Although so near London, and so admirably situate for the occupation of any gentleman whose daily attendance in Town is necessary, the grounds are so beautifully secluded, and the foliage of the trees and shrubs so luxuriant that during the summer months not a house is visible and the quietude is such as can only as a rule be obtained in the country...'

The house was lived in briefly after the sale by the new Lord Mayor, Polidore de Keyser, the successful hotelier. It was demolished in 1895 when the covenants on Knowles' first purchase ran out.

Cubitt next leased another piece of land which eventually led to the building of Clapham Manor Street. However it took him eight years before he did so and a number of builders were involved with a variety of designs but under his supervision. As a result the east side of the street was completed by 1849 and the west side not till 1856.

Battersea and Balham

In Battersea housing development was much slower and the population, if anything, had been slightly lower in the 1780s than fifty years earlier[21]. A turnpike from Old Battersea Village to the City was only created in 1799. Development had begun in 1790 to create Battersea New Town on farmland next to the main east/west route between Wandsworth and Lambeth and this provided 20% of all housing in Battersea at the start of the nineteenth century. Further houses were added at a rate of only about ten a year until 1845. Most of these were small terrace housing for workers – 70% of all Battersea houses were rented for less that £20 per annum, either around the old Battersea Village or on York Road. At this stage there was no evidence of development for the middle or richer classes, although St Mary's, Battersea continued to serve the well off, as recalled by a Battersea resident[22].

> *'All the gentry from Battersea Rise then attended it on Sunday morning and the lines of carriages reached from the Church to some distance beyond the Square (which was then the commercial part of the Village as containing the best shops).'*

The population of all Battersea only doubled during the period 1801 – 1841, growing from 3,365 to 6,687. Little of this increase was in South Battersea which remained in the eighteenth century estates apart from the development around the bottom of Battersea Rise or minor in-filling. Pigot writes even in 1834[23] that:

> *'Battersea is pleasantly situated on the southern bank of the river Thames. The houses are irregularly built, and in detached situations; but the neighbourhood, especially in Battersea Rise is ornamented with several handsome villas In other parts of the parish, much of the land is occupied by market gardens who furnish the London market immense quantities of vegetables, amongst which the asparagus from this part is highly celebrated.'*

And Greville[24] wrote of Battersea in 1838 in his memoirs:

'There is no middle class of tradesmen in good circumstances; they are divided between the extremes of wealth and of poverty; but among the latter there is a considerable amount of knowledge, although their minds are ill regulated and their principles perverted.'

Its rural nature is emphasised by the road renamed Lavender Hill, after the lavender fields of William Pamplin's nursery garden, established in 1820. In the same way, Sir Charles Grove[25] recalled that in the 1820s:

'So clear was the air across Battersea Fields that we could see the coloured sails of the barges going up and down the river, and could hear plainly the drums and fifes at Chelsea Hospital....It was an entirely open space, a good deal of it given up to corn and the rest grazing fields, which were inhabited by an immense heard of cows.'

This may have been a somewhat romantic view, given that a former city missionary of Battersea Fields described it as[26] '...a place out of Hell that surpasses Sodom and Gomorrah in ugliness and abomination.' Matthew Arnold[27] wrote to his wife in 1852, 'Battersea, so far off, the roads so execrable, and the rain so incessant', while Thomas Carlyle would only cross the river from his Chelsea digs 'armed with a good stick in my hand.' This would have been in part because of worries about physical safety on the old Battersea Bridge. A woman had been murdered on the bridge in 1844 in full view of one of the toll collectors who did not intervene because both parties had paid their fares.[28] Even Walter Besant, normally a supporter of South London, remembered Battersea Fields in the 1840s in bleak terms[29].

'I myself remember the old Battersea fields perfectly well; one shivers at the recollection; they were low, flat, damp, and, I believe, treeless: they were crossed, like Hackney Marsh, by paths raised above the level. At no time of year could the Battersea fields look anything but dreary; in winter they were inexpressibly dismal. As a boy I walked across the fields in order to get to the embankment or river

wall, from which one commanded a view of the Thames, with its barges and lighters going up and down – pleasant when the sun shone on the river, but a mere shadow of the ancient glory, when the pleasure barges and state barges swept majestically up the river with the hautboys and the trumpets in the bows.'

12: Barges at Battersea. Edmund Cook 1828

13: Launch of Luisa Shelbourne at Battersea 1864

Both the land and the river at Battersea were used for many activities. Ill 12 shows a range of barges in 1828 with Battersea Bridge in the background, while Ill 13 records the launch in 1854 of

14: Battersea Agricultural Show 1861

the Luisa Shelbourne at a yard in Nine Elms, with a draught of only 4½ feet built for the Baltic trade. It was both the largest ship of its kind ever built and the largest built on the Thames above the bridge. There was also a regular agricultural show in Battersea (Ill 14) and some of the land owned by the London Brighton and South Coast railway at Battersea was used in 1861 for the first full scale trial of the London Pneumatic Despatch Company's system for transporting letters and packets around London. (Ill 15)

In Balham the population was rising slowly, increasing to 712 people in 97 buildings in 1821, including some 20 shops or other businesses and in 1831, 196 families with 1,331 people in 156 houses. Development was chiefly either mansions or large villas, or small dwellings for those who supported the big houses. There was as yet no regular transport from Balham into London other than by picking up a coach from Clapham. But Balham was becoming known; in 1838 R S Surtees described his famous character, Mr John Jorrocks, a Cockney grocer whose every waking hour is filled with thoughts of hunting, as riding from the City to the meet of the Surrey Hounds at Croydon and passing 'Balham Hill Joes's 'Come crack 'em and try 'em stall'.[30]

THE PNEUMATIC LETTER AND PARCEL CONVEYANCE: THE DESPATCH-TUBE AT BATTERSEA.

SECTION OF DISC IN THE ENGINE-HOUSE.

THE MOUTH OF THE TUBE, AND CARRIAGE.—SEE PAGE 147.

15: Pneumatic parcel handling

The increase in population also drew Balham unto contact with
the Clapham Sect, who helped to raise the money for a new chapel.
Benjamin Harrison of Hollywood, Nightingale Lane, was the leading
light but Wilberforce, Henry Thornton and Zachary Macaulay all

attended its opening. It was designed by Francis Hurlbatt who was also responsible for the portico of Holy Trinity, Clapham Common.

In 1821 James Morrison, a millionaire from the drapery trade, bought a small estate on Balham Hill near Balham House at what would now be between Cathles and Gaskarth streets with a view of the Streatham hills. Meanwhile the chances of development gains meant that the Bedford Hill area was beginning the change from farming to residential development. Richardson Borrodaile, Chairman of the Hudson's Bay Company and a prosperous merchant of the East India Company, purchased Bedford Hill Farm from another property developer and built his house in 1809 on the highest part of the estate with fine views to the west. This was widely regarded as the principal residence in Balham and was described in 1823 as 'a beautiful mansion', Another house, the Priory, an example of Victorian Gothic, was built nearby in 1812 and shared the carriage way. It was called the Priory because it stood on the site of an old abbey founded by Anselm, Abbott of Bec and subsequently Archbishop of Canterbury. The connection to Anselm caused the nearby common to be called Tooting Bec.

16: 207 Balham High Road

Borrodaile promptly began to build 16 modern styled stuccoed villas, two of which at 207 and 211 Balham High Road still exist (Ill 16). Some of these may have been the houses advertised in The Times in March 1827.

> '*Six new built and commodious detached villa residences, erected in the most substantial manner, of chaste elevation, and possessing every accommodation for a family of respectability; held for about 30 years, at small ground rents, and most suitably and pleasantly situate on the high road, but at a convenient distance therefrom, between Balham and Tooting, only 6 miles from the city and 5 from Westminster. Each containing well proportioned eating and drawing rooms about 22 feet by 17, morning room, gentleman's dressing room, 4 principal bedchambers, 2 dressing rooms, 3 servants' chambers, 2 spacious kitchens, housekeeper's and footman's pantry, good cellars etc, coachhouse, and 3 stall stables.*'

Borrodaile then moved on, selling his house in 1843 to William Cubitt – the brother of Thomas and Lord Mayor of London in 1861.

(Endnotes)

1   Roy Porter. 1994 London A Social History p222, 209
2   Private communication from Pamela Hunter, Archivist to the Hoare family
3   Quoted in Edward Walford. 1897 Old and New London – The Southern Suburbs
4   Richard Barham. 1840 Ingoldsby Legends The Lay of St Odile
5   W M Thackeray quoted in Pevsner London 2 South 1983 p 379
6   W M Thackeray. 1853 The Newcomes p15,17
7   Horace and James Smith. 1813 The Spread of London
8   Hermione Hobhouse. 1967 Country Life
9   Pigot. Guide to Surrey
10 Thomas Allen. History of Surrey 1830 p290
11 Pigot. 1823/4 Guide to Surrey 1834
12 Ibid
13 Richard Barham. 1840 Ingoldsby Legends Babes in the Wood
14 Oxford Dictionary of National Biography
15 Hermione Hobhouse. 1971 Thomas Cubitt p 254
16 Edward Brayley. 1850 History of Surrey Vol III
17 Hermione Hobhouse. Ibid p 253
18 Illustrated Account of Clapham and Balham 1893. quoted by Hermione Hobhouse. Ibid

19 Sir Walter Besant. 1912 London South of the Thames

20 Hermione Hobhouse. Ibid p 247

21 Keith Bailey. 1980 Battersea New Town p 6

22 Thomas Winter quoted in J G Taylor 1925 Our Lady of Batersey p 285

23 Pigot. 1834 Guide to Surrey

24 Greville. Memoirs Vol IV p136-7

25 Charles Graves. 1903 Life and Letters of Sir Charles Grove p 5

26 Quoted in Battersea Park, An Illustrated History 1996

27 Matthew Arnold. quoted on local estate agent's web site

28 Chris Roberts. 2005 Cross River Traffic p 63

29 Sir Walter Besant. 1898 Pall Mall Magazine Vol XVI

30 Jorrocks' Jaunts and Jolliities. 1838 quoted in Arthur Porritt Ibid p 10

CHAPTER 4

THE SUBURBS COME TO SOUTH WEST LONDON – QUICKLY

Improved transport enabled people to live further from the centre than before, but there were also forces persuading or compelling people to move. Improved wealth was one of these, as tradesmen no longer wanted to live over the shop, but many families were displaced directly or were driven to look for more congenial surroundings by the displacement of others. Building the railways was also an important factor; some 76,000 people were displaced by railway schemes in London between 1853 and 1902, half of which were between 1859 and 1867[1]. Economic factors also stimulated the move out of central London as the high land prices drove developers to seek more intensive use of the land, replacing residential use by offices and retail, maintaining the process which had been continuing since the development of Belgravia and Pimlico. All these redevelopments drove the poor out, stimulating in turn further moves.

As a result the second half of the century saw much more rapid growth of housing, accelerating in the last quarter so that by 1900, very little land was left to be developed. This required the development of a variety of infrastructures, chiefly local government, transport, and the financial resources for new housing. Not all of these developed at the same pace, and some led while others followed the population moves.

Local Government

Local government before 1855 in what became the London County Council (LCC) area has been described as 'an interesting study of inadequacy'[2]. One estimate is that local government in London was carried out by more than 300 different bodies, deriving their authority from over 150 local acts. It was still based on local vestries, formed by the existing ecclesiastical parishes, operating on a voluntary basis and largely concerned with the operation of the Poor Law, with few powers. For example, building of sewers and taking precautions against epidemic diseases fell outside their terms of reference.

The four relevant vestries for this part of London were: Streatham – in which Balham fell, Battersea – where St Mary's covered what became South Battersea - , Clapham and Wandsworth. Although local boards of health had been provided for in the 1848 Public Health Act, London had been excluded, despite active lobbying from the Battersea vestry. There were continuing problems with sewers, even when the 1848 Act created the Metropolitan Commission of Sewers, which proved amateurish and ineffective. The problem for the legislators was, as ever, to produce a scheme for effective local government in London which kept the Corporation of the City of London happy - that is, as independent as possible.

Local government in London was reorganized in 1855 and given greater powers. The authorities could now build sewers and drains, pave roads and provide street lighting. Equally importantly, they were empowered to borrow money for the implementation of their plans. Their involvement in public health was emphasized by the requirement to appoint a chief medical officer to advise on, among other things, the checking of infectious diseases. This latter point was a real one, given the cholera epidemic in 1848, which none of the vestries thought it their role to take action against.

Two types of local authority were created; those such as Lambeth that were thought large enough to warrant administrative bodies of their own and remained parishes, and 'smaller' ones that were grouped together into local boards. Overseeing all these were the Metropolitan Board of Works which had some powers of direction and could override local decisions. To vote in the vestry elections, a ratepayer had to have been assessed and paid rates for a year, and for most vestries, the qualification for standing for vestryman was a rate assessment of at least £40 per annum. Alexander Corsellis, the clerk to the Wandsworth Board, believed that the collection of rates from those rated between £20 and £30 per annum was very difficult because they moved so frequently that they could often either not be traced or felt able to evade payment anyway.

Battersea, Clapham, Wandsworth, Putney, Streatham and were combined into the Wandsworth Local Board of Works with the addition of Tooting. However the Wandsworth Board rapidly created subcommittees to take decisions about its six individual components and provided little or no overall coordination. In practice, the pre 1855 vestry structure was maintained, albeit with greater powers, and the authorities gradually became more effective. For example the Wandsworth Board built 197 miles of sewers between 1860 and 1869, and a further 88 miles between 1870 and 1888.

Battersea never liked being brigaded with the other vestries, and argued that it was underrepresented on the Board. A Ratepayers Association was formed and the more prosperous traders formed the Bolingbroke Tradesmen's Club which nominated candidates for local offices among its members. Eventually, the Clapham vestry itself proposed that its own representation should be decreased to allow an increase for Battersea's from 30 to 36 out of 81 Board members in 1882. It was not enough to satisfy them and, with the support of the local Board, Battersea finally gained its independence in 1888. This was confirmed in 1899 when it became one of the 28 London metropolitan boroughs on the creation of the London County Council. By then Battersea was the ninth most populous borough with the tenth highest rateable value. Clapham and Streatham were then part of Wandsworth, only changing, in the most part, to Lambeth when the Greater London Council (GLC) was created in 1965.

Transport

The availability of transport, in terms of capacity, frequency and price, was of course important in determining who and how many lived in what became the suburbs of London. More and better roads and bridges opened up outlying areas that had been too distant in the past. While this literally paved the way for improved public transport, it also facilitated walking to work over much longer distances than would be considered today. 200,000 walked to the City every day from Camberwell[i] in the 1850s[3] and one historian

---

[i] Camberwell is about 1½ miles south of London Bridge.

cites his grandfather, a clerk in the Admiralty, who in the 1860s used regularly to walk from his home in Stockwell to Whitehall[4]. Meanwhile the new bridges stimulated movement across the river, although until the tolls were abolished in 1879, they were too expensive for the low paid to commute daily even by walking.

Over the nineteenth century the capacity of road-based public transport increased as new modes became available. First came stage coaches which carried a handful of passengers; then in turn horse drawn omnibuses carrying a dozen, horse drawn trams taking up to 50, and by the 1890s electrical trams. Relative costs fell as capacity increased and the transport became useable by wider groups of the population. This process was facilitated by the 1883 Cheap Trains Act which gave the Board of Trade power to require railway companies to provide cheap fares on early trains that could be used by workmen.

The coming of the railway changed everything, although not always as quickly as some have imagined or necessarily in the expected direction. The first passenger railway in South West London was the line to Southampton, started in 1834 by what became the London South Western Railway (LSWR), reaching Woking in 1838, and open in its entirety in 1840. The average journey was 21 miles with return fares from Wandsworth to the terminus at Nine Elms costing 1/6 first class and 1/- second class. It was not designed for suburban transport and its inner southern suburban stations remained relatively underused. Indeed the railways' first effect was to enable the well off to live further out in the countryside, as did Cubitt himself when he left Clapham in 1851. His own routine demonstrates the ease of commuting. He would leave his house near Dorking for the 9.55 train, arriving at London Bridge at 10.45 and leave London at 4.30 giving him time, as he wrote to a friend, to enjoy his rural quiet and peace.

Railways and Clapham Junction

The LSWR line passed through a cutting in Wandsworth Common (the land sold by Earl Spencer) and had a station called Wandsworth on what is now Battersea Rise. This name had to change when another company built a line to Richmond with a station roughly where Wandsworth Town is now and naturally also called Wandsworth. For some reason LSWR changed the name to Clapham Common, another example of the continued efforts by the railway companies to avoid naming anything after the supposedly socially inferior Battersea.

No further lines opened until 1856 when the West End of London & Crystal Palace Railway (WECPR) ran its line through another Wandsworth Common cutting with a temporary terminus roughly where the present Wandsworth Common Station is now. This station closed after only eighteen months to be replaced by one on Battersea Rise called 'New Wandsworth' – no doubt to distinguish it from the Wandsworth station on the Richmond Line. The next two railway lines were more geared up to suburban commuting. A branch of the London, Brighton and South Coast Railways (LBSCR) ran between Pimlico and Crystal Palace. Balham and Upper Tooting stations on this line opened to passenger traffic at the end of 1856 and what is now Balham station moved to its present position in 1863. It was a significant improvement on the only previous direct means of getting to London, an omnibus that ran about six times a day at the very expensive fare of one shilling, but since it still took about 45 minutes to get to Victoria, it did not itself stimulate much house building. A third main line arrived in 1862 when the London Chatham and Dover Railway (LCDR) completed the extension of their main line from Bromley to Herne Hill and then to both the City and Victoria, carefully avoiding houses in Clapham so that only 38 houses had to be demolished between Herne Hill and Battersea.

By this time all the railway companies were beginning to accept the inevitability of a single station handling all their lines and each contributed, with varying degrees of willingness, to the construction of a new station, Clapham Junction which was opened in May 1863. This provided a limited exchange facility allowing changes of destination between Nine Elms, Waterloo and Victoria with limited access to Ludgate Hill in the City.

Clapham Junction eventually took over the role of New Wandsworth station which was closed in 1869 with a new Wandsworth Common Station (the present one) opened the same day. The local inhabitants were so keen to have the station that they offered a contribution of £2500 to the cost[5]. It had an extensive goods yard as well as passenger facilities and Tim Sherwood explains that this was used as a base 'to cart general merchandise to the substantial houses and shops in Nightingale Lane, Trinity Road and Balham.'[6] However the name 'New Wandsworth' lingered on, particularly with reference to the roads to be developed on the north side of Nightingale Lane and at least three of the people in the Dictionary of National Biography are described as having lived in New Wandsworth.

To start with, the coming of Clapham Junction did not stimulate great growth in the population of South Battersea. Its principal effect was to add to the creation of railway jobs in Nine Elms and the other railway operations in Battersea. There is little evidence that railway workers lived in South Battersea, although they comprised almost 10% of the working population in North Battersea with well paid jobs and steady employment.

The effect of the developing railways on the south west suburbs was complicated and localized. By 1860, the railways were beginning to play more of a role in commuter traffic from the inner suburbs but still preferred to compete with the omnibus and trams by providing a quicker journey rather than on price. The companies' approach was set out by the Chairman of the LCDR[7],

> '*The first thing a man does when he is settling South of the river is to ascertain what will be the accommodation, what has been the character of the Railway Company with respect to punctuality, and so forth. If he finds that a place is very accessible early and late and at frequent hours, he will go there, but if he does not find that he will not go.*'

In 1875 The Builder Magazine spelt out the effect of railways on house and land prices[8]

> '*...it might be that a locality had become dotted over with gentleman's residences, occupied by persons of good means, all able to keep their carriages and saddle horses, and that the comparative remoteness of the neighbourhood was an element of value...The establishment of a new railway station in the immediate*

*vicinity of this select locality would obviously much
lessen the value of existing house property. Vacant sites
would no doubt improve in value...to be occupied by
clerks and business people .. and .. the old residents
would leave the neighbourhood.'*

There is little doubt that this happened in Clapham and South
Battersea.

Housing development

How the housing then developed in the suburbs was crucially
dependent both on the structure of land holdings, by then already in
relatively small parcels, and on whether the owner was prepared to
sell. In turn this depended on the age of the owner/occupants which
largely determined their propensity to move elsewhere. It was also
affected by what was happening nearby. There was a great desire for
social segregation so that the different classes were not forced to live
too closely together. The lack of large estates, the unwillingness – or
inability - of owners to impose controls on development, the paucity
of what we would know as town planning, the lack of large-scale
building firms and the financial structure of the building industry - all
pointed towards small-scale development.

There was one exception to this concentration on small actors
- the Land Societies. These were originally formed to exploit the
retention in the Reform Act 1832 of the ancient forty-shilling
freehold. This gave the right to vote in parliamentary elections to
all owners, whether or not resident, of freehold property worth
more than £2 in ground rent or £50 capital. This did not apply to
voting in parliamentary boroughs, but if the owner was resident
in a parliamentary borough, he acquired the right to vote in the
county in which the borough was situated. In the 1850s that would
have meant Surrey for Battersea and Clapham. The going rate in
practice for securing votes during county elections had been £50
each and the Radicals began to realise that it would be cheaper to
purchase estates wholesale and divide them into forty-shilling parts.
It took ten years and many court cases to establish the various
tests that had to be met to ensure the success of this approach.

Land Societies were invented to collect funds from shareholders to allow such purchases[ii].

At first their interest was only to sell the small freehold plots – it was the freehold ownership, not the existence of a house that guaranteed the vote – and The Times commented[9] 'The erection of houses is seldom or never to be attained in those societies'. However many of those who invested in the Societies' shares benefitted from the increases in the value of the land bank and the societies rapidly changed from being driven by political concerns to being developers in their own right. They also became one of the important channels of finance to both potential occupiers and small builders.

The largest such Society was the National Freehold Land Society created in 1849 with the radical MPs and chief architects of the freehold land movement, Richard Cobden and John Bright, as two of the directors. Although Conservatives opposed these means for creating new voters, they saw no option but to do likewise and they formed the Conservative Land Society in 1852.[iii] Both were active in South West London where the National Freehold Land Society was prepared to advance to builders the whole of the price of the land and two thirds of the value of the proposed building. In many ways, the Land Societies were the forerunners of today's building societies and indeed the National Freehold Land Society eventually became the Abbey National Building Society.

As a result, unlike many continental cities, virtually all the development in South London, certainly in inner suburban areas, was financed by the private sector speculatively and in relatively small

---

[ii] The mechanics of this were complicated, since Land Societies were not permitted to hold land themselves, only to lend money against it. This was circumvented by their directors making the purchases, although they carried the financial risk personally. The problem was solved when general limited liability became available in 1856 and societies formed joint stock subsidiaries to perform the land buying and selling roles.

[iii] Dyos gives an example whereby the Westminster Freehold Land Society had purchased thirty acres in 1850 in what is now East Moseley, adding 260 voters to the electoral roll for West Surrey for £4,700 or about £18 each. This was important because the Conservatives had recently lost their seat in East Surrey The Conservative Land Society purchased the St Margaret's Estate in Twickenham in 1854, dividing it up into 272 plots of different sizes to differentiate themselves from the identical plots favoured by Liberal estates!

lots of only a few houses, usually following a sale by one particular owner as they moved or a relation died. Each individual development could be, and usually was, tailored to the particular constraints and opportunities of the specific site. There were few large-scale builders such as Cubitt. Much of the investment was channelled by solicitors, either acting on behalf of individual clients or on their own behalf, to builders and developers that they knew.

We explore this further in later chapters but it should not be assumed that there was anything inevitable about the way that London suburbia developed. London's essentially small scale and entirely private sector development is very different to what took place in Paris or Vienna.[10] Although a few suburban villas had been built in the outskirts of Paris, the seriously rich had created a new urban district, the Chaussée d'Anton, on the Right Bank at what was the north west edge of the city. The buildings were imposing apartment blocks with each apartment taking a whole floor and the exterior copying the classical forms of the eighteenth century aristocratic mansions. However these were expensive to build and required more capital than was readily available, even to the upper middle classes and those who might develop for them.

This position was radically changed as a result of Haussmann's redevelopment of Paris. He reserved prominent sites for apartment blocks, and supported their financing through a state-sponsored mortgage bank which resulted in the savings of small investors and notaries effectively being channelled to the large builders and developers. This in turn made it even more difficult for the necessarily riskier small builders and developers to find finance. The middle class moved into these apartments with alacrity, and it was the less well off working class who had to move out of the centre. Vienna's Ringstrasse was supported by similar government involvement in the financing, and with the same result - imposing apartments for the upper middle class.

The rich move on: Clapham 1850 -1875

How did all these factors play out in Clapham? We have seen that in the eighteenth century, Clapham became accessible safely by horse and carriage but this was only really useful for the affluent who had neither to arrive at work early nor stay late. Travel to London was further improved by the availability of Waterloo Bridge (1817) and Southwark Bridge (1819) and by Macadam's work on roads, although Balham was still difficult to reach by what passed for public transport. By 1845 Punch's Mrs Caudle told her long suffering husband 'The time has come to have a cottage out of town.' [11] Roy Porter[12] explains that improved access made South London an attractive, or at least affordable, place to live and described Clapham at that time as 'classy'. T W H Crosland was less enthusiastic about suburban London, which he despised, writing of its beginnings,[13]

> 'The prosperous urban who had lived over his shop for years finds himself after much grubbing, so encumbered with superfluous wealth that he determines to acquire 'a sweetly pretty place a mile or two out'. To and from this rural retreat he drives daily in a gig.........If the site chosen by our adventurous gig-drivers has been propitious, all the rest follows. Clapham was started that way,'

But it was not necessary to rely on one's own transport. By 1825 there were frequent short stage coaches running between Clapham and the City increasingly supplemented - and replaced - by horse drawn omnibuses. These did however remain middle class, serving those who would not themselves be able to afford their own carriage and starting at eight in the morning, long after the working classes had started work. Nor were they cheap, with a fare of 6d from Clapham to the City. Nevertheless these buses allowed considerable middle class commuting and Clapham became increasingly attractive to the commercial classes.[iv]

---

iv It was on one of these buses in 1853 that the German chemist, Frederick Kekule, was woken abruptly from his sleep by the cry 'Clapham Road' at the end of the route - and luckily his own stop - to realise the tetravalency of carbon, its ability to form chains and so became the founder of organic chemistry.

By 1850, upwards of 50 return journeys from Clapham were made every weekday by either stagecoach or omnibus to the City and several other parts of London.[14] However Clapham was no longer solely populated by bankers and merchants. Rich businessmen leaving their homes in the City as its population started its permanent decline looked first to Piccadilly or Mayfair, and then to Bayswater and Marylebone. In some circumstances even parts of Pimlico were viewed as socially acceptable, but Clapham was not viewed as an alternative, and the rich preferred a move out of London entirely. Those moving to Clapham on the other hand were precisely described in Tallis' Illustrated London.[15]

'Dulwich, Camberwell, Clapham etc on the south side of the river consist, mostly, of the houses of tradesmen and others who daily visit the city in pursuit of business. The prevalent fashion among the Londoners of fixing their abode in the suburbs has been greatly encouraged by the easy communication afforded by the omnibuses and coaches which run to and from at all hours of the day, and until late at night.'

This is confirmed in a slightly later guidebook to London[16] 'City men such as stockbrokers, merchants and commercial agents, affect Tyburnia, Bayswater, Haverstock Hill, Brixton and Clapham'

The changes over the first 60 or 70 years of the nineteenth century had taken place relatively slowly as the horse drawn omnibus gradually introduced the middle class to Clapham. The growth of horse drawn trams continued this process. They increased the transport capacity further but still catered for the relatively well off, and encouraged more of those engaged in the City to live in Clapham. The first tram arrived in Clapham in 1871, carrying 46 passengers and charging 1d a mile and its effect was summarised by Edward Walford[17].

Since the construction of the Chatham and Dover Railway, Brixton and Clapham are much more accessible than formerly. There is also a good service of trams to the Borough, Westminster and Blackfriars bridges and an excellent service of omnibuses to London Bridge and Regent Street. The omnibuses, especially in the morning

*and evening ones, are horsed in a way that reminds
me of the old coaching days, and the rattling pace at
which some of their teams travel is quite contrary to the
ordinary notion of a 'bus horse's pace'*

In due course the companies were compelled to operate
workmen's trams at 1/2d a mile before 7am and after 6 pm. This in
turn increased the pressure on railways to provide corresponding
facilities, formalized in the Cheap Trains Act. Once a workmen's
train was available, the middle class did not wait too long before
moving onto somewhere more salubrious. The social structure of
the suburbs had been controlled by their geographical and social
isolation but Roy Porter[18] captured the change.

*'Before the arrival of the railways, inner suburbs served
by omnibuses had generally been rather elegant and
moderately populated. Once railways invaded, street
after street went up, row after row of houses. Much
development was still large and spacious, three and four
story houses for families with maids; but the density and
monotony of it all robbed Brixton and Brockley and all
such places of any pretensions of gentility, and made
them hopelessly vulnerable, within a couple of decades,
to multiple occupation and the slide into shadows.'*

Clapham then entered the second stage of development during
which the original mansions began to be knocked down or lose
their grounds to have large villas built in their place. But Clapham
was not yet finished, and superior houses (not apartments) were
still being built. One such development was Cedars Terrace built by
James Knowles in 1860 and named after the former house on the
site. Priscilla Metcalf describes the property as[19]:

*'a long, narrow, piece of some seventeen acres, extended
downhill from Clapham Common to what is now
Wandsworth Road continued as Lavender Hill, the old
turnpike to Kingston. Beyond it, the meadows of a great
dairy farm still in the early 1860s lay between the upper
ground of Clapham and the riverside Battersea fields area.'*

The first development was of massive five and six storey French Renaissance terraces on the North Side of Clapham Common, built as the gateway to Knowles' Park Town development. The other houses were built in Victoria Rise and Cedars Road which followed the demolition in 1851 of two eighteenth century mansions, The Wilderness (former home of the Fleet Street banker Henry Hoare) in 1851, and The Cedars itself in 1860. Edward Walford[20] wrote of the area that 'Clapham Park was long the Belgravia of Clapham but a newer and perhaps more attractive quarter has since sprung up in the Cedars.' While Priscilla Metcalf says that the estate was inhabited at first 'especially by well-off young couples with City connections, interspersed with a few retired people and comfortable widows', her overall description is less favorable[21] 'a solid undisastrous development completed within ten years and inhabited for almost a century by solid and, for the most part, undisastrous people.' Only four of the large houses remain, still acting as the Clapham end of the Park Town estate for which they were designed. The rest, including most of Victoria Rise and Cedars Road were either bombed or those remaining demolished in the 1950s to build the LCC housing estate. The Chase, however, still stands. It was a development on what had been an existing road for a long time, albeit a private one, at the back of the mansion built by Sir Denis Gauden. These too are massive detached or semi-detached villas of the mid 1870s

Smaller houses were now being added as well. Park terrace in Cavendish Road was built in 1856 on the edge of Clapham Park by William Nash, a builder and plasterer from Balham Hill, and is in contrast to Cubitt's grander building. The Clapham Rise estate, around Gauden, Sibella and adjoining roads was developed by E B I'Anson with serious, if much less substantial, houses than the villas being built by Knowles. I'Anson had been the surveyor and architect to the Hankey family who had owned the large house on the estate called Clapham Retreat. It was briefly a private lunatic asylum before being sold off by the Hankeys. Smaller houses were also built around Larkhall Rise and North Street to cater for the population moving out of central London as a result of the wholesale demolition of houses and the erection in their place of non-residential building. This demonstrates that Clapham was no longer as fashionable as it once was, and there is further evidence a few years later that the cohesiveness of suburban life so near to London was being diminished by more efficient public transport.

One of the features of suburban life at that time was the existence of local societies that discussed a range of matters, intellectual, artistic, and sometimes political. Clapham had at least one such, the Clapham Athenaeum, founded in 1841. John Knowles junior was a prominent member, but others included the architects and builders Edward I'Anson and Thomas Cubitt, John Gassiot, wine merchant and an FRS for his work on electricity, the geologist Gideon Mantell, the musicologist Charles Grove, and the astronomer Charles Pritchard who founded the renowned local grammar school. But by 1868, this society was disbanded and essentially replaced by a metropolitan version, The Metaphysical Society. This society, largely organized by the younger Knowles, included everybody, Gladstone, Huxley, Tennyson, James Morley, Leslie Stephen and many others. But it met in London, not Clapham. Eventually Knowles found it harder to attract London-based members or speakers to Clapham to prepare meetings, and in 1883, he himself moved to London, taking a lease on Queen Anne's Lodge, where the Home Office was located until recently. Even someone who had been a pillar of Clapham society for a long time felt the need to move closer to the centre of things.

Other changes were also taking place and, according to Charles Booth, Clapham became 'one of the greatest centres for Catholicism in London' and there were no more examples, as there had been on Guy Fawkes night in 1850 - just after Cardinal Wiseman had been enthroned in Southwark - of the parading and burning of an effigy of a Cardinal in scarlet hat and robe mounted on a donkey. Indeed Booth reported that by the turn of the twentieth century[22].

> 'Not only is there a very large congregation at the Church of Our Lady of Flowers in the High Street, and a convent on the Common, but the Catholics also have one or two middle class schools, occupying the old houses of the Clapham Sect, where may have been held some of the first meetings of the Church Missionary Society, or of the Bible Society, a hundred years ago.'

This had driven Trevelyan to write (in about 1876) in his life of Macaulay[23].

> 'At Clapham, as elsewhere, the old order is changing. What was once the home of Zachary stands almost within the swing of the bells of a stately Roman Catholic chapel; and the pleasant mansion of Lord Teignmouth, the cradle of the Bible Society, is now turned into a convent of nuns.'

Nevertheless, towards the end of this period there were strong signs that things were changing. Building News wrote in 1869[24].

> 'We can point to estates and localities, once open and healthy, which have given place to these close set nests of bricks and mortar in the neighbourhoods of Brixton, Clapham, and Camberwell; but as houses built readily let; any remonstrance appears to be useless.'

But this may have been too confident. The recession of the late 1860s brought the bald statement from the Architect magazine [25] that even in distant suburbs such as Highgate, Dalston, Clapham and Kennington, there were 'whole streets... full of houses let off from ground floor to attic in single rooms.'

Battersea and Balham 1850-75

Other development in Battersea was very much in two parts, confirmed by The Suburban Homes of England in 1881[26].

> 'Lavender Hill is somewhat curiously divided into two neighbourhoods. That on the right hand and lower side, reaching towards Battersea is, as we have already pointed out, of a somewhat poorer character while that on the left or Clapham Common side is very much more aristocratic. Probably the rents range from £55-100 pa.'

As we shall see, South Battersea proceeded slowly in this period. North Battersea on the other hand began to accelerate. The pace of building picked up from an average of 10-15 houses a year in the first 40 years of the century to 80 in the 1840s and 120 in the 1850s. But 5,800 were built in the 1860s and almost 7,000 in the 1870s. By 1875 there were over 11,000 houses in Battersea compared to just 335 in 1791. The vast majority of these were in terraces of two or three stories, between 15 and 20 feet wide, and would have rented for less than £30 pa. This rapid growth of housing naturally brought its recompense and the building cycle turned down rapidly towards the end of 1869. Builders went bankrupt and there were 1,345 empty houses in Battersea in 1871 with a further 435 under construction.

During this period, pressure built up to link Battersea and Clapham with Chelsea. Chelsea Bridge had been built and a road constructed south from it along the east side of Battersea Park in 1858, but went no further. Most, if not all of Clapham's communication was with the City, but many wanted to have direct access to the West End (Hyde Park is directly north of Clapham). In addition the various builders and developers in Clapham saw commercial advantage to their properties if such a road could be built – as first suggested by Cubitt in 1844. He of course had interests on both sides of the river, in Belgravia and his Clapham Park estate. James Knowles was waiting to build the Park Town estate on behalf of the Australian developer Philip Flower which would be absolutely dependent on the road.

The problem was the railways. They already had their eyes on routes to London through Battersea and the new road to Chelsea Bridge (Queenstown Road) had to cross no fewer than three railway lines. The complicated story of how this was achieved is told by Priscilla Metcalf[27], but it is an example of the power that Clapham could bring to bear. Its lobbying committee, consisting entirely of people living around Clapham Common, included Sir Charles Barry, the architect of the Houses of Parliament and whose sons were developing Victoria Rise, James Hopgood, solicitor to the late Thomas Cubitt, William Herbert, a successful retired builder, one of the Lucas brothers who had helped to build the 1862 Exhibition, John Gassiot, and finally as secretary Edward I'Anson a future president of the RIBA and active in Clapham development. The railways opposed fiercely, as did the Battersea farmer concerned who claimed that while there might be advantage to Clapham there would be none to Battersea. However in the end the road was built, but possibly more because of the lobbying of the developers than the assembled great and good. Although the developer of Park Town, Philip Flower, had completed the arrangements for buying the lease of the necessary land in December 1862, the enabling Queen's Road Battersea Extension Act was not passed until June the next year. It still took some time for some of the practical cooperation to be established and, in the interim, labourers from the LCDR regularly removed the roadmakers' tools and filled in their trenches every time they went to lunch. The toll on Chelsea Bridge, of 1/2d for pedestrians and 2d for horses, was not abolished until 1879.

The road, eventually called Queenstown Road, was only adopted by the local authority in 1869 but progress was slow since, as elsewhere, building stopped in the Park Town estate during 1870-2. There followed a constant struggle to let the properties. Attempts to let the better houses on three year leases with rents paid quarterly (as opposed to weekly rents) were generally unsuccessful; certainly, whenever the estate provided extra amenities, the properties tended to fall back into the estate's hands and were converted into flats.

Balham was still relatively select and Punch's Mrs Caudle said of Balham Hill in 1845[28].

> '*Now Brixton and Balaam Hill I think delightful. So select ! There nobody visits nobody, unless they're somebody. To say nothing of the delightful pews that make church so respectable.*'

The pews in St Mary's, Balham, were the usual three-decker high and were equipped with two pew openers, sisters called Stafford. The St Luke's parish magazine recalled.

> '*It was not for strangers that their services were required, for they were few and far between, but for the well-to-do seatholders, who had to be solemnly escorted up the isle and securely fastened into their pews, which, by the way, were provided with locks and keys dating, I suppose, from the time when St Mary's was a proprietary chapel.*'

Building in Balham still proceeded slowly. What was then Grove Road (renamed Cavendish Road in 1892) was being developed and by the 1860s a number of typical large Cubitt Clapham Park style boxes had been built along its north side. This part of Cavendish Road with the adjoining Balham New Road and Devonshire road was the first area of development away from Balham Hill in an expansion towards Clapham Park followed by the building of Balham Grove and Holly Grove in 1860. An idea of the social life comes from a description[29] of Christmas 1864 written by a sister living in what was then 5 Old Devonshire Road to her brother in school in Germany.

> 'On Christmas Day we dined with Aunt L. We mustered fifteen. We had for dinner oxtail soup, salt beef, roast turkey, boiled chicken and ham, potatoes, greens, plum pudding, mincepies, baked pears, clotted cream, blancmange, jam tart, and champagne. After dinner we played at Pope Joan and went home at 12.30'

The greater availability of building land on the north side of the railway line eventually led to quicker development. The opportunities were appearing by the end of the 1860s as evidenced by the large number of advertisements for sale of land with development potential. Two such appeared in the South London Press on 20 June 1868, the first, while headed 'Clapham, Surrey' consisted of a substantial family residence (5 Balham Terrace) and gardens bordering Balham High Road and Cavendish Road. The advertisement demonstrates how development was driven by the profit motive.

> 'The whole contains nearly eight acres, is immediately available for building purposes, and offers to freehold land societies and speculators an opportunity seldom to be met with for a highly profitable building scheme, as by a judicious arrangement and the formation of new roads several thousand feet of available frontage would be secured.'

The second advertisement, from the same auctioneers, offered both half-acre building plots and the purchase of rented accommodation.

'Messrs NORTON, TRIST, WATNEY and CO have received instructions to OFFER for Sale, at the Mart, City, on Friday, July 5 at 2o'clock, in 24 lots, a very valuable BUILDING ESTATE, containing about 12 acres, situate at Balham, within a few minutes walk of the Balham station, on the London and Crystal Palace Railway, and within about six miles of the City. It has extensive frontages to first rate roads, known as the Balham Park-road, and Boundaries Road, leading from the high road, Balham, to Wandsworth and presents eligible sites for the erection of detached and semi-detached residences, so much in demand in this favourite locality. Also Leasehold Ground-rents, amounting together to £219 per annum, amply secured upon substantially built, detached and semi-detached residences, situate in the high road from London to Tooting, and in Balham Park Road, together of the estimated value of about £1300 per annum.'

It is not surprising therefore that a number of roads were laid out in the 1860s, Ramsden, Oldridge, Temperley and Rossiter, but the recession meant that no building started on any of these until well into the 1870s. The one speculative development that did proceed was a range of more than eighty cottage-type properties built for city clerks on low incomes by Daniel Dendy. Known for a time as 'New Balham' they were built between Grove and Boundaries Road near an old trackway lined with chestnut trees that later became Chestnut Grove .These were demolished in 1973 to make way for Chestnut Grove School. Balham's population increased steadily, but by the late 1870s had only reached 3,000.

Large scale development: 1875-1900

By 1875, the majority – but not all - of the very wealthy had left Clapham, whether for homes in Surrey or elsewhere made possible by the trains, or back to the West End. Such an exodus was not confined to Clapham. F M L Thompson writes of Hampstead[30] at the same time.

'Upper class and uphill Hampstead ran into a sort of twilight time towards the end of the [19th] century, becoming thought of as either too near or too far from central London by the kind of people who were in the market for really expensive houses. Certainly, a second and almost final, retreat of the gentry occurred at this time, as those who had survived into the 1870s from the early village decided that the time had come to sell up and move out into more rural settings. By 1900 all the earlier mansions and their mini parks had disappeared.'

17: Clapham High Street

As the wealthy moved, their houses and gardens became available for redevelopment, if only on a piecemeal basis with the new housing supplied by small developers and builders taking individual sites as they came up. The middle class were now moving out of central London as shopkeepers and minor professionals no longer wanted to live above the shop. Smaller villas or semidetached houses were built for them, not just to match their pocket, but because the supply of horse buses allowed suburban middle class families to dispense with carriages and hence with coach houses and mews and the associated stable hands. As Thompson[31] points out, this allowed households to be run with only female servants and consequently houses could be smaller. The postcard (Ill 17) shows both horse trams and individual carriages in Clapham High Street. There were also changes in the social environment which required different kinds of public buildings which could provide public rooms for the use of respectable ladies. 'Ladies Coffee Rooms' began to appear in respectable hotels such as the Alexandria Hotel at Clapham Common in recognition of the change described in 1897 by Escott[32] as 'the transition from the eventless, purely domesticated existence to the locomotive, semi-public, generally unsettling, and exciting life of the future wives and mothers of middle-class Englishmen.'

The new developments on a range of different sites allowed a greater differentiation of the types and sizes of house and hence promoted greater segregation of classes. This in turn encouraged people with choice to move when they no longer felt comfortable that their surroundings properly matched their circumstances, whether environmentally or in terms of their neighbours. Booth[33] comments:

> '*A fair number of detached houses with large gardens occupied by the wealthy remain round Clapham Common, but the tendency is for their dwellings to be replaced by houses built for and tenanted by the middle and lower middle classes. The servant keeping classes of Clapham have moved either out of London altogether or to the new houses and flats in more central London, and their places taken by the fairly comfortable out of Kennington, South Lambeth and Stockwell. The law of successful migration is again seen. On the west side of the common there is a continual shifting in a westerly direction, leading to a general level of lower middle in place of middle classes.*'

Many of these changes were driven by the new forms of work as the number of clerks and shop assistants grew. The employment of clerks rose geometrically in the second half of the century and by 1901 7,000 clerks were to be found in Camberwell, the highest concentration anywhere[34]. Many others had already moved from Camberwell to South Battersea and we shall explore this in more detail in the next chapter.

Journeys to work were made even easier by the coming of the tube from the City to Stockwell in 1890, extended to Clapham North in 1900 and Clapham Common (Ill 18).

18: Clapham Common underground station c 1904

These stations have an underground island platform between north and southbound trains, the only two remaining stations to do so. The tube made public transport available to clerks and shop workers who could not previously have afforded the travel to London. Although this first deep tube had been planned without electrification, cable cars were abandoned in favour of electric traction just before it opened. Percy Fitzgerald[35] commented:

> 'The traveller who would not encounter the monotony of the protracted but cheerful Clapham Road, can find a pleasing diversity by diving into the boundaries of the earth, through the agency of a lift, and taking the electric railway to Stockwell - a curious experience. Indeed one can make choice of steam, omnibus, tramcar, cab, or electric line to Clapham.'

What Punch called the 'sardine-can' line attracted too many passengers and the City and South London reduced fares to 1d for workmen's trains before 8am, raising them to 3d between 8 and 10 am for the middle classes. In fact it turned out that the tunnels were too narrow and the electric power too weak to allow the line to carry the volume of traffic that it needed to compete profitably with the horse trams overhead. (More powerful electric locomotives were developed in time for the Waterloo and City Line, 'The Drain', which was built during 1894-8 and was an economic success)

T S Eliot[36] wrote memorably of those leaving London Bridge Station in the morning.

'A crowd flowed over London Bridge, so many,
I had not thought death had undone so many.
Sighs, short and infrequent, were exhaled,
And each man fixed his eyes before his feet.'

The same daily commuters into London were described rather more romantically, by Walter Besant in his book about South London[37].

'If you want to form some idea of the South London folk, go stand inside Cannon Street station and watch the trains come in, each with its freight of those who earn their daily bread within the city. See them pass out – by the hundred – by the thousand – by the fifty thousand. The brain reels at the mere contemplation of this mighty multitude which comes in every morning and goes out every afternoon. As they hurry past you observe on each the same expression, the same set eagerness, with which the day's work is approached. ....His face means battle, daily battle with which the weapons are superior knowledge, earlier knowledge, keen sight, readiness and ruthlessness, while there is as much need for success, of courage, tenacity, and bluff as in any battle between contending armies.'

What did these changes mean for south west London? The 'Handbook to the Environs of London' said in 1876[38].

*'Clapham has increased so largely of late years in houses
and population (27,347 inhabitants in 1871) that it has
become a town in size and appearance if not in name
.....Skirting the common are several of the roomy old
brick mansions, with good elms before them, the abode
of wealthy citizens which once nearly surrounded it but
are now giving way to brick and compo Gothic and
Italian villas.'*

Generally all three areas moved further down market and the
houses became smaller, giving rise to clear social distinctions among
the inhabitants. The Architect reported, drawing on a comment of Mr
Caudle to Mrs Caudle 30 years earlier, '...wholesale Clapham declines
the acquaintance of retail Clapham.' Many regretted the changes. John
Grover, writing a history of Clapham in 1886, was depressed.[39]

*'One by one the great houses are passing away – formal,
ugly terraces are taking their place – and it will be soon
the melancholy task of some suburban Gibbon to write
'The Decline and Fall of Clapham Common' The hand
of the speculative builder is heavy, and it effaces old
landmarks in the same ruthless fashion as the Goth and
the Hun swept away the magnificence of imperial Rome.
It is time to try to rescue the past from the oblivion into
which it is rapidly falling, and the object of my task is to
accomplish this, to some small extent, before it is too late.'*

Put another way, the City Press in August 1887 declared that
'Wilberforce and Macaulay now would scarcely know the scenes of
their boyhood.'

Certainly Clapham was no longer fashionable and a final
comment comes from Mrs Panton's 'From Kitchen to Garret'. It was
published in 1887 but sufficiently popular to run to 11 editions in 10
years and which, having made clear received wisdom that the most
desirable areas of London are the south and west, fails to mention
Clapham as at all desirable[40].

*'While I most emphatically taboo those [suburbs] on the
north side, I can as emphatically recommend those on the*

south. ......I always consider that the southern suburbs are at least twenty-five years in advance of those in the north; the houses are more modern; they are much more tastefully arranged; I wish I could say that they were more sensibly built; and the shops are better; the society is undoubtedly infinitely superior; the churches are not to be compared for a moment. .....But... one has to consider the vileness and uncertainty of the train service.....

'Penge and Dulwich are dreary and damp, they are evidently well supported and much lived in. But the higher parts of Sydenham are to be preferred; while Forest Hill, the higher parts of Lordship Lane, Elmers End - where there are some extremely pretty and convenient villas - and the best parts of Bromley, Kent, are all they should be. Still, to those who do not mind the north side of London, Finchley, Bush Hill Park – where the houses are nice to look at and excellently arranged – and Enfield are all worthy of consideration.'

The fortunes of the building industry fluctuated with both booms and busts. Tarbuck's 1875 Handbook of Household Property[41] quoted an anonymous poet.

'The richest crop for any field
Is a crop of bricks for it to yield.
The richest crop that it can grow
Is a crop of houses in a row.'

But the building peak in 1881 led to the inevitable result and the Chairman of the National Freehold Land Society, the forerunner of the Abbey National Building Society, said in 1885,[42] 'An array of unoccupied houses meets the eye in all directions and even where some of the buildings have recently succeeded in finding tenants, at greatly reduced rentals'. There continued to be adverse comments on the speculators and the housing density they achieved. Writing a book on 'Landlordism' Henry Lazarus[43] complained of the greed of the great landlords in 'abolishing altogether breathing space from their estates, compel the better-to-do tenants to move into healthier neighbourhoods, and leave only the very poor behind.' Building News confirmed this point in 1890[44].

> 'Clapham, Brixton, Dulwich and Norwood on the south are already being irretrievably spoiled by the reckless speculator..... while every acre of land is allowed to be crowded with from fifty to sixty houses, which is the average density in many of the new localities, the higher class of suburbs are being brought down to the level of those in poorer districts.'

Commentators still spoke highly of the west of the Common, so for example, Edward Walford[45] writes in 1897.

> 'At Battersea Rise, which forms the north western extremity of Clapham Common many pleasant villas and superior houses have been built, this being a most desirable situation and respectable neighbourhood'

This is echoed by Besant[46], who observed the juxtaposition of old and new on the West Side of Clapham Common.

> 'Along the western edge are many old mansions standing back in freely timbered grounds, each with its encroachment of posts and chains railing in portions of the Common and keeping their privacy by directing the footpath from their doors. Behind them are deep old fashioned gardens with stretches of new houses at the foot in strange contrast.
>
> The Common as it stands today is beautifully kept; trees and grass alike are protected, but the gorge is steadily disappearing, the last of it being at the Nightingale Lane side, where are also some of the finest trees, many of which are said to have been brought from abroad and planted by Captain Cook, the great navigator, whose wife passed her last years in the High Street of Clapham.'

But as late as 1893 there were still those who saw at least a faded gentility in Clapham. Percy Fitzgerald[47] wrote, perhaps a little condescendingly.

> '[Clapham] has really an inviting air of rusticity. The natives, too, seem to be rustic in their way. These are Claphamites who would never ask to leave its placid precincts; their tastes are simple and pastoral. ...... On the fringe of the Common, and notably at Battersea Rise, are seen substantial mansions, with their grounds and gardens tenanted by the 'well-to-do gentry, who have a society of their own, 'keep their carriages' and give dinner parties now and again. The confectioners in The Pavement often have a busy time of it, 'send out dinners' and equip parties in London fashion. It seems like some thriving country town. There are concerts and 'Philharmonic Society', lectures, readings, string quartets galore. And yet London is but twenty minutes away. The air is restoring and especially to the smoke-dried lungs of the 'jaded Londoner'. Indeed the wholesome breezes sweep from Wimbledon and Putney Heath in the west and thus the Claphamite stands on a plateau far above the great city, and there is nothing between him and Brighton.'

This picture is confirmed, at least by Thomas Burke's perhaps rose tinted memory writing in 1937[48].

> 'Clapham.... was for many years after its early growth a district of large houses kept by well-to-do people of the conservative sort. They helped maintain its original rural atmosphere and to protect it, in the eighties and nineties, from 'development'... Some of them even had meadows and cows'

Nevertheless, by the end of the century, the picture was clearly a very different Clapham from even fifty years before. As Booth put it[49]:

> 'Old and wealthy Clapham has gone to dwell in Kensington or Surrey, and the new Clapham of £40 householders has moved in from Kennington and

elsewhere... Rents of the best old houses round Clapham
Common and even of middle class residences have fallen'

We end this piece about Clapham in 1900 by quoting the possibly tongue in cheek and certainly unfair comments of T W H Crosland in his book The Suburbans[50], where he describes Clapham as the 'capital of Suburbia'.

'If you walk down the Clapham Road, you will have seen the best part of all that Suburbia has to show you. You will comprehend the why and wherefore and raison d'etre of halfpenny journalism. And you will perceive that whizzers, penny buses, gramophones, bamboo furniture, pleasant Sunday afternoons, Glory Songs, modern language teas, golf, tennis, high school education, dubious fiction, shilling's worth of comic writing, picture postcards, miraculous hair-restorers, prize competitions, and all other sorts of twentieth century clap-trap, have got a market and a use, and black masses of supporters.... From its youth up it has enjoyed a reputation for respectability, and no man has dared to hold it up to opprobrium. Cunning persons, however, have latterly and of their cunning hazarded correct surmises as to the true meanings of it. They have said to themselves, 'Behold, herein is the strong city of the foolish and the vapid and the empty headed. The citizens thereof have a little money, and a paucity of brains, and, if we mistake not, they will e'en purchase such and such mediocre merchandise. Lo. We lay that merchandise at the simple feet of Clapham.'...They have concluded with a creditable sagacity that what Clapham accepts today will be accepted by all Suburbia and all Provincia tomorrow. ...... If, on the other hand, it fails to meet with the approval of Clapham, it will fail to meet with the approval of snobbery, brainlessness, and suburbanism in the mass.'

Balham

We have already mentioned the Priory in Balham. It became a centre of great notoriety in 1876 when the owner, Mr Bravo, was poisoned by antimony. Many believed that the murderer was his wife, Florence, possibly abetted by her supposed lover, Dr Gully, who lived in nearby Bedford Hill. The inquest was held in the Bedford Hotel and lasted many weeks. Crowds came from all parts to watch the arrival of Mrs Bravo at the inquest and also of the well-known barristers including, on behalf of the Crown, the local John Gorst QC. He later became Sir John but was at the time MP for Chatham and formerly the Conservative party's central agent. He lived on the Dents estate and Gorst Road was named after him in 1883. While there was not enough evidence to secure a conviction, people still wandered up to the Common to gaze at the Priory and removed the fence palings as mementoes. Recent books into the case argue that Florence was guilty[51], and one even claims that she had murdered her previous husband by the same method.[52]

Despite this cause célèbre, life in Balham in the 1880s was described by Arthur Porritt[53]

> 'as strangely placid, and over the quiet High Road mighty oaks and elms spread their branches until they almost mingled. The southernmost terminus of the London tramway service was at Nightingale Lane. Stately houses in ample garden stood well back from the main road, shielded from the common gaze by high walls. Behind them, stretching to the Tooting Bec Common, were the spacious grounds of still larger mansions, homes of wealthy merchants and professional men.'

The last quarter of the century at last saw real growth in Balham. By the mid 1880s, most of the open ground on the north and more fashionable side of Bedford Hill had been given over to housing with a mixture of styles suitable for an aspiring middle class. Perhaps to our surprise, Walter Besant[54] could link Balham with Sydenham, Highgate, Hampstead, Barnes and Richmond as containing 'the richer sort of City tradesmen'. Grander houses, with yearly rents of £70-200, appeared near Tooting Bec Common and

Ramsden Road was completed. The Suburban Homes of London reported in 1881[55].

> 'Balham Hill Road is fringed with a succession of fine houses, all of which have extensive gardens, and not one of them would be of less rental than £100' making the road 'about as pleasant a place for a promenade as we know.
>
> For a long time, the residents of Balham were confined to what are termed 'carriage people' and a few labourers or gardeners; but when the Brighton company constructed their West End route to Crystal Palace, they opened a station at Balham; and the place soon became revolutionized. A large proportion of the land was cut up into building plots and at the Clapham end a series of fine roads was made. In the angle formed by Balham Hill Road and Nightingale Lane are a number of handsome thoroughfares with just that mixture of the practical and the picturesque which appeals at once to the taste of the suburban house seeker... there will be found a capital choice of houses ranging from £40 to £60 or £70 per annum.
>
> It is a great recommendation of Balham that it has no back slums. All is of an 'eminently respectable' character, and no wonder that it has been chosen as a place of residence by so many of the wealthy.'

However the writer did see one problem.

> 'There is perhaps a little drawback as far as its suitability for a place of residence for businessmen is concerned – the communication with the City is not very good. Some of the Clapham omnibuses from London Bridge come as far as Tooting and Balham but the ride, though pretty, is tedious. It makes it the suburban residence of the businessmen of the West End, rather than of the denizens of the City.'

Ill 19 shows one of the horse-drawn trams in Balham High Road.

19: Horse drawn cab, Balham High Road 1899

The major residential housing development of that era in Balham was the 100 acre Heaver estate built from 1890-7 on the grounds of Bedford Hill House and the nearby Elms farm. Although the cheaper properties had rents starting from £38 – in keeping with other local estates -, the larger houses near Tooting Bec Common and the Heaver Lawn Tennis Club could command £80. The rapid increase in population (and Balham grew from 3,000 in the late 1870s to 38,000 in 1901) did result in Balham becoming a real shopping centre. It had its own department store, John Holdron's, where staff lived on the premises, and Harper's drapers' store lasted until the 1960s. John Sainsbury opened his sixth shop in the Balham High Road in 1888, viewing it as a part of his expansion into middle class areas. This only closed in 1969 when the shop moved into larger premises which are still a Sainsbury's supermarket. Most of the chain store owners were there, Marks and Spencer, Cullens, Liptons, Freeman Hardy and Willis, Lilley and Skinner and the Home and Colonial. It was this concentration of shops that, no doubt, led the developers of the Hyde Farm Estate in the first few years of the twentieth century to claim[56] 'Balham is well provided with first class shops and stores, allowing a careful housewife to shop more economically than in other parts of London.' Ill 20 and 21 show some of the shops in the Balham High Road at about this time.

20: Balham High Road c 1907

21: Balham High Road c 1911

This remarkable retail development would have been directed at the prospective occupiers who were, in the main, city clerks paying a rent of as little as 10/- per week for a flat and up to 18/- for a six room house. However by 1900 Booth[57] reported 'that the incoming population was of lower middle and working class' and the Vicar of St Mary's, Balham had seen 'the rich almost all gone', perhaps anticipating Arthur Ransome's comment on staying with relations in Balham in 1904 'Balham was the ugliest and most abominable of London's unpleasing suburbs.' But while putting Balham between the 'fashion though faded' Clapham and 'pure working class Tooting', Booth's overall comment was that 'socially the district may yet drop a little'. It would have been the continued improvement in transport which made this possible, with the transport difficulties being rectified by the electrification of the horse tramway line from Westminster to Balham Hill, then extended to the terminus at Totterdown Street, Tooting – inaugurated by the Prince of Wales in 1903 (Ill 22).

22: Opening of Electric trams to Totterdown 1903

This opening was connected with the LCC's purchase of the land on which the Totterdown estate of almost 1,300 houses was built from 1903 to 1911. Besant commented on this development:[58]

'Tramway terminus to Tooting, with its threepenny fare to London, calls to mind the fact that only a few

*years ago the daily trips of the coaches from Clapham
Common to London averaged about 5 a day, while now
the service here is a five minute one from early till late.'*

The rent for a five room house on the Totterdown estate was
10/6d a week, said to be up to 3/6d a week cheaper than for
comparable accommodation in central London, leaving a substantial
2/6 a week saving after the workmen's return fare (2d return starting
before 8 am) had been paid, incidentally very much greater than the
saving of only 1/- a week to be made on the comparison for a three
room flat. Not surprisingly, the estate filled up quickly, with half the
first 75 tenants working in central London on an average wage of
32/- a week. The number of workmen's tickets leapt from just over
0.5m in 1902/3 to over 4m in 1909/10. Not everyone was happy with
this. A letter to the Evening News in 1911 complained,[59]

*'I have used the Tooting and Westminster service for
six months and have rarely been able to travel thereon
with comfort. Last night, at Nightingale Lane, Balham,
I was twice turned off a full car for Westminster at 9.30
am and have had to board one for some other place
and change to the tube in Clapham..... At Westminster
Bridge, the Tooting cars at 5 o'clock were already full
upon arriving there every evening but one last week... It
is on the Tooting and Streatham routes that conditions
are the worst.'*

As has been seen, this is not the first nor will it be the last
complaints about the Northern Line or its equivalent.

The next chapters start to narrow down the focus of the study
by concentrating on South Battersea.

(Endnotes)

1 Jack Simmons. Ibid p 297
2 Janet Roebuck. 1979 Urban Development in 19th-century London p 4
3 H J Dyos. Victorian Suburb p 69
4 Jack Simmons. 1973 The Power of the Railways in The Victorian City Ed Dyos and Wolff
5 Tim Sherwood. 1994 Change at Clapham Junction p 46

6   Tim Sherwood. Ibid p 45
7   Tim Sherwood. Ibid p 59
8   Quoted in Tim Sherwood. Ibid p 83
9   The Times. 27 Nov 1848
10 Robert Fishman. 1987 Bourgeois Utopias p 108-16
11 Mrs Caudle's Lectures. Punch 1845
12 Roy Porter. 1994 London A Social History p 224
13 T W H Crosland.1904 The Suburbans p 10
14 Edward Brayley. History of Surrey Vol III
15 William Gaspey. 1851 Tallis's Illiustrated Guide to London
16 G F Pardon 1862 Routledge Shilling Guidebook to London
17 Edward Walford. 1897 Old and New London – The Southern Suburbs
18 Roy Porter. Ibid p232
19 Priscilla Metcalf. 1980 James Knowles   p 167
20 Edward Walford. Ibid
21 Priscilla Metcalf. Ibid p 166
22 Charles Booth. 1900 Life and Labour of the people in London, 3d Ed p182
23 G O Trevelyan. 1876 Life and Letters of Lord Macaulay
24 Building News 1869 quoted in Donald Olsen 1976 The Growth of Victorian London
    p134
25 The Architect 1871 quoted in Olsen Ibid p119
26 W S Clarke. Ibid
27 Priscilla Metcalf . 1978 The Park Town Estate and the Battersea Triangle
28 Mrs Caudle's Lectures Punch 1845
29 St Luke's parish magazine 1933
30 F M L Thompson. Hampstead 1974
31 F M L Thompson Ed 1982 The Rise of Suburbia p 11
32 T H S Escott. 1897 Social Transformations of the Victorian Age.
33 Charles Booth. Ibid p 192
34 H J Dyos. Ibid p 192
35 Percy Fitzgerald. 1893 Victorian London Vol II– The Suburbs Ibid p 161
36 T S Eliot. 1922 The Wasteland
37 Sir Walter Besant. South London 1907
38 James Thorne. 1876 Handbook to the Environs of London
39 J W Grover. 1886 Old Clapham p 11
40 Mrs Panton. 1896 From Kitchen to Garret 9th Edition p26
41 Tarbuck. 1875 Handbook of Household Property
42 H J Dyos. Ibid p 80
43 Henry Lazarus. 1892 Landlordism; An illustration of the Rise and Spread of Slumland
44 Building News 1890 quoted in Roy Porter. 1994 London A Social History p232
45 Edward Walford. Ibid
46 Sir Walter Besant. 1912 London South of The Thames
47 Percy Fitzgerald. Ibid p 161
48 Thomas Burke. 1937 London in my time
49 Charles Booth. Ibid p 192
50 T W H Crosland. 1904 The Suburbans p 82
51 James Ruddick. 2001 Death at the Priory
52 John Williams. 1976 Suddenly at the Priory

53 Arthur Porritt. 1930 A Home of Fellowship p 17
54 Sir Walter Besant. London in the Nineteenth Century 1909
55 W S Clarke. 1881 Suburban Homes of London
56 Graham Gower. 1996 Balham A Brief History p 31
57 Charles Booth. Ibid p 103,4
58 Sir Walter Besant. 1912 London South of the Thames
59 Evening News 17 January 1911 quoted in Alan Jackson. 1973 Semi-Detached London

CHAPTER 5

SOUTH BATTERSEA.
THE START OF DEVELOPMENT

The pattern of development seen in the last chapter for the area as a whole is repeated in South Battersea but some tens of years later than for Clapham itself. That is: first the building of large houses with estates for the wealthy, then gradual replacement by smaller villas for the upper middle class, and finally rows of terrace or semi-detached housing. In South Battersea, most of the large houses were in place by the mid nineteenth century at the latest, whether on Bolingbroke Grove, Battersea Rise or the west side of Clapham Common. Their gradual replacement and the growth of the population sometimes followed and sometimes stimulated improved transport. The very rapid net overall growth of the population conceals movement in different directions both into and out of London and which need to be understood to explain the change from Georgian to late Victorian suburb. An outline of this development between 1851 and 1900 is given in Roger Logan's 'South Battersea' reprinted as 'Between the Commons' in 2007[1].

In the middle of the nineteenth century, South Battersea, or its modern name 'Twixt the Commons', was still semi-rural. There were only a few houses around its periphery; five along what was becoming known as Bolingbroke Grove; one on the Battersea side of Nightingale Lane; seventeen on the West Side of Clapham Common; and five on Battersea Rise. Broomfield House, later to be renamed Broomwood, was the only one in the middle. Almost all the houses had been built or extended in the last quarter of the eighteenth century and no more than two or three substantial houses were built in the first half of the nineteenth century. There were still a number of working farms with associated cottages. A stream, known from the seventeenth century as the Falcon Brook, with sources rising in both Balham and Tooting,[2] still ran into the Thames above ground in its valley between the two commons. This name, as for the pub and road, stemmed from the crest of the former Lord of the Manor, St John, a falcon rising.[3] The brook was covered in and used thereafter as a main sewer in 1869. This is captured in Map 6, produced in 1862 by Stanford.

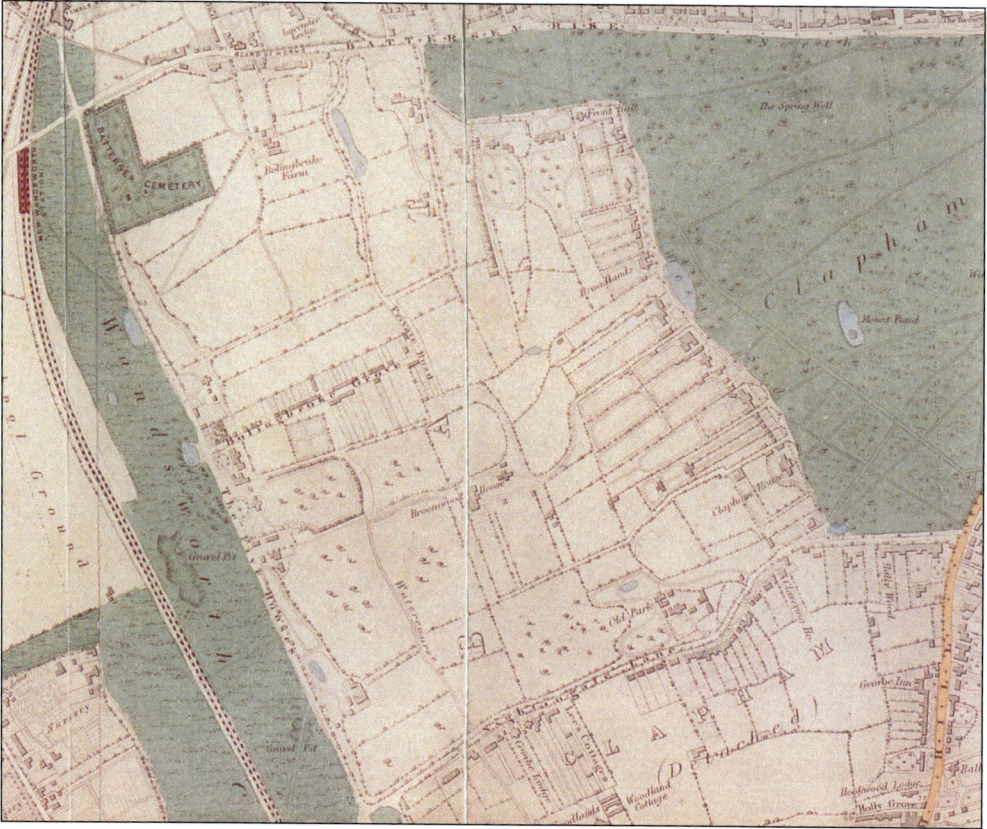

Map 6: Stanford map 1862

Although the houses had remained unchanged, that does not mean that the occupants did. Merchants and bankers, or their families, did not have the same emotional ties to property as the aristocracy, who traditionally depended on the income from land and had - or believed they had – long standing and permanent ties to a locality. There is no example of entail around the Clapham area; indeed there were many substantial families who were content with a long lease. For the rich of Clapham, property was no different from any other investment. They moved elsewhere when it suited them.

Most were happy to sell up and take their profit, usually children selling up at the death of the surviving parent. The only exceptions to this were the Thorntons who remained in Battersea Rise House, bought by Henry Thornton in 1792, for almost 120 years. Even this sale, virtually the last of the big houses, was accelerated by the breakup of the family as a result of a dispute about a marriage.

We also find some ambivalence about the name of the area, giving greater weight to the confusion about the local boundaries that we saw in previous chapters. Those living in the houses on Bolingbroke Grove described themselves variously in their wills as living in Battersea Rise, Battersea, Wandsworth Common and Clapham. It is doubtful if the traditional boundaries mattered very much to the inhabitants who attended the church that suited them best, whichever parish they lived in. Henry Thornton, living in Battersea Rise House on Battersea Rise in the parish of St Mary's Battersea owed his allegiance to the church of Holy Trinity, Clapham, the church attended by his father who had also bought the right to choose the vicar. Robert Dent on the other hand, living in a house off Nightingale Lane and certainly closer physically to Holy Trinity, was a supporter of the less evangelical St Mary's Battersea.

By the early 1850s, the population growth had created a demand for infrastructure. Local services were needed; retail shops, schools, churches and hospitals, all of which needed people to work in them. However the most pressing need was for a new burial ground for the parish, caused by a relatively high death rate of about 20 per 1000. In 1852 an Act 'To amend the law for burial in the Metropolis' provided for special vestry meetings to be called to discuss the problems of insanitary burial places should ten or more ratepayers request them. Although the Battersea vestry took no immediate action, the Battersea Burial Board was created in 1855 and after some consideration decided:[4]

> 'to apply to Henry Willis Esq, the owner of land at the corner of Five Houses Road (Bolingbroke Grove), Battersea West Common, the contemplated site for the Cemetery, to ascertain the terms and price for the purchase of the said land'

This land, consisting of just over eight acres corresponding to a particular field in the 1836 tithe map and the site of the present cemetery, had been left unsold when Henry Wheeler, bought Bolingbroke House, his home for six years, and some of its land in July 1858. This had been sold by Henry Willis following the death of his widowed mother Sara in 1857. There were a number of local objections[5], both to having a cemetery nearby and, most importantly having to pay for it. The Battersea Vestry refused to allocate the necessary money, which of course the ratepayers would have had to pay, claiming that the proposed cemetery was far too large for the population of the parish of about 10,000 and too expensive. They argued there were perfectly good cemeteries available at Lambeth and Norwood, the latter being used by Clapham in preference to acquiring their own, and that any paupers could continue to be buried at Woking for an inclusive annual charge to the Vestry of between £50 and £60. As a result of this refusal, the Burial Board appealed to the Home Secretary[6] complaining that the Vestry meeting which discussed it had been:

> 'of a most disorderly character, the objectors, many of them indulging in gesticulations, groans, hisses and personalities, which rendered it impossible for anyone to hear what was going on, much less have an opportunity of calmly discussing the subject'

The Home Secretary upheld the Burial Board in October 1859 and the land was purchased for £5,000 at the end of 1859 and a further £3,000 spent on the fencing, laying out and draining to the specified depth of seven feet together with the building of the chapels, lodge, and other buildings. The new cemetery came into use in November, 1860, but there was continued arguing about whether all the expenses had to be met out of the £8,000. In the end the Home Secretary was forced to publish the correspondence between the Burial Board and himself. The need for the cemetery became very evident soon after, since between its opening at the end of 1860 and the middle of 1874, no fewer than 10,595 people were buried there, more than the total population of Battersea in 1851 and more than half the population in 1861. By 1871, and with a total population of 54,000, some 1,100 deaths a year would have to be dealt with. The cemetery was full by 1885.

This and the subsequent two chapters describe how South Battersea was developed over a period of about half a century and the final result is shown in Map 7.

Map 7: Twixt the Commons street map

This shows all the roads, whenever built, and will be helpful in understanding the references to individual developments.

The first development: Chatham Road

At the same time as the land for the cemetery was being purchased and prepared, the first new road in South Battersea was laid out with the standard width of forty feet, and building started. This followed the death in 1852 of the owners of one the Five Houses on Bolingbroke Grove, Miss Elizabeth Hoper at the age of 92. She was the sister-in-law of the previous occupier, Matthew Chalie and more details of their history are given in Chapter 7. She left the house to her three nephews; it then changed hands a number of times and was finally purchased by the British Land Society, the land dealing subsidiary of the National Freehold Land Society. It was the location of the offices of the Wandsworth District Board of Works from 1856 until they were given notice in 1858. James Lord, a barrister lived there until 1863 while building was going on round him, and the house was demolished in 1864.

This was not the only local purchase by the National Freehold Land Society which was also active around St John's Hill near Clapham Junction. It seems likely that the road was laid out as early as 1855 (possibly by Charles Dungate, a grocer living and trading in Clapham at 19, The Polygon) because it was never approved by the Metropolitan Board of Works which came into existence in 1856. If so, this would also have been before the Society had been enabled to establish its land trading subsidiary and so would have been more likely to be fulfilling its original aims of increasing the number of voters and promoting owner occupation.

The first evidence of building intent was a building notice in 1857 for a single house on Bolingbroke Grove – that being the original name of Chatham Road which still appears on the Stanford Map of 1862. This was followed by a number of other building notices, all of which now referred specifically to Chatham Road. The reason for calling the road 'Chatham' is not clear, although Logan[7] has advanced a number of possibilities. One, favoured in the latter part of the nineteenth century[8], seems to have been after William Pitt, Earl of Chatham, who was closely associated with the Thorntons at Battersea Rise House and whose library he had designed. Logan suggests that the name may have been chosen by Dungate as the developer or by the National Freehold Land Society and there are plenty of examples elsewhere of the Society naming roads after politicians such as Bright and Cobden, even though Pitt might not have come so naturally.

By March 1860, ten houses had been built, and there was an unusually high percentage of owner occupation, a characteristic of early National Freehold Land Society financed developments. Most of the new houses were small, with an annual rent of about £20. Houses of this size were not designed to attract the middle class who would have needed more room to accommodate their servants but any freeholders would have met the electoral test for parliamentary elections.

It is not always easy to establish which houses these were, since the numbering in both the Poor Rate Book, and the 1861 Census a year later, tends to represent the order in which the houses were planned or built (or even the order visited by the census official) rather than their eventual order in the street. The houses in Chatham Road were not renumbered in a systematic way until the beginning of 1879. Although Charles Dungate is listed as owner of four of the houses, it is unlikely that he actually lived in any of them; Similarly John Collyer, a farrier living in Battersea Rise, was identified as the owner of two of the houses.

The others are, perhaps, surprising examples of home owners in the mid 1800s. James Havard was a carpenter, aged 28 with a wife and four children when he bought the house which became 18 Chatham Road; the 1862 Rate Book shows him as owning the next door house as well. Havard was still living there in 1901, a widower with his youngest son Alfred's family.

Next door to him were the houses occupied by the Godfreys. Thomas Godfrey senior, born in 1796, was a skilled metal chaser or embosser, a trade continued by his eldest son James. His other sons, Lewis, Thomas and Reuben were wood carvers, and the four families lived next door to each other. The Godfreys were an early example of those moving across the river from Chelsea. While it was possible that they returned there each day to work, that would have provided some drain on their pockets since the toll on Chelsea Bridge was ½d. The fact that Thomas junior was soon paying rates on a workshop in Chatham Road suggests that they intended to do most of the work in Battersea. The Godfrey families continued to live in

Chatham Road until the next century. Reuben died in 1862 and his younger brother Thomas married Reuben's widow, Fanny, the next year and took care of their three children.[i] Thomas was still living at 27 Chatham Road in 1891, but by 1901 he had moved next door to his other house, 25, where he lived with his youngest son, Montagu, and his wife and child.

Of the other two original occupants, Francis Newman was the son of a Lambeth greengrocer and described himself as a millwright/engineer in the censuses. By 1871 he had moved to a house in Plough Lane which could accommodate his wife and seven children and he was by then a corn dealer. He died in 1877 but his wife Sarah kept the business going until their son, William, took over. Her second daughter, Phoebe, married their lodger, William Oulds, a candle maker, perhaps at Price's Candles. By 1901, Sarah was living on her own means at 69 Battersea Rise with her unmarried daughter, Alice, now aged 47, and Phoebe and her family which included two children. Sarah appears to have been concerned to conceal her true age, since while she was married she declared her year of birth in the three censuses during her married life as 1831 – which would have made her only 18 at the time of her marriage in 1849, rather than an adult 23, but as soon as she became widowed, she declared her year of birth as 1826 – which would have made her two years older than her husband Francis. It is this age that is recorded on her death certificate in 1902.

Joseph Stapleton was a carpenter from Ampthill in Bedfordshire and moved across the river from Westminster to Chatham Road in 1859 with his wife Lucy and three children. His house was, or became, a beerhouse –which he had advertised with a sign. Following complaints, the District Board was advised that it did not have the power to remove it because the road was still private[9]. By 1861 this had become the Bolingbroke Arms, clearly a successful pub since Stapleton extended it to take in three houses, although he still described himself as a carpenter. The pub may have financed further business since by 1871 he was living in Falcon Road and describing himself as a builder, although this appears to have been on a fairly

---

[i]   A marriage of this kind was not legalised until 1921 by The Deceased Brother's Widow Marriage Act.

small scale. He was responsible for 42-4 Bennerley Road in 1877, 62-4 Shelgate Road in 1879-80 and 95-7 Mallinson Road in 1886. In1881, Stapleton moved to a new house in Shelgate Road with his second, younger, wife Louisa, Lucy having died in 1878. They shared the house with another household headed by an accountant. One of Stapleton's grandsons was born in Australia, suggesting that his son Frederick, also a carpenter, had travelled or emigrated and then returned.

During this period there were six pubs in Chatham Road, three of which were still operating in 2000 - the Bolingbroke Arms, the Eagle, and the Gardeners Arms. The Bolingbroke Arms was the only example remaining in the twenty-first century of the houses built before 1860 in Chatham Road, having been spared the 1971/4 redevelopment of that area, although it did not last much longer. The pub (Ill 23) was closed in 2003 and its site acquired (again) for development in 2006 with demolition in 2007. The names of two of the pubs, the Gardeners' Arms and one long since gone, the Carpenters Arms, may have reflected the high concentration of those occupations in the road and the Carpenters' Arms resident and possible licensee, Samuel Cutler, was himself a carpenter.

23: Bolingbroke Arms pub

The Gardeners Arms was where 'The Friends in New', a local Court of the Ancient Order of Foresters, met from 1866.[10]

By 1861, Chatham Road had 36 houses occupied and one empty. The small houses with relatively low rents were occupied by people whose earning power was restricted or, like those in the building trade, subject to uncertainty. Ten of the heads of households were carpenters or of other building trades. Five were gardeners and three were agricultural labourers, one describing himself as a cow keeper. He also paid rates for a cow house, reflecting the part that agriculture still played in Battersea. Only two houses had live-in servants (a wine merchant's clerk who lived next to Stapleton and a civil servant) and seven took in lodgers.

Only three or four people might have had aspirations to middle class; a German teacher – who later moved to 2 Bennerley Road, a clerk to the Duchy of Lancaster – who owned the house and lived there for ten years or so before moving to Croydon, and a cab prefactor. As Logan points out[11], it seems unlikely that the original occupants of Chatham Road had been stimulated to move to South Battersea by the creation of the railways since they would have had no need to travel to the City for their work, nor generally could they have afforded it. There were few 'early' trains before 9.00am from Clapham Junction[12]. The potential buyers for the houses was probably either the people needed to service the increasing population of South Battersea and Clapham, or for those displaced from north of the river in Kensington, Mayfair, Pimlico, Belgravia and Chelsea by the massive redevelopments taking place there.

The small scale of the houses in Chatham Road contributed to the street becoming less attractive and, over time, the standing of the street declined. Poachers who went for game to the Wimbledon Woods were reputed to live there. Certainly none of those living in the road bothered – or could afford – to pay to have their names in any of the street guides produced for Clapham. By 1871, the road had about 70 houses but few of the original occupants were still there; there was increased multi-occupancy and a high proportion of unskilled. The road had 14 labourers, nine gardeners, one of whom differentiated himself by claiming to be a 'gardener to a gentleman', and ten in various building trades. There was a musician and a bookmaker, and the only two in the road who kept a live-in servant were a theatre box office keeper and a retired civil service clerk. This downward trend continued in later years as more houses were added in the 1870s although there were still some oddities such as the retired German Army officer, by then a naturalized British citizen, Edward Albrecht de Nevers, living at 66 Chatham Road in 1881.

The next development

Development nearby continued slowly in the 1860s. In 1862, Charles Dungate built a further four houses on what was in due course to become part of Northcote Road and, in 1865, a Mr Stonell created a new road, named after himself, only half the normal width at 20 feet wide with small cottages which were completed by 1867 (Ill 24).

24: Stonell's Road

In both cases the District Board refused permission for the building but was overruled by the Metropolitan Board of Works. At the beginning of 1866, at the request of both local residents and Sir Charles Forbes, a successor to Wilberforce as the occupier of the Broomwood estate to the south of Chatham Road, the District Board agreed to adopt Chatham Road and so make it up and pave it. The cost of so doing, – but not future maintenance, was apportioned between the owners of the adjoining property who were not always happy to pay for it, fuelling the development of ratepayer associations. George Todd, a builder employing some 60 men, then proposed three new roads in the Chatham road area, Darley – parallel to Chatham and which was demolished in the redevelopment of 1971/4, Skeldon, which was never built, and Swaby Road which was renamed as part of Northcote Road in 1896, the houses being now the odd numbers from 157-173. Although the houses on Swaby/Northcote road were a little larger than in Chatham Road, they catered for the same market of the less well off.

The Church had not forgotten its role and a curate, the Rev Henry Boutflower Verdon who lived in Auckland Road, was appointed to take charge of the Chatham Road district of the parent church, St Mary's Battersea. A Sunday School for the Chatham Road children was held by Miss Jones at her home, High Trees, on the corner of Nightingale Lane and Clapham Common.[ii]. This arrangement became too crowded, and in August 1872 an iron room was built on Chatham Road that served as a school on weekdays and a church for Sunday evening. The land and building were paid for by Philip Cazenove, the founder of the stockbroking firm who lived on the Chatto estate off Clapham Common and who, following his wife's death in 1860, had increasingly devoted his time and energy to charitable and church activities.

Meanwhile Christopher Todd, a prominent member of the Wandsworth District Board of Works, was beginning a series of developments on Henry Wheeler's former land at the other end of South Battersea from Chatham Road, where Battersea Rise crossed the Falcon Brook. By 1861 Christopher had moved from Chelsea to Lee in South East London and his census return describes him as employing 300 men and 60 boys; his younger brother George was also a substantial builder employing 120, although he soon changed to be an auctioneer and surveyor and became a member of both the Battersea Vestry and the Wandsworth Board of Works. He described himself as a 'landed proprietor' in the 1871 census and his household in Battersea Rise had four live in servants.

[ii] the precursor of the present Art Deco block of flats which was made famous, at least to lawyers, by one of Lord Denning's more radical judgements

Christopher Todd's building activity included three houses in 1863 on the corner of Battersea Rise opposite what is now St Mark's Church and two years later a row of six commercial properties, Hopefield Terrace, in Battersea Rise which are still used as shops. He lived in one of them himself, 3 Hopefield Villas, which probably gave him a good chance to supervise the rest of his building. Following the opening of Clapham Junction in 1863, he gained permission for three roads, only two of which were in fact built, Auckland and Middleton; the third, Pelling Road, was replaced with a small 20 foot path along the cemetery. The District Board opposed these roads, but was again overruled by the Metropolitan Board of Works.

The houses in both these streets are larger and more substantial than those in the Chatham Road area. They are all similar despite being built by different builders, which suggests that Todd exercised some control even, it has been suggested, designing them himself. As usual, the roads were only built up slowly although their existence persuaded the District Board to agree to the 'fixing and lighting of a new lamp on Battersea Rise between the lamp at Bolingbroke Grove and the lamp at the Railway Tavern' and to a further light near Auckland Road in 1865. Auckland Road only had three houses occupied in 1865 with 14 of the existing 19 houses occupied in 1867 and all 19 by 1869. Todd continued to build, and the 1871 census shows that 16 houses were empty, a further nine were being built and 17 occupied. The houses were occupied by people with higher income, reflecting their rateable values being £28, more than twice that of many houses in Chatham Road. More than half of those occupied had living in servants, although there were also two lodging houses. Arthur Collings at 35 Auckland Road who was described as 'clerk of works', may have been living on the job and been employed by Todd – who still owned 12 of the houses in 1873.

A similar pattern applies to Middleton, later Buckmaster Road. While only half a dozen houses were occupied by 1869, the vast majority were filled a year later. Their rateable value was £26 and the houses were occupied by law clerks, civil engineers and widows living off annuities. More than half had live-in servants. In 1871, one occupant was an Inland Revenue clerk at Somerset House and another a secretary to an MP, so clearly they could have taken the new horse drawn trams or the opportunity of proximity to Clapham

Junction to travel regularly up to town for work, as probably did a (male) shorthand writer. One of the residents, at 9 Middleton Road, was Alexander Rolfe, one of many children of the artist William Rolfe. Alexander had moved from Richmond and was a painter of landscape, still life and sporting pictures, obviously generating adequate income since he employed a servant.[iii] John Cazenove, an elder brother of the founder of the stockbroking firm, lived at 13 Middleton Road. He was a political economist and is reputed to have been the anonymous editor of the second, posthumous, edition of Malthus' Principles of Political Economy.[13]

Another occupant of wider interest was the plumber, Thomas Crapper, who invented and patented the valveless lavatory system. Born in Yorkshire in 1836, he was apprenticed to a master plumber in Chelsea. Having served his apprenticeship and worked as a journeyman plumber for three years, he set up his own company in 1861 in Robert Street, Chelsea, later moving to what is now part of Draycott Street. He had a new approach to marketing and caused a sensation when he installed large plate glass windows at pavement level displaying his toilets for all to see. He was another example of tradesmen no longer living over the shop and moving across the river. He lived at 1 Middleton Road from 1867 to 1874 when he moved to 8 Middleton Road which he had built himself. By 1891 he was living in Brighton and describing himself as a sanitary engineer rather than a plumber but returned to Anerley in outer London at the end of the century. He and his elder brother, George, built 8 and 10 Middleton Road in 1873-4 and between them also owned 1-7 and 19-35. Thomas' nephew, also George, lived at 19 Gorst Road for some twenty years and eventually took over his uncle's share of the firm since Thomas' only child had died in infancy. George was active in local charities and a sidesman at St Luke's church.

Some indication of the distribution of house sizes can be gauged from research commissioned by the Battersea Vestry in June, 1866. Although this is divided up by West and East Battersea (with no definition), there can be no doubt that what was called West Battersea would include the West side of Clapham Common and the streets

[iii] He was moderately successful in his time and a picture of his of fishing at Twickenham went for almost £10,000 at Christies recently.

between Clapham and Wandsworth Common. As can be seen, there are very many more highly rated houses in the west part of the borough but even so there are at most 80 very large houses.

Distribution of House Size in Battersea 1866

Rateable Values	East Battersea		West Battersea	
£	houses	%	houses	%
Less than 20	1645	63	2253	63
20-29	722	28	708	20
30-39	140	5	241	7
40-49	43	2	133	4
50-59	22	1	80	2
60-79	26	1	53	1.5
80-100	10	0.4	19	0.5
More than 100	9	0.3	70	2
Total occupied	2381	91	3301	93
Total Houses	2617		3547	

Source Battersea Vestry Minutes

We shall see in Chapter 7 that 1866 brought the sale of the estate around Old Park and agreement to a number of new roads to be built on it. However this did not result in any immediate building. The next development came on Henry Wheeler's Bolingbroke Park estate, although Wheeler remained in the house. The estate had been sold in 1866/7 to Newnham Winstanley and James Goodson MP acting for the National Freehold Land Society's rival, the Conservative Land Society, through its land owning subsidiary the United Land Company. They too had purchased other land in Battersea, including a few years before the Plough Estate near to Clapham Junction, and used it to create new Tory voters. However, the 1867 Reform Act widened the franchise by giving the vote to every male adult householder living in a borough constituency, thereby removing the original rationale of the Land Societies. From then on their land dealing subsidiaries acted in the same way as any other speculative land agents and developers. No better evidence for this is an advertisement for some land in Balham in the South London Press for 6 June 1868 which identified an eight acre site.

> '..*immediately available for building purposes, and offers to freehold land societies and speculators an opportunity seldom to be met with for a highly profitable scheme, as by a judicious arrangement and formation of new roads several thousand feet of available frontage would be secured.*'

Even before the Conservative Land Society had obtained permission for their intended layout, they advertised the first tranche of plots in the South London Press on 16 May 1868, although managing to call the estate by three different names in a few lines.

> *THE CONSERVATIVE LAND SOCIETY*
> *THE SOUTH-WEST LONDON ESTATE,*
> *Clapham Junction*
>
> *The Bolingbroke Park estate is a large property having two frontages, one of considerable extent on Wandsworth Common, and the other to Battersea Rise. It is within 4½ miles from the General Post office, close to Clapham Junction and New Wandsworth stations. The Clapham Junction estate is one of the most valuable building properties in the suburbs of London. The first portion to be offered for sale comprises 113 plots, with frontages to five new roads. A subscription is being raised for a church near the Clapham Junction Estate. Water and gas are laid on in the high roads. The plots range from £58 up to £1000 each.*

This sale was obviously successful and the second tranche was advertised for sale in the South London Press only a few weeks later.

> '*Most eligible Suburban Building Land – South West London Estate (Second Portion), the Clapham Junction Estate (Bolingbroke Park), Wandsworth Common and Battersea Rise, East Surrey. The sale of the first portion of the above valuable estate fronting Wandsworth Common*

*and Battersea Rise, close to Clapham Junction and New
Wandsworth stations, will be commenced at the offices
on the 24ᵗʰ of June. The first portion has been entirely
disposed of. Prospectuses of the Land, Building, Share
and Deposit Departments with lists of Villas and Houses
for Sale will be sent free of charge, together with printed
instructions how to acquire land and pay for the houses
or plots by easy instalments.'*

Soon after this sale James Wyslon, who had been surveyor for
the National Freehold Land Society before taking the same role with
its rivals, submitted proposals on behalf of the Conservative Land
Society for a number of roads which were agreed in 1869. These
were Salcott, Bennerley, Mallinson, Shelgate, Cairns and Abyssinia
Roads and part of what was Northcote Road, thereby establishing
the existing road pattern at that end of South Battersea. The land
society was very much operating in its new standard procedure of
only laying out estates, including paying for the roads and sewers,
rather than developing themselves. The plots were auctioned once
the roads were laid and the services provided. This more commercial
approach also resulted in larger houses than in Chatham Road[iv]; most
buyers of the land were from the construction industry although there
were a few individual investors. Mortgages were offered through
their own Conservative Benefit Building Society. The reference to the
existing subscription for a nearby church was part of establishing
the respectability of the area. No church was ever built on the estate,
although 1868 saw permission given for an iron church nearby as
the precursor to St Marks on Battersea Rise.

London wide building recession began in 1868 and this was
reflected in a slow development of these roads and large numbers
of vacancies. This is illustrated in the position revealed by the 1871
census.

---

iv The National Land Freehold Society adopted the same presentational technique.
   Their subsidiary, The British Land Company, purchased a site in 1872 near
   Denmark Hill which ended up with substantial two or three storey houses. Their
   advertisement also had a reference to a subscription being started for a new
   church without one ever being built.

Bolingbroke Park Estate development 1871

Road	Occupied	Unoccupied	Building
Salcott	4	8	9
Cairns	5	9	
Mallinson	10	18	
Abyssinia	8	10	
Shelgate	17		
Bennerley	15	30	20
TOTAL	59	75	36

Source 1871 Census

Cairns Road and Abyssinia Road (the latter of which was redeveloped in 1977/8 by Wandsworth Council) were slightly less attractive than Middleton/Buckmaster with rateable values of £15-19. Nevertheless, Cairns had living in it a teacher, a civil servant, a commercial clerk and a butler while the inhabitants of Abyssinia Road included a stationer, a number of clerks, an accountant, a bookmaker's manager, as well as a House of Lords messenger, demonstrating that the area was beginning to be used by those who travelled up to London to work. Most of the houses in Abyssinia Road were owned by a George Luff, but one occupant - of 17 Abyssinia Road - was Edward Heaver, the brother of Alfred Heaver who became a very active builder in South West London, building over 4,000 houses and who later developed the Heaver Estate in Balham. Alfred Heaver himself lived in 3 Shelgate Road, next door to his long time collaborator, Edward Coates. 2-12 Bennerley Road were probably the first Battersea houses to be built by Heaver.

Other occupants included Jesse Moham, an assistant secretary of the RSPCA who lived at 10 Shelgate Road, and people who described themselves as 'gentleman' or 'land owner' side by side with a prison warder, a map draughtsman and a coachman. George Washington Bacon, an American who took British nationality and became a prolific and successful map publisher, lived at 42 Shelgate Road until 1886, when he moved to Wimbledon. The wide variety of occupants suggests landlords were letting to whomever they could rather than trying to keep standards up in a difficult housing market. The same was true of Bennerley Road; Number 1 was shared between two households, one a gardener and the other a writer/music critic. The street had a retired barrister, one of Her Majesty's Inspectors of Schools and a number of plasterers and carpenters.

There was also one rather surprising occupant, Horatio Wraxall, who with his wife shared 5 Bennerley Road with another household and described his occupation as 'a baronet and author of light literature'. Although in the previous two censuses his occupation was 'railway clerk' and 'solicitor's general clerk', he had indeed succeeded his brother (also an author) and become the fourth baronet in 1865. His brother was moderately well known at the time having written a biography of Queen Caroline, the sister of George III, as well as a number of stirring tales of foreign parts. Little if anything remains of Horatio's writing, although it is known that he published a short story entitled 'The Naked Truth'. He came to a sorry end, being convicted of fraud in 1878. His scheme was to advertise for shop manager positions in South Africa with passage paid. Candidates were interviewed, received an offer of a post, and were asked to pay a deposit of a guinea to confirm their willingness to take the position. When they arrived at Southampton to take their passage on a named ship, they discovered that it did not exist. Apparently this was not the first time that Wraxall had been involved in such schemes and he was imprisoned for 12 months and subsequently committed to the Wandsworth Lunatic Asylum. He died destitute in April 1882.

At the start of the last quarter of the nineteenth century, the development of South Battersea was well under way, but growth was still relatively slow, hampered by the collapse in the housing market in the late 1860s. The vast growth of Victorian suburbia in South London was still to come and the next chapter looks at the most intensive period of the development of South Battersea, the last quarter of the nineteenth century and the first few years of the twentieth.

(Endnotes)

1   Roger Logan. 2007 Wandsworth Historical Society Wandsworth Paper 15
2   N J Barton. 1962 The Lost Rivers of London p 42
3   J G Taylor. 1925 Our Lady of Batersey p 15

4 Roger Logan. 1977 South Battersea The Formative Years 1851-1900 p 9
5 Battersea Burial Ground 1861 HMSO 158
6 Ibid
7 Roger Logan. 1977 Ibid p 8
8 Canon Erskine Clarke in St Luke's Parish Magazine
9 Roger Logan. 1977 South Battersea The formative Years p 9
10 Sean Creighton. 1999 Ancient Order of Foresters in Battersea and Neighbouring Districts
11 Roger Logan. 1977 Ibid p14
12 Tim Sherwood. 1994 Change at Clapham Junction p 24
13 Dictionary of National Biography. John Cazenove

CHAPTER 6

SOUTH BATTERSEA – COVERED IN TERRACED HOUSING

The last thirty years of the nineteenth century saw South Battersea covered with terraced and semi-detached houses, but only slowly at first. There was less development in the 1870s than in the previous decade, influenced by the recession at the end of the 1860s and the consequent large numbers of empty houses awaiting tenants. In July 1869 the South London Press commented that there were more than 1,000 houses empty within a one square mile area in Battersea. In an editorial on 'The Free Bridge Question' it argued that abolishing the toll on the private Waterloo Bridge would save lives because people could then afford to move from 'overcrowded hovels in Westminster to the more roomy houses now gasping for tenants in Camberwell and Battersea'.

The recession hit both builders and developers hard, and one such affected was James Lord. When Elizabeth Hoper's old house was demolished in 1864, he moved to St John's Lodge, opposite the Plough Pub[i]. He was there in 1871 in some comfort with his wife, married daughter and six servants all of whom carefully characterised themselves for the census as domestic servant, cook, kitchen maid, laundry maid, and nurse (for the baby grandson). The Rate book records him as owning six houses in Chatham Road, three of which had shops, but virtually all were empty. A year later, St John's Lodge was unoccupied and a resident[1] recalls that 'Lord was said to have lost his fortune by embarking on building speculation before the district was ripe for it, and ...had left several rows of unfinished 'carcasses' of house in Bolingbroke Grove and elsewhere.'

---

[i] He still had plenty of money in 1868. In May The South London Press reported him as giving a donation of £1,000 as the nucleus of a fund to oppose Gladstone's disestablishment of the Church of Ireland and funding scholarships with the Scottish Reformation Society to train reporters 'to counteract the Jesuitical influences in the Reporters gallery' in order to change Parliamentary reporting.

One of the issues that had to be sorted out was the extent of development that would be allowed on Wandsworth Common where the Lord of the Manor, Earl Spencer, was looking to realise the potential increased value of his land. His first step had been in 1857 with the sale for £4,000 of 55 acres to the Royal Victoria Patriotic Asylum which housed orphans of those killed in the Crimean War. Since then he had been enclosing and then selling off small parcels of the Common. He had been defeated earlier on proposals for a massive building scheme for Wimbledon Common, of which he was also Lord of the Manor, to be followed by one for Wandsworth and the outcry over these two proposals had resulted in the Metropolitan Commons Act 1866 which empowered any 12 ratepayers to apply to Parliament for a statutory management scheme of a particular common.

Development may also have been slowed – at least in the short term – by the flamboyant campaigning of one John Buckmaster[ii] who lived at 2 New Road, off St John's Hill.[2,3] He was a tireless campaigner and used his skills for some time to maintain public access to the Common. He began in 1865 when he had torn down fences put up by the railway company which had closed a footpath from Bolingbroke Grove across the Common to the New Wandsworth Station but his arguments with those trying to enclose the Common continued. In 1867 he spoke against enclosure to a crowd of 4-5000 – there were handbills saying 'Cursed is he who removeth his neighbour's landmark' and complaining about 'the filching and reselling of the common at enormous profit.' In 1868, the rights of the Lord of the Manor were tested by Mr J Anderson Rose and 'two or three public agitators' by persuading some gypsies to camp on the Common. Unfortunately, the gypsies chose a part of the Common near Nightingale Lane close to Mr Rose's own home. He was so inconvenienced personally that he asked the Inspector of Nuisances to intervene to move them on without

---

[ii] He began work, aged 10, as an agricultural labourer in Slapton, Buckinghamshire, becoming a trained carpenter and joiner and then a paid campaigner for the Anti-Corn Law League He went on to train as a chemistry teacher, teaching first at the local college in Battersea and then at Imperial College. His elder two sons both got Oxford firsts and his third son Stanley, who did not, went on to become Lord Chancellor in Asquith's coalition government in the First World War and subsequently Viscount Buckmaster.

testing the Lord of the Manor's rights. The South London Press much enjoyed his discomfiture.

Earl Spencer kept on trying and in 1869 attempted further encroachments on Wandsworth Common. By that time, there were many influential people around the Common who could afford the costs of litigation and of procuring their own private Acts of Parliament. Sir Henry Peek, MP for Surrey (which of course included both Wandsworth and Wimbledon) owned land on both Commons, and had been an important actor in securing the Metropolitan Commons Act. Buckmaster formed a committee of local people to raise £5,000 to take Court action against Earl Spencer and promote a local Bill to protect the Common for all time. In due course this led to the 1871 Wandsworth Common Act which transferred the Common from Earl Spencer to conservators funded by ratepayers for an annual fee of £250 in return for the Earl giving up the income from the gravel dug from what are now the ponds.

Buckmaster soon took a further opportunity to protest against development on the Common. We have already seen that the WELCPR had bought land from Earl Spencer to cut a rail line through Wandsworth Common and some of the land that ended as surplus to their requirements was near Christopher Todd's Auckland Road development described in the last chapter. Auckland Road itself was already doing well and the adjacent shopping parade along Battersea Rise had ten shops full including grocer, greengrocer, and fishmonger as well as tailor, chemist and coffee shop. The forthcoming development of the 50 ft wide Northcote Road encouraged Todd to capitalise on this success. He had bought the surplus land from the railway in the 1860s and naturally maintained its enclosure. Local opinion was firmly opposed to building on what had formerly been common ground and Buckmaster led a group of about 2,000 people to tear down the fences erected on the Common opposite the cemetery to allow the land to be built on. As a result, he appeared in court to answer a summons for 'wilfully and maliciously destroying the property of Mr Christopher William Todd, at Wandsworth Common'. Buckmaster conducted his own defence, attacking the encroachment by what he called 'speculative builders', and succeeded in having the case dismissed. In practice this caused no more than a delay and Todd obtained permission in 1872 for a new road first called Mabel Road but now Chivalry Road. Buckmaster's role was remembered much later, when Middleton Road was renamed Buckmaster Road in 1936.[iii]

Only two new sites were developed in the 1870s. The first, part of the Dent family estate, is covered in more detail in the next chapter. The other involved the demolition of the house - and associated elm trees - occupied for many years by the Ashness family of Battersea Rise and the development of Almeric and Lindore Roads as the Clapham Common Gardens Estate. The house was sold at auction in 1875, following a family dispute and litigation over the inheritance. The scale of the house can be judged from the advertisement in The Times.

> '*The valuable FREEHOLD PROPERTY, situate on the south side of Battersea formerly occupied by the Ashness family and latterly by Mrs Wells, within a few minutes' walk of Clapham Junction and Wandsworth Road Stations, and about a mile from Clapham Station, possessing frontages on two sides and having every facility for immediate development as a building estate. There is an old fashioned residence, containing, on the second floor, four attic rooms; on the first floor, four bed rooms, dressing room etc.; on the ground floor, dining room, library, drawing room with bay, and convenient offices; a four-stall stable, a coach-house, and an extra timber built carriage-house. At the rear is a pleasure-garden, with lawn and flower beds, greenhouse, and some grassland.*'

[iii] Buckmaster was well able to conduct more than one campaign at a time. The list of rateable values in Battersea quoted in the last chapter had been commissioned by him as part of his campaign to dismiss the secretary to the Battersea Vestry, Alexander Corsellis, for not ensuring either the fair rating of properties or the collection of the rates. It was Corsellis who had commented that it was not worth collecting the rates from the smaller houses and he was also simultaneously the secretary to the Wandsworth Board of Works. Buckmaster eventually prevailed after Corsellis had refused to open any letters from him or to attend angry meetings of the vestry faithfully reported in the local press. Buckmaster was obviously remembered with some affection, because as a church warden of St Mary's Battersea in 1872, he was invited back to the 35th anniversary of Canon Clarke's institution as Vicar in 1907. He had planned to come but was prevented by his doctors by 'the inclement weather that February day'.

All the houses in Almeric Road were built in 1877-8 by the same builder, John Miller, who had just finished the odd numbers in Sibella Road. Six builders were involved in Lindore Road but, although there is a wide difference in the houses' rear elevations, the fronts are very similar except for minor variations in the detail of the eaves. The positioning of these two roads reflects the nature of the site being developed. With building already on Northcote Road, and the other side of Webbs Road still occupied by the Webbs estate, the only practical approach was to build them parallel to Northcote road, in distinction to all the other roads between Webbs and Northcote Roads, and to accept that there could be no houses facing onto Webbs Road. (Map 8)

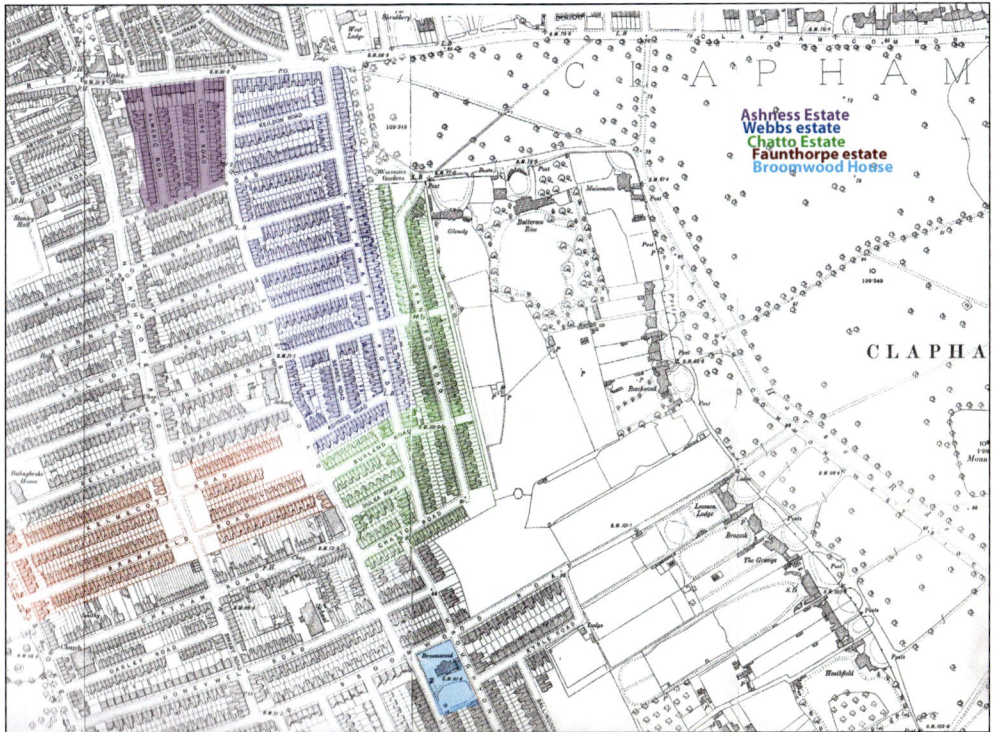

Map 8: Roads and land boundaries

The remaining development involved building on the part of the Bolingbroke Park Estate closest to the eighteenth century house. Henry Wheeler had died in 1873 and, although his wife, Portia, and daughters continued to live there, construction began of the southern extension of Northcote Road and the eastern part of two new roads running up to Webbs Road, Belleville and Wakehurst. Although the Wheeler family were still heavily involved in local church affairs, they moved out after a few years to Worcester Park House in Long Ditton where they continued to entertain the Battersea Mothers' Union meetings in the summer. With the family gone, the Conservative Land Society was able to gain approval in 1878 for laying out the western sections of Belleville and Wakehurst Roads running up to the Common. As luck would have it, Bolingbroke Park was conveniently placed between the roads and was not demolished to enable these roads to be built. This final part of the development of the Bolingbroke Park estate also allowed the houses to be given a rational sequential numbering system, rather than reflecting the date of building or a series of names or numbered villas.[iv]

The population of Belleville and Wakehurst Roads was somewhat different from that of the houses in Salcott and Bennerley in 1871. Many of the houses were built with a servant's door at the side[v] (Ill 25) and a high proportion did indeed have live in servants. Given that the first group of houses were built in the very late 1870s, the 1881 census gives a good profile of those who moved into the new houses. Almost a third of the houses in Wakehurst Road were occupied by clerks of one kind or another (including half a dozen working in solicitors' or barristers' offices). There were five in professions related to building such as surveyors and architects. There was only one manual worker; and only three houses had lodgers or boarders (as one might expect in a street so recently tenanted and therefore with less time for the changes in fortune that often required the taking in of lodgers), two of them unemployed and one widow. One third of the houses had live-in servants.

There was an analytical chemist, two butlers (one of them

[iv] Bolingbroke Park estate was the first to be renumbered, but that does mean that all the census details up to and including 1881 are on a different basis to the existing numbering and can be difficult to match up.

[v] This was narrower than the main front door and allowed the servants to enter the house without going past the front room and seeing - or being seen by - the family.

25: Servants' door, Wakehurst Road

unemployed), and an artist, William Hargreaves, who lived at 13 Gloucester Villas, now 34 Wakehurst Road. John D Wood, an estate agent, the founder of the firm by that name, lived at 1 Gloucester Villas, now 10 Wakehurst Road. He later moved to 11 Honeywell Road and then out to Warlingham. Edward Thomas, the war poet, was born at 49 Wakehurst Road and later moved to 61 Shelgate Road where there is a blue plaque to commemorate his residence. The extent of some of the families would make any twenty first century person blanch to live in a house that size. John Clayton, a solicitor's clerk, lived with his wife and seven children in 10 Gloucester Villas (now 28 Wakehurst Road), and William Saunders, a commercial clerk, lived with his wife and eight children (aged from 18 months to 18) in 8 Gloucester Villas (now 24 Wakehurst Road).

There is much greater uniformity of design in Belleville Road than in Wakehurst Road which has a wide variety of designs, originally with series of house names rather than numbers. This must have been because of the controls imposed by the builder and developer, Alfred Heaver, working with the Conservative Land Society architect,

William Poole. John Rowe, one of the builders, lived at The Acacias, now 48 Belleville Road, and Poole himself lived at 62 Belleville Road.[vi] The occupiers are very similar to those in Wakehurst Road, with clerks forming almost a third of the heads of household, and almost no manual workers. Occupants included a 'surgeon/dentist', and one who described his occupation as 'gentleman'. Alfred Robinson at Oak Lodge, now 7 Belleville Road, was a manager in a church furnishing business employing 10 men and three boys. He must have been doing very well given the large expansion of churches in this part of Battersea. Another artist, Joseph Whitehead, lived at The Hawthorns, which is now 18 Belleville Road.

This distribution of occupations reflects the overall change in the neighbourhood since the early 1870s and was not that different from Salcott and Bennerley themselves in 1881. The population growth was stimulated by the removal in 1879 of the tolls on the bridges across the Thames, the continuing redevelopment across the river, and the desire of white collar clerks to move out of Inner London. Most of the population worked locally, remembering that even middle class people were used to walking three or four miles each way to work. By 1881 those two roads had changed to have 25% clerks, 25% with servants and 10% manual, with a fair smattering of small builders, including the future builder of Old Park Avenue, David Kettle, then employing 2 men and living at Rosric House in Salcott Road.

By now there were five roads running in parallel between Wandsworth Common and Webbs Road but no decent connections between them. Northcote Road was only being built up slowly and in any case provided no link between Chatham Road and Belleville road where the Board School had been built. What was then Webbs Lane (now Road) was still private so the District Board felt free to refuse to pave or light it. However, in 1879, the District Board adopted all the roads on the Conservative Land Society's Bolingbroke Park

---

[vi] Alfred Heaver had by then married his second wife, Patience, younger sister of his first wife, Isabella, who had died in 1874. This marriage, another which breached the prohibition on marrying one's deceased wife's sister, ended with Patience's death in 1877. Heaver married for the third time, but this ended tragically when he was murdered in 1901 on the way to his local church in Dorking by his brother in law who apparently felt that the rest of the family were benefiting insufficiently from Alfred's wealth.

Estate, the Clapham Common Estates and that part of Webbs Road from Battersea Rise to Shelgate Road where they put up a couple of gas lights. This decision was, as often, opposed by many of the ratepayers who were becoming increasingly aware of the costs that they were being asked to shoulder. The aggregate length of the roads in Battersea doubled from 25 to 50 miles between 1870 and 1888 and reached 65.5 miles in 1894. Most of these were roads on new estates and paid for by the owners of the property. The number of street lamps was also growing, from 605 in 1868 to 826 in 1874. Originally these were at least 75 yards apart, but this caused problems because the South Metropolitan gas company was not obliged to provide gas to a lamp more than 75 yards from an existing one. Accordingly the District Board was prevailed upon to install more lamps with gaps of 50 yards or less and the number of street lights in Battersea trebled in the 20 years to 1894.

Canon Erskine Clarke

We know a lot about how South Battersea appeared in the late nineteenth century from John Erskine Clarke (Ill 26).

26: John Erskine Clarke

He was instituted into the post of vicar of St Mary's Battersea by Bishop Samuel Wilberforce (son of William) on February 2 1872 and remained in Battersea until his death in 1920. He played a key part in building up the infrastructure of the area and the St Luke's parish magazine contains a number of his reminiscences on the substantial changes he saw during his 48 years in the parish.

After curacies in Harrogate and Lichfield, he became Vicar of St Michael's and then St Andrews, Derby, where he invented the parish magazine in 1859, then much more substantial than now with extended stories and commentary. He also inaugurated what was described[4] at his funeral as 'an entirely new branch of bright and wholesome literature for children in his publications, Children's Prize, Chatterbox, and Sunday and he commenced the issue of Church Bells.'

He was already well off but these publications made him a rich man, and the parish of Battersea was also well endowed, paying him £1,000 a year, a large sum in those times. Earl Spencer had presented him to the parish on hearsay knowledge of his capacity, not least in providing for the growing railway population of Derby.[5] Even so, the parish historian[6] quotes Erskine Clarke's first reaction on a two months' acquaintance with the size and needs of the parish as being almost overwhelmed by the challenges 'It would have made me wonder at my own temerity did I not believe I had obeyed a definite call of God's providence in attempting it.' Booth[7] later described the work of his churches being inspired by:

> '..the broad, genial, kindly spirit of the rector, who has held his office for twenty-eight years. His sympathies are wide, and those who work under him are of various shades of churchmanship from not very High to not very Low.'

Stephen Potter[8] describes him in graphic terms when in his eighties.

> 'Canon Clarke was a huge figure of pale faced geniality, a sort of temperance Falstaff, with spacious Victorian side whiskers, and a waistcoat as wide as a sail rigged with chains for gold crosses, a spectacle case and a fat watch which he would pull out clankingly as a signal for

*guests to go. He was certainly kind and lovable, though
it was a surprising fact, never admitted or mentioned
by anybody, that his sermons (now he was older) were
a little boring and watery.'*

He was also clearly at home with the wealthy and made good
use of his ability to raise money. He later described his choice of
accommodation in Battersea in a way that makes this quite clear.[9]

*'I was called from Derby to Battersea in 1872. It was a
very different Battersea from the present. In those days
Clapham Common, Wandsworth Common, St John's
Hill, Lavender Hill, were occupied by large houses
with grounds and gardens. One large family house,
with spacious garden, The Elms, stood where the Town
Hall now stands. When I came to review the situation,
I saw that to live in the Vicarage in Battersea Square,
close to the river, would not give me much chance of
influencing the residents in these houses, so I rented a
house at No 6 Altenberg Gardens, which was about the
centre of the parish....The house was the centre one of
fifteen detached houses which had not all been built
when I came in 1872. When I first went to live there,
I looked out of my top window across wooded fields
and gardens right to the back of Cedars Road. So rural
was it that one day a cuckoo dashed itself against the
dining room window'*

Erskine Clarke rented the house from the builder and lived
there in some comfort with two or three women servants and one
manservant. His sister, Emma, an invalid who had lived with him
in both his appointments in Derby, moved down with him but died
two years later.

The 15 houses in Altenberg Gardens had been built by a Mr
Hiscox on the grounds of a mansion, West Lodge, that he had
acquired from its previous occupier, Mr Sumner, brother of the then
Bishop of Winchester. It had a fine cedar tree in front and survived
some years before being demolished for further building, although
part of the stabling/coach house remains. One of the tenants, Erskine

Clarke recalls[10], was apparently a respectable gentlemen but it transpired that he had:

> 'committed clever robberies of bonds in transit from the Continent on an extensive scale, but who long outwitted the police who had him under observation. I remember seeing his wife in the garden with their children who had a donkey with panniers on either side and were a picture of domestic happiness.'

It would seem that this "respectable gentleman" was Adam Worth, the notorious and successful criminal who stole among many other things Thomas Gainsborough's portrait of Georgiana, Duchess of Devonshire. He was nicknamed "the Napoleon of Crime" by a Scotland Yard detective and was probably the model for Conan Doyles's Moriarty.

27: The Shrubbery

It is difficult to imagine what the area was like when Erskine Clarke described the area when he first moved in, when even if hard to present as countrified, there was certainly plenty of green and unbuilt-on land[11] .

> 'In those times, Battersea Rise and Lavender Hill were
> both rural roads, connected by St John's Road, which
> was of the same character. Lavender Hill was no more
> than a broad gravelled pathway and Battersea Rise had
> a line of poplars on Mr Tom Taylor's estate and on the
> opposite side from the common to Webb's Lane there
> were the fine trees of Mr Webb's estate.'

He must have had some previous knowledge of the area because he describes a visit that he made in 1848, having taken an omnibus from Charing Cross to Clapham to visit the family of an Oxford University friend, William Humphery, at their house, The Shrubbery. This house, built in 1796 by George Scholey a hop merchant and distiller who was Lord Mayor of London for 1812-13. He was reported[12] as being 'remarkable for the neatness of his person, and often appeared well mounted on the Clapham Road'. The house still stands in Lavender Gardens, albeit converted into flats in 1987. Ill 27 shows a picture of the house as it was after being extended in 1843 and Erskine Clarke gives his memory of it[13].

> 'The house belonged to Alderman Humphery....[who]
> had just then added a new suite of rooms, dining
> room, circular drawing room and state drawing room
> a hundred feet from end to end, and I was one of the
> house party when they were opened with a great dance.'

His friendship with William Humphery was obviously an important one. Humphery was captain of the Wadham College Boat Club at the same time that Erskine Clarke was the secretary. They were both good oarsmen and between them won the University Sculls for three years running 1848-50. Humphery also rowed bow for the University in 1849, but Erksine Clarke commented that they had rowed together in a famous Wadham Crew. This turns out to be the Eight that won The Grand, The Ladies and the Wyfold Cup (all famous races at the Henley Regatta) in the same year. [14][vii]

Humphery's house, The Shrubbery, was also described by Erksine Clarke on his arrival in Battersea as Vicar in 1872[15].

> *'The next house was called 'The Shrubbery', with a long frontage to the Common, and two pairs of handsome gates for entrance and exit. It was tenanted, when first I knew it, by Mr Spartali, the Greek Consul. The grounds extended to Lavender Hill, and included a large field, in which we used to enjoy seeing the hay-making from our windows. There was a wooded path along which we used to see Mr Spartali hurrying to his morning train by the wicket door on Lavender Hill.'*

Michael Spartali, who was a merchant as well as the Greek Consul, had two beautiful daughters who modelled for Whistler, Rossetti and Burne-Jones as well as the photographer Julia Margaret Cameron. Swinburne[16] said of the elder sister, Marie Spartali 'She is so beautiful that I want to sit down and cry.' She became the pupil of Ford Maddox Brown and had a substantial career as a Pre-Raphaelite painter as well as a model. Following her marriage

---

[vii] Erskine Clarke tells the story.
'In 1849, the Grand Challenge was fixed so early that the Oxford term was not over. As there was some doubt whether the College authorities would let the men go to Henley, the Wadham Boat was entered as ''The St John of Malta', and the crew under pseudonyms. On Monday June 11, the crew attended their lectures up to 2, and then started in a drag with four post-horses at 2.30, dining at Benson on the way, and getting to Henley at 5. They had not been over the course before the race. The Ladies' Challenge Cup was rowed on the first day. Wadham won the toss and beat Second Trinity, Cambridge by one length with Oriel a further two lengths behind. Bell's Life, the one sporting paper of those days wrote, 'It was a most spirit stirring race, and the crews rowed beautifully and most determinedly throughout, amid the vociferous cheering of vast numbers who ran along the meadows, many of them from start to finish, when some were so 'blown' that they had to recline on the hillocks of hay till they could regain their wind'. There was much cheering and excitement when the drag got back to College about ten. The next day, having beaten Trinity in the Grand when the latter, having crossed the finishing line a third of a length up, was disqualified for a foul, the drag did not reach the College till halfpast twelve, but the Sub-Warden of the time had much sympathy with rowing men, and so the lateness of the 'Gate' was condoned; indeed the achievements of the crew were celebrated by a grand supper in Hall on the Thursday evening for which they had been given permission to entertain the beaten Cambridge crew, with the only stipulation that there should be "no hot lush".'

to the American journalist William Stillman, they lived for a short time in the early 1870s near Clapham Common which Stillman[17] later described as 'the comparative quiet of that then delightful neighbourhood'.

The Shrubbery's next owner was the Rev F H Baring, described by Erskine Clarke as a wealthy clergyman, and indeed he was one of the banking family. After a couple of years Baring returned to his mission work in India, the site began to be developed by Heaver, and in 1888 Erskine Clarke bought the house for use as a school, finding time to influence the choice of road name[18].

> '*When the property was sold to the builder the mansion stood clear of the road, while the stables and greenhouses were swept away. There was a Shrubbery Road elsewhere, so the Metropolitan Board would not have that, but they accepted the builder's name 'Malone Road'. I suggested 'Lavender Gardens', but the Metropolitan Board said that there were too many Lavender names in the neighbourhood, and that the Post Office would object. I wrote to the Postal Authorities and found that they preferred to have adjacent streets grouped under one general name, so that street became Lavender Gardens, which was appropriate, as there used to be real lavender fields in the district.*'

Erskine Clarke clearly got on well with his own, the better off of the parish, but he was also able to relate to others in different stations. A good example of this is given by Percy Thornton, the great nephew of Henry Thornton of Battersea Rise and the Unionist MP for Clapham from 1891-1911 as well as church warden at St Mary's. He recalled[19] an incident in the late 1880s when unemployment was very high in Battersea.

> '*organized bands of unemployed workers insisted on the right to attend Divine Service at St Mary's Parish Church coupled with a demand that the Vicar of Battersea, The Rev Canon Erskine Clarke, should preach from and upon the injustice of those asking for bread being given a stone: an allusion to needy men out of work having to*

labour in the parish stone yard before receiving the small assistance that could properly be bestowed.

Ultimately the Canon faced the situation and preached the sermon with great success, improving the occasion of getting as many poor men into the Parish Church who were strangers to the worship there. But the going and returning to and from the church of large masses of unemployed escorted by police caused many of us a time of anxiety on behalf of the peace of Battersea.'

These skills were important in helping him stimulate the building of churches, schools and a hospital in Battersea.

New churches

While the original parish church in Battersea of St Mary's had been rebuilt in the eighteenth century, it was not substantially increased in size and could not now deal with the increased population. The north part of the borough was served by Christchurch in Battersea Park Road and St Philip's, donated by Philip Flower for the Park Town estate and completed in 1870 but these did not provide for South Battersea. By the last quarter of the nineteenth century, more churches were thought necessary, St Mary's parish had already built an infants' school in 1866-7 on Battersea Rise financed largely from donations from Philip Cazenove and this is recorded in an inscribed gable shown in Ill 28.

In 1870 a new iron church was constructed on the school's playground. This soon became overcrowded and the present brick church was built in its place in 1874 (Ill 29).

Apparently its dedication to St Mark arose from what Erskine Clarke[20] called 'a curious economic reason'. The infants' school had also been known as St Mary's, but it became increasingly confused with the parochial school of the same name in Green Lane, Battersea and it was decided that a new name was required. The school had an inscribed stone in the gable shown above, but 'an ingenious person' was able to change the 'Y' in St Mary to a 'K' and the iron church was given the same dedication. Ill 30, a more detailed picture of the gable inscription, still shows the signs of this change.

28: St Mark's School gable

29: St Mark's church

30: St Mark's School letter change

It had an unusual construction for the time, being built of cement with a diaper patterned brick external skin, but this led to a problem described by Erskine Clarke.

> 'There were however some greater problems with its construction. The crypt had been built with a beautiful groined roof resting on a single central pillar. While the nave was being built many cartloads of gravel for the concrete for the walls were led into the nave and shot onto the crypt roof. Then came very wet weather, which so increased the weight of the gravel that it crushed in the roof of the crypt, which now had a different arrangement of pillars.'

> 'The other incident was that the nave pillars originally were of brick – as may be gathered from the responds at the east end – but when some of the bricks were tested by hydraulic pressure, it was found that all were not to be relied on to carry the weight put upon them, so before the wooden framework under the arches was withdrawn, the brick pillars were hacked away and the present Pennant stone pillars were swung into their place.'

These problems may have been the reason for the building work taking longer than had been anticipated by the Building Committee, but the final product was worth waiting for, and Pevsner[21] rates it the best of the architect William White's Battersea churches.

Charles Booth's investigation[22] of London at the end of the nineteenth century covered its churches in great detail. He commented that St Mark's prominent position on Battersea Rise helped it to become a locally fashionable church - to the detriment of St Michael's on Chatham Road. It collected its congregation from all around, being well filled on Sunday morning, packed on Sunday evening, and with over 500 Easter communicants. Booth also noted a "remarkable" Church Literary Society with over 400 members with an average attendance at meetings of 200. It is hardly surprising that Booth described it as 'on the whole a happy and successful church', a judgment that could also be applied to the present operation under the Holy Trinity Brompton flag.

St Mark's was only the first of many churches (and other public buildings) built under the aegis of the new and energetic vicar of Battersea. He became well known for his success. Battersea had moved from the Winchester diocese to that of Rochester in 1877 and visiting his new domains in 1881, Anthony Thorold, the Bishop of Rochester praised him[23].

> *'Anyone who wishes to see good sense combined with economy in church building should visit the churches of Canon Erskine Clarke in Battersea. Avoiding both sordidness and extravagance, he has just built effectively, and yet cheaply, a new church at the cost of £6 per sitting. £10 is the usual cost and thought cheap.'*

His activity after only his first twenty five years was summarised by the third Bishop of Rochester he had served under[24].

> *'During these twenty five years, the 13 Parochial Clergy have become 49; 8 Churches have become 19; Church sittings have increased from 5,460 to 12,410. Over £100,000 had been spent on Churches, Schools, and other buildings for religious or benevolent purposes. The moral of the Vicar's successful work was the value of patient continuance in well doing. He had been content to keep to one place and had not grown stagnant in it. He had also adhered to the central line of Churchmanship which was sometimes contemned as 'safe' or 'dull' but which has undoubted power when taken in a generous and contemplative spirit.'*

In the end, Erskine Clarke built twelve churches, one coming after the bishop's speech. This was a prodigious programme for which he either raised the money or used his own and it is notable that the advice he gave to other clerics[25] was 'One of the first steps in connection with any piece of work is to appoint as treasurer a layman, as good a businessman as might be, so as to try to run on business lines.' Erskine Clarke was very good indeed at this, having access to many successful and wealthy businessmen in his parish, and making good use of them. There was an underlying vision behind his distribution of churches since he was very keen that his church-going parishioners should attend a church within the original parish of St Mary's Battersea rather than go outside. Their location was chosen to implement 'my plan of trying to place a church near the boundaries of the parish [of Battersea] so that parishioners should have to pass a church of their own when they sought one out of the parish'.

The churches are shown in the Table below. Many of them employed the same architect, William White, who also designed the pulpit and lectern at St Luke's. We shall return to the building of St Luke's church in the chapter on the Dents and Old Park estates.

Churches built by Erskine Clarke

Church	Date built	Architect
St Marks, Battersea Rise	1874	William White
St Peter's, Plough Lane	1876	William White
St Matthew's Gowrie Road	1876	William White demolished
Ascension, Lavender Hill	1876-98	James Brooks
St Michael's Bolingbroke Grove	1881	William White
St Mary-le Parc, Albert Bridge Road	1883	William White Never completed
All Saints, Queenstown Road	1884	F W Hunt
St Stephen's Battersea Bridge Road	1885	William White
St Andrew's, Patmore street	1886	demolished
St Luke's, Thurleigh Road	1889	F W Hunt
St Barnabas, Clapham Common North Side	1898	W Bassett-Smith
St Bartholomew's, Wycliffe Road	1902	G H Fellowes Prynne

Source: Pevsner Buildings of England: London South

Although the Established Church was the most prominent in constructing new churches, other denominations were also active. According to Booth, the non conformist churches were mainly supported by the lower middle classes. A 'new' Baptist Church was built in Chatham Road in the 1860s and the Northcote Road Baptist Church opened in 1889. Methodists from Battersea Park Church who had been meeting in the upper part of a house in Bennerley Road built a church on the site of a stonemasons' yard in Mallinson Road. Another Methodist group, which had originally met in a house and then a shop in Swaby (Northcote) Road, used the Baptist Church in Chatham Road when that was vacated and then an iron building in Swaby Road, known as the 'Tin Tabernacle', before moving to their permanent building with a seating capacity of 1,000 in Broomwood Road in 1900. Roman Catholic churches were built at St Vincent de Paul and Nightingale Square. The South West London Synagogue opened at 104 Bolingbroke Grove in 1915 and was extended into a purpose-built building in 1927, but closed in 1997.

Despite this enormous building effort, it is not clear that the enterprise was entirely successful. Booth[26] quotes a clergyman as saying 'These people do not come to church much, and are difficult to visit parochially, but are good responsible people, and not to be called irreligious.'

And the Salvation Army found '...the whole of the district bad for its work; too respectable, on the one hand, with too great a love of pleasure on the other.'[viii] A further explanation came from the local Methodist Minister[27].

> '..the growth of Sunday visiting, which marks the strength of their home life, acts as a hindrance to religious observance. The pianos are going on Sunday evening; and, in explanation of non appearance, even church-going people will say, 'We had so-and-so come to see us."

[viii] In the 1902/3 Mudie/Smith census of religious undertakings there were 18 Anglican churches and 51 other chapels, churches and mission rooms. The maximum attendance at evening services was 14,605, which represents only 8-9% of the 1901 population, low by Victorian standards.

The growth in church sittings over the previous quarter century so praised by the Bishop of Rochester was in fact only a 227% rise compared with an increase in the overall population of 313%. We shall see that St Luke's Church played (and indeed continues to play) an important role in the social life of the parish, but it is easy to exaggerate the role of the church in Victorian society. The 1851 religious census, taken on 30 March, revealed that the national average of those attending church in urban areas was 23.9% in the morning, 10.5% in the afternoon and 13.3% in the evening. The figures were slightly higher in the Wandsworth registration district at 33.7%, 10.2%, and 21.3% respectively. This prompted the Registrar General[28] to comment 'The most alarming fact which this investigation as to attendance brings before us is, unquestionably, the alarming number of non attenders.' This was caused, the Registrar General argued, by two factors, first that the working classes were '... unconscious secularists – engrossed by the demands, the trials, of the pleasures of the passing hour, and ignorant or careless of a future.' and second, that the social divides in the church (such as the arrangement of pews and free places) had the result that 'Working men, it is contended, cannot enter our religious structures without having pressed upon their notice some memento of inferiority.'

Many others have commented that the wealthy put on their best clothes to attend church or found other ways to display their affluence. One such is Anthony Anderson[29], the biographer of H M Bateman whose cartoons in the early part of the twentieth century satirized the suburban lifestyle.

> 'Social display revealed much of the folly of the new
> breed. They liked to puff themselves up, and show off
> their feathers, and it was in the drawing room or out
> in the street after church on Sunday that they took the
> opportunity to do so. It has been said that the middle
> classes only went to church because they thought it
> important to set an example to the lower classes – who
> were probably miles away – but it was also important
> that everyone should show exactly what they thought
> of themselves and everybody else. The church parade

was an occasion which called forth all the resources of the wardrobe, and the whole vocabulary of glance and gesture.'

Schools and the hospital

As elsewhere, the number of school places before 1870 was unsatisfactory and the national shortage led to the 1870 Education Act and the setting up of School Boards. A survey of provision in Battersea suggested that there was no place for about 40% of those of school age, and the charges, just over eight shillings a year for National Schools or 3 – 6 pence a day for private schools placed a burden on the poor, when the average earnings were £1 a week. Absenteeism was rife. The average teacher earned 5s-6s a week, less than half a washerwoman. We have already seen church schools set up next to both St Mark's and St Michael's. On his arrival, Erskine Clarke consulted Her Majesty's Inspector of Schools who advised that the chief educational need of the parish was a Superior School for Girls, above the elementary ones. As a result, one of his first acts in 1872 was to set up a school in the Battersea Vicarage (which was empty since he lived elsewhere). He persuaded a Miss Crofts, who was then governess of the Derby Training College for School Mistresses, to come and start a new school in the Vicarage. He explained the history in his 'funeral oration' for the school when it closed in July 1911[30] .

'In the real Vicarage House, the School did good work for fifteen years. Most of the Falcon Lane was then a quiet road, with the garden wall of Mr Fowne's mansion on one side and with the post and rail fence of a cabbage field on the other.

Gradually shops came, not of a high order, and parents in this part of the parish [ie South Battersea] complained of rudeness to the pupils... Falcon Lane had become far from pleasant for the daily walk of the pupils from the upper part of the parish and so I bought what was then called The Shrubbery, which had just then come into

the market, and that has been the delightful home of the
school for twenty-three years.'

By the time Erskine Clarke gave this speech, much had changed.
The School Board had built a school at Belleville Road in 1877 which
led to the closure of St Michael's School although the headmistress
moved across to be head of the new infants' school. This school
also put pressure on the road system, and by 1882 there was further
pressure to improve Webbs Road and a petition signed by 323
residents drew attention to the almost impassable conditions of the
lane which was now used by hundreds of children attending the
school. There was no path on either side of a considerable portion
of it which rendered it extremely dangerous for foot passengers
– there was of course still no link along the bottom of the Falcon
valley between Chatham and Belleville Roads. The next school was
at Honeywell Road where temporary iron buildings were erected
in 1889 with a permanent brick building completed in 1894 and
in Broomwood Road where the County Secondary School for Girls
was completed in 1907. These cost about 2-3d a week in 1877 and
provided education for the ages five to thirteen. Schools in the less
built up South Battersea tended to be cheaper to build than in the
north of the Borough, for example the site for Belleville cost £1,661
compared to over £3,000 for the schools in Gideon Road and Holden
Street.   Mr J T Pilditch, the Surveyor of Battersea, claimed in 1895[31].

'We have erected in the parish no less than 18 public
schools, maintained by the ratepayers, accommodating
23,617 children, and erected at a cost of £396,738.
In addition to this, there are new schools in course
of erection, or in contemplation, as also enlargements
to the existing schools, which will provide additional
accommodation for over 2000 children, at a further cost
of about £50,000.'

There were also many private schools, often located in private
houses and catering on average for 20 to 30 pupils. These were
almost entirely located in South Battersea, where the market was.
Against this background, it was not surprising that the numbers
attending the Vicarage School had dropped from nearly 300 to

about 160. Erskine Clarke described this as 'a remarkably large private school, but not yielding the funds to maintain it efficiently', and the fact that he was by then 83, and that Miss Crofts 'friends thought that the time had come when she ought to have a rest from her strenuous labours and responsibility' meant that 'I felt myself too old to undertake the anxiety of financing and directing the school under a new headmistress.' and the school closed.

The next local need was for a hospital. Usually, development of an estate led to demolition of the original house and it would have been expected to be no different for the Wheelers' house on the Bolingbroke Park estate. However, by luck, after the stables and greenhouses had been cleared away, the house stood between the two new roads Belleville and Wakehurst and its demolition was not immediately essential for their development.

Salvation appeared, by the intervention of the indefatigable Erskine Clarke, He had been impressed by his experience as a member of the Board of Guardians of the Battersea Dispensary. This had been operating since 1844, providing medical advice and drugs for those could pay something for their treatment in return for a modest regular subscription,. Its membership was largely artisans, labourers and domestic servants. When the prospect of Bolingbroke House becoming available arose, he responded to 'the wish of the men of the Battersea Dispensary for a hospital where they could pay what they could afford rather than having to accept charity at one of the big hospitals meant for the poor'.

The house was saved at the cost of £6,000 to become a pay hospital, receiving its first patients in 1880 with the intention was that it would be a "self-supporting" hospital where those who could pay more than their cost would help those who could only pay less. (Ill 31)

31: Bolingbroke House/hospital

An early advertisement appeared in The Times on 6 December.

A HOME in SICKNESS
BOLINGBROKE-HOUSE PAY HOSPITAL
Wandsworth Common
Trustee - The Rev Canon Erskine Clarke

This Institution is now open, and ready to receive sufferers from acute sickness upon payments according to their means, and it offers them the advantages of hospital treatment and nursing with home comforts. There is a ward for children as well as for adults, of both sexes. It is situate on the verge of one of the most healthful and extensive commons near London, and has a medical staff and resident surgeon and nurses.

Ladies and gentlemen interested in the scheme of assisting those who are willing to help themselves may view the Hospital any day but Sunday, between 12 and 4 o'clock

DONATIONS and SUBSCRIPTIONS are necessary until the Institution is sufficiently well-known to be self-supporting.

Prospectus will be forwarded by the Honorary Secretary, Mr J.S. Wood, Woodville, Upper Tooting , S.W.

A new dispensary, the Wandsworth Common Provident Dispensary, was set up in the basement. Even at the time, this hospital was recognised as a significant experiment by The Illustrated London News[32].

> 'If only the majority of the London parochial clergy were as practically minded and as alive to the material wants of the population under their charge as is the Vicar of Battersea. He had resolved to meet a local want and to try an important social experiment. There had long been among the middle and upper middle ranks of the population a desire for hospitals conducted on cooperative or quasi cooperative systems.'

The first patients included two clerks, a commercial agent, a game keeper, journalist, labourer, music master, an ostrich farmer (from the Cape), and six servants. Only two years later the same journal wrote again about the hospital[33].

> 'It is not opened as a 'financial speculation' but to give well-to-do artisans and middle class people an opportunity of obtaining treatment during sickness without the loss of self respect which must result from their resorting to one of the general hospitals as objects of charity It is situated in the middle of a great and growing middle class population four miles distant from the nearest general hospital.'

However, financial difficulties arose at regular intervals. The average weekly contribution was £1/10/6 but the costs were £2/2/0. As a result, five years later there was not enough income to finance the hospital. The Committee decided to sell the property, but they found that it had increased in value by £2,000, so they abandoned the sale plan, took out a mortgage and repaid their debts.[ix]

The next crisis, in 1889, was resolved by Mr Bryant, the President of the Royal College of Surgeons, sending his patients to the Bolingbroke

---

[ix] The hoped for security resulted in the medical superintendent, Dr Cecil Lyster, promptly marrying the lady superintendent or matron, Edith Thompson.

rather than to Guys Hospital; and three years later the hospital started taking patients from local accidents rather than their being sent up to St Thomas's or St George's in the centre of London. This began to change the character of the hospital; a new outpatients department was built in1901, a new wing in 1906 was financed in part by the King's Fund and a further wing financed shortly afterwards by a legacy from Benjamin Weir. Ill 32 shows a ward of around that time.

32: Bolingbroke hospital ward

The original eighteenth century house remained until its eventual demolition in 1937 and the hospital survived bomb damage in 1941 and a nearby V1 rocket in 1944. After the war, the hospital's Board resisted joining the NHS[34].

> 'The people of the area would greatly regret to see it merged into a system of state hospitals if that should come to pass under the plans for post-war reconstruction.'

However, come to pass it did, and the Bolingbroke joined the NHS in 1948. Against this background it is hardly surprising that the Bolingbroke hospital was held in such high affection locally, even though it has gradually lost more and more of its functions and a decision to close was consulted on and finally confirmed in 2007.

Remaining development

This section runs quickly through the remainder of the development in South Battersea. which continued briskly over the last two decades of the nineteenth century and into the twentieth. It is, of necessity, fairly detailed and those more interested in the analytic part than in how their particular road came into being could skip to the next section.

In July 1880 approval was given for the largest estate development then proposed in South Battersea. This was for the 41 acre Broomwood Park Estate which consisted of what Erskine Clarke called 'charmingly wooded meadows and shrubberies'. The estate was approached by a narrow lane 'fringed with gnarled and twisted oak'[35] which was eventually widened to become the eastern end of Broomwood Road and part of Kyrle Road and entered Clapham Common between Broadlands and Leveson Lodge. Formerly occupied by Wilberforce, it was then lived in at time by Sir Charles Forbes. The grounds were substantial running from Thurleigh Road to Chatham and Darley Roads and from about the present Wroughton Road to the Falcon Brook. The estate had grown further since Forbes had bought the corresponding slope up to Bolingbroke Grove which had belonged to one of the original five houses, The Elms, last lived in by Charles Lambert, a cigar merchant and cofounder of Lambert and Butler with a factory in Battersea. At the end of Webbs Road – then called Mud Lane - there were high boarded gates leading into the Broomwood fields owned by Forbes and no public right of way. This caused some difficulty for Erskine Clarke since it made longer the journey from his house in Altenberg Gardens to St Luke's. Sometimes he avoided this through the good services of Mr Holmes, Sir Charles Forbes' gardener and father of the verger at St Luke's, who would let him out at the estate's Chatham Road gate.

The estate was bought for £43,000 by John Cobeldick, a Cornish born land agent and builder living in Stockwell. The development resulted in the early demolition of The Elms, its site to be crossed by Honeywell Road although Broomwood House was retained until 1904 when William Wilberforce's former presence was recorded in a brown plaque on the east wall of the corner house with Wroughton Road. There followed the construction of Honeywell, Broomwood,

Montholme, Gayville, Devereux, Hillier, and Wroughton Roads plus extensions to Northcote and Webbs Roads. Part of this was 44 houses by the Working Man's Cooperative Housing Society.

While this development was taking place, other old houses came on the market as their occupants died and their children sold up. The next was on the extensive West Side Estate, once the residence of the antiquary Thomas Astle, and lived in for forty years by the Webbs, who were wine merchants. The house was bought by two prominent developers and builders, Thomas Ingram and William Bragg a year after the widowed Mrs Webb died. This estate had entrance gates at the end of the present Webbs Road and also gates on Clapham Common. The house stood about where No 44 Leathwaite Road is and, according to Erskine Clarke, that house is the only one on the West Side with a basement which had been part of the old mansion. Her son Edward Webb then moved to Byrom House which later became the Manor House School.

There was not much that could be done with this long thin estate other than to extend the existing Wakehurst, Salcott, Bennerley, Mallinson and Shelgate Roads across it in an easterly direction. Webbs Lane was widened and improved and one new road, Leathwaite created, shortly afterwards extended southwards to Ashness Road. Two small roads were added to maximise the number of new houses, Berber Road and Keildon Road, eventually reorientated from its original course to run parallel to Webbs Road. These roads were adopted and paved in 1886 although Webbs Road continued to pose problems until the objections of the owners of the properties (many of which contained retail shops) to having to pay their share of the costs were finally overruled.

The next development was of the Chatto estate, whose grounds and fields ran back to Chatham Road. This was owned by Mr Chatto but tenanted by Philip Cazenove who had died in 1880 and the estate purchased by Alfred Heaver the next year. However he failed to develop it and sold the land on to Ingram and Bragg; the house was lived in until 1885 when it was demolished to make way for Grandison, Chatto, Burland, and Dulka Roads. St Michael's Church, Bolingbroke Grove was built in 1881 in Cazenove's memory as well as that of the Rev Henry Boutflower Verdon who had died of rapid consumption a few months after marrying one of the daughters of

Henry Wheeler (the owner of Bolingbroke Grove House) and shortly before becoming vicar of St Mark's. Boutflower Road, next to St Mark's, was named after him.

Meanwhile Cobeldick who, like others, may have been affected by the slowdown in building in the early 1880s, sold the remaining 30 acres of the Broomwood Park estate in 1886 for £45,000, slightly more than he had paid for the whole a few years earlier, again to Ingram and Bragg, with a further partner James Brown. They raise additional funds and pressed on with the building. A further extension was approved following this sale with the formation of the sections of Broomwood and Kyrle Roads bounded by Wroughton Road. This development was described by Sir Walter Besant[36] in 1912.

> 'East of Bolingbroke Grove to Clapham Common and from Nightingale Lane north to Battersea Rise, there has swept within the last few years a wave of building, and now, with very few open spaces the entire block is covered with houses... Along the western edge of Clapham Common are many old mansions standing back in finely timbered grounds, each with its encroachment of posts and chains railing in portions of the Common and keeping their privacy by diverting the footpath from their doors. Behind them are deep old fashioned gardens with stretches of new houses at the foot in strange contrast. At Broomwood Road the estate has been cut through from the common and the land is now drained and prepared for building.'

The first of the large houses on Clapham Common West Side to go for development was Broadlands, one of the many developments by Henry Corsellis (the son of Alexander Corsellis, the Clerk to the original Wandsworth Vestry). This land, coupled with an attached meadow, provided the scope for a row of three story houses facing the Common , for a striking set of houses at 196-222 Broomwood Road, the only listed Victorian domestic buildings in 'Twixt the Commons'. They have a high spirited Gothic elevation with considerable decoration, inside as well as outside. (Ill 33)

33: examples of 196-222 Broomwood Road

The final approval in this decade was for the development in 1890-96, again by Henry Corsellis, of the estate of the Rev John Pincher Faunthorpe, the Principal of Whitelands College, Chelsea who moved out to a house overlooking Bromley Common. He had married Elizabeth Champion's companion, Charlotte Blackman,, who had been left a life interest in the house. There had been previous attempts to extend Northcote Road directly to Thurleigh Road or even as far as Nightingale Lane, but this was finally rejected in favour of the existing position which places Montholme Road in an offset position so the gardens on the west side of the road run down to the Falcon Brook. Faunthorpe's estate provided the land for this final piece of Northcote Road together with Bramfield and Kelmscott Roads.

Thus, by the turn of the century, South Battersea was laid out, but not fully built, on all areas except those closest to the West

Side of Clapham Common where the big houses still retained their substantial gardens. This state of affairs was not to last. Four of the villas were purchased by Thomas Ingram, including Leveson Lodge, Broxash, The Grange, once the house of Charles Baldwin who organized the draining of the Common in the eighteenth century, and a fourth unnamed house. These were demolished for a range of smaller houses on Amner and Broxash Roads, a continuation of Kyrle Road with a housing density of 24 per acre being the highest in the whole area. Ingram appeared to be trying to maximise his return but he did allow somewhat larger houses on Clapham Common West Side. The next year it was decided to incorporate the southern section of Amner Road with Ballingdon Road and rename it Roseneath Road in the belief that it would eventually be extended as far as the Common. Beechwood was then developed for Culmstock and Winsham Road – renamed Grove in 1902 as a result of a petition from the inhabitants who felt the trees in the street justified a more impressive name than Road.

Manchuria Road was approved in 1901 and John Cobeldick returned to the area by purchasing Heathfield House designed at the very end of the eighteenth century by James Barton. For once, the original house was not demolished, perhaps because Cobeldick liked to live in it himself. It remains as 21 West Side. Even so, 44 houses were built in its garden to form Sumburgh Road as well as houses in Thurleigh Road and West Side Clapham Common. Thurleigh Road was extended to the Common in 1903 (although not built until 1906-7) and its original route to Nightingale Lane was renamed Thurleigh Avenue. As a result Thurleigh Road has two bends to go round the earlier houses in Thurleigh Avenue, built in 1870 and 1890, and still avoid Heathfield. The remainder of he houses in Thurleigh Avenue were not constructed until the early 1930s.

The next change was the demolition in 1904 of Broomwood House which had been left standing when most of Wroughton and Hillier Roads were built. It is still shown in Map 8, based on the 1891 Ordnance Survey. This allowed those two roads to be completed 15 years after the rest. In keeping with the change in fashion, the last 21 houses on each road where Broomwood House had been are faced with red brick rather than the gault bricks used for the rest of the road. (Ill 34)

34: Hillier Road change from gault to red brick

While these houses were being built, The LCC decided to honour William Wilberforce with a commemorative plaque. The purchaser of 111 Broomwood Road, Miss Florence Higgins, the first woman to graduate as a Bachelor of Music from the University of London, agreed to have it placed in the wall on the Wroughton Road side of the house, where it has remained to this day.

The largest estate left was the 22 acre site of Battersea Rise House, including the two nearby houses of Glenelg and the Maisonette which, although smaller, still had 10 and 9 bedrooms respectively. The site was bought at auction by Edwin Evans in 1907 for £51,000. The map attached to the sale (Map 9) shows the extent of the housing development at that time.

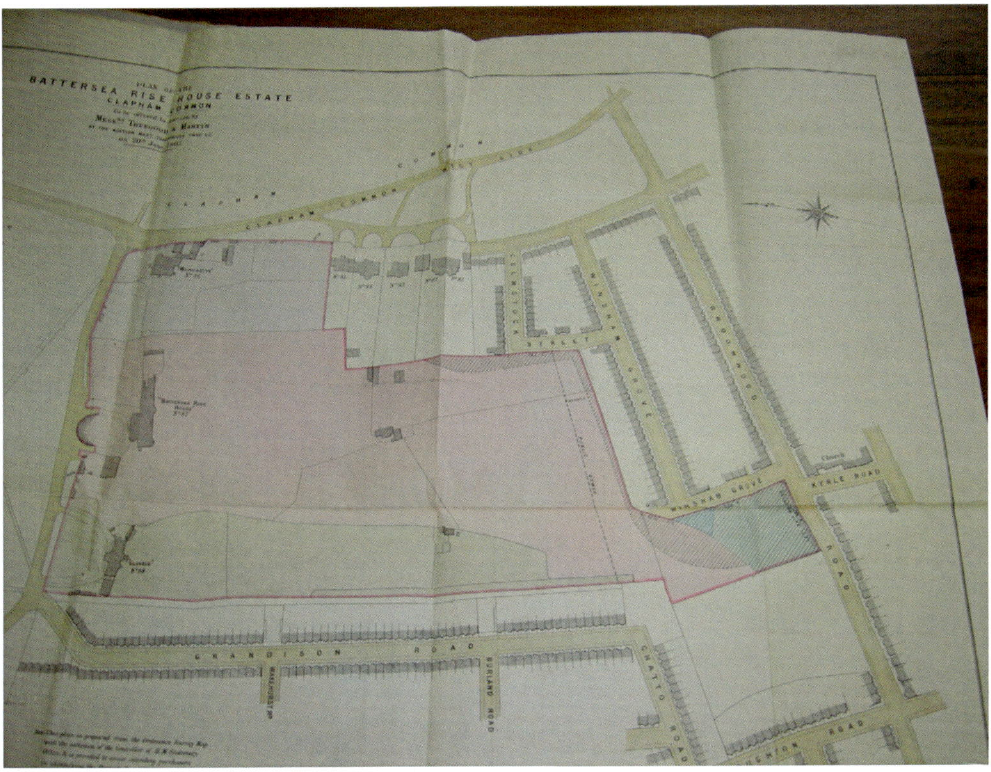

Map 9: Sale of Battersea Rise House

There was an attempt to save Battersea Rise House because of its historical connections, but although Edwin Evans offered the house, together with two acres of woodland, to Battersea Borough Council at cost for £7,945, it was declined. The progressives who opposed the proposal on 'social, ethical, and sentimental grounds' saw no reason for burdening the ratepayers with the building's costly maintenance, nor in all probability did they wish to react positively to a proposal from a prominent Conservative. A tender for £800 for demolishing the various houses was accepted, although some of the chimney pieces and a carved mantel piece were sold for £160. An Adams mantelpiece was resold for £275 three months later, and it is believed that one of the chimney pieces from the house is now at Wittington House on the banks of the Thames between Marlow and Henley, apparently installed by Garfield Weston in the 1930s.

Erskine Clarke felt strongly that there should be some means to commemorate the members of the Clapham Sect and raised £1,350 to purchase part of the Battersea Rise estate on the corner of Alfriston and Culmstock Roads, half way between St Luke's and St Barnabas for a church to be called the Church of the Holy Redeemer. He began a campaign to raise a further £5,000 to build the church, but this was one of his few failures and it was never built. Instead, the estate was developed to produce Bowood, Canford, Muncaster, Alfriston and Wisley Roads with some extensions to Wakehurst, Chatto and Culmstock Roads. These are transitional houses leaving the Victorian/Edwardian behind and including many Art Nouveau details. Edwin Evans produced a number of Art Nouveau designs with different builders and the glass, tiles and interior decorations still remain in many houses. There are some good examples on West Side, Culmstock Villas, and Muncaster Road.

Building did not stopp then because approval of the roads was by no means the same as building the houses. Many of the houses in Roseneath Road were built in 1914-25. Sudbrooke Lodge on Ramsden Road was built in 1915 by Edwin Evans, financed, it is claimed, by the building and sale of 1-6 Sudbrooke Road, which occupy a piece of land about the same size as the Lodge. The south side of Sudbrooke Road remained unbuilt on for some time because it was still the gardens of the house in Nightingale Lane, while much of the north side were allotments for some considerable time. The last road to be laid out in South Battersea, Holmside Road, was on the former Beecholme Estate in 1926. It was developed, together with 88-118 Thurleigh Road and Thurleigh Avenue, over the next four years by F J Wooding and Sons. The original intention had been to call the road after the house, Beecholme, but this was changed before completion of the building.

The enormous amount of building in Battersea increased the amount of household refuse and the vestry struggled to find private contractors to take care of this satisfactorily. Eventually it decided to take the matter into its own hands, using what we would call a direct labour force for the horse-drawn age. They bought land at the end of Culvert Road and, at a cost of £12,000, erected a 12 cell waste destructor together with stabling for 20 horses, wheelwright and blacksmith's shop and residence and office for the horsekeeper and manager. The household refuse was burnt and the residue crushed and converted and sold for tar paving for the footpaths of the parish at an annual profit of £2,000.[37] This was only one example of the municipal socialism pioneered by Battersea Council which was controlled from 1894 by the Progressive Alliance, a grouping of the local labour movement and radical and liberal organizations.[x] They went on to open state of the art baths, wash houses and libraries. The Council even refused to fly the Union Jack from the town hall for six years or pay the 1902 Coronation expenses, which caused the Daily Mail to proclaim 'it is a case of Battersea against the British Empire.'[38] Its support of the anti-vivisection movement also caused national controversy.[39] This sense of a separate if not unique identity remained in Battersea for a long time. A journalist on the patriotic 'British week' wrote in 1924[40] that Battersea had 'a feeling for the underdog.. and instinct to repudiate authority and commonly accepted standards…It is predisposed to support any one who prefixes his creed with 'anti' .. it backs the minority whether wise or otherwise.'

THE COLOSSUS OF BATTERSEA.

The Right Hon. John Burns (to his native borough). "SHIFT ME, AND YOU BECOME A 'BLASTED HEATH'!"

["If he were defeated the borough would never recover from the indelible stigma of rejecting him."—Report, in "The Times," of Mr. John Burns' speech at the Battersea Town Hall.]

35: John Burns – Colossus

---

[x] Their leader was John Burns, who had been elected to the LCC in 1889 and became MP for Battersea in 1892. He was a towering figure locally (Ill 35), and important nationally, becoming the first working man to be a Cabinet Minister in 1905.

(Endnotes)

1   St Luke's Parish Magazine
2   Sean Creighton. 2005 History of Battersea
3   Oxford Dictionary of National Biography
4   St Luke's Parish Magazine
5   J G Taylor. 1926 Our Lady of Batersey p 293
6   J G Taylor. Ibid p293
7   Charles Booth. Ibid Vol 5 p 162
8   Stephen Potter. 1959 Steps to Immaturity p 48
9   St Luke's Parish Magazine
10 Ibid
11 Ibid
12 Quoted by Peter Burton in Wandsworth Historian No 97 p2 2009
13 Ibid
14 Erskine Clarke. 1898 Wadham College Gazette
15 St Luke's Parish Magazine
16 Quoted in Wikipedia and elsewhere
17 William Stillman. 1901 Autobiography of Journalist Vol 2 Chap 25
18 St Luke's Parish Magazine
19 Percy Thornton. 1912 Some things we have remembered p 422
20 St Luke's Parish Magazine
21 Bridget Cherry and Niklaus Pevsner. 1983 Buildings of England London 2 South pp 61, 667
22 Charles Booth. 1900 Life and Labour in London Religious Influences Vol 5 p 179
23 The Times 14 November 1881 p12
24 Bishop Edward Talbot quoted in St Luke's Parish Magazine
25 Charles Booth. Ibid Vol 6 p 166
26 Charles Booth .Ibid Vol 5 p 177
27 Charles Booth. Ibid Vol 5 p 180
28 Religious Census 1851 p clvii
29 Anthony Anderson. 1982 The Man who was H M Bateman p 55
30 Charles Booth. Ibid Vol 6 p 166
31 John Pilditch. 1895 Ibid
32 Illustrated London News 13 November 1880
33 Illustrated London News 20 February 1882
34 Consultation document on closing of Bolingbroke Hospital 2007
35 Erskine Clarke in St Luke's parish magazine
36 Walter Besant. 1912 London South of the Thames p 240
37 John Pilditch. Ibid
38 Daily Mail 22 May 1902
39 Andrew Prescott. 2002 Freemasonry in London
40 British Week 11 December 1924

C H A P T E R   7

THE DENTS AND OLD
PARK ESTATES

So far we have described the development of the west side of
Clapham Common and the housing associated with the Thorntons on
Battersea Rise, but we have made little reference to the development
of the Dents and Old Park estates and the adjacent land. This is the
next stage in tightening the geographical boundaries and looking
in more detail at a small part of South Battersea over the timescale
covered for the larger area in previous chapters. We will study in
more detail the various transactions by which the development was
financed. They demonstrate all the features that have already been
mentioned; sale of the original estate following the death of the first
or second generation occupant; finance for the developer raised from
solicitors or the clergy; and refinancing of the builder's or developer's
costs by sale of the ground rents.

None of the original owners of the land in South Battersea
undertook development themselves. In the early stages some of the
estates were sold to the freehold land companies, but as time went
on it was more usual for them to be bought by individual investors/
speculators. We have already seen how James Lord lost his money.
Sometimes these speculators developed the land themselves, but more
often they either subdivided the land to sell to other speculators or
sold building leases to individual builders. This spreading of the risk
helps to account for the very large number of builders involved in
most of the roads in the area.

The Dents and Old Park estates illustrate these patterns. Although
occasionally owned by the same person, these estates were generally
owned by different parts of the Dent family and were developed
at slightly different times and by different people. However, they
provide one of the few examples of restrictive covenants being used
to ensure that larger houses were built on the land. Even though most
of the other covenants were not enforced as strictly, or for as long as,

the corresponding ones were for, say, the Dulwich Estate, they have had a lasting effect by influencing the type of houses built, most of which remain. Many of the freeholds (and hence the ground rents) in these roads were owned by the Governors of Queen Anne's Bounty and it has therefore been possible to examine many of the original deeds which run to some 55 pages for each estate and give at least a partial account of the history of the development.

The five houses

In the eighteenth century, a small number of houses were built on the east side of Wandsworth Common and on the part of Battersea Rise closest to the Falcon Brook, although in most cases it is difficult to establish the exact date of their construction. The land, at least from 1763, was largely owned by Earl Spencer but as we have seen he was starting to sell pieces of it. The houses were occupied by people of wealth and, often, of distinction. Apart from Isaak Ackerman, the former owner of Battersea Rise House, three of the landowners were Thomas Astle, the antiquarian, Robert Lovelace, a partner in Childs' Bank, and Robert Dent who became a partner in the same Bank only three years after Lovelace.

Robert Dent first appears in the Battersea rate book in 1767 and his own account book shows that he bought a further 88 acres from Earl Spencer and Thomas Parker in February 1773 for £5,650, building a house on that land in 1776 for which he paid the builder, Richard Morris £5,496/7/0. Over the next twenty five years he was involved in a number of land deals in Battersea, both selling and buying, resulting in three large estates, two smaller ones, and five substantial houses along what became known as Bolingbroke Grove, together with a couple of farms and associated cottages. Lovelace, who owned the land on the Clapham Common side of the Falcon Brook, sold it in 1797 to the owners of the first four of the houses on Bolingbroke Grove, allowing them to extend their plots across the stream. After these transactions, the pattern of land ownership remained almost unchanged for 60 years and the result is shown in Map 10, based on the 1836 Tithe Map.

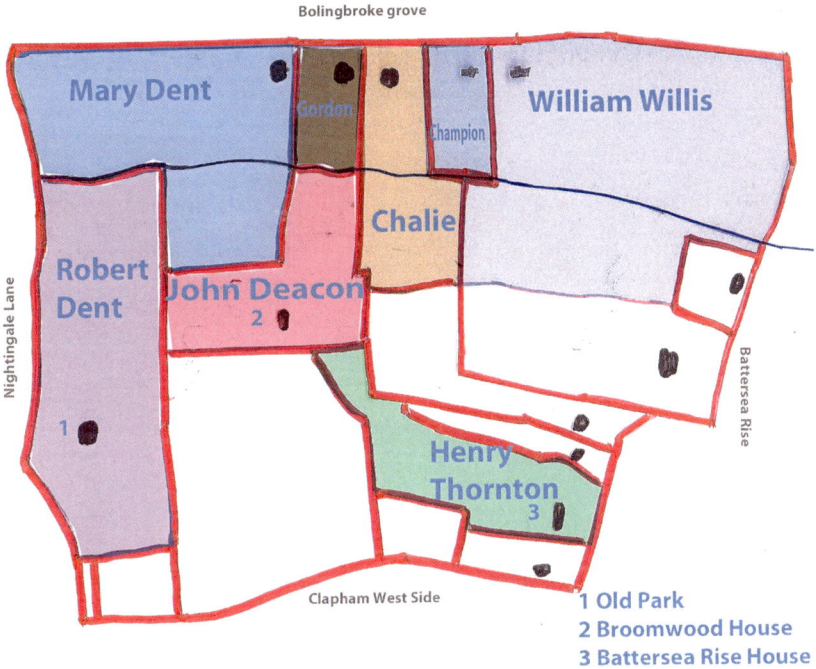

Bolingbroke grove

Mary Dent

Gordon

Champion

William Willis

Chalie

Nightingale Lane

Robert Dent

John Deacon

2

1

Henry Thornton

3

Battersea Rise

Clapham West Side

1 Old Park
2 Broomwood House
3 Battersea Rise House

Map 10: Boundaries from 1836 Tithe map

The five houses gave their name to the road in the 1790s and were described as 'very genteel modern built brick houses which overlook the common towards the west.'[1] Illustrations 31 and 36 show two of the houses.

36: Bolingbroke Grove House

One of the larger transactions involved Robert Dent selling the land on the corner of Battersea Rise and Bolingbroke Grove, including a house that was called Bolingbroke Grove House, to the eminent banker, William Willis, partner of the bank Willis Perceval. As we have already seen, this was the only house of the five to survive into the twentieth century, having been rescued by Erskine Clarke to become the Bolingbroke Hospital.

Willis also owned the next house along and this was occupied for some time by Edward Fawkes (reputed to have been the man who dug the ditch along the border between Clapham and Battersea). Fawkes was succeeded for a short period by Henry Barchard, a wine merchant, before the house was taken by Alexander Champion. He was the son of a father of the same name and a prominent whaler, appearing regularly before the Committee of the Privy Council for Trade and Plantations as spokesman for the Southern Fishery. One of the Galapagos Islands is named after him. He was obviously a rich man because his daughter and co-heiress, Harriet, was described[2] as bringing a 'considerable fortune' to her husband, the antiquary Thomas Streatfeild.

Alexander's wife, Ann, continued living there after his death in 1808 with her two daughters Maria and Elizabeth. Ann died in April, 1837.[i] The two daughters were left the leasehold of the house and stayed there for the rest of their lives, Elizabeth being the last to die in 1870, having bought the freehold from Willis' successor as owner.

The third house was occupied first by Thomas Hinchcliffe and subsequently by Matthew Chalie for over forty years. Chalie came from a Huguenot family; his grandfather, Pierre, had fled Montauban and settled in Holland. Pierre's sons, James and John, were already connected with the wine trade and established a business in Mincing Lane in the City describing themselves as 'Wine Merchants, General Merchants and Bankers.' Matthew was the son of James and it is not surprising he moved near to the Huguenot community in

---

[i] There was a problem with her will because it could not be found at first. Finally her brother found it together with five codicils in a sealed envelope locked in a drawer in Ann's bedroom in which she was reputed 'to keep her papers of moment'. Unfortunately, some of the codicils were written on sheets of notepaper which had the top torn off and it was necessary to swear that they were in that state when the envelope had been opened.

Wandsworth. In 1785 the firm shipped twice as much claret to London as any other firm and just over 20% of the total. Matthew Chalie, with his new partner Wiliam Parry Richards, created the firm Chalie Richards which supplied the six successive monarchs from George IV through to George VI and is still trading, albeit as a subsidiary of a larger group. One of their trademarks is a picture of an eighteenth century man and is called 'Old Matthew'.

Matthew's first wife, Marianne, died in 1786 and he then married Mary Anne Hoper whose sister, Elizabeth, lived on in the house after the Chalies had died. Matthew had one daughter, Jane, who married the lawyer Robert Vaughan Richards. In turn they had one daughter, Marianne, who married Field Marshal Ramon Cabrera, the Carlist general who had been created Count of Morella after his victory there but was driven out of Spain and eventually settled in England. As Countess of Morella and great niece of Elizabeth Hoper, she was well known in the area and gave her name to Morella Road.

The fourth house was occupied by Benjamin Cole at the end of the eighteenth century and was then bought by Sir James Mansfield. He was a distinguished lawyer, having represented John Wilkes on his application for bail when he returned to England in 1768. He became Chief Justice of the Court of Common Pleas in 1804 and presided over the trial in 1812 of John Bellingham for the murder of the Prime Minister, Spencer Perceval. Following Mansfield's death in 1821, the house was occupied first by John Gordon, a solicitor, and then his son Alex. The land for this house, which was called the Elms, lies between Broomwood House and Bolingbroke Grove and John Deacon had bought it when he bought Broomwood House and Sir Charles Forbes later became the owner of both houses. After a short occupation by Frederick Mangles, a merchant trading with India, it was rented by Charles Lambert, the cigar merchant, until it was knocked down for building when he moved to Streatham.

Old Park

The land that became the Old Park estate was assembled about the end of the eighteenth century by the Dent family. As we have already seen, Robert Dent built a house on land near Clapham Common in 1776. He sold some of his land to his brother William who also built a house, this one being the fifth on Bolingbroke Grove and the nearest of the five to Nightingale Lane. William's first intention was to leave his house to his nephew, Robert's son, John Dent, with an annuity charged to the estate and payable to John's sister Jane Sophia who had married a Captain Trotter. He also gave his daughter Mary, who may have been illegitimate, the right to live in the house for a year after his death together with the income on a substantial sum of money. However, three years later he changed his will giving her the right to live in the house for life. She exercised this right and lived there after his death in 1822 until she died on December 27, 1867.

There is potential confusion about the exact location of Robert's 1776 house. The well known map of Clapham Common produced by Smith around 1800 (Map 4) does indeed show Robert Dent as living around Clapham Common, but on the West Side. However, two other maps by James Edwards and Thomas Milne, both published in 1801, show no house where Smith puts it, but rather a house halfway down Nightingale Lane, exactly where we know Old Park was situated and with the same curving drive which is shown in Batten's map of 1826 and in the Tithe Map of 1836. By then there are two houses at the Nightingale Lane end of West Side, Hightrees House and Heathfield House. However, Hightrees does not appear in any maps/records until 1805 and Heathfield, although building commenced in 1797, was not finished and occupied until 1806. Moreover, there is no evidence from the rate books that Robert Dent ever owned this land. Henry Cavendish was the owner of the land on which both Hightrees and Heathfield were built.

The most likely explanation is that Smith was just a little lazy about the exact location of Robert Dent's house, recognising that it was the last on the West Side but not bothering to indicate – as he had done for the house of the major public figure Wilberforce – that it was some way down the side. This is consistent with what we know of the land that was left to Robert Dent's son John, which did not extend as far as Clapham Common itself. This is confirmed by the text of James Edwards' map which describes all the houses on or near the road to Brighton. Having listed the houses at the start of Nightingale Lane, he goes on[3].

*'About one quarter mile west of the last described, and
a small distance north of a road leading from hence to
Wandsworth Common is the seat of Robert Dent, banker,.
The house stands on an eminence with a view to the west.'*

The final confirmation is a detail from a map (Map 11) by J Cary,
published in 1790, which not only marks a house where Old Park
was located but shows it as occupied by Mr Dent.

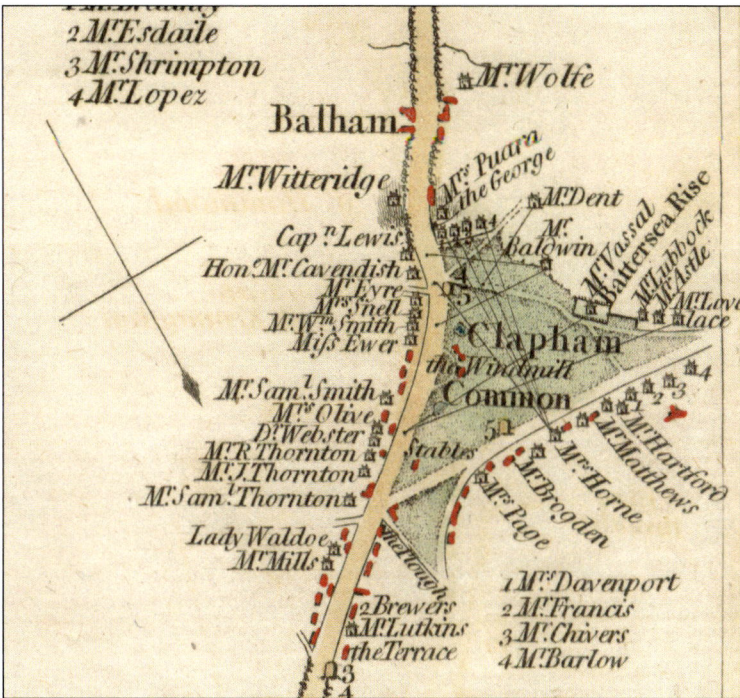

Map 11: John Cary's map of 1790 (detail)

There is also a picture of Old Park, commissioned in 1830 (Ill 37)
and while it is very likely that the house was altered in the 1820s, it
does have an appearance consistent with having been built in 1776.

Following Robert Dent's death in 1805, his eldest son John
became the owner of Old Park, although he did not himself use the
house extensively, spending more time in his London residence in
Hertford Street, Mayfair and his Hampshire villa at Barton. John
followed his father in becoming a partner in Child's Bank in 1795 but
he was also developing a more public career, representing Lancaster

OLD PARK, CLAPHAM.
The Residence of JAMES COLES Esq.

37: Old Park 1830

as an MP, which he won in 1790 and five times subsequently until he retired from the seat in 1812. It was an expensive seat to fight and his father's account books show a donation in 1790 of over £3,000 for electoral expenses. No doubt he also made best use of a family connection because not only was Robert from a well known Westmorland family but he had purchased a share of the manor at Cockerham near Lancaster, costing over £20,000. This was settled on John at the time of his marriage in 1800. John Dent was also a voracious book collector[4] and was elected a FRS in 1811. His collection included a 1462 Latin Bible and the first three Shakespeare folios and realised over £15,000 when sold by auction after his death. However he was best known to his contemporaries by his nickname of 'Dog Dent' following his proposing a tax on dogs in 1796 and vehemently denouncing the species. He died in 1826, and this part of his land ended up with his second son, John Villiers Dent who succeeded to it when his elder brother died unmarried in 1832.

Old Park was occupied briefly by Francis Freeland in 1808-11 and subsequently by W H Cooper in 1820 for three years and then William Hughes from 1823-1829. William Hughes was a silk mercer, haberdasher and linen draper in Mincing Lane in the City and may have been the link with the next occupier, James Coles, with Villiers Dent clearly continuing as the freeholder. Although Coles is not recorded in the Rate Book until 1835, one of his descendants[5] has established that he moved to Old Park in 1830 from a house in Denmark Hill where his two youngest children (of eight) had been born a few years earlier. Coles was also a silk merchant, having started his own firm Leaf, Coles and Co in 1821, operating from premises at 39 Old Change, St Paul's Churchyard and had a large warehouse occupying the corner of Old Change and Watling Street. Leaf, Coles and Co grew to become one of the biggest haberdashers in the country. As a result of their extensive use of the Post Office to deliver their goods, Coles was repeatedly invited to give evidence to Parliamentary Select Committees on the need for a universal postal system. Another branch of the Coles family started the largest store group in Australia with the same name.

James Coles also commissioned in 1830 the print of Old Park (Ill 37) and remained there until his death in July 1851, with Villiers Dent still the freeholder. It was a large house, with 13 or 14 bedrooms, stabling, coach house, servants' hall and 'a vinery and conservatory about 80 ft. long'. The grounds contained a pond famous for water lilies. The earth excavated from the pond was heaped round a circular brick shaft and in the winter ice from the pond would be dropped in for use in the summer. This mound of Old Park had four scotch pines on it and a small thatched summerhouse nearby.

He lived in some style in Old Park, no doubt reflecting the grant of a Coat of Arms in 1840 to both James and his wife Elizabeth (in her own right, as the heiress of Timothy Horsman, the High Constable of the North Riding of Yorkshire). By 1841 there were seven servants, including coachman, footman and a married gardener living in the lodge. James Coles had furnished the house in a sumptuous style with an extensive library, a grand piano, porcelain dinner and breakfast services and plenty of silver.

By the mid 1840s the rising cost of capital forced many City of London merchant companies to incorporate and bring in other investors. James retired in 1847 but, following a dispute, cut his son (also James) out of the business six days after his son's marriage in early 1851 to a woman fifteen years younger than him and from a working class family.

William Leaf, James Coles' partner and probably his wife's cousin, had lived in Herne Hill, near to Coles, before moving to the house he had had built for him in Streatham, Park Hill. Leaf continued with the company after Coles' retirement and was joined by his sons in due course.[ii][6] Park Hill was subsequently acquired by Sir Henry Tate who lived there at the time he endowed the Tate Gallery. It was then a convent for some long time with its grounds occupied by the Park Hill Estate.

[ii] However, his eldest son William died in 1871, William senior died in 1874, and his second son George became ill at about the same time. As a result, George's son, Walter, took over. Walter was at 23 already a distinguished classical scholar and had certainly not intended to become a businessman. He wrote in his diary shortly after 'for the first time taking his seat on an office stool' that 'I made no pretence of liking the drudgery, but it had to be faced; and from the very first day I determined that it should not make me forget the higher intellectual interests.' While finding time to become recognised as the foremost Homeric scholar of his day, he sorted out the financial issues, converting the firm into a limited company in 1888 and amalgamating it with another company to form Parsons and Law Ltd in 1892. Walter Leaf then left the board and became a banker, ending up as chairman of the newly merged Westminster Bank in 1918.

Following Coles' death in 1851, Old Park was occupied by Joseph Wakefield for three years and then, according to the rate book, was empty for 10 years, while still owned by Villiers Dent. It is not clear that the rate book gives a correct record. There are a number of references elsewhere to Old Park being lived in by John Thornton, the son of Sam Thornton (brother of Henry), and his wife Eliza after their terrace house in Clapham was demolished in 1861. John had nine children and had left banking to join the Audit Office and subsequently became a Commissioner of the Inland Revenue. His father, who was very much a banker, wrote in his 'Year Recollections'[7] in November 1823, 'His occupation at the Audit Office appears to be congenial to his turn of mind. And I have only to wish that the emoluments of it were adequate to the support of his large family.' Given the number of references to his living in Old Park, it may well be true, but it cannot have been for long. The 1861 census, conducted in April, shows John Thornton still living at his house in Clapham and Villiers Dent, the owner, living at Old Park. John Thornton died later in 1861; his wife only lived until 1863 and, as we shall see, when Old Park was offered for sale in 1866, it was described as having been for a long time the residence of Villiers Dent.

Nightingale Lane south side part I

The first local reference to Old Park comes from the local vestry minutes in July 1864 which record a complaint from Messrs Debenham and Tewson, acting on behalf of the owner, that the fence of Old Park was being damaged because Nightingale Lane had been raised. The surveyor reported that a retaining wall was required on which the fence could be rebuilt and he had discussed the cost of this with Mr Jennings, presumably the George Jennings (of whom more later) who was building on the other side of the road. Mr Jennings agreed to contribute half the cost and Mr Dent also agreed to the wall being built on his land rather than on the road side of the fence because that would be cheaper. The cost was £42, half of which was met by Mr Jennings and half by the vestry. There were no houses on this (north) side of Nightingale Lane, which formed the edge of the

Old Park estate, recorded in the Stanford map of 1862 (Map 6) and this incident confirms that there was still no building there by 1864.

There had been houses at the south side of the Clapham Common end of Nightingale Lane for some long time (including Hollywood and Broadoak from the eighteenth century) but these fell within the parish of Streatham (later Balham). One such house was advertised in The Times in 1838.

'To let in Nightingale Lane, Clapham Common, a detached house, in excellent repair, on lease containing drawing and dining rooms each 22 feet long, large productive garden, with lawn and field,, coach house and three stall stable, and a well of superior water; lately occupied by J S Schweuck Esq. For further particulars enquire of the gardener, on the premises.'

38: Nightingale Pub

While most of the houses in Nightingale Lane were large, some smaller cottages were built in 1853 in what is now Western Lane. At first they were known as Lee's cottages after the Lee family which owned the land as well as that around their home, Balham House. They sold the Nightingale Lane frontage to George Jennings and most of the remainder in 1868 to the British Land Co which laid out a number of roads and sold off the frontage in small building plots. The other building of interest is the Nightingale Pub, built in 1853 by the publican Thomas Wallis. He rebuilt it in 1869 (Ill 38) and an advertisement appeared in the Clapham Observer on July 10 that year saying 'Thomas Wallis, proprietor of the Nightingale Wine and Spirit Establishment, has entirely rebuilt and considerably enlarged his premises so long known as 'The Nightingale." More large houses had been built further down the same side of Nightingale Lane since the early 1850s and that process was virtually complete by 1860. Unlike the houses facing Clapham Common at the start of the road, these were in the detached part of the parish of Clapham, and so neither Battersea nor Streatham (Balham). This led to continuing arguments about how responsibility for Nightingale Lane was divided between the various parishes and on 12 February 1868 we find the Wandsworth Board of Works ordering the footway on Nightingale Lane to be paved with Purbeck kerb at the joint cost of Battersea, Streatham and Clapham parishes.

The houses on Nightingale Lane were, and still are, substantial houses built for the wealthy with lodges and stables. Those living there in 1861 included a ship broker, sugar refiner, brewer, wholesale furrier and wine merchant as well as three describing themselves as fund holder or landed proprietor. All had many servants as well as coachmen. Two of those living there were famous names. Charles Spurgeon, the famous Baptist preacher, had made such a success of his first post as pastor of a small church near Cambridge that he was invited at the early age of 19 to take charge of the church in New Park Street, Southwark. Despite its considerable enlargement, it could not cope with the numbers wanting to hear him preach and, during the construction of the Metropolitan Tabernacle at Elephant and Castle, he preached in the Surrey Music Hall to 10,000 or more for two hours at a time. The Tabernacle was built by William Higgs who, although most of his work was for government contracts, became a close friend of Charles Spurgeon and was a deacon at the Tabernacle. Higgs also built a chapel in Chatham Road and we shall see that he built a number of houses in Nightingale Lane. Spurgeon used his money from the church and from sale of his sermons house to buy a house, Helensburgh, in Nightingale Lane in 1856 and he moved the pulpit stairs from the New Park Chapel when it was sold to his garden in Clapham, fixing them to a large walnut tree there. The location was described even twenty years later by The World as in 'Nightingale Lane – a quiet nook hard by Wandsworth Common.'[8] This allowed him to escape from Central London after preaching at his Tabernacle. His wife wrote in Spurgeon's autobiography[9].

> 'We left the new Kent Road, in 1857, to reside in Nightingale Lane, Clapham. This was then a pretty and rural, but comparatively unknown region, and our delight in the change and interest it afforded, was unbounded. On the right hand side of the road, if the visitor came from Clapham, stretched a glorious park, which, with its residential mansion, was then the property of J. Dent, Esq. Our house stood on the left side, facing the park and its palings. I do not think there were more than five or six houses, besides our own, the whole length of the 'Lane' from one end to the other. This secludedness was a great attraction to my beloved.'

The second famous name was the leading sanitary engineer (Josiah) George Jennings who lived at Oak Lodge with his second wife Sophie (whom he married when he was 35 with four children and she was 16). They had a further 11 children of their own and subsequently moved down the road to Ferndale which, like Oak Lodge, he had built himself. Born in 1810, he started as a plumber in Southampton, but moved to London to work for a firm for which his father had been a leading foreman. He was an effective innovator, and was awarded the medal of the Royal Society of Arts by Prince Albert in 1847, which helped him, against opposition, to install public conveniences, called monkey closets, at the Crystal Palace ,essentially a private cubicle with a water flush,. He charged a penny, not for their use, but for a clean towel, a comb, a clean seat after each use, and a shoe shine. They were used by 827,280 visitors to the Exhibition and generated an annual income of £1,000; this was the origin of the euphemism 'to spend a penny'.

The Metropolis[10] magazine claimed that knowledge of his name extended from 'Zembla's shores unto the far Peru' and his public conveniences were widely praised, as by this poem written to commemorate the opening of the first, more elaborate, underground convenience at the Royal Exchange, which contrives to mention both the Battersea sanitary kings[11].

> I'front the Royal Exchange and Underground
> Down gleaming walls of porc'lain flows the sluice
> That out of sight decants the Kidney Juice
> Thus pleasuring those Gents for miles around,
> Who, crying for relief, once piped the sound
> Of wind in alley ways. All hail this news
> And let the joyous shuffling queues
> For Gentlemanly Jennings' most well found
> Construction, wherein a penny ope's the gate
> To Heav'ns mercy and Sanitary wares
> Received the Gush with seemingly, cool obedience,
> Enthroning Queen Hygeia in blessed state
> On Crapper's Rocket: with rapturous ease men's cares
> Shall flow away when seated at convenience !

Development of Old Park estate

Before considering how the estates on the Battersea side of Nightingale Lane were developed, it is worth summarizing their history. As we have seen, the Dent family, albeit different branches of it, owned the roughly 75 acres of land alongside Nightingale Lane between Bolingbroke Grove and Hightrees House immediately facing the west side of Clapham Common, They had two houses, Bolingbroke House just off Wandsworth Common and Old Park off Nightingale Lane, which were originally the property of the brothers William and Robert Dent. Their wills left both of the houses to Robert's elder son John. It is not clear how much John Dent lived in either house, but following his death in 1824 he gave his daughter Mary the right to live in Bolingbroke House for the rest of her life, which she exercised until her death in December 1867 at the age of 86. Old Park appears to have become the property of John Dent's eldest surviving son, John Villiers Dent, although we have already seen that the house was let for much of the time.

Mary's longevity resulted in the houses going down different sides of John Dent's family since he left the ownership of Bolingbroke House, where Mary lived, to his wife Ann. Although she died in 1856, long before Mary, the future beneficiaries were determined by her will which also covered her wedding settlement. She left her property to her younger children, Villiers Dent having taken the eldest son's portion following his elder brother's early death. As a result, the two pieces of land were developed at slightly different times and at a different pace.

The Stanford Map of London, dated 1862, (Map 6) shows the two estates unchanged since the 1836 Tithe Map, but change followed when Villiers Dent divided his time between his family house and land in Hampshire and his house in Bryanston Square and took the opportunity of the then current building boom to seek to sell the land for development. The first of the Old Park land was sold in February 1866, resulting in the break-up of the estate, although the house itself and immediate grounds were lived in for another 20 years. The land was purchased by Joseph Welch, a warehouse manager, and Henry Hughes a wool broker, although they mortgaged the property to the auctioneers, Debenham, Tewson and Farmer (a new partner). The intent to develop was indicated by the firm of architects, Wimble and Taylor, promptly applying the next month to form four new streets which they proposed should be named Thurleigh, Sudbrooke, Westerdale and Winchelsea. Westerdale became Ramsden, presumably because it was a continuation of the road on the other side of Nightingale Lane which was approved in 1868 as part of the British Land development and which had houses on it first. Winchelsea became Rusham Road. Having secured this permission for development from the Metropolitan Board of Works on 23 March 1866 (planning permission did not take long in those days!), the original land was divided up into four separate pieces in preparation for sale and development, and it was possible to proceed with the sale of the house itself. Accordingly, Messrs Debenham, Tewson and Farmer (who were the predecessor of the international property firm DTZ) advertised for auction on Tuesday 17 April 1866 the four acre property of Villiers Dent esq, 'A first-class Family

Mansion, with its surrounding grounds of great beauty, kitchen garden, stabling, etc, to be Sold, with immediate possession.' A copy of the advertisement, which appeared in the South London Press on 31 March and 7 April that year, is shown below at Ill 39.

SALES BY AUCTION.

OLD PARK, CLAPHAM COMMON.

A first-class Family Mansion, with its surrounding grounds of great beauty, kitchen garden, stabling, &c., to be Sold, with immediate possession.

MESSRS. DEBENHAM, TEWSON, and FARMER will SELL, at the London Tavern, on Tuesday, April 17, at 1 (unless an acceptable offer be made in the meantime), the first-class FREEHOLD FAMILY MANSION, for many years the residence of Villiers Dent, Esq., and so well-known as Old-park, Nightingale-lane, Clapham-common, a remarkably healthy, open, and agreeable neighbourhood, within an easy five miles' drive of the City and West-end. It is surrounded by residences of a superior class, each having extensive grounds, and contains 13 or 14 bed and dressing-rooms, store and linen rooms, spacious corridors, capital entrance-hall with portico, dining-room about 22 by 17, elegant drawing-room 29 by 18, library 20 by 15.6, study, kitchen, scullery, pantry, &c., on the ground-floor, and other good offices in the basement, including servants' hall, housekeeper's room, &c.; there is also an ample range of out-offices, a seven-stall stable, two loose-boxes, harness room, large coach-house, two rooms for coachman, a walled kitchen garden, with vinery and conservatory about 80ft. long, also a small farmery; the lawn and pleasure grounds are well-timbered and planted with choice shrubs. The whole comprises about four acres, and the purchaser can, if wished, have the option of buying additional land adjoining. The property is well supplied with water, is thoroughly dry, and in every respect adapted for a gentleman's establishment. Particulars of T. G. Bullen, Esq., solicitor, 7 and 8, Barge-yard-chambers, Bucklersbury; of Messrs. Wimble and Taylor, architects, 2, Walbrook; and of the auctioneers, 80, Cheapside, who will give cards to view, and are prepared to treat by private contract. N.B.—In reply to numerous inquiries, the auctioneers are instructed to state that the property will not be let.

39: Old Park sale advertisement 1866

A similar advertisement appeared in the Times on April 5, although by then the land had grown to be almost five acres!

Most people must still have regarded the land between Old Park and the bottom of the valley as part of the estate and it continued to be described on plans of other land sales as 'The Clapham Old Park

Estate' until at least 1877 even though it had had no connection with the owner of the house for over ten years. However the house was not sold at auction and, despite the advertisement claiming that the property would not be let, Villiers Dent was still listed as the owner of the site in the 1868 and 1871 rate books and the property was indeed let.

The sale of the Old Park estate stimulated other sales in the area. An advertisement appeared in the South London Gazette on 23 January 1869 announcing the sale by auction of nearby land.

> 'In lots, a further portion of the eligible FREEHOLD BUILDING LAND, situate in Nightingale Lane and the new road called Ramsden-road, leading from Nightingale Lane to Balham Station. The property is situate between Wandsworth and Balham stations about five miles from the City and West-end, and about ten minutes walk of Clapham Junction and Balham stations on the London, Brighton, and South Coast and South Western Railways. Nine-tenths of the purchase money may remain on mortgage or contract at five per cent, to be paid in nine years by equal half yearly instalments; but the whole or any part of the balance may be paid off at any time without notice.'

Not for the last time, the estate agent's blurb contained some exaggeration, since it is at least 20 minutes walk to Clapham Junction from Ramsden Road.

There was no move to demolish Old Park itself and by 1871 Edward Tewson (of the firm of auctioneers) had purchased Old Park and its immediate land from Welch and Hughes who had also sold the land adjoining it to a number of different purchasers. It is probable that it was at that time that the restrictive covenants were imposed. All the houses on Nightingale Lane in the late 1860s were large and detached and it seems likely that the developers believed that they would get the best return by maintaining the status of the area. Accordingly they imposed restrictive covenants requiring any houses built on the site to be either detached with a minimum cost of £800 or semi-detached with a minimum cost of £1,200 a pair.

They also imposed a covenant ruling out a range of activities that might lower the tone of the neighbourhood, including running any business or trade, hotel or tavern. These are given in more detail in Chapter 9.

One plot had been sold to William Newmarch for his house, Beechhome discussed later; a second to William Higgs for building 42-50 Nightingale Lane; and the third to Thomas Bullen, a lawyer who had been involved in helping to finance the original purchase from Welch and Hughes. Erskine Clarke later bought Bullen's plot for £1,150 for a future church selling a small strip of his purchase to William Newmarch who had been trying to buy a part of it which had 'good trees'. The resulting layout of the land around Old Park is illustrated in the advertisement (Map 12) for its later auction in 1876 on behalf of Jane Simpson by the surveyors Debenham, Tewson Farmer, and now a fourth partner, Bridgewater.

After a period of uncertain occupation, Old Park was rented at least from 1870 by a retired tavern keeper, Thomas Simpson, his wife Jane and ten children, not to mention a niece and grandchild, four servants in the main house with married servants living in coach house and lodge. Thomas died in 1872 and Jane continued at the house, finally buying it from Tewson in October 1873 and disposing of it herself in May 1876 to James Horatio Booty, an oil merchant. She then moved, first to what had been the Webb's West House and then to Craven House at 50 Nightingale Lane, allowing her to overlook the building taking place on her former Old Park. She died in 1893.

Development on the former Old Park estate was slow and concentrated for the time being on Nightingale Lane itself, leaving the old house in place. This reflected the recession in building generally at the end of the 1860s and perhaps the restrictive covenant that required semidetached houses costing no less than £1,200 a pair. While the census records for 1871 show a number of empty houses and one under construction, there were only six occupied, Sherbrooke Lodge, Nightingale Lodge, what are now 3 and 5 Thurleigh Avenue, Beecholme and Dudley House.

Beechholme was built by the banker, William Newmarch, as he moved from Kensington and is described graphically in the rate book as 'house, lodge building, stable, garden and pleasure grounds' and

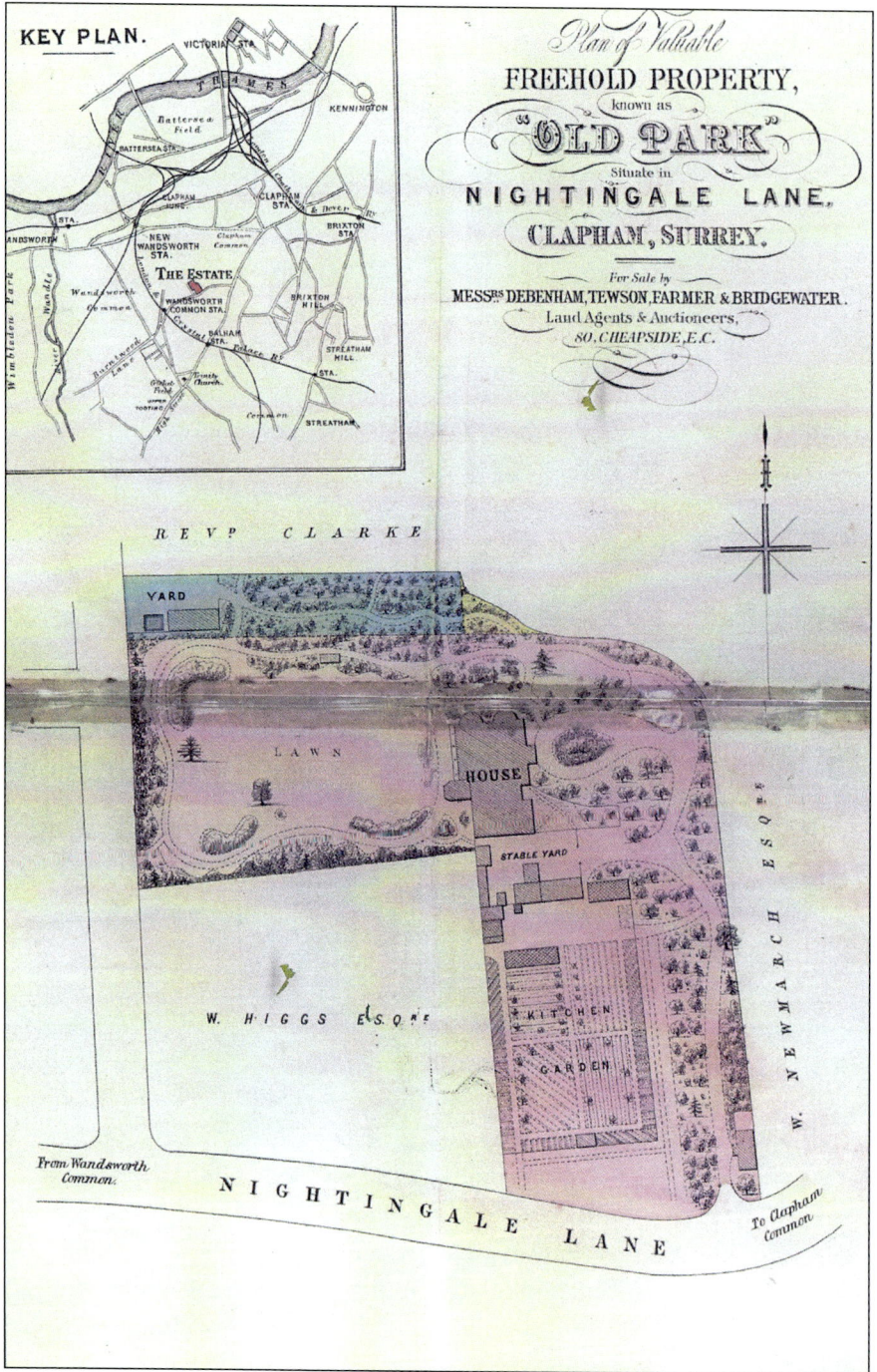

KEY PLAN.

Plan of Valuable
FREEHOLD PROPERTY,
known as
"OLD PARK"
Situate in
NIGHTINGALE LANE,
CLAPHAM, SURREY.

For Sale by
MESS^{RS} DEBENHAM, TEWSON, FARMER & BRIDGEWATER.
Land Agents & Auctioneers,
80, CHEAPSIDE, E.C.

Map 12: Sale of Old Park, 1876

referred to by Erskine Clarke as 'quite a farmyard'. He also reported that[12] 'Lord Penzance had a rose garden adjoining Beechholme on which he built a thatched cottage to which he used to come on Sunday afternoons. It is said that the famous 'Penzance briars' were first grown in that garden'

Newmarch had a remarkable career He left school at an early age to start as a clerk with a stamp distributor and became a renowned economic statistician, FRS, manager of the prominent banking firm, Glyn, Mills and Currie, and successor to Gladstone as President of the Statistical Society. He wrote the Annual Commercial History of the Year for the Economist and invented their first price index. He did much research on monetary economics, being a fierce opponent of the quantity theory of money, and in a speech to the 1861 British Association for the Advancement of Science, claimed that the most important advance in economic science in the 30 or 40 preceding years was the use of systematic observation rather than deduction arrived at by geometric reasoning. He retired from the bank in 1881 and died in Torquay the next year.

We have less full detail about the other early inhabitants of this (north) side of Nightingale Lane but they were clearly affluent merchants and traders. George Lawford, who lived in Sherbrooke Lodge (replaced by a block of flats at 58 Nightingale Lane in 1961) was a stockbroker born in Antwerp (but keen to make clear in the census that he was an British subject) with six children and five servants in a strict hierarchy with both housemaid and under housemaid as well as an under nurse.

As we have seen, William Higgs, who knew the area from his work for Spurgeon, had bought the land fronting onto Nightingale Lane each side of Ramsden Road and his first houses, built in 1869-70 were 52-56 Nightingale Lane of which only 56, Dudley House, remains. This was built as a speculation by a city solicitor John King Farlow who was later involved in building Rusham Road. Its first occupier was Henry Green, a widower with four children and four servants. He was a wine and spirit merchant who had formerly lived in Park Place, Lambeth. A later occupier, turf accountant James O'Connor, remodelled the coach house and stables as a games room in 1898. These still remain and the splendid interior includes a number of frescoes, one of which is reported by the Clapham Society as depicting the Prince of Wales, said to have been a frequent visitor.[13]

Higgs went on to build four large semi detached and three detached villas in the early 1870s. All but one of these still remain. No 50, formerly called Craven House, was bought by the Polish community shortly after the war and renamed Thomas Arciszewski House. It is now part of Broomwood School. Further down the road, Fairseat, 72-4, and now also part of Broomwood School, designed by Rowland Plumbe, is an outstanding example of the high Victorian design described by Pevsner as 'Bankers Italianate', having the characteristic embellishment of a picturesque campanile. 'The Buildings of Clapham' draws attention to 'massive folly structures on the boundaries'[14], but the local gossip is that the occupier, Austrian born jeweller Joseph Lindner, was very keen to preserve his privacy and built the walls to stop anyone looking into his garden.

Nightingale Lane south side Part II

The nature of the houses in the area was changing as a result of both new technology and, of course, fashion. Spurgeon found that his house on the other side of Nightingale Lane, which he had moved into only some ten years earlier, 'was becoming antiquated and lacked suitable conveniences'. His wife described it as follows[15].

> 'The house was a very old one, and in its first estate, I should judge it had been an eight roomed cottage, with underground cellars afterwards turned into kitchens. Some bygone owner had built another storey, and thrown all the eight rooms into four better size ones, but even with this improvement, they were narrow and incommodious.'

He pulled it down and his friend William Higgs rebuilt it in 1864. The new house, still called Helensburgh was described by a visitor, G H Pike[16]

> 'Helensburgh House struck the visitor as being not only an elegant villa, but one which was well planned to suit the requirements of the family. There was a neat garden in front, charming grounds of some extent in

*the rear. When you entered the house from Nightingale
Lane, all the domestic arrangements would strike you as
exceedingly comfortable, but there was nothing provided
for mere show. At each end the dining room opened
into a conservatory which was also an aviary, where
feathered inmates maintained a kind of cheerful chorus.'*

Much of the activity on the same side of the road as Spurgeon's
house involved George Jennings, who had developed a patent
bonding brick which opened new ways of using structural terracotta
and facing blocks. He set to work applying these in south west
London. Many of these still survive including 49-52 Clapham
Southside where Noel Coward lived in No 50 during the First World
War. A number were built in collaboration with the architect, Mark
Chamberlain, including 70-82 The Chase, 33-41 Stormont Road, and
73-83 Rush Hill Terrace on Lavender Hill which had to be mortgaged
to Jennings to pay for the stonework because money had run out
during their construction. There are also many examples of Jennings'
terracotta around Nightingale Lane. 2-10 Endlesham road were built
in 1873 in the same style as he had just built 81-95 Nightingale Lane
although it is only the latter that display barley sugar twist columns.
Thomas Colcutt, who had been introduced to terracotta by Jennings,
designed 69-79 Nightingale Lane and these were built in 1879 with
extravagant terracotta embellishment on the basement. (Ill 40) at
the same time as Colcutt had come to prominence by winning the
competition for the design of Wakefield Town Hall.

Jennings came to an unfortunate end shortly after, as recorded
in the South London Press[17].

*'It is with feelings of regret, which will be joined in by
all who knew him, that we have this week to record the
death of Mr George Jennings of 'Ferndale' Nightingale
Lane, Clapham, universally known as the celebrated
engineer of Palace Wharf, Lambeth. Mr Jennings' death
occurred under the following painful circumstances. On
Thursday evening, according to his usual custom, he,
together with his son George, drove home in his gig. The
horse, of a very restive character and hard in the mouth,*

whilst crossing over the Albert Bridge, shied and threw Mr Jennings and his son against a dust cart. Mr Jennings jnr escaped with only a shaking, but Mr Jennings' collar bone was fractured. He was conveyed home and attended by Dr Edmonds and two other physicians. His recovery from the injuries proceeded favourably up until Sunday, when against his doctors' orders, he would get up. On Sunday night a relapse and congestion of the lungs set in, and he expired on Monday evening about six o'clock. He was 72 years of age.

40: 69-79 Nightingale Lane, T E Colcutt 1879

The funeral took place on 23 April 1882, and was attended by large numbers of friends, employees and mourners acknowledging Jennings' kindness and thoughtfulness of the interests of the labouring classes, and marking the respect of the community in which he lived.'

Jennings' former house, Oak Lodge, was bought by William Bradbury, the publisher of Punch as well as some of Charles Dickens' early work including David Copperfield. By this time, however, the two had fallen out over Bradbury's failure to include a disclaimer in the magazine to counter allegations of Dickens' marital problems printed elsewhere. Ferndale itself was sold the next year, with the auction being advertised in The Times.

> 'Nightingale Lane Clapham Common - By order of the Trustees – a choice Freehold Residential Estate, with noble mansion and delightful pleasure grounds,, charmingly situate midway between Clapham and Wandsworth Commons , known as Ferndale, the residence of the late George Jennings Esq., the well known sanitary engineer; and a long Leasehold Residence adjoining, the whole containing about 3½ acres.

> The mansion, in the Italian style, was erected by the late George Jennings Esq. for his own occupation, is in all its appointments complete, and was built and finished under his personal superintendence regardless of expense, and with all his well known care for sanitary arrangements. It is well set back from the high road, and approached from Nightingale Lane by a carriage sweep, and contains the following accommodation; - Elegant and lofty drawing room and dining room, billiard room, morning room and library, fine entrance hall, with very handsome principal staircase to first floor, seven principal bed and dressing rooms, eight secondary bedrooms, secondary staircase, bathrooms, and most complete and convenient domestic offices. The drawing room, dining room, and back hall open onto a raised terrace walk with ornamental balustrading, and steps to lawn and glass houses, leading into a magnificent

*conservatory, communicating with a large and lofty
fernery, into which the billiard room also opens. The
grounds are studded with fine, large, park-like trees.
Divided from the lawn is a paddock , and shrubbery
walks lead to the walled-in kitchen garden, amply
stocked with fruit trees in full bearing, range of hot
houses and forcing pits. The stabling and coach-house
premises are ample. The whole forms one of the most
compact residential properties to be found anywhere
within such a short distance from the metropolis, being
only a few yards outside the four mile radius from
Charing Cross. Also a detached residence adjoining,
known as Wilby Lodge, containing five bedrooms, box
room, two reception rooms,, conservatory and usual
effects, with stabling and coach house and extensive
grounds well stocked with fruit trees and shrubs.'*

In due course these two houses formed the core of the Nightingale
Home for Aged Jews.

By 1881 both Nightingale Lane itself and the part of Rusham
Road at the bottom of the former Old Park estate closest to
Nightingale Lane, were filling up with large houses, mostly developed
by J K Farlow and probably the work of the architect Frederick
Notley. Many of them were occupied by successful merchants,
some of whom lived in the road for a considerable time. George
Lawford lived in Sherbrooke Lodge for twenty four years until his
death in 1895 when his son Herbert, a solicitor, moved in with two
of his sisters and one brother. Ann Lindner, the widow of Joseph
Lindner, was still living in Fairseat in 1901, twenty eight years after
they moved there. Most of the people then in Nightingale Lane still
working would fit Booth's model of a prosperous part of London[18].

*'They breakfast everyday at 8 or 8.30 and travel first
or second class by season ticket to the City by the 9.15
train. By day the place is destitute of men. The wives
and daughters lunch at one and take tea at five. The men
reach home in time for a bathroom wash before dinner
at seven, which is in this district the natural hunger-*

prompted time for the evening meal. And the usual thing,
except when a party is given and eight is made the time.
Bedtime is at ten o'clock, or soon after.'

It was still possible to imagine a rural feel to the area. Besant described the view looking west along Nightingale Lane[19].

'*Behind these houses to the South all is open fields as far*
as the railway line, with Nightingale Cottage, a small
old fashioned house, at the Common corner where the
roadway leads through the trees and park to Fernside
which stands alone in the fields facing a detached portion
of Wandsworth Common. At the railway station west of
the Cottage, building has been started on Wexford Road.'

Nevertheless times were changing. By 1881 Spurgeon wanted to go to a more secluded spot than the 'once rural Nightingale Lane' had become, perhaps remembering the time during an election campaign when the front gates and walls of his house had been plentifully daubed with paint 'to correspond with the colours of the Conservative candidate for that division of Surrey'. He commented: 'It is notorious that I am no Tory.' and waited for those who had put the paint on to take it off, which in due course they did. It seems too that the salubriousness of the area was less obvious than in the past, since he wrote in his almanac for 1881 'We have often been advised to rise from Nightingale Lane to higher ground to escape a portion of the fogs and damps which hang almost always over our smoky city.'[20] He moved to a new house built for him on South Norwood Hill in 1884.[iii] Helensburgh House still remains to this day, extended and renamed first Glenbrook House, and now Queen Elizabeth House.

Spurgeon's move indicates that the status of the area was beginning to decline, albeit slowly, and a steady stream of people flowed out to the leafier suburbs of Wimbledon, Epsom, or even further. The very substantial 'Bankers Italianate' houses began to

---

[iii] Nevertheless, the climate was obviously regarded as more than acceptable by some, because it was chosen by the founder of the Balham Congregational Church, Rev John Gilbert, on being advised to find a milder climate than Brighton where he was the congregational minister.

give up their grounds to infill development of semi- detached or even terraced villas for people who were well enough off, but did not expect to employ their own coachmen. By the beginning of 1888 it was thought necessary to re-number the houses in the road and from then on they are referred to by number rather than by name. [iv]Nightingale Lane is still an attractive street. Pevsner recognises that it has 'rather more character' and Wandsworth Council describes it in its conservation area character statement as follows: 'There is a sense of the picturesque about its winding configuration, grand houses with broad frontages and a wealth of mature trees.'[21] This is not too different from Walter Besant in 1912.[22]

> 'Nearer Nightingale Lane, however, the style is better, and in the Lane itself, from the corner of Bolingbroke Grove to Clapham Common, with the inevitable exception of the shops at Ramsden Road, the buildings are of a much better class.'

A final view on Nightingale Lane can be gained from the postcards of the area. Three are shown in Ill 41-43, all taken in the early 1900s. The bottom one, looking towards Clapham Common, shows the original Hightrees House, demolished in 1936 to build the present block of flats.

41: Post card Nightingale Lane

[iv] Ironically, the addition of houses around the turn of the decade meant that a further re-numbering would be required.

Nightingale Lane, Wandsworth Common.

42: Post card Nightingale Lane

43: Post card Nightingale Lane

Development of the Dents estate

The rest of the estate continued to develop at a steady pace. We have already mentioned Jennings' houses in Endlesham and Ramsden Roads. The style and character of houses in those roads tends to be more attractive the closer to Nightingale Lane they are. The next nearby development was on the land between Rusham Road and Bolingbroke Grove which had been the Dents House Estate lived in by Mary Dent. We have considerable detail of how this was developed from the deeds retained by the Church Commissioners after they purchased the ground rents some years later in 1898. It is worth rehearsing some of this which, although very detailed, does give a very good illustration of why the particular patchwork of roads and types of building emerges.

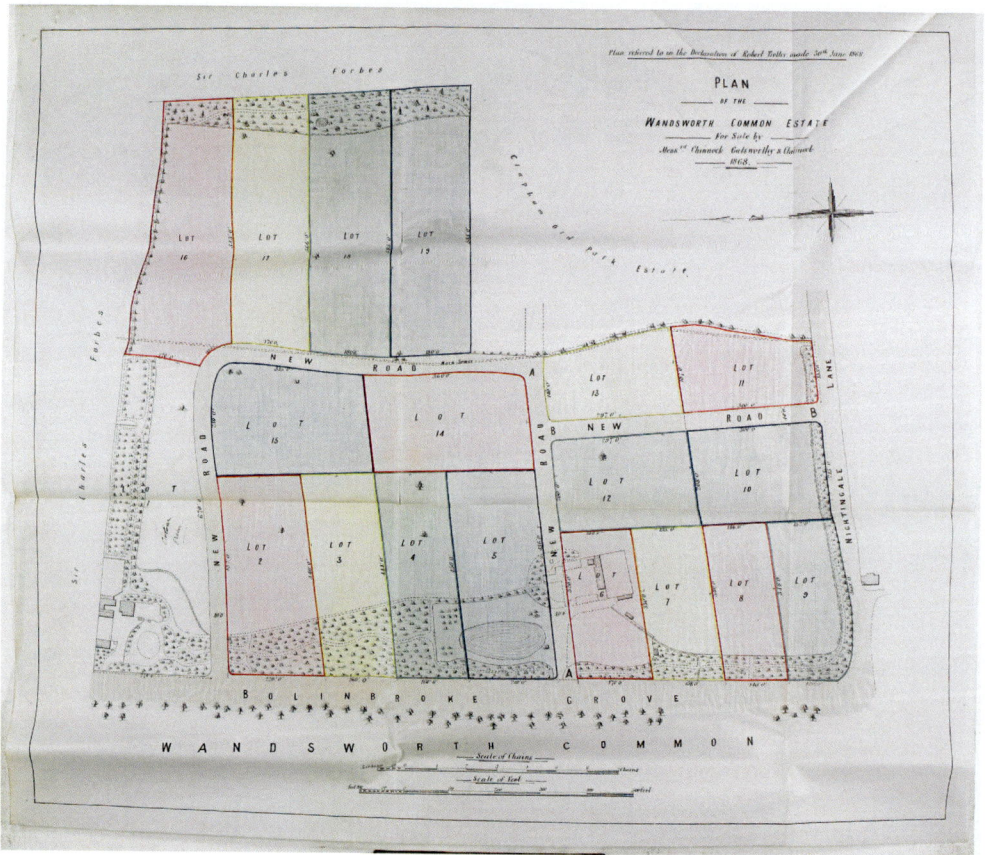

Map 13: Sale of Dent's estate, 1868

Following Mary's death in 1867, her unmarried cousins who had inherited the estate were already well into their sixties and living in comfort in or around Bryanston Square in the West End. It must have made sense to them to realize the capital and the whole estate (then given the title Wandsworth Common estate) was offered in lots for sale in June 1868 by Messrs Chinnock, Galsworthy and Chinnock as shown in Map 13.

The new roads proposed on the map (which had not had official approval) are not the same as those that were eventually built. At first sight it may seem odd that the proposed new road along part of the Falcon Brook does not continue along it the whole way but this is explicable in terms of the land boundaries. Where the estate owned the land on both sides of the Brook, it made sense for a road to run over the Brook (by then covered and converted into a sewer) with houses on both sides, corresponding to the pattern adopted in Northcote Road. However the Brook was the boundary with the Old Park Estate and clearly it was not possible to lay out a new road along this line without reaching agreement with the other owners. As a result the proposed plan displaces the road to allow a house with a garden running down to the Brook. In any case Sir Charles Forbes, the owner of the adjacent Broomwood estate, bought the land on the east side of Falcon Brook and in August 1872, the Dents sold the remainder of the land to John Galsworthy for £15,528. Map 14 gives a good idea of the resulting layout with the Dents House at the north east corner; the farm buildings further south show a path running down to the bottom of the valley which eventually became the top part of Thurleigh Avenue.

Galsworthy was a Kingston solicitor as well as an auctioneer and was clearly speculating in his own right. He sold the Dents House – confusingly called Bolingbroke House in the deeds - together with just over five acres of land to John Eldon Gorst in 1874 and the remaining 21 acres to Charles Appleby the next year for £17,790/15, making a tidy profit in the process.

John Gorst lived in the house on Bolingbroke Grove until about 1881. As well as being a successful QC – we have already seen he was chosen to represent the Crown at the inquest of Charles Bravo in Balham– he had been the Tory party's central agent helping to mobilise the enlarged urban electorate to secure the Tory 1874

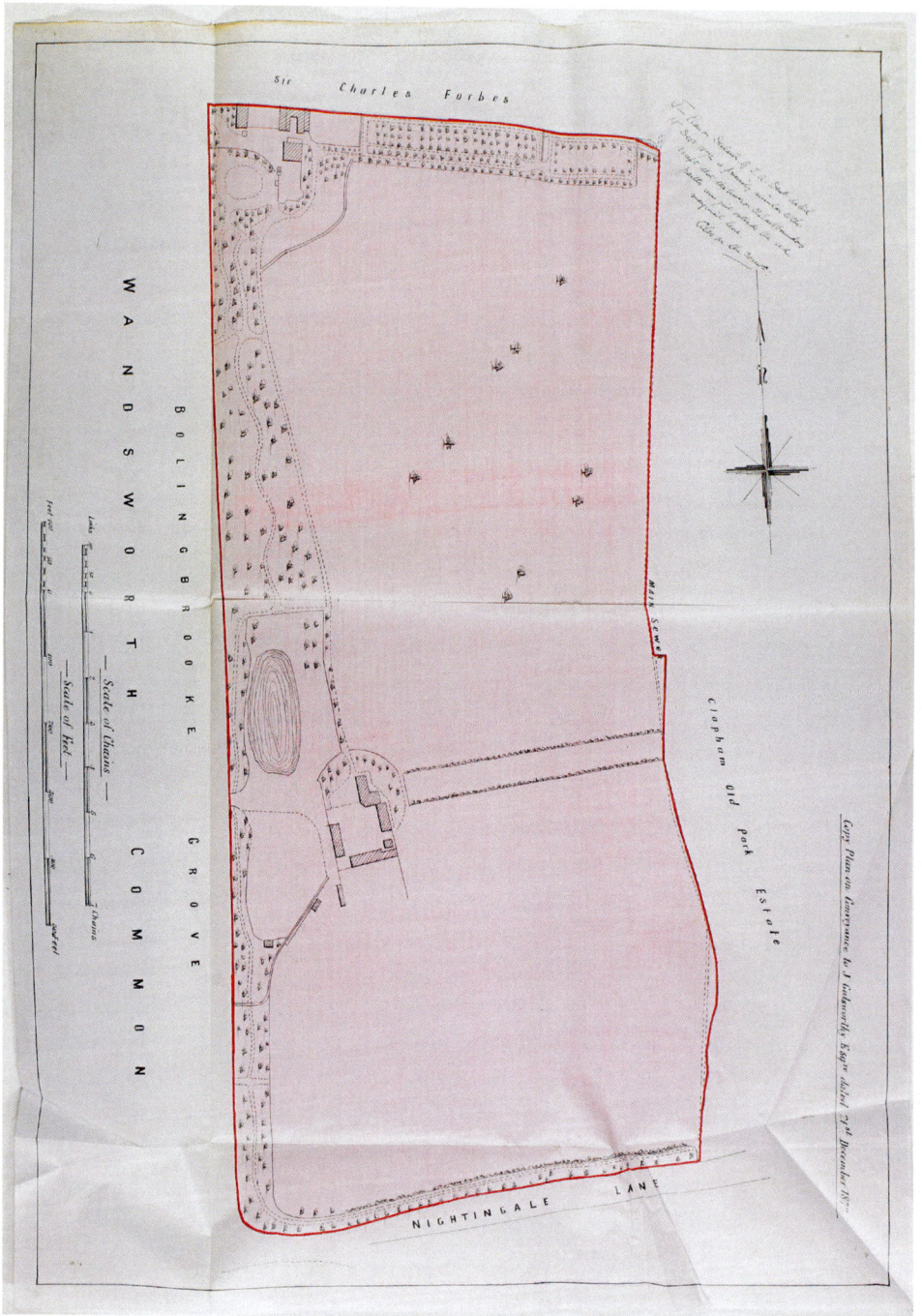

Map 14: Residual Dent's estate, 1872

election victory. He was MP for Chatham during his time in Battersea and when the Conservatives returned to power in 1885 he became Solicitor General and was knighted. His son Sir Eldon Gorst succeeded Lord Cromer as British Agent in Egypt in 1907.

Charles Appleby, who was the next link in the development of the Dents estate, was a civil and mining engineer aged 39 in 1875, and also the proprietor of the Cornish company, Tamar Terracotta works. It is tempting to think that he was attracted to the area because of George Jennings' interest in terracotta, but there is, alas, no evidence for this. He was related by marriage to the prominent architect E R Robson who designed many of the iconic Board Schools when he was architect for the London Schools Board, including Belleville School in 1876.[v] It may have been this connection that persuaded Robson to include some domestic architecture in his portfolio by designing nine houses for Appleby, all but two in Bolingbroke Grove. 23-26 Bolingbroke Grove were built in 1875-6 and No 8 in 1879 which may have been built for Appleby himself. All these are still standing (Ill 44a-d) but Elmshurst (No 19) was replaced by flats after being bombed in the war, while Haresfields, set well back from Bolingbroke Grove on Blenkarne Road, has also been replaced by flats. Robson also designed two houses at 5 and 7 Blenkarne Road, originally known as Blenkarne and York House. Blenkarne Road had been a name insisted on by the Metropolitan Board of Works which preferred to name the road after a former local landowner, Thomas Blenkarne, than take up Robson's proposal of Nightingale Grove.

26 Bolingbroke Grove was the first house to be completed, the land having been sold to Marjorie Peddie in 1875 who named the house Linden Lodge. She had been the governess to the large family of Sir Robert Dalrymple-Horn-Elphinstone, and then been for 20 years or more the headmistress of Manor House School on East Hill, Wandsworth. Map 15 shows Robson's original plan for the development of the site. Blenkarne Road still curls round to end in Nightingale Lane, but is now well away from the Falcon Brook and contains a small crescent.

---

[v] Chapter 10 has more material on Robson from an architectural point of view and on the Queen Anne style.

44a-d: E R Robson houses

Robson's houses were designed for the upper middle class, and it would seem that Appleby and Robson were planning to build 50 or so large houses, rather like the ones they had already built on Bolingbroke Grove. Once Marjorie Peddie's house was built they contrived an article in 'Building News' which described the house as 'first of a series of houses in the old English style, somewhat incorrectly called "Queen Anne"'[23].

However although similar, even larger, houses were readily filled in Nightingale Lane, it took longer in Bolingbroke Grove. Marjorie Peddie died in May 1879 and when the house was auctioned later that year, it was purchased by The School of the Indigent Blind of St George's Fields, Southwark for £4,100, slightly less than her original costs of £900 for the land and £3,500 for the construction. Although this may have reflected the general trend in house prices at the time, there was little demand for houses of this kind in Bolingbroke Grove and by early 1881 the school was the only long term occupier of the seven houses designed by Robson.

Appleby had financed the original deal by borrowing £10,000 at 5% from two individuals, one of whom was the Rev Augustus Gedge, the Rector of Louth in Lincolnshire. Two years later they in turn mortgaged the land for £14,000 to the National Freehold Land Society and Appleby decided it was time to reduce his borrowings. He first auctioned the six houses in one lot, and the remaining 12 acres of land in another. The houses were advertised[24].

> *'Wandsworth Common. Bolingbroke Grove, facing the common, five minutes from station. Delightfully situate Queen Anne Residences, of superior construction and perfect from a sanitary point of view, each standing in about half an acre of finely timbered ground'.*

Only one house, No 24, was sold at this time, for £2000, the remaining ones had to be sold later by private tender and the land repackaged to make it more attractive. The architect Thomas Wimperis moved into No 8, by then called Rockfield, and subsequently purchased the freehold in 1885. Wimperis' main residence was 25 Sackville Street in Mayfair and he was a churchwarden at St James Piccadilly in 1880/1 where a memorial

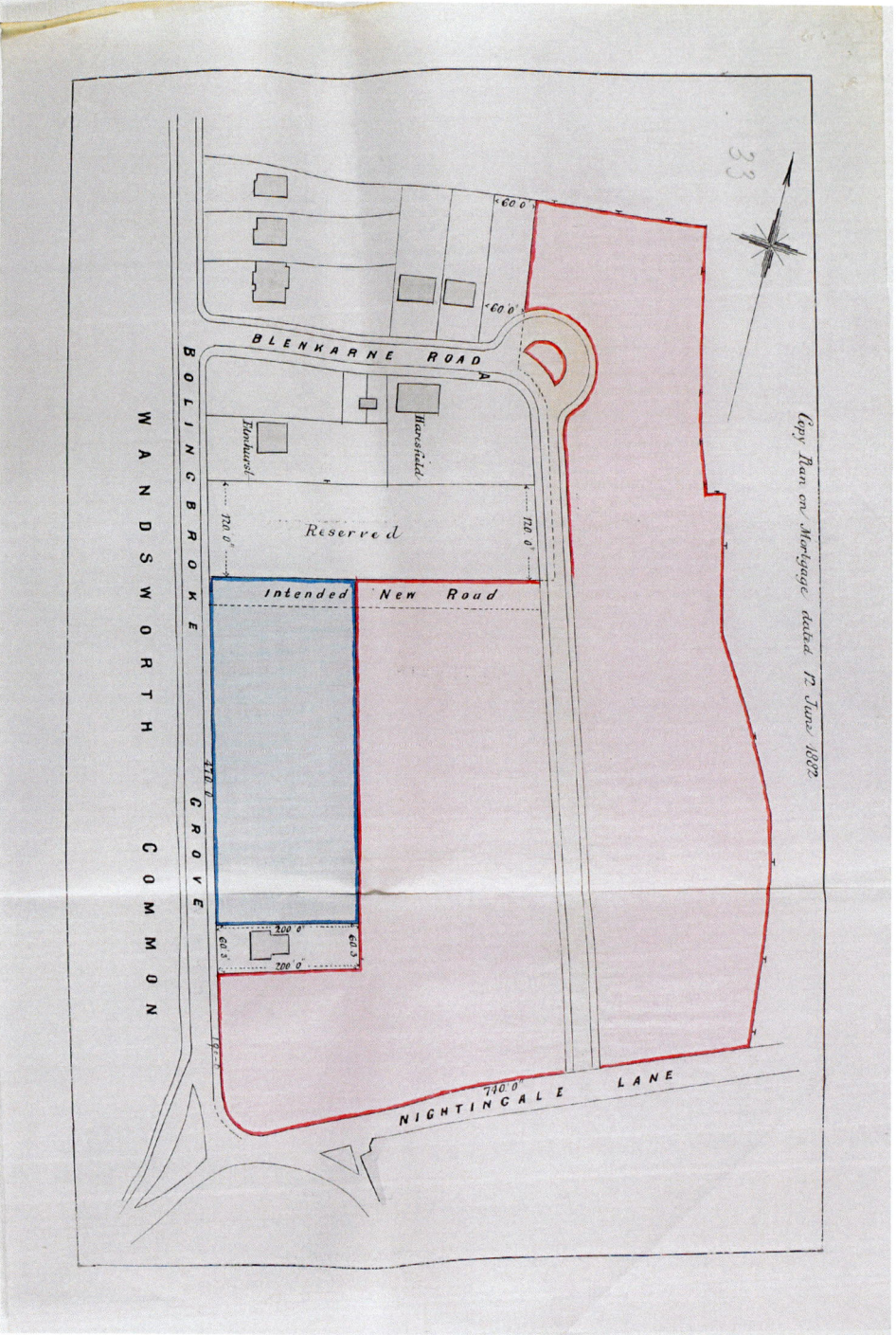

15: Original plans for land in mortgage, 1882

to him is on the north side of the west end of the church. It is not clear how he divided his time between the houses but he appears in the 1891 Census in his Battersea home. He may well have valued living in a house designed by Robson because The English Heritage Survey of London describes him[25] as being 'a representative Queen Anne designer of varying accomplishment' and 'Though often a speculating architect he could ascend the social scale too.' He designed the first Queen Anne style building in Oxford Street (443-451) and has a number of surviving buildings in the West End, including 130 Mount Street, 34 Berkeley Square and 51-4 Green Street.

Adding a further one and a half acres of land next to the original Dents house, Appleby made the 13½ acres of land more attractive by removing the covenants so that 'negotiations could be entered into under conditions presenting perfect freedom to a purchaser.'[26] He finally achieved a sale in 1882 for £19,710 to a group of builders and developers whom we have already encountered, Thomas Ingram, Henry Bragg and Frederick Snelling They paid off the mortgage and borrowed £14,000 from Charles Percival, a contractor from Tulse Hill at 5.5%, and £6000 at 5% from a London firm of solicitors, Simpson and Palmer (whom we shall come across later). Despite his offer Appleby retained control on future development that might impinge on his own house. He did this by imposing a restrictive covenant on the sale that required houses built on the piece of land on Bolingbroke Grove between his house and the Robson houses at 23-26 to have a minimum frontage to the road of 25 feet and the same depth of plot of 200 feet as his house.

Snelling, a builder in his thirties, may have had difficulty in financing his share of the development, and he soon sold a half share in his third share of the profit to a solicitor Henry Leonard for £1100. Ingram and Bragg bought this back six months later for £2000 and bought out Snelling as well. Meanwhile they changed the plans of the road. The proposals of Map 15, consistent with substantial houses with large gardens, did not appeal to Ingram and Bragg who clearly believed that, while there was a market for comfortable houses, they needed to be built at a higher density than envisaged by Robson. This was why they had declined to buy the land with the restrictive covenants.

Ingram and Bragg used a well known local architect, Charles Bentley, who often worked with Heaver, and was well used to getting as many high class houses on a site as possible. He moved what is now Hendrick Road closer to Falcon Brook to reduce the gardens, and offset it from Blenkarne Road, while introducing three new east-west roads, Roy, Granard and Morella. Roy Road ran down the hill from Bolingbroke Grove in the same line as Thurleigh Road and the developers had planned it to stop there with Estcourt (Hendrick) Road being built across it. This gave rise to another of Erskine Clarke's interventions and he was just in time to purchase the site of two houses for £100 and use it to join up Roy and Thurleigh Roads. His purpose was 'to give direct and easy access to St Luke's from all the district' and this secured access to the west of its parish. Map 16 shows the result.

Ingram and Bragg started Granard Road in 1882 and built Morella Road, Bolingbroke Grove and Nightingale Lane from 1883-5. They continued to use Charles Bentley to design all the houses, except those built by David Kettle in Bolingbroke Grove. For the first road to be built, Granard, they used only one builder, J T Robertson (who by 1891 lived himself in No 33 with his six children under 11), but for Morella Road, which started the next year, four different builders were used. Bragg obviously got on well with Robertson because they also worked together on 118-30 Nightingale Lane. Although they put semi-detached houses on Granard Road and at the Bolingbroke Grove end of Nightingale Lane, all the others are terraced, albeit with recesses between the houses to give the appearance of being semi-detached. The terrace houses are a direct consequence of Appleby having to abandon the restricted covenant to sell the land.

By 1885, they must have found the development too much for them to finance by themselves, and they sold off parts of the estate to builders that they were already working with. The land for Nos 1-13 Thurleigh Road and 9-18 Bolingbroke Grove went to David Kettle, the other side of Thurleigh Road (Nos 2-30) to John Miller who built terraced houses, and land for two houses in Blenkarne Road to John Robertson, although he continued to build other houses there for Bragg. The result of these sales was to leave Ingram and Bragg with the 115 houses colored red on the 1893 plan (Map 16).

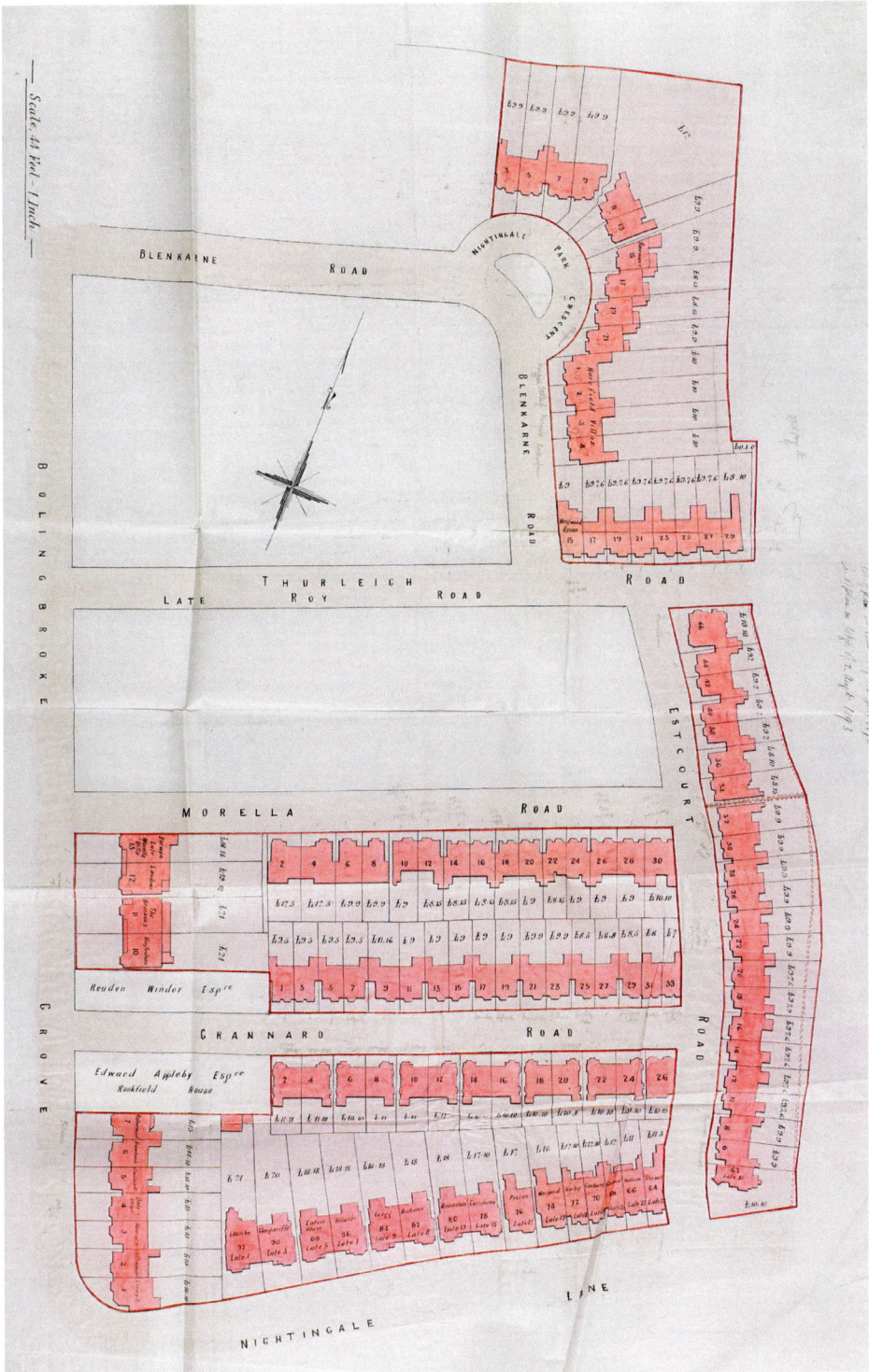

16: Sale of ground rents, 1893

They obviously form a coherent group given that the houses on the northern side had been sold previously. No 9 Bolingbroke Grove, formerly known as Elstree, was designed specifically for Reuben Winder, a partner in the firm of solicitors, Simpson and Palmer, which had lent money to Ingram and Bragg and was the developer of Old Park Avenue. We shall hear more about him in Chapter 9. The run of houses, 10-18 Bolingbroke Grove, was not built immediately by Kettle until four years after No 9 because he wanted to wait 'until he could ascertain what class of property is most desirable'. Under Appleby's sole surviving covenant, the only choice was detached or semi-detached and it is not surprising that after the earlier problems with Robson's larger houses, Kettle decided on semi-detached. The resulting houses have good Arts and Crafts details and it is possible that they bear the hand of N.S. Joseph and Smithem, the same architects who worked with Winder and Kettle a few years later in Old Park Avenue.

Given all this nearby development, it is perhaps not surprising that John Gorst also sold up. His house was demolished in 1881 to create Gorst and Dents Roads as well as 27-35 Bolingbroke Grove. The development was carried out over the next three years by J W Everidge, again to the designs of Charles Bentley who was forced by the shape of the site to make the road double back on itself as a U shape. Everidge had originally proposed that the whole road should be called Dents Road, but the Metropolitan Board of Works intervened to require that half the road was named after Gorst himself, the last inhabitant of the eighteenth century house. There are still some remains of the original house built by William Dent where the stable building of the main house was altered and extended in 1883 to form 1b Gorst Road. The Georgian boundary wall between the Dent's House and The Elms survives between 35 and 36 Bolingbroke Road.

We should not assume that this level of building meant that the roads were made up and widely used. An account of a Confirmation at St Luke's towards the end of 1885 reported[27].

> 'The day was bright and pleasant so that those who
> had a long walk to and from were able to enjoy it.
> Omnibuses were provided for female candidates from
> the St Mary district as St Luke's is about two miles

distant from their homes, and some of them did not even know the way to it.'

This area was the major part of what was sometimes known as 'New Wandsworth', a name originally created for what became Wandsworth Common station, and which had a reputation for thinking itself a little better than the surrounding parts. Surveyor Pilditch referred to this in his speech on the Progress of Battersea in 1895[28].

'There are a certain portion of the parishioners who prefer being known by any other address than that of Battersea, and studiously ignore the fact, except when reminded by the call of the tax collector; and I refer more particularly to those portions of the parish known as New Wandsworth, Lavender Hill, Clapham Common, North-side Wandsworth Common, Nightingale Lane Balham, St James's Road Upper Tooting etc.,etc., all of which are in the parish of Battersea, but are little known as such. And I trust the time is not far distant when the parish of Battersea will be known and distinguished in its broadest sense. (This was greeted with applause by his audience.) An attempt was made some few years ago to carry this into effect by adding the name Battersea to the name of the road on the street name plate, but this caused so much annoyance, public meetings had to be held, that they had to be removed. And so Upper Tooting and Balham remain as names better known than Battersea.'

It is noticeable in Post Office directories of the times that many of the roads in South Battersea do not appear in the Battersea part of the directory, but rather in the Clapham part (eg houses on Clapham West Side and Battersea Rise) and in Wandsworth (labelled 'New Wandsworth' for the streets between the commons). The postcard of St Mark's church (Ill 31) bears the appellation 'New Wandsworth' and presumably this reflected how the occupiers wished to be thought of. This phenomenon has been repeated in more recent times when the inhabitants of Sudbrooke Road objected strongly to the suggestion of Balham appearing on their street name on the grounds that it could reduce the value of their houses.[29]

The next financial deals took place in the late 1880s when the developers sold out to the contractor, Percival, from whom they had borrowed the £14,000. This resulted in a number of deals amounting to £27,572/16/3. By then Percival was the owner of the ground rents, which he sold on in July 1890 for £35,913/3/-, equivalent to an interest rate of 3.57%, usually expressed at the time a multiple the ground rent, in this case 28 years. In turn these were sold on by auction in 1898 to Queen Anne's Bounty for £37,500.

Ill 45 shows the advertisement for the sale, described as 'Abundantly secured on High-class Property' and 'An investment of exceptional character not often to be obtained'.

45: Bill of sale for ground rents

The rents amounted to £1,282/13/3 per annum, an equivalent interest rate of 3.42% or in the parlance of the time, 29.2 years purchase.

Detailed examination of this development highlights a number of themes about the local townscape. To the casual observer, Victorian suburbs appear to have been constructed en masse of virtually indistinguishable houses. Yet as we have seen for South Battersea as a whole, there are almost infinite variations which reflect the original (or at least eighteenth century) pattern of land ownership. Disposals could depend on when the oldest inhabitant of the house died, any covenants restricting development, or whether it made sense to build in large or not so large gardens. The final factor was the effect of the bombs in World War Two.

In a rational world, there would have been a road along the bottom of the valley, following the path of the Falcon Brook, already converted in the late 1860s to a main sewer. This did indeed happen where the land on both sides of the brook was owned by the same person, which is why Northcote Road runs only as far as Broomwood Road; by contrast, on the south side of Broomwood Road, that is from the Dents Estate on, the brook was the boundary between two land owners, at least after Sir Charles Forbes had bought the land east of the brook and the rest of the Dents land had been divided. When houses were built on the land west of the brook, it made more sense to have their gardens going down to the lowest point than to have the road at the bottom since there was no incentive to lay out a road only half of which would benefit the developer.

The pattern of land ownership explains the rather odd feature of Nightingale Park Crescent, the circle of houses off Blenkarne Road. The developer was faced with the problem of how to make the most use of the land in the north east corner, to which there was no obvious access, once the two large houses had been built in Blenkarne Road. The circle, apart from being almost the only planning features in 'Twixt the Commons' allows an additional three or four houses.[vi] Map 15 shows the route of Roy Road as originally intended, and

vi The little patch of grass in the middle of the semicircle allowed the Crescent to be classified as a Square for the purposes of the Royal Commission on London Squares that reported in 1928.

Erskine Clarke's purchase of enough land to allow it to connect with its continuation of Thurleigh was probably quite attractive to Ingram and Bragg because it gave them a good excuse to implement Bentley's proposal to move what became Estcourt Road closer to the brook with smaller gardens for those houses and, overall, more land for building.

While the larger houses built on the Dents estate have remained; the large gardens with the 200 foot plots on Bolingbroke Grove have been used for infill. Charles Appleby's house had two houses built in the garden in 1938, and both sides of Blenkarne Road were built on, one in 1925, and the other in 1935 when Haresfield was demolished. The block of flats, Lane Court, was built in 1947 by Wandsworth Borough Council to replace bomb damage to 19 and 20. The garden of the blind school was used to construct a block of flats on Dents Road in 1994. As in so many places, he detailed topography of the area, which at first looks haphazard, is essentially determined, and demonstrably so, by the variety of local events over the last two hundred years.

Of the roads above, only Thurleigh Road was developed slowly, possibly because of the structure of the land ownership. While the lower numbers had been part of the Dents estate and were built between 1885 and 1888, the next set of terrace houses, up to Wroughton Road on both sides, was built between 1896 and 1903. The larger houses at the top of the hill on both sides were generally built individually by a Norfolk architect, Henry Bignold, over a twenty year period from the mid 1880s. They usually had their own names which sometimes changed with change of occupier although most of the house names were lost from the postal addresses when the road was renumbered in 1903. Names remain on some houses and one such is Edith Villa at 3 Thurleigh Avenue where a blue plaque commemorates the music hall star Gus Elen who lived there from 1898-1910.[vii]

The large back gardens of Nightingale Lane went the same way as those in Bolingbroke Grove, being combined with the allotments

---

[vii] This was considered part of Thurleigh Road until that was extended in 1906 through to Clapham Common and the road to Nightingale Lane was renamed Thurleigh Avenue.

to allow the building of houses in Sudbrooke Road. Edwin Evans developed the corner of Sudbrooke and Ramsden Roads with a large detached Queen Anne Style House designed by Edgar George, allegedly financed by the construction and sale of 1-6 Sudbrooke Road in 1911. They went on to purchase 52-54 Nightingale Lane, replacing the two original Higgs houses with eight smaller semi-detached houses in 1925. Of the two old houses in Sudbrooke Road, Parkhurst built in 1899 survives and the other, Thorne House, was pulled down to build 7-10a in 1923. Nos 11-24 Sudbrooke Road were built in 1903.

A further change occurred in March 1912 when the LCC decided to change the name of Estcourt road to Hendrick Avenue. This was not universally liked. An anonymous correspondent wrote to the parish magazine[30].

> 'On the 9th of this month Estcourt Road will cease to be known by that name, unless in the meantime the residents will have been able to take advantage of the invitation of the London County Council to show cause why the name should not be changed. It would be more satisfactory if the Council had seen fit to inform us why it is desirable that one of the oldest roads in the parish should have its name altered to the meaningless and singularly inappropriate 'Hendrick Avenue'. Perhaps a friend is right, who suggests that it has been called Estcourt long enough, and that it is time for it to 'ave a new' name. The reason does not sound altogether convincing, but we suppose that in these giddy days of revolution it will serve'

An answer came quickly from Mr J T Richards, the Borough Councilor involved[31].

> 'To die as a Road, and be resurrected as an Avenue, is in the general view by no means lamentable, as your contributor in the March Magazine would see, if he possessed more snobbery.
>
> As it was on my motion that the borough Council agreed to the change proposed by the County Council,

you will perhaps let me say that the reason was not founded on the whimsical humour that he has thought of. There is another Estcourt Road in London, S.W., namely at Fulham. It is of considerable length, and, though probably not half as good, is better known than ours, which contains only twenty-three houses. Since the L.C.C. is trying, for postal and other reasons, to abolish duplication of street names, as far as possible, it was right that we should accept a change, and the residents here may find some confusion avoided.

I can say nothing as to the name 'Hendrick', except that it is difficult now to find names unlike any others in use, and that this has nothing similar to it in our neighbourhood. Trees planted in a road, as here, can give it the dignity of an Avenue. Winsham Street, as it was called at first, was changed to Winsham Grove, this name also being justified by trees, on the petition of its residents.'

Although the First World War made a major impact on the parish with many men being called up and the war memorial paying tribute to the number that lost their lives, the earliest impact was felt by the arrival of refugees from Belgium in September 1914. St Luke's put up over 200 with the Hall being used by Red Cross Headquarters as a clearing house while more permanent places were found. The Parish Magazine said that the priests and nuns from the Roman Catholic church in Nightingale Square, some of whom were Belgian, helped with the 'language difficulty' but reading between the lines of the report, not everything went smoothly. The magazine explained that the church members 'did everything themselves, with the occasional assistance of some of the Belgian women', while the comment on the refugees themselves was, 'The refugees were of different social ranks; some few were educated people, but most were of the middle class. With few exceptions they were grateful.'[32]

St Luke's Church

We have already seen that Erskine Clarke had bought a site in 1874 from the Old Park Estate with a view to building a church on it. However a covenant in the title deeds prevented the raising of any public building, a restriction incidentally carried forward in the deeds of Old Park Avenue houses. He had asked for this permission from a neighbouring resident, somewhat anxiously, but later reported[33] that 'he obtained it with the good humoured encouragement that the church would be "convenient on wet Sundays"'. At about this time, the iron church used previously for St Mark's, Battersea Rise became available since it had been superseded by the new brick church. It was moved to the St Luke's site and dedicated on 14 November 1874. The purchase of the iron church cost £500, the removal £400, and various extras, including choir stalls, light and the laying out of the grounds cost a further £360.53. It did sterling service for eight years. (Ill 46)

AS IT WAS, 1874—1883.

46: Iron church

Recalling his purchase much later, Erskine Clarke wrote in his Christmas message in 1901[34].

> 'St Luke's, Nightingale Lane, which 25 years ago we spoke of as our 'little rural outpost', is now a truly magnificent church. In 1874, the iron chapel was moved to a picturesque corner of the Old Park Estate, where there were five trees and a pond famous for water lilies.'

Ill 47 gives a colour picture of the iron church which emphasises its rural setting.

47: Iron church

By the harvest festival in 1881, the steady increase in the number of houses and population meant that the little iron church was full to overflowing and many were unable to hear the preacher. Following Erskine Clarke's initiative, a committee was formed to promote the building of a brick church as an answer to the stimulus of Dr Thorold, the Bishop of Rochester.

'It may be worth considering whether we have not had enough of Gothic churches, with their difficult acoustics and expensive ornamentation.. Why not try a basilica, with a font big enough for immersion, and a pulpit in which the preacher can both move and think, and space in which people can see, hear, and worship? ...A fine red-brick basilica is the one thing of all others I wish to see. Who will build us one?'[35] [36]

This is exactly what he got. St Luke's church was designed by F W Hunt (who had built a church and schools in Derby) to produce what Pevsner describes as 'An impressive red brick Lombard Romanesque exterior ...... the interior is indeed basilican, with no chancel arch, although the arcades are pointed and rest on early Gothic capitals.' In 1883, the Chancel was built as far as the centre of the first arch and, together with the south transept, was dedicated on November 15. The St Mary's parish magazine reported that 'This portion of the church will contain 288 chairs – so that with the iron Church annexed there will be room for about 600 worshippers with ample choir arrangements.'[37]

The effect of the slow development of Thurleigh Road meant that some felt there was little hope of St Luke's being filled because of the bad state of the roads leading to it. Even so the nave was finally completed in 1888 and the iron church removed and the tower - still a prominent landmark - finished in 1892. A contemporary postcard shows St Luke's as it looked at the turn of the century. (Ill 48)

St Luke's became a parish in its own right in 1900 and, by special dispensation, Erskine Clarke was allowed to add vicar of that church to his other roles. In 1901, he decided to build himself a vicarage for St Luke's next the church hall. His architect, J S Quilter, produced what is a splendid vicarage with nine bedrooms. Erskine Clarke lived there with a housekeeper and one male and two female servants.[viii] (Ill 49)

[viii] The vast house was, however, wholly inappropriate for late (or even mid) twentieth century priests who shivered in the enormous draughty spaces, until it was sold to Broomwood Hall School in the 1990s and the vicarage moved to a house slightly down the hill in Thurleigh Road.

48: St Luke's church c 1904

At the end of the century, Booth reported that St Luke's had won a prominent place in the hearts of the comfortable residents of the parish[38].

> '*It is now the most fashionable church in the neighbourhood. It provides a beautiful musical service and is attended by large numbers, coming mostly from this end of the Common where the streets are, and perhaps always will be, occupied by well-to-do people.*'

The church did indeed help to promote an active social life. It had a flourishing hall for which Erskine Clarke reverted to his previous architect William White. It opened in 1885 when the church itself was only half-built. It could hold up to 350 people and provided a base for the traditional church societies, as well as a girls' gymnastic class, a cycling club which had at least monthly 'runs' to places such as Sutton, Coulsdon or Windsor, a choral society, and a whist drive which had 180 players. The men's club, open 7.30-10.30 every night but Friday, laid on gymnastics, chess, draughts, two billiard tables as well as smoking and reading rooms, and there were regular concerts and plays in the hall.

AS IT IS, WITH THE HALL AND VICARAGE.

49: St Luke's church, hall and vicarage

St Luke's vital statistics
Averages 1895-1915

Baptisms	93
Confirmations	55
Marriages	51
Easter Communions	623
Sunday Communions	145
Annual Offering	£792/10/3

Source: Parish magazine

The annual offering was, as is always the case, the subject of some discussion on how to enlarge it. The commentary in the parish magazine on this subject also allows us to get a better measure of the size of the congregation. They kept detailed records of the coins given and in February 1907 the Vicar wrote in the parish magazine[39].

> 'The £780 annual offering is made up of thousands of small coins – more than 65,000, but less by 1,100 than the year before. In these coins there were, in round numbers, 250 half crowns, 440 florins, 2,400 shillings, 9,200 sixpences. 5,800 threepenny pieces; in copper 35,750 pennies, 11,370 halfpennies, 400 farthings – roughly 18,000 silver coins and 47,500 copper coins.
>
> It has been reckoned that there are 300 heads of families in the congregation, and that they ought to give at least a shilling a Sunday – not a very adequate offering for the privileges of worship at St Luke's.'

A shilling was the price of participation in the whist drive or attending one of the concerts and 300 shillings a week for 300 families would have provided £780 a year. However eighteen months later, things were no better and the November 1908 magazine contained the following analysis of the morning collection on Sunday 11 October. That service was chosen because the 'morning congregation is undoubtedly more well-to-do that that which meets in the evening'.[40]

> 'Our examination has led to the following distressing results. The collection contained 449 coins. Our church is seated for 800 persons, and would look noticeably empty with a congregation of 449. It is therefore certain that many made no offering at all. Let us, however, suppose that all these were children, and that the 449 coins were the gift of 449 adult persons. Their value amounted to £5 18s 2d, so that the average offering made by each individual was rather less than 3 1/4d.
>
> This of itself does not point to any excess of generosity, but the sad state of the case is even worse. Givers of a

*shilling or more numbered less than one fourteenth of
the whole adult congregation, and gave considerably
more than a third of the entire collection; while of the
total of £5 18s 2d, no less than £4 6s was contributed
by 111 persons out of 149 in units of 6d and upwards.
We are sure that they do not grudge their gifts, but the
burden laid upon them is most unfair, for it appears
that the average offering of the remaining 338 adult
worshippers was almost exactly 1 1/4d.*

*We know that there are some few among us whose
small gifts are the amount that out of their poverty
they can afford. There are others, too, whose principal
offering is made at 8 a.m. But, all these apart, it is
too evident that the alms of not less than half of our
morning congregation are inadequate, for persons in
their circumstances, to a degree which, if it were not
deplorable, would be ridiculous.*

*Doubtless, their inadequacy is unrealised and
unintended.....'*

The offering increased the next year (1909) from £779 19s 7d
to £816, stayed at that level for one more year and then fell back to
£713, £755 and £787 in the three years after that.

There were further financial stresses for the parish in 1913.
When Erskine Clarke finally resigned from the position of Vicar of St
Mary's Battersea in 1909, he naturally gave up the four-figure income
associated with this. He then had to rely entirely on the St Luke's
endowment of about £270 a year together with a grant of £120 for
taking services at the Royal Patriotic School, which was becoming
hard to do because of the growing demands of St Luke's. Until he
left St Mary's, he had used part of that endowment to provide one
or even two curates for St Luke's in addition to that provided by the
Churchwardens, but it was becoming more difficult for him to fund
the second curate himself. He did not think that 'St Luke's could be
administered, even by a young and vigorous Vicar, with only the
curate provided by the Wardens' and therefore suggested the creation
of a Second Curate's Fund. This was accepted by the Church Council.

Even Erskine Clarke could not go on forever and in 1913, aged 86, he resigned from the position of Rural Dean of Battersea, a post he had held for 34 years since its creation in 1879, and from St Luke's. He was succeeded by his nephew Charles Erskine Clarke who had been a curate there for some years and lived in Old Park Avenue. Erskine Clarke suffered a severe stroke in 1916 and died in 1920.

The main income of the church, other than collections, was from pew rents. The Church was advertised as having 800 sittings of which 500 were free, implying that 300 were not. Pew rents essentially reserved a particular pew for a family, although seat holders had to be reminded from time to time that the written receipt for their rent made clear that the seats were only reserved until the bell stopped ringing before the service. These rents raised £215 per annum, or almost one third of the money raised for general church expenses, and so was not easily given up. During the First World War, there was continued lobbying against the principle of pew rents; one correspondent wrote in 1916 to the parish magazine (anonymously but describing himself as a 'non-seat-holder') 'When our men come home they will never feel able to submit to the restrictions such a system must have attached to it.'[41] Even so when the Church Council did finally discuss the future of pew rents in February 1917 it could only agree that 'the whole subject be dropped'.

It is surprising that there were pew rents at St Luke's at all because Erskine Clarke had been one of the pioneers of the "free and open church" movement, and had removed the pew rents in St Mary's Battersea as soon as the 100 year leases, used to help finance the building of the church in the eighteenth century, came to an end in 1876. Erskine Clarke had told a meeting of the heads of families of that church[42].

> 'The seats in the centre of the Church really belong to all
> parishioners in common; and although, for convenience,
> certain seats are reserved for certain persons, yet it is a
> great stretch of privilege that they should expect them
> to be kept vacant for them or should think that other
> parishioners can only enter them on sufferance.'

In 1924 an interesting change came for the congregation of St Luke's when Charles Erskine Clarke moved on to be Rector of St John Redhill, and for the first time in its fifty year life, the parish had to decide how much to pay the incumbent. (Charles, like his uncle had a private income). After taking into account the heavy cost of the upkeep of the Vicarage, and considering[43] ' the importance of the Church, the population and character of the parish, the increased cost of living since the War, and the general effort which is now being made to improve the stipends of the Clergy,' they decided on a stipend of £500 per annum.

After an interim appointment, the Rev W T Havard became the vicar of St Luke's. He was a great success and later became the Bishop of St Asaph and subsequently of St David. He raised the subject of pew rents as soon as he took up his incumbency in 1925. He argued strongly that such rents were 'a survival of Victorian days and a contradiction of our Lord's religion.' He proposed that they replaced the pew rent system by one of weekly offerings and even offered to reduce his and the curate's stipend if there was a financial shortfall. The congregation agreed within a few months, Stephen Potter's father, Frank, saying that a free church was an ideal which Canon Clarke would have been glad to have consummated. The result was all that Havard could have asked for, with the overall giving to the church increasing; 366 people gave an annual amount of just over £1,125.

The organ

Given the appeal in 2007-9 for restoration of the organ at St Luke's it is interesting to see how the Edwardians went about it. By 1911, the church was struggling with the problems of the organ that had been installed six years earlier with a modern electric action and blowing apparatus. It had taken some time to pay off the debt incurred to buy it and Charles Erskine Clarke claimed that the organ had never worked properly. Stephen Potter[44] describes it as having a tendency to produce an unwanted and continuous high pitched note on a piercing reed stop as soon as the motor was switched on. This was because, if Potter is to be believed, the new organ had been put in cheaply by two men from Fademan's, the plumbers, working at a cut rate (after hours only). He claims that the then organist, Mr Drummond, 'became expert in constructing a sequence of voluntaries based on this permanent note'.

It seems that the organ had been built on a modern and relatively untried design based on electro-pneumatic action and the recommendation, endorsed by Sir Frank Bridge, the organist of Westminster Abbey, and by the organist of St Michael, Chester Square, was that it should be reconstructed on the more old fashioned but established tubular pneumatic principle. This could be done at the cost of about £500. Frank Potter, who was a member of the organ committee, 'because of his musical knowledge', was also appointed Churchwarden and wrote in the introduction to the Summer Fair programme [45].

> 'What then is still wanting? Well what about the Organ? Can any thinking person, musical or otherwise, consider our present Organ to be satisfactory? The writer of this note remembers keenly, if not bitterly, the long delays in its construction, the constant breakdowns, and the extraordinary and uncouth noises with which it was wont to embarrass the clergy and disturb the minds of the congregation - troubles which have by no means ceased.'

In March 1914, the organ committee recommended the reconstruction work be carried out at a cost of £500, plus a further £60 for a new blowing apparatus, and £25 for future extension. Having raised almost £300, the Organ Committee then proposed to invite 60 members of the congregation to guarantee £5 each, so that the order might be placed quickly with Messrs Lewis in June. This was agreed and work to raise the guarantees was set in hand.

Finally, after nearly seven months in reconstruction and enlargement, the organ was reopened on Wednesday, June 16, 1915, and dedicated by Bishop Hook who afterwards preached on the value of music and its right employment in divine worship. The total cost ended up at £650, of which there was a balance of £33 to be raised with £233 outstanding in guarantees by the congregation. Matters then went quiet, until a question was asked some time in 1917 as to when the guarantees would be repaid. While the Vicar and Wardens undertook that they would repay without delay anyone who needed the money urgently, it was only in August 1918 that a serious appeal was made 'to remove the slur on the congregation for having made no attempt during the last three years to repay those who so kindly lent their money in 1915'. This was partly stimulated by a generous donor who promised to pay the last £15 if the remainder could be raised by a deadline that was extended twice until the end of January 1919. In thanking all for paying off the debt, the Vicar was able to say that 'The Church will be able with clear conscience issue the appeal for contributions towards our War Memorial which will shortly have to be made'.

This was not, alas, the end of expenditure on the organ. In May 1932, the Parish magazine reported that a lady had recently died and left £25 to the church and that this 'and a little more' had been spent on the organ. In 1942, however, the annual general meeting heard that the 'organ was in a bad condition, causing the weird noises that have been heard lately during the services, and might break down at any time'. Further repairs were done to the organ in the 1950s and the recent appeal raised £250,000 for a major restoration.

(Endnotes)

1   James Edwards. 1801 Companion from London to Brighthelmston. Part I p 25
2   Dictionary of National Biography. Thomas Streatfeild
3   James Edwards. Ibid Part II p 12
4   Dictionary of National Biography. John Dent
5   Ken and Suzanne Smith. private communication
6   Quoted in David Knyaston. 1994 The City of London Vol I p304
7   Sam Thornton. 1891 Year recollections p 187
8   The World 4 October 1876
9   Mrs Spurgeon in C H Spurgeon 1897 The Early Years p 498
10 Quoted in Friends of West Norwood web site
11 George Young 1854 The God Loo Guide quoted in website above
12 St Luke's Parish Magazine
13 Clapham Society. 2009 April Newsletter
14 The Buildings of Clapham. 2000 p 180
15 Mrs Spurgeon. Ibid p 499
16 G H Pike. 1894 Life of Spurgeon
17 South London Press 24 April 1882
18 Charles Booth. Life and Labour in London Religious Influences Vol 6 p 164
19 Sir Walter Besant. 1912 South of the Thames p 232
20 Charles Spurgeon. 1881 Almanack

21 Wandsworth Borough Council. Conservation Area Character Statement no 6
22 Sir Walter Besant. Ibid p 231
23 Building News. June 1876 p 620
24 The Times. 20 May 1881 p 15 and 13 August 1881 p15
25 English Heritage. Survey of London vol 39 p 150
26 The Times. 13 August 1881
27 St Luke's Parish Magazine
28 John Pilditch. 1895. The Progress of Battersea
29 Phil Brown. private communication
30 St Luke's Parish Magazine
31 Ibid
32 Ibid
33 Ibid
34 Ibid
35 The Times 14 November p12
36 St Luke's Parish Magazine
37 St Mary's Battersea Parish Magazine
38 Charles Booth. Ibid Vol 5 p 177
39 St Luke's Parish Magazine
40 Ibid
41 Ibid
42 J G Taylor. 1925 Our Lady of Batersey p 294
43 St Luke's Parish Magazine
44 Stephen Potter. 1959. Steps to Immaturity p 68
45 St Luke's Parish Magazine

CHAPTER 8

HOW IT HAPPENED AND WHO MOVED IN

It is often assumed that the movement of people into south west London was determined by transport capacity. However, although the development of public transport was important for the development of Balham, it is less clear that it was so significant for Clapham and Battersea. The wealthy had long since been able to move out to Surrey and commute comfortably from there and while many of the clerks travelled into London, there would have been plenty of clerical jobs locally. Such public transport as there was still tended to be directed to the middle class. The 1870s saw the development of the horse drawn tram and The South London Tramways Company obtained the necessary legal powers in 1879 to lay down some six miles of tramways. While this helped to promote development, what brought people into the parish could also take them out and some opposed (unsuccessfully) the introduction of the trams on the grounds 'that the introduction of tramways would afford facilities to the Battersea residents to leave the parish and trade in other parishes, to the detriment of the local tradesmen.'[1]

Even by 1895, when bus services in Battersea had improved in quantity and price, they still catered for the middle-class market and were concentrated on central and south Battersea where their clientele lived. The horse tram network peaked in 1895 and was shortly to be electrified, but only 480 seats were provided on the early workmen's trams. While a proportion of those working will probably have done so in the City or the West End, it is not obvious from their occupations that a large number would have done so. Many may have moved from North Battersea as their income improved. Booth[2] commented on the Park Town estate there in the late 1890s, observing that 'The tenants tend as time goes on to become slightly poorer, consequent on the outward drift to the new houses being built near Clapham Common.' It was not until 1914 that there was a substantial number of early trains from Clapham Junction into London, 49 before 8.00 am as compared with the seven before 9.00am in the 1870s.[3]

The growth of the population stimulated retail and retail employment. An advertisement in The Times[4] in 1881 made this clear.

> 'TO LET by AUCTION four acres of highly valuable FREEHOLD BUILDING LAND, situate St John's Hill, close to Clapham Junction Station, having an important frontage to the best part of the main road, immediately available for the erection of shops and dwelling houses, which are in very great demand in this favourite district. A lease will be granted direct from the freeholder for 99 years'.

Messrs Arding and Hobbs moved from their first shop in Wandsworth High Street to five shops in Falcon Road in 1881 and built their first department store on the corner of St John's Road and Lavender Hill in 1885. Ill 50 shows the site in 1871.

50: Site of Arding and Hobbs store

One writer commented about how it had looked at that time[5].

> *'In those days, the bottom of Lavender Hill ran between the grounds of the house of Mrs Shirley, the well known actress, and the house where Tom Taylor, the famous playwright, wrote many of his popular comedies, and unaltered practically from the days when the Falcon meandered peacefully from Tooting through Battersea to the Thames.'*

This building burnt down in 1909 after which the present store was built. Ill 51 shows a contemporary postcard of the then new building.

The largest Furnishing and Drapery Store South of the Thames.

51: New building of Arding and Hobbs store

It was the largest furnishing and drapery store south of the Thames and the writer of the card had described it, with perhaps some surprise, as 'rather a big business, in fact they sell pretty well everything there.'

Let us now examine who moved into South Battersea in the nineteenth and early twentieth centuries, not least as a route to understanding why the area developed as it did. There are several contemporary sources, such as Canon Erskine Clarke, who has already been cited frequently, and Charles Booth. Booth's 1902 study, 'Life and Labour of the People in London', is of major importance, providing a comprehensive commentary on all the streets of Inner London (for which South Battersea was on the outer fringe). Booth, or a colleague, walked the streets of London making notes on all he saw and grading the streets by class and/or wealth adding commentary as well as comments from policemen or other locals. There is also considerable detail in the various censuses, of which the two most recently published in full are for 1901 and 1911. Some information on what happened in the period between censuses can be found in the Rate Books which record those responsible for paying the rates.

Sources of finance

We have already seen that, apart from Cubitt's Clapham Park, there was little or no large scale development in south west London. Typically, individual pieces of land became available as the original occupants died or moved on and the owners, with no great emotional attachment to the land, wanted to realise the proceeds. It is in this context that the ground rent system, a vital element in developing London's housing and reflecting a mechanism particular to England and to its urban areas, came into its own.

An owner seeking to profit from his land had two main options, apart from undertaking the development himself. He could sell the freehold of the land to a developer, taking some profit but leaving most of the increase in value – and the risk of achieving it – to the developer. Alternatively, he could retain the freehold but grant a building lease, of between 50 and 100 years, with a ground rent secured on the land and buildings and with reversion of all to him at the end of the lease. In turn, a builder would sell on a lease on an individual property either to someone who wanted to live in the house or more often to someone who would let it out and take the risk of collecting future rents. In both cases, the builder would charge a ground rent, significantly higher than he had paid for the undeveloped land. This increased ground rent was often attractive to an investor since it was more secure than the rent for the house itself although of course giving a lower return. Builders could then sell the income stream from the ground rents for a capital sum which could be used to repay borrowings, whether for the land or building. This early manifestation of financial engineering meant that the barriers to entry to the house-building business were very low; many tried their luck, but many failed on the way as the market turned against them. In virtually all cases this was how housing was created in south west London.

Investors were therefore able to invest in housing in a number of ways. They could buy ground rents, they could lend money on a mortgage for someone else to buy the property, or they could buy the property and collect the rents themselves. The return increased with the risk. In the 1880s, ground rents yielded about 3-3.5%, a slightly higher return than the 2.75% on Government stock, mortgages gave in the region of 5-5.5%, while rents had the highest returns, depending on the risk. While speculators would often buy land in the expectation (or hope) that it would increase in value, no one gave much thought to the possibility of house prices increasing and indeed inflation was very low or even negative in the 1890s.

When they reached their forties, the Victorian professional middle class tended to prefer predictable income from property investment to more speculative equity investments, no doubt as a means to ensure finance for their old age[6]. What interested them most was sound middle class property with sound middle class occupiers. They looked to people like Galsworthy's Soames Forsyte who had a reputation for having 'a talent for bricks and mortar' and being 'not content with less than four per cent for his money'.[7] The rent on working class property offered much higher returns - an average return in Stepney of 36% in 1906 is quoted[8] - but with much more potential aggravation such that a London estate agent wrote in 1886 'Investors of the better class will not touch a kind of property which brings them into such unpleasant relations with a class below them.'[9] One estimate puts this borderline in London as a rent of about £41 per annum[10] - below the rents in Old Park Avenue but above those in the roads off Northcote Road.

The middlemen in these transactions were almost invariably solicitors who were also a common source of funds for investment in housing, whether using their own money or acting on behalf of their clients Solicitors often managed funds from widows' inheritances, marriage settlements or other trust fund. Trusts were first allowed to invest in mortgages in 1859, and Dyos[11] was one of the first local historians to recognise the significance of this.

> 'We come at last to a source of building capital which has scarcely been noticed in the business annals of the period; the solicitor. He must be one of the most obscure characters, not only in the history of the Victorian period at large, but in a field of business activity in which he may well have been at one time the real fulcrum for the bulk of the capital movements. There is little direct evidence of solicitors being used to any extent as channels for house-building investment before the second half of the century, and it seems quite possible that they did not become important until building society advances to builders began to flag for the first time following the recession of 1868-72. In many cases they were acting as trustees, although the Trustee Act of 1888 extended the right (without express provision) to invest in freeholds to leaseholds of over 200 years.'

Dyos' observation was followed up by Avner Offer's work[12] which sheds considerable light on this world. He showed[13] that the general public, usually acting through solicitors, were the largest lenders of conventional mortgages at the end of the nineteenth century, accounting for about 80% of the value of loans compared with only about 6-9% lent by building societies, the successors of the land societies. Solicitors were able to play this role because they were intimately involved in all land transactions as well as dealing with probate and investment of the resulting funds. Land and related transactions were the most important part of their business with conveyancing alone providing at least 50% of the income of solicitors overall. For many the proportion was much higher[i]. There was no register of title, and deeds were voluminous and complicated. The original deeds to houses in Old Park Avenue ran to 55 pages with

---

[i] Offer estimated that about one third of all the solicitors in England and Wales worked within a ten mile radius of the centre of London. The great majority worked alone or in small partnerships and their work was almost entirely probate, conveyancing and associated litigation.

all previous transactions recorded and covenants repeated on each occasion, often with minor variations which may or may not have been relevant. In addition, the deeds contain annotations which show that the originals of other related transactions had been read and checked. It is hardly surprising, given their monopoly of conveyancing work, that this was such a fruitful source of income for solicitors. Despite regular attempts to introduce registered title, this was resisted fiercely and the Law Society only finally withdrew its opposition in 1972.

Costs and income

To understand the finances of South Battersea houses we need to look at the costs and rents of the time. There are a number of sources for these, including individual deeds but the most general is the weekly sale price reports of auctions in The Builder[14] which give an idea of the going rate for houses in many parts of London, including streets in Battersea. The ground rents, annual rents, and auction prices for an 80-90 year lease, on houses in nearby roads during the last half of the 1890s are shown below.

Rents and auction prices in 1890s for South Battersea houses (£sd)

Road	Ground Rent	Annual Rent	80+ years lease
	£	£	£
Belleville	6	31	325
Bennerley	6	28-34	
Dents	7/10/-	44	400
Gorst	6/10/-	40	400
Granard	9	45	400
Honeywell	6/6/-	35	300
Kelmscott	7	34	345
Mallinson	6/6/-	30	255
Salcott	6/10/-	35	315
Thurleigh	8-9	46	470
Wakehurst	6-7	34	300
Winfrith	5		230

Source: The Builder

This general picture is confirmed by the details of a contemporary mortgage. Adolphus Spencer, who was in the tin plate business, moved in 1892 from Frith Street in Soho to 45 Kelmscott Road. The builder William George had taken a 99 year lease from the developer Henry Corsellis in return for a ground rent of £7 per annum. As the first occupier, Spencer purchased all but a few months of the lease for about £375. Spencer had five shares in the West London and General Permanent Building Society and this entitled him to a mortgage of £250 amounting to about two thirds of the cost, as was standard practice. His six year mortgage at 5½ % cost £4/4/5 a month, or £50/13/- a year, appreciably more than the rent of about £34, quite apart from having to find his deposit.

To understand who could have paid these rents, we can consider the finances of those on the fringes of the middle class. Clerks at the Railway Clearing House in the Edwardian years were advised not to contemplate marriage until their income reached at least £90 a year[15]. They could then just about afford a two-bedroom Victorian cottage or a new half house, at a rent of between 7s 6d and 9s a week (£19/10/- to £23/8/- a year), leaving enough for the other necessities of life. Third Class season tickets ranged from £6 to £10 or more a year, so the minimum 'safe' salary for marriage in the white collar class for those without subsidised fares was probably about £100. One writer[16] estimates that three-bedroom houses were generally available at £25-£30 annual rent plus another £10 or so for local rates and water and a salary of about £150 a year was necessary before a three-bedroom or modest four-bedroom house was within reach. Looking at South Battersea, this suggests that an income of at least £150 was needed to rent a whole house off the Northcote Road but getting on for £200 was necessary for the larger houses in the roads such as Dents or those off Thurleigh Road. This was at a time when the average clerk or shop assistant rarely received more than £120-130 and the skilled worker at most £110-120.

Booth gives an interesting insight into the Sunday of the 'ordinary' non church-going clerk[17].

> *'[He] breakfasts on Sunday about 10.15, half dressed.*
> *So do his womenkind. A bare arm may be seen stretched*
> *round the door to, take in the morning's milk. After*

breakfast, the man goes for a walk, with pipe or cigar. The public-house, when it opens, does not attract him. It is not 'the thing' to go there and he has no club. At 1.30 or 2 is Sunday dinner. After that, sleep; and tea at five. Such is the programme of a lazy day. On an active Sunday, he meets a friend and they go off on bicycles, sometimes for an all-day ride, perhaps to Brighton and back, at other times for the morning or afternoon only.'

52: Cycling in Battersea Park, 1895

Cycling has already been mentioned as a recreational activity. Battersea Park played an important role in the development of cycling since it was the first in London to allow cycling on carriage drives.

Those who had once been enthusiastic horse riders in Hyde Park forsook their old haunt to join the fashion conscious in Battersea with their new clothes. Richard Church[18] recalls 'the rest of the bloomered and knickerbockered cyclists, figures in a parade which appeared every afternoon in Battersea Park during the spring and early summer of those years about the turn of the century'. Ill 52 catches this picture.

But cycling was not only for the well off.[19] Many clubs were founded for the working class and there were at least two successful clubs in Battersea. The Clarion included better-off workers and clerks while The Pioneer, formed in 1881, comprised professionals and businessmen. It included John Pilditch, the Borough Surveyor, and Percy Thornton MP. One can only speculate whether the effect noted by The Builder in 1896[20] had much influence in Battersea. 'We can scarcely doubt that it [cycling] has improved the value of many houses. It has brought houses at some distance from railway stations into touch with railways.' On the other hand, the large number of bicycles left daily in 2010 at Clapham Junction and Clapham South stations may suggest The Builder had a point.

The housing market - a steady decline in status

The comments of Erskine Clarke and others have demonstrated that while South Battersea was only just beginning to be developed by the late 1880s, housing then came quickly. This trend is captured in a description of the area given by Patricia Hansford Johnson in her book "An Impossible Marriage". She had herself lived with her musician grandfather at 53 Battersea Rise since her father was a colonial administrator in West Africa. The house in the novel is no doubt drawn from her own experience.[21]

> 'He was a retired civil servant augmenting his pension now by letting the two top floors of the large Victorian house on the extreme edge of the Common, in the borough of Clapham and not of Battersea by the width of a street. When my grandfather bought the house in 1886 the neighbourhood had been much favoured by professional men in some way or other connected with

the theatre. At that time the south side of Battersea
Rise had consisted of open fields, a few hawthorns,
and sheep safely grazing. He had bought his own house
chiefly for the view, but within ten years the view had
been obliterated by a sudden seepage of lower middle-
class houses and shops, and within another ten the
seepage had streamed down through stratas of villas and
potential slum to the very edge of the river.'

This also identifies the perception of continued social decline as
the land was filled with more and more smaller houses built for the
lower middle class. E M Forster, referring to his attempts to identify
the former location of Battersea Rise House which he had known
well as a boy, makes similar observations[22].

'I have identified the area with difficulty. It is completely
covered with very small two-storied houses. A couple
of roads run through it, north to south, intersected
by crossroads. The site was cleared at a time when
development was unusually ruthless. Not one tree
survives. Clapham Common survives, but so messed
about, so full of roads and railings and notices and huts
and facilities and infelicities, that Marianne and her
mother would not recognize it.'

As with most things at that time, the housing market was very
clearly stratified, and in a world where class differences were finely
observed, the range of rents identified in the table above reflects
two separate markets. The first is the development on the Dents
and Old Park estates; houses on them were not as large as those
along Nightingale Lane, but were larger than those in the second
market consisting of the roads off Northcote Road. Rents in Dents
and Old Park houses were up to £10 per annum higher and they
were accordingly occupied by more affluent people. The second
market was by far the larger, and had probably been set by the first
development there in the 1870s. It was where most builders saw
the market and had the advantage of having no covenants trying to
maintain status by requiring a minimum cost of the houses or that
they be semi-detached. There was less risk in smaller houses which

could be finished quicker and were less trouble to let, all of which was helpful to the small builder who preferred to finance only a few houses at a time. Builders' ability to finance their work is one explanation of why it sometimes took as much as 10 years after permission had been given for a road to be developed.

The houses in this second market off Northcote Road were extremely flexible. As Booth explained[23]:

> *'they had the great advantage of being specially built to suit the classes that have occupied them. The object has been to provide self-contained dwellings of from three to seven rooms, each having its own kitchen, scullery and washing copper, and each with its own front and back door. Great ingenuity has been shown, and a type of house produced which can be arranged for one or two families, and which not only fulfils these requirements, but has some external architectural merit; far more, I think, than can be claimed for the contemporary three-storey houses of the class above.'*

It is hardly surprising therefore that Booth[24] records:

> *'there is a never-ending demand for small two-storyed houses, arranged for either one or two families. These as fast as they are erected are occupied by people who have enough to enable them to live comfortably; though, having probably little or nothing saved, they depend on continued prosperity. Among them are many newly married couples, and there is no sign of any reduction in the birth-rate'*

The flexibility of the houses was particularly important since it allowed for many different types of occupation. For example, one way round a lessee's problem of finding the rent was to sublet one or more rooms. Booth[25] gives a detailed example of this for one of the streets off Northcote Road in what a police inspector described as an 'old-fashioned ' street paying £36-38 rent per annum.

> *'The tenant himself, with his family, would occupy two rooms and kitchen on the ground floor and retain one*

upper room, and would let out the first floor, containing front and back room and box room (which although very narrow, is often used as a bedroom) for 7s a week; while above that would be one room, which may be let to a single old lady unfurnished for 4s, or perhaps to two single men furnished at 5s or 6s, according to whether they sleep in two single or one double bed. Thus first floor at 7s would pay £18/4/- per annum; second floor at 4s would pay £10/8/- per annum, leaving £8 to £10, plus an equal (or more probably larger) amount for rates and taxes as the share of the tenant in chief, always supposing that the rooms let out are never vacant and the rents regularly paid.

The first floor occupants make the front room their best room, using it as a bed sitting room. For cooking they have a range in the back room. Where there are young men lodgers they usually take all their meals out, except Sunday dinner, paying a regular sum for eating this with their landlord. If the top floor is taken by an old lady, she will cook all her meals over her own little fire; on the rare occasions when such a facility may be needed, she would have the use of the oven downstairs without charge.'

Note the policeman's use of the phrase "old fashioned". Landlords would be reluctant to let houses in a 'new' street to those who would have to sublet, since that would lower the tone, although they might well reckon that a proportion of their tenants might later find the need to do so. But in any case Booth[26] points out:

'The demand is for new houses not old. There are those who will only live in new houses, and move when the street becomes 'old' – move 'simply to change their house and start fresh painted' Young newly married people, who, as soon as the brass handle is tarnished move elsewhere.'

The success of these houses, repeated all over South London, may have been the reason that the builders of the time seem to have been more consistently successful than their counterparts of twenty five years earlier. Building began to be more concentrated in the hands of larger builders who had a longer period of activity. They built more houses, both in total and in larger groups at a time and they stayed in business. In many cases a whole road, even a long one, was constructed entirely by one or two builders. For example, 70 of the houses in Bramfield Road were built either by William George or his father James; Abel Playle built all the houses in Ballingdon Road and, between them, Playle and George built all of Culmstock Road. George also built half of Muncaster and all of Winsham Grove and Bowood Road. John Smith built 50 of the houses in Hillier Roads, all the original houses in Sumburgh Road, and he and Playle one side each of Amner Road, John Stanbury a third of Kelmscott Road. William Kerwen built much of Alfriston Road and one side of Wisley Road. All of them contributed to Broomwood Road.

Many of these builders lived in the area, often in houses they had built themselves or near houses they were building. William Steer moved from Broomwood Road first to a double fronted house he had built in 1888 at 38 Honeywell Road with his wife, nine children aged 3-19, and a 75 year old aunt, and subsequently for a short period in 1891 to 64 Honeywell Road. The 1891 census gives the roads that each of the children was born in and so documents their six previous homes in Lambeth and Battersea. William George lived at 1 Kelmscott Road while he was building 1-33; he then moved to 10 Broomwood Road and on to 89 West Side Clapham Common while he was building 89-114 West Side and subsequently 62 -90 Alfriston Road. Many of these houses have Art Nouveau details and the house George built for his son, Edgar, at 90 Alfriston Road (Ill 53) has been described[27]:

> 'an architectural gem in roughcast render over red brick with '1914' set in clay tile above the door. A tour de force in whimsical Art Nouveau style, utterly unspoilt, one of the delights of the west side of the Common.'

53: 90 Alfriston Road

Most of these builders were living fairly modestly, without servants but this was not always so. Stanbury was the son of a small builder, but the 1901 Census shows that by then he had moved out to Cheam, describing himself as a retired builder, and employing a governess, cook, housemaid, groom, coachman and gardener to support his family which included three sons. He was only 38!

Booth's walks and the Census

Booth's walk round South London gives considerable insight into the area although it is worth checking it against the details in the census. He colour coded the neighbourhoods from semi-criminal to wealthy as shown in the table below. Map 17 gives the details for the area.

Map 17: Charles Booth Poverty map

Category	Colour	Description
A	Black	The lowest of occasional labourers, loafers and semi-criminals
B	Dark Blue	Casual earnings, very poor, below 18s a week
C	Light Blue	Intermittent earnings, 18-21s a week
D	Light Blue	Small regular earnings
E	Pink	Regular standard earnings – above poverty line
F	Pink	Higher class labour – fairly comfortable earnings
G	Red	Lower- well-to-do middle class
H	Yellow	Wealthy

Source: Charles Booth

Only a few houses entirely in Nightingale Lane or West Side, Clapham Common were graded yellow. The most common classifications in South Battersea are pink and red corresponding to the different gradations of the middle class although Booth differentiates still further by using a category 'pink barred', or 'pink b', which is pink with red stripes, or half way between the two. Booth tended to devote less time to these streets, finding the blue and black streets more interesting.

Categories C and D comprised what Booth described as the "poor" and he estimated them to comprise about 22.5% of London's population; category B was about 11% while category A was only 1%. He gave this category a more extended definition which was not afraid of value judgements[28]:

'the lowest class which consists of some occasional labourers, street sellers, loafers, criminals and semi-criminals. Their life is the life of savages, with vicissitudes of extreme hardship and their only luxury is drink.'

There were no black streets in South Battersea, and few in the rest of Battersea, although Clapham Junction generated some interest[29].

'The gay and crowded streets at Clapham Junction are one visible result of the surging life of this new population, and *here a good deal of vice floats to the surface. Prostitution is rife, and the Commons at night are scenes of disorder.'*

Booth or his researchers were accompanied by a local policeman who gave his own views and comments on the streets. The area of South Battersea was visited in two walks, one from Battersea Rise to Mallinson Road with Police Constable George in July 1899, and the other with Police Constable Nilmes in October 1899 covering essentially the area between Mallinson Road and Nightingale Lane. Describing, the first walk Booth picks up the changes identified by Pamela Hansford Johnson and others[30].

'The notable feature is the steady progress from pink b and sometimes red to pink and the tardy demolition of the yellow west side of Clapham Common which has withstood the builder so much longer that the north and south. Even now the greater portion remains intact.'

He describes the second walk .[31]

'a wholly uninteresting area, almost exclusively upper and lower middle class. Though it is almost impossible to tell it from the exterior, according to George's evidence there has been considerable decay in the streets between Wandsworth Common and Northcote Road. Those on the map are red or pink b but George says that they are now universally let to two families and are servantless. Indeed in his opinion there are not six families in Battersea that have a home to themselves.

Some of the roads close to Wandsworth Common [he mentions particularly Auckland and Chivalry] were, and I think from George's tone still are, a good deal frequented by prostitutes who ply their trade on the Common. The only poor road in this otherwise well-to-do district is Chatham Road and the streets off it. In this short road are no less than four beer houses and one public house.'

There are two groups of streets in this walk, the first being all those from Salcott Road north which are either, according to George, let as half houses or tenanted, and the second group comprising the larger houses on Thurleigh Road and those built on the Dents and Old Park Estates. He sees the roads east of Northcote Road (ie further from Wandsworth Common) as slightly better than those west - 'but not much' - and Mallinson as a little better than Bennerley. There were signs of poverty in Abyssinia and west Bennerley Roads. Apparently, the costers[ii] and their stalls had been evicted from St John's Road by the opposition of the tradesmen and moved to Northcote Road but the tradesmen were already beginning to regret it. Even so, only a few costers were out when the walk was done. The state of Chatham Road is no surprise. The 1891 Ordnance Survey shows there was still a smithy in the road and it is clear that many of the houses were distinctly smaller than those in surrounding roads.

We also have information about these roads from the various censuses, the 1891 census taking place not long after the roads were first built -sometimes - a long time after permission was given for them. We will look at four roads in more detail, Hillier, Honeywell, Kyrle and Wroughton, all of which were approved for laying out in 1880. Honeywell and Wroughton Roads were built quickly, but building hardly started for ten years in Hillier and Kyrle Roads. As a result, the people who lived in the two sets of roads were different, as shown by the tables at the end of the chapter.

Houses on all the roads have a high proportion of younger heads of household but in the newer roads, Hillier and Kyrle, they are more likely to have been born in or close to Battersea and almost twice as likely to have a servant. There was a wide range of occupations, with clerks of one kind or another making up 20-25% of all households and retail being the next largest. There were virtually no professionals (one solicitor and two accountants) and of the 229 households in these roads in 1891, only ten had heads of household aged over 60, two of whom were over 70, reflecting both life expectancy and the funds available to older, often non-working people.

There is a clear difference between the houses on those four roads and the larger ones built by 1891 on the Dents and Old Park estates which include both sides of Thurleigh Road up to 29/30 and Granard,

---

ii 'Costers' is Booth's word. We would probably use the word costermongers or street traders.

Morella, Hendrick and Rusham Roads.[iii] These houses have what a modern household would regard as five or six bedrooms rather than the four in the houses lying between Northcote and Webbs Roads, and they attracted different kinds of people. There were few clerks, at least not without some qualifier, such as first division civil service, and no manual workers. They were journalists, managers, employers and manufacturers, civil engineers or merchants, more professionals and a good few retired or living 'off own means'. James Hobbs, a draper and co-owner of Arding and Hobbs, lived at 1 Thurleigh Road. On average there was slightly more than one live-in servant in each house and Rusham Road had an average of almost 1.7 servants per household, demonstrating that they were comfortably off, if not on the scale of the larger houses in Nightingale Lane. As we might expect for more expensive and larger houses, the heads of household tended to be older, and there were distinctly more over 60 (indeed 5% are over 70), and a higher proportion, significantly over half, born outside London.

Age of Head of Household (%)

Road	20s	30s	40s	50s	60+
Hillier	39	39	22	0	0
Honeywell	23	36	26	12	4
Kyrle	23	23	23	25	6
Wroughton	7	55	20	12	6
Average	17	43	23	11	5
Dents	9	27	27	14	23
Estcourt (Hendrick)	5	50	23	23	0
Gorst	8	40	31	18	3
Granard	0	17	36	23	23
Morella	3	33	16	37	10
Rusham	0	30	20	20	30
Thurleigh	0	27	27	27	19
Average	4	33	33	18	12

Source: 1891 census

iii Old Park Avenue was built later, but followed the same pattern, being subject to the same covenants.

On the other hand, the proportion of owner occupiers (ie freeholders or long leaseholders) in the South Battersea area was much higher than the overall London average of about 10%, illustrated in the table below for 1901 when all the houses were occupied. There seems to be no particular correlation between the size or price of the houses and the amount of owner occupation, since Wroughton and Hillier Roads have smaller houses than those in Estcourt or Dents Roads.

Owner occupation in 1901

Road	% owner occupied
Bennerley	15
Dents	15
Estcourt (Hendrick)	19
Gorst	22
Hillier	37
Honeywell	20
Rusham	20
Wroughton	31

Source 1901 Census

As we have seen, the policemen with whom Booth walked round South Battersea were clear that virtually all the terrace housing was sublet to at least two families per unit. However the evidence from the 1901 Census suggests that it was not widespread in the larger houses and that the policemen may well have been partly wrong about many of the streets in South Battersea. No more than 10% of the houses in Wroughton Road were recorded as being in multiple occupancy, although the Census reveals that a few more had boarders. The picture is somewhat different in the roads crossing Northcote Road. Salcott Road had about 20% multiple occupancy, concentrated on the houses nearest to Wandsworth Common, while no fewer than 55% of the houses in Bennerley Road were in multiple occupancy, perhaps picking up the policemen's comment about poverty in that road. And some of these houses were, at least to our standards, extremely crowded. Examples include:

- 19 Salcott Road – three households

  William Clark (41, a fruiterer), wife Sarah(32), seven children aged 1-11

  William Nunn (aged 25 a plumber), wife Mary and two children aged 2 and 3

  Edward Springwall (22, a carman), wife Lily aged 22 and a baby

- 17 Bennerley Road – three households

  Lucy Dodgson (42, no husband and charwoman) 9 children aged 1-19

  Henry Wilkins (62 grocer), wife Louise (42) and two children 15, 17

  John Holmes a 72 year old widower and his adult son

- 30 Bennerley Road – two households

  William Moore (41 railway guard) wife Emily, six children 1-14, widowed father

  William Harrison (43 railway guard) wife Miriam and three children 2-12

Overcrowding was not confined to those houses in multiple occupancy. Samuel Chapman (a grocer aged 52) lived in 11 Salcott Road with his wife Florence (aged 42) and eleven children under 21.

One road that was not built in time for Booth's study was Blandfield Road, for which we have a witness with a different viewpoint. The poet, Edward Thomas, his wife Helen and first child Philip, had little money when they got married and moved into the top maisonette in what was then 7 Nightingale Parade in Blandfield Street opposite Old Park Avenue off Nightingale Lane[iv]. Helen describes it in graphic terms[32].

[iv] This was re-numbered to be part of Blandfield Street (now Road), and would now be 6 Blandfield Road.

'[Philip] found, in a new street in what was obviously doomed to become a slum, a half- house of which the rent was seven shillings and six pence a week, and to this we moved. It had a good sitting room which, very much to the builder's surprise, we chose to have distempered a warm grey; a bedroom which just held our bed, the child's cot and a chest of drawers; and a little kitchen with steps leading from it to a tiny squalid back yard, used by the downstairs people for keeping ramshackle rabbit hutches and hanging out washing which was always wet and never clean. There was a notice printed in the rent book which at first puzzled me – 'Broken windows must be repaired by the tenant,' but we had not been there a week before we understood the significance of this regulation. The downstairs people frightened me rather because of their way of moving out in the middle of the night. Very seldom did the downstairs tenants stay longer than a fortnight, because, as I heard later, they could not be sued for rent under a fortnight's tenancy. Sometimes they were quiet, but more often noisy, quarrelsome, rough men and women and pale dirty children, often with a frightened dog tied up to a barrel in the back yard. All were terribly poor and degraded.'*

She may have been a little unfair, since a number of people did stay in Nightingale Parade for many years – including their neighbour at No 8, but it is also true that many of the houses had no one on the electoral roll for years at a time, a sure sign of a street in which tenancies change frequently.

Conclusions

There were essentially two markets for housing in the South Battersea area by the end of the nineteenth century. The first consisted of the larger houses in roads near to Nightingale Lane on the land originally owned by the Dents where there had been covenants requiring houses to be built of a minimum value amounting in practice to at least five bedrooms. These were occupied by established middle class families, usually with two servants. Few of them had been born in the neighbourhood, which of course had not existed then, and more than half had been born outside London even if in many cases they had lived elsewhere in south London first.

The second market consisted of the somewhat smaller houses on the roads off Northcote Road. Most of them were reasonably soundly built, despite the regular tirades against "jerry-building".ᵛ While their first letting was usually to a single family, many brought in lodgers or in some cases they were let to two families or even more. The balance depended on the family finance which could change without notice. Many of the occupants were moving out of central London as their status or income improved. Sometimes they moved up the hill from North Battersea as their status improved or out of Camberwell (home of clerks) as that area went into decline. They probably met the poet Robert Church's description of Battersea as 'a slumbrous suburb, largely peopled with artisan folk, clerks and minor civil servants.[33]

We also see a lot of turnover within the area, reflecting the three-year leases that were prevalent, both towards newer or bigger houses or further away from Wandsworth Common where the houses were more likely to be occupied by dysfunctional or unruly families. In general newer houses were lived in by younger people.

On the supply side, two things are clear. First, those who lived in the larger older houses did not seem inclined to leave for elsewhere. Houses were only redeveloped when the original owner or surviving spouse died. By then the children had established themselves elsewhere and had no desire to return to an area that was clearly urban and without much pretension to being upper middle class. The few exceptions were the Thorntons who hung on in Battersea Rise House until 1912 and some of the houses on West Side and Nightingale Lane, but even these usually sold their gardens for development. The future was clear to see. The last house to sell up was Beecholme, when Holmside Road was built in 1926.

ᵛ The Builder opined in June 1893 that 'There is no class in the community which more largely inhabits jerry-built houses than what may be called the class of clerks; these persons wish to have respectability and a higher standard than the artisan, and for them the jerry-built villa has to a great extent been constructed, because the clerk cannot afford a more substantial structure.

We have already seen in Maps 8 and 10 the connection between the present road structure and the original estate boundaries. Map 18 illustrates further the contention that the pattern of the roads in South Battersea was determined by the original land holdings and the relative time of their development or sale of gardens.

Map 18: Roads and boundaries

It shows the road pattern in black with the boundaries between the various 1836 land holdings in red. These two developments provide a good illustration of how the pattern of the roads was determined by the shape of the long standing land holdings and the order in which they were sold off. The Webbs estate, unlike the development on the Ashness site, did allow the continuation of the roads running from Wandsworth Common, but the site narrowed towards its end, resulting in smaller houses being built on Berber Road, itself squeezed in to maximise the number of houses built. The Chatto estate was developed five years before Kelmscott and Bramfield Roads were built, which explains why Ashness and Burland Roads are not quite their continuation and have different names while the small square of roads formed by Burland, Dulka and Chatto fills the little square of land at the end of the Chatto estate, the last two roads being displaced from Chatham Road to maximise the houses built. (Map 10)

(Endnotes)

1 Quoted in John Pilditch. 1895 The Progress of Battersea given to Bolingbroke Ratepayers Association
2 Charles Booth. Ibid Vol 5 p 158
3 Tim Sherwood. Ibid p 24
4 The Times 20 May 1881
5 History of Arding and Hobbs. 1907 Wandsworth Historical Library
6 Richard Rodger. Housing in Urban Britain 1780-1914 1989
7 John Galsworthy. 1906 The Man of Property Penguin edition p 19, 25
8 A Offer. Property and Politics 1870-1914 p 123
9 Quoted in A Offer Ibid p 122
10 A Offer. Ibid p 122
11 H J Dyos. 1982 Exploring the Urban Past. Eds David Cannadine and David Reeder. p 169
12 Avner Offer. Ibid
13 A Offer. Ibid p 143
14 The Builder. 1895-1900
15 Alan Jackson. 1973 Semi Detached London p 41
16 Alan Jackson. Ibid p 42
17 Charles Booth. 1900 Life and Labour in London Religious Influences Vol 6 p 163
18 Richard Church. 1955 Over the Bridge p 35
19 Sean Creighton. Organized Politics and Cycling in the 1890s and 1900s in Battersea
20 The Builder. July 25 1896
21 Patricia Hansford Johnson. 1955 An Impossible Marriage p 20
22 E M Forster. 1956 Marianne Thornton p 9
23 Charles Booth. Ibid Vol 5 p 187
24 Charles Booth. Ibid Vol 5 p 177
25 quoted in Fried and Elman. 1968 Charles Booth's London p 211
26 Charles Booth. Vol 5 p 187
27 The Buildings of Clapham 2000 p 163
28 Charles Booth. Ibid Vol 1 pp 33-62
29 Charles Booth. Ibid Vol 5 p 189
30 Charles Booth. 1900 Notebooks B369 p 232-3
31 Charles Booth. 1900 Notebooks B366 p 226-7
32 Helen Thomas. 1935 As it Was...World Without End p 127
33 Richard Church. Ibid p 62

CHAPTER 9

OLD PARK AVENUE

As we have seen, towards the end of the 1880s, building was taking place at the top of Thurleigh Road and St Luke's Church had been completed. It must have seemed obvious to builders to look for other opportunities for clearing big estates to make way for dense housing.. Chapter 7 recorded that James Horatio Booty lived in Old Park and the four to five acres that remained of the original estate from 1876 when he bought the house from Jane Simpson. He was clearly in some degree of comfort with his wife and eight children, together with five servants and a coachman and his wife living in the lodge. Two of his children were born there and were baptised at St Luke's (Mabel in October 1876 and Stanley in July 1878). However, it would appear that his affairs took a turn for the worse, starting in 1886. Hee borrowed extensively from The City Bank Ltd with the house as security, and the bank foreclosed on him in 1888.

The start of development

By this time, the bank had already discovered (or been approached by) a potential developer for the site. Edward Hammond Thompson was a local land owner and developer, born in Tottenham and established in Brixton as a linen draper. His business must have gone well and developed further because he described himself in the1881 census as a land agent. He was the freeholder for the development of the Clock House estate in Clapham and tried to maintain some control over the design of the housing there.[i] Thompson's affairs continued to go well and he moved to Clapham House on Nightingale Lane in

---

[i] The original house had been home to the King's printer, Charles Eyre who died in 1795 and was sold in 1885 by the owner of almost 25 years, John Kemp-Welch, proprietor of Jacob Schweppe and Co.

1887, where he described himself in the 1891 census as 'living off own means'. He lived there until 1892 when the house was knocked down and replaced by the present block of flats on the site, Clapham Mansions, and he moved out to Shepperton. He must have known the area well and could identify possible development sites where the owner would contemplate selling.

Accordingly, in early 1888 a request was received by the Metropolitan Board of Works from Edward Thompson asking to create Old Park Avenue. It an unusually shaped road, as it is a simple dog leg rather than the natural route straight from Nightingale Lane to Thurleigh Road. This is because it followed the land ownership and was confined to what were the remaining grounds of Old Park. The developer could take in neither the land already owned by Erskine Clarke for the Church nor that occupied by William Newmarch's house, Beecholme. It is perhaps a sign of the aspirations for the street that it was, at the time, the only road in South Battersea given the appellation of 'Avenue'.

According to normal practice, the Superintending Architect for Battersea, T Blashill, wrote on 22 March to the Battersea Vestry (which became independent from Wandsworth on 26 March) to consult them. On 3 April, the Vestry referred the application to its Works/General Purposes Committee, which took it at their meeting of 18 April and decided to object. The objection was endorsed by the Vestry itself without a vote on 25 April.

Meanwhile, the Superintending Architect went ahead with his own report, produced on 18 April which went to the Metropolitan Board of Works on 27 April who referred to their Building Act Committee. This committee considered it in turn on 25 May and minuted.

> *'It is proposed to lay out a road of the full width of 40 feet to lead out of the N side of Nightingale Lane for a distance of about 300 ft, whence it extends in a westerly direction and forms a communication with Ramsden Road. Your Committee sees no objection to the proposal and recommends*
>
> *That the application be granted, upon condition that no barriers be at any time erected, or other obstruction*

caused to the free use by the public of the road, and that
the name "Old Park Avenue SW" be approved.'

The Metropolitan Board of Works approved this recommendation on June 1. It is not clear why the Vestry had objected to the road, not least because a number of its members were builders, including until the 1888 elections in May one of the two men who eventually built the road. It was one of the first pieces of business considered by the newly independent Battersea Vestry, and it may be they were seeking to demonstrate their presence; alternatively they may have found some minor deviation from the rules which had often been the cause of their objection in the past. It was not unusual for the Metropolitan Board of Works to overrule or even ignore the views of the local vestry, and it is interesting to note that the decision could be considered by six committees and the local body overruled without appeal in no more than 10 weeks from start to finish.

The developers

Thompson himself was not the eventual developer of the road. He sold the property in December, 1889 to two solicitors, Reuben Winder and William Palmer. It was a good deal for Thompson. In a back to back deal he had bought the house and land from City Bank for £5,000 and immediately sold it to Winder and Palmer. They raised a mortgage of £4,950 from Palmer's wife, Julia, and paid Thomson £6,200. The land and its layout are shown in Map 12, based on the sale to Booty in 1876. Booty moved out of Old Park - to Hammersmith - first to Loftus Road and then to Wood Lane, living in very much less style with only one servant.

The law firm that developed Old Park Avenue was originally Simpson and Palmer, the two original partners being Henry Simpson, who lived in Cedars Road, and William Palmer who lived with his parents in Bromley. Their offices were at 9, Three Crowns Square in Southwark, where Reuben Winder had lived with his father and elder brother, Edwin, for at least ten years by 1861. Reuben's father was a savings bank messenger and Reuben, just 15, started work as a clerk in the solicitors' firm. Edwin, seven years older, was a hop factor's assistant, probably working at the nearby Hop Exchange, whose building still remains in Southwark Street. Both brothers were out to improve themselves Edwin had become secretary of the Southwark Savings Bank while Reuben had been promoted tomanaging clerk of the solicitors' firm and had married. Managing clerks earned between £150 and £350 a year and ran the office as well as overseeing the detailed processes of the law, most of which was conveyancing. The partners concentrated on clients and on bringing in the business.

Henry Simpson died in 1883, aged 58, and William at 31 became the sole partner, marrying next year Julia Courtney who had been living with her sister, recently married to an elderly rich land owner who lived three houses down the road from William's parents. Julia was wealthy in her own right since her father was dead, and she had access to more funds, not just through her sister but from a childless uncle. William and Julia moved to Beckenham, but he clearly needed a new partner who would do the work and make some local contacts. It is possible that Reuben benefited from the dispensation allowed for granting articles to long serving clerks as 'ten year men'. As Offer explains[1], these were not generally highly regarded and in the early twentieth century, Beatrice and Sidney Webb were told in the course of their study of the solicitors' profession: [2] They lack education and breeding of the ordinary articled clerk, as well as the needful money and influence.'

This does not seem to have been true of Reuben Winder. He took his chance, qualified as a solicitor and, by 1887, had become a partner. He then moved from Battersea Park Road to a new, more select, house at 9 Bolingbroke Grove, one of a row of detached houses built by David Kettle on the land which used to be Dents Farm. Like any good local solicitor, Reuben played his part in the local community and even became a churchwarden of St Luke's, an important source of occupants for his future buildings.

The firm was by now known as Simpson, Palmer and Winder, although it sometimes dropped the Simpson. There would seem to have been good links between the Winder brothers because in 1897 the firm moved to 1 Southwark Street, where the Southwark Savings Bank had its offices. It is possible that the bank could have been an additional source of funds for building speculation, although Offer points out[3] that many building societies were based in solicitors' offices and were only a slightly corporatised version of solicitors lending on their own account. Reuben's second son, Sydney, and William's eldest son, Courtney, joined the firm when they qualified as solicitors and the firm remained at that address until 1978.

It appears that Old Park Avenue was financed largely by the two solicitors rather than by the builders. There is no evidence from deeds of any involvement by the builders in financing the houses although the Rate Books show that they took out long leases on a small number of houses. It seems therefore that the builders were working, and being paid, by the developers rather than speculating on their own behalf..

Palmer and Winder were 37 and 43 respectively when they bought the freehold of the land for Old Park Avenue on 17 December 1889 and the eventual leases, when signed a few years later, were for ninety nine years from 25 December 1889, with peppercorn rents until the houses were occupied. However, the deeds show that the purchase was financed not by their client's funds but by a mortgage from William Palmer's wife, Julia.

Attempts were sometimes made by land holders to keep up standards on a development in Battersea, for example Cubitt's Clapham Park or Flowers in Park Town for largely commercial reasons, or the Shaftesbury Estate in Battersea for high minded reasons as well as commercial. But there were very few estates like the Dulwich Estate or The Crescent in Clapham that kept a close eye on development and were able and willing to maintain this control indefinitely – and do so still. We saw in Chapter 7 that the original freeholders had wanted to ensure from the start that the Old Park estate would be attractive to the relatively well off middle class. The chief restrictive covenant in place to protect their investment read[4].

'No additional houses or outbuildings other than detached or semidetached residences with the requisite detached or semidetached stables for private purposes shall at any time hereafter be erected upon any part of the hereditaments to which this part of the Schedule refers each detached house or residence to cost not less than £800 and each pair of semidetached houses or residences to cost not less than £1200 and in each case

the cost to be estimated at the current wholesale price
of material and labour employed and to be exclusive of
the cost of stabling outbuildings and fences.

No trade or business whatever shall at any time
hereafter be commenced or carried on on any part of
the same hereditaments and premises and no tavern
hotel teagarden livery stables beershop or other shop or
manufactory or trade premises shall at any time hereafter
be opened commenced or carried out on nor any fair be
held nor any goods or wares be exposed for sale therein
nor any bricks or tiles be made or burnt on the said
premises or any part thereof nor shall any building or
any part of the said premises at any time hereafter be
used as a Hospital Sanatorium or Asylum of any kind or
for Public Charitable or Religious purposes.'

It was a phrase such as the last (which may of course have been
the source of the Old Park Avenue covenants) that had required
Erskine Clarke to seek permission from the Estate for the building
of St Luke's church. The covenants also required that builder's
costs (not sale price) be at least £600 each for the semi-detached
houses, suggesting an intention to put Old Park Avenue near, but
not necessarily at, the top of the local housing market at that time.

Some other covenants were added for No. 18 whose lessees were
required to insure the property with North British and Mercantile
Insurance Company.

'Maintain hereafter obscure white glass on all the
lower sashes of windows of the back additions and
outbuildings and in both sashes of all windows lighting
he staircase, bathroom and wc or in the said back
additions and outbuildings and to paint in every fourth
year all outside and in every seventh year all inside
wood and coinwork twice over with proper oil colour
and to pay proportion of repairing Old Park Avenue
until taken to by Parish.'

The builders

Houses started being built in Old Park Avenue at the end of the 1880s and the development took place in two stages. The builder for 1-7 and 2-12 - that is most of that part of the road closest to Nightingale Lane -was Robert Francis Saker, who lived in Fentiman Road, Kennington. There is no record of him being active in house building in Battersea or Clapham before and indeed it was only in 1891 that he gave his occupation in the census as builder, In 1861 he had been a sawyer like his father; in 1871 he gave 'carpenter' as his profession; and in 1881 he described himself as 'carpenter/joiner'. This relative reticence was not uncommon and larger builders than he still described themselves as carpenter.

However, he was moving up the social scale. He had been living in a small house in Lyham Road just behind Clapham Park which was then in the Stockwell ward, but a road which Cubitt had been careful to keep separate from his own up-market development. In the early 1880s he moved to a three storey house at 199 Fentiman Road, Kennington, where he lived with his wife and two younger children, the youngest of whom, Herbert, was already a builder's assistant at 18. He could afford a live-in servant, perhaps helped by a medical student lodger, and also had a 'works' at Heyford works, Old South Lambeth Road. His finances were such that he had taken the trouble to make a will in 1889 which not only again described himself as a builder but made specific provisions for any buildings that he had on hand to be completed and then sold or mortgaged.

Although permission for the street had been granted on June 1 1888, it was some time before the houses were built to allow time for the demolition of Old Park itself. This also allowed the building of houses on the Nightingale Lane frontage on either side of the new road, which followed the drive up to the old house. These are now 32-36 Nightingale Lane on one side of Old Park Avenue and 38-40 on the other, although at the time they had names rather than numbers. They were all built by David Kettle. He had moved down from Scotland and was already established as one of the few local builders to have built over 100 houses between 1878 and1900. Half his output, 73 houses in all, was in South Battersea where he himself had first lived in Rossie House in Salcott Road (which he had built) before moving to 1 Vardens Road. He recorded himself as an employer in the 1881 Census.

He started with smaller houses in Salcott, Belleville and Bennerley roads, but gradually took on larger houses, building in Bolingbroke Grove, Hendrick and Thurleigh Roads. His application in May, 1890 to build the last two of the houses on the Nightingale Lane frontage of the Old Park estate made clear that they would use the Old Park Avenue sewer, then described in his application as a 'new road'. He must therefore have been engaged on these when Saker was building the first houses in Old Park Avenue.

The first ones built by Saker were two detached houses, 1 (Ill 54) and 7 and one pair of semi-detached, 3 and 5.

54: 1, Old Park Avenue built by Saker

Detailed designs for the road's layout and disposition of houses was provided for the developers by the architects N. S. Joseph and Smithem and it may be that the first houses were their design. An application for the next tranche, three pairs of semi-detached houses (2-12) on the other side of the street, followed on June 16, 1890. The street must have been in existence by 1891, because it is mentioned in the description of the relevant enumeration district of the Census although there is no record of any of the houses being in course of building. Saker put in an amended version of the drainage plans for 10-12 Old Park Avenue on 2 January 1893, describing them as 'in course of erection' and the Ordnance Survey map of 1894 shows these ten houses, so we can assume they were all complete by then. This comprised all the building in that part of the street before the bend in the road. At this stage the road had not been adopted by the local authority, and there was a covenant in the deeds to No. 3 requiring the lessee to contribute to the maintenance of the road in the meantime.

These houses appear to have been built with a view to letting them. The rate book shows Saker as the owner of No. 2 and that house was let very quickly – to Milton Bradford, a solicitor who had previously moved to Beckenham from Camberwell and who subsequently moved out of London in 1900 to combine being a Sussex farmer with his legal role. However, the others were owned by either (or both) of the two solicitors responsible for the development, Reuben Winder and William Palmer. The rate books over the next 15 years show a variety of combinations, both the two partners together or separately, and many changes between them. It is not clear whether this represents real changes, perhaps to balance the books between the two, or confused record keeping.

This part of the street filled up slowly although the house leased by Saker, No. 2, was occupied from 1891 and No. 7, Fairholme, has a date of 1891 on one of its walls. We do not know how fast the houses were built but the sale of the freehold of 1-6 and 8 (to E S Morphew) was only completed in 1894. Indeed we can only be sure that 3-6, 10 and 12 were occupied by 1894. 1896 saw 1, 7 and 8 occupied. This is captured in the table below.

Occupation of first houses in Old Park Avenue

House number	Drainage Application	Occupied
1	1890	1896
3	1890	1894
5	1890	1894
7	1890	1896
2	1890	1891
4-6	1890	1894
8	1890	1896
10-12	1892	1894

Source: Drainage applications and Rate Book

There were probably other short-term occupants, and it may well have taken a few months for occupation to be reflected in the various records. For example, it seems likely that Beaumont Grover, a printer, lived at 7 Old Park Avenue in 1897, because he gave that address on the baptismal certificate of his daughter who was baptised at St Luke's in 1897. But according to the various directories and rate books at the time, Mary Gilson was the occupier and it may have been that Grover preferred his children to be baptised in a more fashionable church than might otherwise have been available. It would appear that some houses (particularly the two detached ones, 1 and 7) either stayed empty or had a series of short tenancies until the road was complete, possibly because then, as now, people do not like living in or near a building site. On the other hand, the rateable values of the houses, supposed to be some reflection of the attractiveness of a house, started off at a relatively high value but decreased as the rest of the houses were built, ending up very much the same for all the houses, except No. 7. This is illustrated for typical houses below.

Rateable value (£)

House Number	1891	1896	1900	1910
2	70	70	63	42
4	-	53	46	42
12	-	55	50	42
26	-	-	44	46
1	-	50	50	50
7	-	63	63	59
15	-	-	44	46

Source: Ratebook

Robert Saker died in 1896 leaving £1,505 gross, nil net, but enough for his wife to continue living 'off her own means' in the same house. Winder therefore had to find another builder. David Kettle had recently completed the houses on the Nightingale Lane frontage of the Old Park grounds and would already have been well known to Winder. Kettle had also built Winder's own house in Bolingbroke Grove and had been a well established member of the Battersea Vestry, an important contact for a local solicitor. It is no

55: 30,32 Old Park Avenue

surprise therefore that the next tranche of building was undertaken by Kettle, who built the rest of the street with all his houses roughly the same pattern. (Ill 55)

As far as we know, the only difficulty encountered during construction was connected with the lily pond that had been in the gardens of Old Park. One of the tenants of the house had thought the pond unhealthy, and Erskine Clarke had agreed to it being filled up.

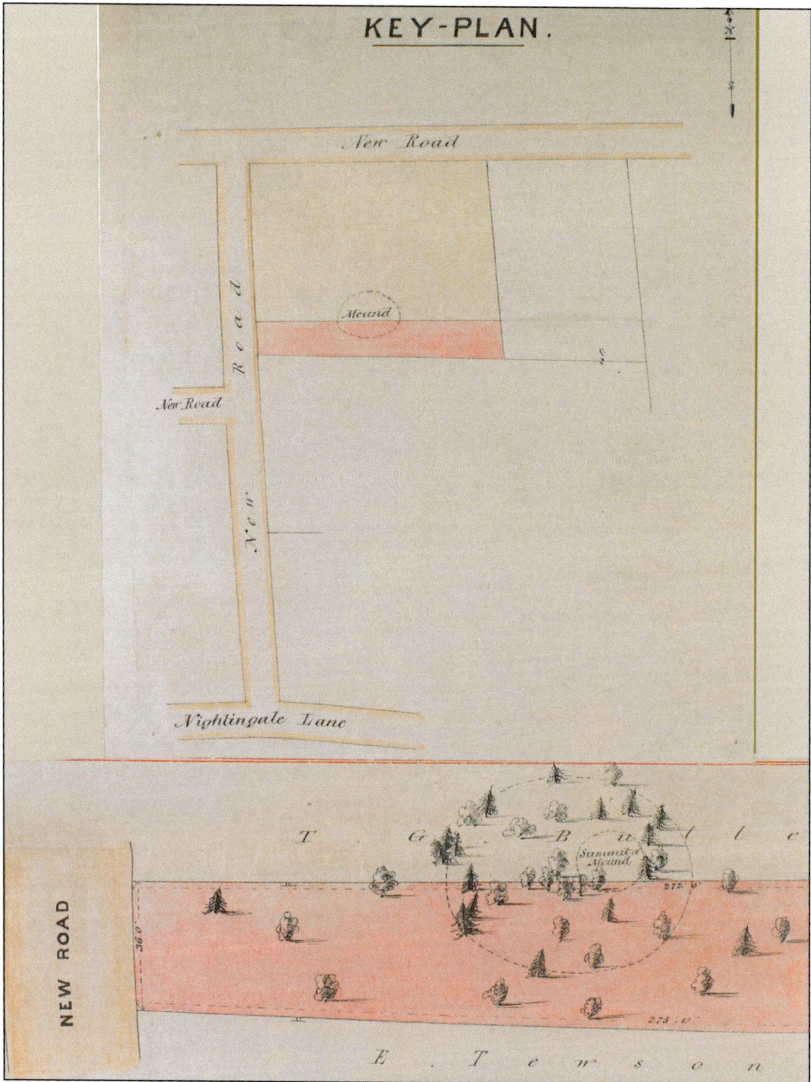

Map 19: Location of the mound

But the mound remained, with the ownership divided between Erskine Clarke and the developers of Old Park Avenue. Its exact location is shown in Map 19 which goes back to the early 1870s, just after Tom Simpson had taken a lease from Edward Tewson. Kettle found that the mound would have made impossible the building of the last four houses in Old Park Avenue, and asked Erskine Clarke's permission to remove it.

This, Erskine Clarke says in the Parish Magazine[5], he did with regret, 'for it was a picturesque feature, though we were sometimes afraid of adventurous boys tumbling into the pit at the top.' The deeds record the exchange of letters between Erskine Clarke and Winder who wrote explaining that 'As I understand it has now become the playground of children, it is desirable to remove it'. Erskine Clarke replied.

> 'I am not at all anxious for the removal of the ice mound. I have always rather liked it and have thought that when houses were built in Thurleigh Road at the South End of the Church, it would be a sort of finish to the garden.
>
> I hear that the trees on it are dying – the bigger ones – and so it will not be so picturesque as it once was, when it had the lake with water lilies at its base from which the earth had been dug which formed it.
>
> But I do not want to be seen unneighbourly, and if it is advantageous to you to remove it, I make no objection to your doing so at your cost, provided you put up a suitable fence along the boundary.'

Winder replied, thanking him for 'removing an annoyance of which they complain'. This correspondence, between the vicar and one of his former churchwardens, was cast in the most formal of terms, each referring to the other merely by 'Dear Sir'. The correspondence, of course, proceeded in all cases by return of post.

The mound and pond live on in another way by the creation, presumably by Erskine Clarke, of an additional restrictive covenant[6] still applying to those houses.

'Not to erect on any part of the hereditaments… within a distance of Twenty feet from the piece of land bounding the same on the north unless with the consent of the owner of such piece of land any building whatever except a lodge or cottage or any ornamental garden structure (every such building not being more that one storey in height)' and

As to the site of the mound (which is marked on the deeds)

'(Such mound having been levelled in or about the year 1898 with the consent of the person having the benefit of the following restrictive stipulations) Not to at any time hereafter build or erect or set up or cause or suffer to be built erected or set up upon the said mound or upon the slopes thereof or any part thereof any building or structure whatsoever except a fence only and not suffer any part of the said mound belonging to the covenanting parties to be used for any purpose whatsoever other than and except a portion of a pleasure ground garden or shrubbery'

There were also a series of difficulties with the fences on Nightingale Lane about which Kettle repeatedly clashed with the district surveyor. He wrote to Mr Pilditch on 19 October, 1891 reluctantly agreeing to move the fencing to a new position 'thereby adding considerably to the amount of land on Nightingale Lane agreed to be thrown onto the public highway.'[7]

The financial strategy and costs

Whatever the partners' financial strategy, they took the opportunity of refinancing their activity by selling the freehold of the houses, and hence the ground rents, as soon they had either tenants (the Saker houses) or had sold the leasehold (the Kettle houses). We know the freeholds were probably sold in four tranches[8] at different times.

Houses	Purchaser of freehold
1-5, 2-8,?10-12	E S Morphew
7,?14, 16	L M Langston, Clerk to Warden and Corporation of St Saviours, Southwark
9-23	Viscount Sidmouth
18, 22-36	Queen Anne's Bounty
20	F W Garston and Mrs E L Wheeler

The freehold produced an annual income per site of £10/10/-, again relatively high for the area where comparable ground rents were in the range of £6-9.

We do not know how much the first two tranches of ground rents realised, but the mortgage from Julia Palmer was repaid in March, 1896, about the time the sales must have been completed. The proceeds should have been enough either to pay for the land or to make a substantial contribution to the building costs.

The freehold of the 9 of the ten even numbered houses, built by Kettle 18 and 22-36, was sold five years later on March 1, 1900 to Queen Anne's Bounty, one of the predecessors of the Church Commissioners. The language of the time was to describe the price of ground rents in terms of the multiple of the annual rent to be paid. These prices followed the property and interest rate cycles and rose from an average of 26.2 years in 1892 to 30.6 in 1897, dropping steadily to 23.6 in 1912. After some negotiation, the Old Park Avenue houses were purchased at 29.5 years, a little below the peak value. They thus raised £2,781/15/-, or £309/15/- each, for what amounted by then to a lease of just under 90 years. The records of the Bounty still include individual files on each of the houses that they owned, with the correspondence about the ground rents and covenants running over a 50 year period. While there were a number of issues from time to time, there can be little doubt that the houses met the test set out earlier in Chapter 7 of being solid middle class houses with solid middle class occupants. The Bounty was clearly pleased with the purchase. Their surveyor reported.

'*The houses are semidetached and stand upon plots of land each having an average frontage of 27 feet to Old Park Avenue and a depth of about 100 feet.*

The buildings have an ornamental elevation of good design in red brick. Each house contains two good reception rooms, kitchen and usual offices on the ground floor, and five Bedrooms and Bathroom, Boxroom and wc on the upper floors. The interior of the houses are conveniently arranged and are being well finished off.

The houses are very attractive and quickly let or sell as they are finished or even before.'

Sale price of Old Park Avenue Houses

House Number	Date of first sale	Price (£)	Date from sale in Inland Revenue return	Price (£)
18	June 1897	610	July 1903	680
20			August 1897 (freehold)	1010
24	May 1898	615	July 1908	455
26	August 1898	659/10/-	April 1902	695
28	October 1898	625	August 1908	625
30	April 1899	665	April 1899	
32	December 1899	660		
34	September 1899	650		
36	June 1899	675		
3			October 1897	682
7			March 1900	575
17	July 1900	660		
19	November 1900	660		
21	December 1900	660	December 1904	555
23			December 1900	862

Source: Leases and Inland Revenue returns

The surveyor went on to recommend that Queen Anne's Bounty purchase the ground rents of the odd numbered houses being built opposite since he understood that the vendors would be prepared to do so once the leasehold interests were dealt with. In the event, Winder and Palmer declined to do this on the grounds that they wished to be able to give their lessees an option to acquire the freehold, if they wished it.

We also have records, from the Inland Revenue returns[9], of the early sale prices of the remaining leases on the houses.

Apart from 3 and 7, the sales up to 1900 appear to be the first transactions and this is confirmed by evidence from the deeds showing the original sale of No. 21 for £660, the same price as for 17 and 19. The sales shortly after of 26 and 18 allowed the owner of the lease to make a small profit, but subsequent prices were lower, possibly reflecting the reduced attraction of a house with a few years use, or in keeping with the general drop in the value of houses .[10] Prices fell by 20% to 40% between 1902 and 1912 as a result of falling demand, dearer money, and rising taxation. Although it is hard to make a direct comparison, the price of a pair of the Kettle built houses at £1,300-£1,320 is enough above the £1,200 minimum required by the restrictive covenant to have allowed some profit for the builder.

We can see that the freehold price of No. 20, one of the larger houses in the road, is compatible with the purchase price of the house plus the freehold of £307, roughly what the Bounty had paid for them. These prices can be compared with Inland Revenue estimates of the market value of the houses in about 1911. These ranged from £710 and £700 for 7 and 23 respectively, through to around £620-£645 for 1-5, 18-22, to about £560 for the rest. This gives a further example of the decline in value of houses over the first decade of the twentieth century. The market value of the land was estimated by the Inland Revenue at about £190 for all except No. 1 (£225), No. 7 (£240) and No. 23 (£240).

It is also clear that the two partners followed a different financial strategy for the Kettle built houses than for those built by Saker, possibly because they had found difficulty in letting the first houses. The first 10 houses stayed in their ownership for some years, but 99 year leases dating from Christmas 1889 (and in one case the freehold) on the later ones were sold as soon as the house was built, if not during construction, usually to the future occupier. This reduced their financial risk and it is possible this approach reflected the greater building experience of David Kettle. The following table relates the dates that the application was made to build the house to when the leases were signed and then when the house was occupied.

Progress with building and filling houses built by Kettle

House Number	Drainage Application	Lease Signed	Occupied
14-16	October 1894		1896
18	March 1896		1898
20	March 1896	October 1897	1898
22	November 1896	August 1897	1898
24	November 1896	May 1898	1899
26	October 1897	August 1898	1901
28	October 1897	October 1898	1901
30	April 1898	April 1899	1901
32	April 1898	December 1899	1901
34	April 1898	September 1899	1901
36	April 1898	June 1899	1901
9-11	July 1899	Owned by Kettle	1900
13-15	July 1899	Owned by Kettle	1900
17	July 1899	July 1900	1900
19	July 1900	November 1900	1900
21	June 1900	December 1900	1901
23	June 1900	December 1900	1901

Source: Drainage Applications, Leases, Rate Books

Although the freehold of one house, No. 20, had been sold, all the others were leased. Two were sold to the Trustees of St Saviours, shortly to be Southwark Cathedral. David Kettle kept a long lease on two of the houses that he had built (9 and 11) while only three of the other houses for which leases had been sold were not occupied by the leaseholder. Two of these were investment properties, owned respectively by a local solicitor and a retired hotel keeper living locally. The third had been bought by Charles Erskine Clarke's South African mother-in-law for him and his wife to live in while he was curate at St Luke's. Given it stayed in her ownership even when the couple had moved on, it may have been a convenient investment for her too. The original plan was to build two more houses, corresponding to what would have been 38 and 40, but Canon Erskine Clarke bought the freehold of the land from Palmer and Winder for £95 in May 1898 to be the garden of his new vicarage next the church hall in Ramsden Road.

56: View of Old Park Avenue c 1910

57: View of Old Park Avenue 2009

Who lived there?

Tarmac was not laid on the road until 1906 and Ill 56, showing the Kettle built houses, demonstrates how it looked in about 1910. The modern equivalent is Ill 57.

Wandsworth Council describes the road in its conservation area statement.

> 'Its character is very distinctive and very different from anything which surrounds it. The houses are high in relation to the road's width and this leads to a feeling of enclosure, especially compared to the areas nearby. This is magnified by the street trees which tend to fill the available space. Narrow, luxuriantly planted front gardens provide another layer of green. The red brick houses have excellently proportioned facades, good details and are in largely original condition.'

Walter Besant[11] also commented favourably in 1912.

> 'To the South at Thurleigh Road, the square red brick tower of St Luke's Battersea is seen with good open ground opposite and at Old Park Avenue there are several good houses through to Nightingale Lane.'

But what kind of person lived in Old Park Avenue? The houses were close to the top of the range for the neighbourhood with, in modern terms, six good bedrooms, high ceilings and large reception rooms. But they were not unique and there are other houses which are roughly the same size and some, in Nightingale Lane or the top of Thurleigh Road, that are bigger. Certainly, the houses were too small to attract the really well-off middle class.

Consider the costs and hence the finances of the likely occupants. Much was written in the nineteenth century about how much income was required to be able to marry and The Times conducted a lively debate in 1858 on the question of whether one could marry on £300 a year. The answer naturally depended on the style which was expected. The life of the middle class was crucially dependent on servants who ran the complicated arrangements required in the larger houses. The number of servants in Victorian Britain has often been called phenomenal. About one in five families had at least one servant. In the 1890s a peak was reached with about 16% of the working population in England and Wales in service, whereas in 1851 it had 'only' amounted to 13%. In London, female servants numbered 15% of the whole population. The growth reflected increased affluence and hence increased numbers of the servant-employing classes. As more alternative employment was created, often of a much more attractive nature, it became more difficult to find servants and they became more expensive. The border line between servant keeping families and those who had none rose from an annual family income of about £200 in the 1850s to about £300, which had previously been enough to have two servants at the end of the century. By then three servants would have cost three times the £30-60 of the 1850s, and Mrs Beaton reckoned an income of £1000 was needed for that level of service.

This was the income that Mrs Panton[12], writing in the later editions of her book in 1897, probably had in mind at least as a realistic aspiration for the future.

> 'As a rule, the ordinary bride begins her married life with a small establishment of two maids..... If Angelina really intends to marry on an income varying between £300 and £500, she must sit down and weigh the pros and cons very seriously.'

And commenting on dowries[13]

> 'I very much myself disapprove of the way middle class parents have of marrying off their daughters and giving them nothing but their trousseaux. It would not hurt any father to give his daughter £50 a year and would not be more than half what she would cost him were she to remain on his hands a sour old maid.'

Even so, the trousseau was not to be disparaged since[14] '[The] underlinen in her trousseau should last her ten or twelve years at least, and with ordinary care her trousseau dresses, with judicious management, last her quite two years'.

There was a fairly well accepted ratio of rent to income for the middle class, recognizing that the vast majority, even of the better off, still rented. This ranged from rent (or more usually rent and taxes) being between one tenth and one eighth of income. The proportion was often much higher for those with less money, although they did not have servants to pay, having to do all the work themselves.

However, not everyone had to live up to Mrs Panton's standards, which involved shopping in Bond Street, at Liberty and Co, or at Hampton's in Pall Mall. In 1899, Mrs Praga produced her guide entitled, 'Appearances. How to keep them up on a limited income'[15], in which she described what was claimed as her own experience of living on £300 a year. In the guide, having rejected their parents' proposal of Bedford Park as a place to live on the grounds that it was 'too far off and too dull for anyone to come and see them', the Pragas claimed to have found a house in West Kensington – with easy access to cheap good shopping in King Street, Hammersmith. It was quite a large house with four floors including a basement and, by agreeing to take the house for twenty one years (with break points) rather than three, they negotiated the rent down from £50 to £40 and were successful in reducing the rates and taxes to £15. Mrs Praga recruited a fourteen year old maid from the local orphanage and trained an eighteen year old as her cook, so getting her two servants for £15 which compensated for the relatively high rent as a proportion of income. She managed her clothes on £25 a year giving her husband a little more. The house was furnished for a hundred guineas. This was very different from Mrs Panton's advice[16].

> *'I think I may state boldly that a house cannot be furnished at all under £150.... A man may dress himself well on £40 a year, and a woman can do likewise on £70, but this requires, in both cases, the most careful management, while the average cost of a child is from £10 to £15.'*

Against this background and using the lower estimates from Mrs Praga, we can estimate what the expenses and hence the income must have been for those who moved into Old Park Avenue.

	£
Rent (or mortgage)	50
Rates and taxes	15-20
Two servants	40-45
Coal	12
Gas	8

All this points to an income of over £500 a year unless they had accumulated enough capital to purchase the lease outright.

It is difficult to match up exactly the occupations given in the 1901 Census with the current ABC1 breakdown. But what seems clear is that the occupants, while clearly reasonably comfortably off, would hardly now be described as upper middle class. They were mid-ranking civil servants, retired ship's captains, retailers, a bank manager, a builder and builders' merchant and curates of the local church, St Luke's. There were four ladies, whether widowed or spinsters, 'living off own means' and a range of professionals, such as the father of the humorist, Stephen Potter, a chartered accountant in a small London practice, three engineers and a surveyor. But there was also a piano tuner, a science lecturer and a journalist/author. The only solicitor to live in Old Park Avenue during the early days was the first occupant of the road, Milton Bradford. He was the only one of the nine households who lived in Old Park Avenue before 1901 not already living in the area, apart from a series of St Luke's curates[ii] staying in 6 Old Park Avenue.

As we would expect, only four of the households in 1901 had no live-in servant recorded in the census, although obviously that does not rule out either their having been away that night or there being servants who came for the day. Of the 26 houses that had servants, 14 had one, eleven had two and one had three. Generally, if there was one servant, they were described as 'general domestic', while if there were two, one would be a 'housemaid' and the other either a 'cook' or a nurse for small children, although in one house the two servants were described as 'useful help'. All the servants were women with ages ranging from 14 to 34; 15 of them were under 21, with six

[ii] Frank Bell, Arthur Powell, and Percy Tomkins

of these under 18. In any household, the cook was always older than the housemaid and tended to be in her mid twenties or early thirties. The only exceptions to this were the two curates living in the roads, whose cooks were only 18 and 19, and one of whom also employed the 14 year- old housemaid.

Unsurprisingly,there were few young heads of household in 1901, only two under 30 and another five in their thirties; well over half were between 40 and 59. In this they were more like the occupants of Thurleigh and Gorst than Hillier or Wroughton Roads. But a large majority of the occupants had an association with the area, perhaps stemming from Winder's involvement in St Luke's. This was particularly true of the younger ones. Charles Erskine Clarke was curate at St Luke's where his uncle was the vicar; Patrick Milln[iii], a stockbroker and owner of the first car in Old Park Avenue according to Stephen Potter, had married on 15 April 1899 Blanche Drake, the daughter of James Drake. He was a former churchwarden of St Luke's and the then current owner of Beecholme, the house next to Old Park and the last big house to be sold for building. William Laurence's parents in law lived in Clapham and later moved to 120 Nightingale Lane where the two families moved in together

Half the adults living in Old Park Avenue in 1901 were born in central London. 16 of the households had moved from nearby roads and only 11 from some distance. Even of those 11, one of the spouses had been born in South London. Another, Eva Bayne in 34 Old Park Avenue, had been given the house as a wedding present by her uncle, the Cornish philanthropist Passmore Edwards, who for some time had lived off Lavender Hill. Five of the families had a naval or shipping connection and four of those had been born and lived in Devon. Many of the families had lived abroad. There was a retired Indian civil servant, born in India like many of his children; one woman had been born on a sheep farm in Australia; others had been born in South Africa, New Zealand, Chile, Jersey or Ireland. Two thirds of the servants had been born in central London and 12 of them had come from the immediate vicinity; others were from the Home Counties, and one 17 year old housemaid was from Gloucestershire.

[iii] He was, presumably, a member of the Milln family of the stockbroking firm Savory Milln.

The occupiers also illustrated the new household structure that was emerging at the turn of the century. The vast majority were nuclear families with parents and children only, apart from servants. Only six of the households in 1901 were more extensive, including two mothers, one aunt, one sister and two brothers, In total, excluding visitors and taking account of those whom we know were away on census night, there were:

Adults   62,   of whom 6 were 60-70 and 3 were over 70
Children 63,   of whom 9 were over 21 and 4 over 18
Servants 38,   of whom15 were under 21

In many cases, there were other adult children who were now making their own way in life and children continued to be born in the road, with a number being baptised in St Luke's, five up to 1901 and 14 between 1901and 1914. Elder children were catered for as well with eight weddings up to 1914. The children seem to have gone to private schools of which there was a large number locally since there is no evidence of any of them attending the local state schools. That was certainly true for Stephen Potter who went to the junior part of Clapham and Streatham (a Girls Public Day School Trust school for girls that took younger boys up to 10 years), then to Rillo Road Preparatory School, and then on to Westminster. (Stephen claimed to be able to get from his bed to Westminster School in about half an hour by public transport.) Education was clearly important to people in the road because at least three of the children went to Oxbridge, including two girls which was unusual in those days.[iv]

The general pattern of occupation was maintained in the 1911 census which confirms the results obtained from other information but gives some greater detail. Two of the houses were empty on census night, with one of them occupied by a caretaker and his family. Even so the total number of occupants decreased from 163 to 140. Only two houses had boarders. The table below gives more information.

[iv] Stephen Potter's sister, Muriel, got a first in English at St Hugh's, Oxford and, having been senior English mistress at St Paul's, became in 1927 the youngest headmistress in the country, aged 33, and was largely responsible for establishing the reputation of South Hampstead High School.

Age of occupants of Old Park Avenue in 1901 and 1911

Year	21-59	60-70	70+	total	0-18	18-21	21+	total	14-18	18-21	21+	total
1901	51	6	3	62	47	4	12	63	5	11	22	38
1911	56	4	1	60	29	5	15	49	2	2	27	31

Source: 1901 and 1911 census

There were considerably fewer children in 1911 than in 1901 with slightly more adult children living with their parents. The number of servants was also reduced with many fewer below 21 years old.

These patterns continued over the next 10-15 years up to the First World War. During that period 24 new families moved into Old Park Avenue and only three were from outside the immediate locality. Some of them had already had children baptised at St Luke's and their occupations were the same mixture of civil servants, drapers, commercial travellers and retailers. Most of them moved to the street in their forties and many stayed for a long time. In some cases, it looks as though they may have moved on the recommendation of former neighbours. For example, four families moved from Morella Road to Old Park Avenue; three moved from Lynette Avenue. In some cases those moving in were related to each other. George Young, a cane/fibre merchant like his father, moved from the family home at 21 Macaulay Road to rent No. 7 from 1905 to 1915 and was the first person to have a telephone (BAT 824) in Old Park Avenue in 1905. His sister Emily moved into No 1. in 1910 and her widowed sister Eleanor Phillips, nephew James, and cousin Nellie Hussey moved in not long after and stayed there until 1932 when both Emily and Eleanor died.

Marie Stead, who had been living at 186 Ramsden Road moved into 4 Old Park Avenue in 1897, perhaps to be near her daughter Emilie (or Emily), married to Captain Francis Seymour, who had rented No. 5 in 1894. Marie Stead was a widow living off her own means but had an adventurous life. Born in Dublin in 1825 she married an older man, David Stead, in 1851 and left for Australia where her first child, Emilie, was born in Victoria. Marie returned to Ireland where five other children were born and by 1871 was living in Hastings with her husband and six children. He described himself as a retired sheep farmer, and Marie and her eldest daughter described themselves in the census as 'Lady'. David died in 1886 and by then most of the children had left home. In 1891, Emilie, whose husband was away at sea a large part of the year, was living in a mews in Paddington with her two children, Valetta and Norah, and her youngest sister, Alberta. The Seymours clearly liked Old Park Avenue and moved into Marie Stead's house No. 4 in 1901 when she moved to No. 2 before leaving the street later that year. They stayed there until 1908 when Francis retired and they moved to Christchurch in Hampshire. The Seymours and Steads were not the only family to move between houses in the road. Edwin and Louisa Davis rented No. 3 from 1901-1910 and then moved to No. 6 where they lived for another three years before moving to No. 30 in 1914. This had been vacated by the Gamble family which had rented it for six years when the original lessee, a widow, Mrs Ann Cooper, moved to Tulse Hill. Mrs Cooper continued to let the property to Edwin Davis, a bank manager who finally bought the lease when she died in 1918, staying until 1932.

Regular movement between houses was a feature of the time. At the turn of the century, no more than 10% of houses were owner occupied, ie the occupier held a long lease or the freehold. Better houses would usually be taken on a three year lease, and the rent on cheaper houses would be paid on a monthly or even weekly basis. Nor was this necessarily seen as a bad thing, given the desire, or need, of families to move regularly as made clear by Charles Booth[17].

> 'The system of three year leases is objected to as unsettling to the lives of tenants, as well as tending to division of interest between landlord and tenant. But the system has its good points; it fits in with the recurring incidents in the life of a house as well as with the changing circumstances of the occupants. Every three years the rooms require to be papered and painted and done up, and this term is as long as can be looked forward to by most tenants. In three years there may be one or two more children; in three years there may have been a rise in salary; in three years the elder children may be at work, or gone to live elsewhere, or a son or daughter may be married. It is felt that it is well to be free.'

In the same vein, The Builder[18] argued against a proposal in 1899 to allow local authorities to finance the purchase of small houses.

> 'Moreover after all is there any great advantage to a poor
> man in being the owner of a poor house. We are inclined
> to think he can be better off if he can move from house
> to house as he wishes.'

In contrast to Booth's analysis, the pattern in Old Park Avenue, with regard to both tenure and movement was substantially different. Overall, the road started out at about 50% owner occupation, a very much higher percentage than seen in the other roads in South Battersea. The houses fall into a number of groups and we will deal with them in order of complexity. Those built by Kettle are the simplest and can be classified by the owner of the freehold who was entitled to the ground rents.

8 houses	9-23	freeholder Viscount Sidmouth
9 houses	18, 22-36	freeholder Queen Anne's Bounty
1 house	20	freeholder F W Garston and Mrs E L Wheeler
2 houses	14, 16	freeholder Langton St Saviours Southwark

The last were the first to be built by Kettle and, were occupied before the others in 1896. (We do not as yet have evidence that the freehold of No. 16 was owned by St Saviours, but it seems likely as this was true of the only other Kettle built house which became occupied in 1896) The Rate Book shows that both of these houses were occupied initially by the owner of the lease. John Cleminson owned No. 14 and lived in it for eight years until 1904. Arthur Eagleston rented it from 1905-1915, When John died in 1908, Mrs Cleminson became the owner until 1920 when the then tenant Horace Howlett bought the lease. Howlett and his family lived in the house until his daughter Mabel died in 1975, aged 88. The history of No. 16 is similar; Edward Buley bought the lease and lived in the house from 1896-1903 when he let it to Alfred Levet who had bought it by 1910 and whose children were still living in the house at the start of the Second World War.

As for No. 20, it is not clear who Mr Garston and Mrs Wheeler were. Their ownership was sometimes exercised through a local solicitor, R W Duncan, but they never lived in the house. The Rev George Ryley was the first tenant and apparently had good private means and lived there from 1897-1903. He had been a Congregational Minister but then took Anglican orders. According to Erskine Clarke, he had been going to St Mark's, Kennington, but, by mistake, took a house near Clapham Common which the bishop said was too far from his work. Erskine Clarke[19] took him on 'although he was over 50' but although he regarded him as 'a very good and able man and an exceptional preacher, he could not put him in charge of a Battersea parish as he has not had the sort of training which a large knockabout parish requires.' The house was rented for at least the first 35 years of its life with apparently one long empty period from 1910-14 according to the Rate Book, although the 1911 Census shows a married couple living in the house.

The rest of the houses on the even side follow the same pattern. All but one were purchased by the first occupants who with two exceptions lived in the house for some time, three for over 25 years and one for almost 40. Even the house (No. 26) which was sold quickly then stayed in the same family for the next 70 years. It was bought by Lydia Young, the wife of a retired bank clerk, who had two daughters, Mabel and Ella. Lydia died in 1910 and her husband Frederick not long after. The daughters stayed on, at some time changing their name to Robson-Young, possibly because of the involvement of George Gibson Robson, a leather currier[v] who lived in Trinity Road and appears to have taken temporary ownership of the house as executor after the two parents had died. Mabel moved away first to work as a governess and then in 1921 to South Kensington but Ella lived in the same house until 1972, when she died aged 92.

The road must have had an attraction for that generation. The owner of No. 22, Frederick Hudson, rented the house for 23 years

---

[v] Currying is the process of stretching and finishing leather, ready for the saddler or cobbler.

to the Presbury family, but then passed it on to his elder son, also Frederick, from 1935 until the war. He then returned to live in the house himself until 1949 with his younger son Louis and Louis' wife who stayed until 1955. No 28. was owned first by the retired boarding house keeper, Uriah Hucknall, who married his first wife when he was butler and she was lady's maid to the vicar of Harrow. He rented it out for the first twenty years and it was then bought by the Roberts brothers in 1919 and lived in by them and their families until 1948,

No. 24 appears to be the only case of the Bounty enforcing any of the covenants. Isabel Herbert had assigned the lease to her children Alice and Edwin in 1906 when she moved out to Westcliffe on Sea. Shortly afterwards the estate agent John Dean wrote to the Bounty saying:

> 'They had found a purchaser for No 24 who is a designer/maker of tea gowns who would purchase if she could be allowed to continue her work privately. No plate of any description would be shown and can assure you that it would be in no way detrimental to other property in the road. Considering there would be no sign whatever of the business being carried on, would you under the circumstances grant a licence, upon terms of course?'

By return of post the magisterial answer came.

> 'The Governors' solicitor thinks the designing and making of dresses is a trade or business; and the Governors are precluded by the restriction contained in the conveyance to them from giving their consent.'

Kettle himself retained the freeholds of two of the houses that he had built,9 and 11, and they were rented at least until the 1930s, although the long leases were bought by Abraham Putley, a retired butcher living in Camberwell. Putley must have had a long standing interest in Old Park Avenue because his daughter was married from No. 32 in 1905. All but one of the remaining houses, 13-23, were owner occupied and continued to be so with only one of the first owners moving out before 1914. The one rented house was No. 19 which, as we have seen had been bought for Charles Erskine Clarke, curate of St Luke's and his wife, Amy. The purchaser, Amy's mother, the South African Mrs Warleigh, moved in with them in 1911. Charles remained there when he became Vicar of St Luke's in 1914, since his uncle remained in his splendid vicarage. The house was rented for many years after Charles moved to his new post as Vicar of St John's Redhill in 1924.

The Saker houses, in spite of being generally larger and the first built, have a more chequered history. Their freeholds (except for No. 7 which, as we have seen, was sold to St Saviours Southwark) were sold to Edward Morphew, a woollen merchant from Croydon who died in 1912. Saker kept No. 2 but the other leases continued to be owned by the partnership of Winder and Palmer. Evidently they were designed to be let, but while Saker let No. 2 very quickly, the partnership appears to have had some problems with letting the others. The even number houses only moved into owner occupation very gradually. Parr, a retired Principal Clerk in the Inland Revenue, moved from Lynette Avenue to buy No. 2, lived there for 10 years, and then let it to Annie Southworth who then sold her lease to Amy Evans who lived there for a long time. Frank Bodger bought No. 4 sometime in the 1910s, living there for 18 years before moving on. No. 6 was rented until the son of the solicitor, George Nichols, who owned it, moved in after his father's death. No. 8 remained rented, the same family staying there until 1963. 10 and 12 went through many tenants until bought by their respective occupiers from Palmer in the twenties. Again their families stayed in the houses until the late nineteen forties.

The Saker odd-numbered houses again were rented for a long time with a number of vacancies, although No. 3 was sold to another local solicitor in 1907. No. 1 was bought in 1920 by Emily Young who had already lived there for ten years and would live there for another 14, but No. 3 (rented first by the Potters) and No. 5 remained rented. No. 7, the biggest house in the road, was bought by the Cottrells in 1918 (building their garage in 1921, the only one in the road) and they lived there for 14 years.

The overall picture, as we would expect, is that there is greater turnover in the rented houses and a greater likelihood of vacancies, although the vacancies may only be apparent because rapid movement in accommodation is less likely to leave its mark in rate books and electoral registers. The houses which were owner occupied had on average 2.7 different occupants in the 40-45 years of the houses up to the start of the Second World War, while those that were largely rented had an average of five occupants. The average stay of the first occupant was seven years for rented and 15 for owner occupied.

Old Park Avenue was well connected with St Luke's Church just round the corner. Charles Erskine Clarke, the Canon's nephew, was by no means the only curate to live there; at least three others rented houses in the road. Stephen Potter makes clear that St Luke's played a major part in his family's life, if not always for Stephen himself. Frank Potter was honorary auditor to the Parish Council and also served several stints as churchwarden, including an unprecedented stretch of three consecutive years from 1913 to 1915 when he was given responsibility for leading the campaign to raise over £600 to renovate the organ. Stephen recalls[20] 'The Potter family had a good pew, next the aisle three rows from the front. We all felt some pride in each other. I was certainly proud of Father on these occasions, quite at home in his churchwarden's frock coat.' So it is no surprise that Potter says[21]'Edwardian social life for me was connected mostly with St Luke's Church and the Vicarage, the boundaries of which began just beyond our back garden.'

In all cases, Old Park Avenue houses appear to have remained in single occupation, albeit with some extended families, until after the First World War and were occupied by those in comfortable circumstances, albeit by no means in the upper reaches of the middle class. We will study the trends over a longer period in a later chapter but in the first two decades of the twentieth century, there was a slight increase in owner occupation from 42% in 1900 to 53% in 1920 and a small increase in the age of the head of household,

Age of head of household

Year	20s	30s	40s	50s	60s	70s	Average
1901	2	4	11	8	4	1	46
1905	0	3	8	11	4	2	51
1910	0	5	13	7	3	1	49
1915	0	3	11	6	6	1	52
1920	1	1	9	9	6	3	53

Source: Census and Rate books

It is also clear that people stayed in the houses for some time. By 1911, a third of the houses had been lived in by the same family for 10 years, rising to over a half by 1921, with six of the households (20%) having lived in the same house for 20 years.

It is not always easy to determine where former occupants of Old Park Avenue moved to but it seems to have followed the normal pattern from an early stage. People were leaving for the outer suburbs from as early as the 1890s. Milton Bradford moved to Sussex in 1900. A few moved back into London, but these were usually those with money and business connections, such as the stockbroker Patrick Milln who moved to Kensington. Few moved to larger houses in the area although one such was George Young who moved from No. 7 to Stanton House in Nightingale Lane, living there between 1916 and 1925.

Parkstone, or as we know it, 40 Nightingale Lane, became in 1910 the home of the cartoonist and observer of suburban life, H M Bateman, who moved there with his parents from 2 Bonneville Road in Clapham where he had lived since 1905. It was a much larger house and gave him a good large studio for his drawing and was in a more 'desirable' position[22]. He used the people of Clapham as sources for his cartoons of suburbia, for example the series published in The Sketch, 'Outside the Four-Mile Radius: Suburbia'. Bateman's family left Clapham early in the First World War when their fear of bombing caused them to move to Bromley.[vi] [vii]He lived in a number of places in Chelsea and moved out to Reigate with his mother when she separated from his father in 1921.

Further evidence about the people who lived in the road can be obtained from a study of the design of the houses, both exterior and interior, and this is considered in the next chapter. The remaining history of the street up to the present will be continued in chapters 11 and 12.

[vi] This may appear surprising to us, but in the event there were a series of Zeppelin attacks on Clapham Common.

[vii] Another effect of the war was the desire to change names to eliminate any thought of connection with Germany. The most well known of these was of course the change of the Royal family name to Windsor, or the Battenbergs to Mountbatten, but there was also an example in Old Park Avenue. Sidney Presburg, whose mother Emily came from East Prussia, changed his family name to Presbury in 1916.

(Endnotes)

1   A Offer. Property and Politics 1870-1914 p 14
2   James Dodd 1914 quoted by Offer p 14
3   A Offer. Ibid p 144
4   Old Park Avenue Deeds
5   St Luke's Parish Magazine
6   Deeds to No 36 Old Park Avenue
7   Letter in Wandsworth Historical Library
8   Inland Revenue IR58 and Old Park Avenue deeds
9   Inland Revenue IR58
10 A. Offer. Ibid p 308
11 Walter Besant. 1912 London South of the Thames p 240
12 Mrs J E Panton. 1897 From Kitchen to Garrett p 18
13 Mrs Panton. Ibid p 36
14 Mrs Panton. Ibid p 262
15 Mrs Alfred Praga. 1899 Appearances. How to keep them up on a limited income.
16 Mrs Panton. Ibid p 260
17 Charles Booth. 1900 Life and Labour in London Religious Influences Vol 5 p 187
18 The Builder. 22 April 1899 p 353
19 Letter from Rev Clarke to Earl Spencer May 1 1901
20 Stephen Potter. 1959 Steps to Immaturity. p 67
21 Stephen Potter. Ibid p 48
22 Anthony Anderson. 1982 The Man who was H M Bateman p 51

CHAPTER 10

THE HOUSES – INTERIOR AND EXTERIOR

Having got an idea of who lived in Old Park Avenue, we now move to the houses themselves. We have seen who lived there originally, but what kind of people were they actually designed and built for? How do they compare with others nearby? Was their decoration typical for the time? We are helped by the fact that many of the houses still retain a high proportion of their original internal and external features so we have good evidence of how they looked 100 years ago, apart from more ephemeral internal decoration such as paint and wallpapers.

Even though some of the houses were not occupied until 1901, they are not Edwardian. They were conceived in the late 1880s and early 1890s, and the essential design even of the later Kettle houses was finalised by 1893. They are late Victorian with their design having been chosen for occupants likely to have been interested at the start of the last decade of the nineteenth century. Helen Long[1] makes the point that house styles remained fundamentally market led and the conservatism of both the market and the builders meant that design was always at least one step behind the latest fashion.

What the market wanted was privacy - from the outside world, from servants and from other members of the family. This preoccupation underpinned the architects' design of the interaction of the exterior with the outside world as well as the internal layout of the rooms, and even how the doors opened. As Donald Olsen[2] points out, we find frequent praise in the various guides to suburban London for an area's withdrawn seclusion and privacy, but never for its lively social life or its abundant community activities. Building News commented in 1885[3] that 'A certain amount of retirement and seclusion is…. necessary for the resident middle class.' and Robert Kerr, Professor of the Arts of Construction at Kings College, London, told the RIBA in 1894 that[4],

'The English idea of domestic comfort depended very much on privacy, especially as to the complete separation of the family from the servants .... The family as one class demanded and were entitled to their own privacy, and the servants as another class demanded as were entitled to theirs.'

Jenni Calder sums this up[5],

'Even that housing that came a long time after the death of Victoria tends to have a Victorian flavour, not necessarily in design, but in reflection of life style. It radiates a life style that is inward, well ordered, or aspiringly well ordered, behind closed doors, conformist, divided from business and trade – and usually at a distance from shops – by gardens and hedges if possible, and by a general air that life depends on the solidity of brick and the quality of curtains. The Victorian middle class home did not like to be looked in upon.'

As with most things at that time, the housing market was very clearly stratified. Maitland, writing a manual for building estates[6], drew the simple distinction, 'terraces for the working classes, villas for the better classes'. A more elaborate classification was set out almost thirty years ago by Stefan Muthesius[7].[i] The incomes and costs are indicative only and correspond roughly to the last quarter of the nineteenth century.

---

[i] Stefan Muthesius is the architectural historian, a great nephew of Hermann Muthesius, the German architect quoted in the introduction and later in this chapter.

The Muthesian classification of socio-economic classes and their houses

Very wealthy	income £3,000-£5,000+, houses costing up to £5000 and more with rents of £500+. Twenty rooms and up to twelve servants
Rich	income of £1,000+, houses costing £1000-£3,000 to build and at least £100 to rent. Fifteen rooms with butler, cook and two maids and servant quarters
Professional	income £500-£700 with a house worth £1,000 and rent of up to £100. This would have ten rooms kept by three servants but no special provision for servants
Higher clerks	earning about £350, renting a £500 house at £40-£60. Seven to eight rooms and one or two servants
Lower clerks, shopkeepers	earning about £200, living in a six to seven room house costing £200-£300, with one maid and paying £25-£45 rent
Lowest-paid clerks	earning £100-£150 renting a five to six room house costing £120-£200 for £12-£30 rent and with occasional help but no live in servant

Clearly, the the ordinary terraced house does not meet the requirements of Muthesius's top two grades. If houses are not detached, they must either be double fronted or they must have more than two or three floors, or probably both. The larger houses in Nightingale Lane would meet the 'rich' category, but even the original Old Park itself would barely make the 'very wealthy' grade; this would be reserved for mansions such as Battersea Rise House.

We know that there had been a desire to maintain the standards of intended occupants in roads in the original Old Park Estate, expressed both by excluding terrace houses (lived in then by 90% of the London population) and imposing a minimum cost for the house. Old Park Avenue houses, at six bedrooms in modern parlance, were larger at the time than any in the neighbourhood except for Nightingale Lane, some in Rusham and Blenkarne Roads and some of the houses built later at the top end of Thurleigh Road. The effect of the covenants is also seen by the fact that all pre second war houses built on the Old Park Estate are semi-detached or detached.

By contrast, apart from a small proportion of the houses on the Dents Estate, virtually all the other housing in South Battersea is terraced.

To see how the housing needs set out in Muthesius' classification were met, we need to look a little at the history of the Victorian design. In the first half of the nineteenth century, houses were flat-fronted and generally with two rooms each the width of the house on every floor, including the basement. The larger houses, for the wealthier, had more floors although only the servants would be required to go from top to bottom. The kitchen was usually in the basement and the 'ground' floor often somewhat above ground level allowing more light into the rooms and indeed allowing a window into the cellar. The challenge for builders and architects then became to grapple with the challenge of creating more space on fewer floors while still letting in more light.

In the second half of the nineteenth century, a new design emerged. It had at most a small cellar under the hall and no basement. This meant that the kitchen had to be on the ground floor and therefore necessitated a larger overall footprint. But the economics of land division and development prevented making the house any wider. The only solution was to build further back, but this could not be across the whole width of the house because any room in the middle would then not receive natural light. The solution was to build an extension across part of the rear of the house, thereby still allowing a window for the back room and creating what was called the back addition, usually two steps lower than the rest of the house. A scullery and outdoor toilet were often added onto the kitchen.

For both terraced and semi-detached houses, the back additions of adjoining houses were built together to give greater stability. In terraces, but not necessarily for semi-detached houses, the front doors were placed next to each other either side of the party wall with the stairs, halls and passages running through to the back addition, helping to minimise noise on one side at least but creating a long and often dark passage. A further innovation, generally introduced in the 1880s, was to have lower ceilings in the back addition which, by taking in some of the roof space, created the capacity for a partial third storey and so an additional bedroom. Thus was created the three-up, three-down house with its slightly larger cousin with two and a half storeys and seven rooms. These became the standard houses built by speculative builders. They did however maintain the Victorian principle of segregating the various functions and users of the rooms which were themselves differentiated in size and decoration.

In the middle of the century the abolition of both the window tax and the duty on glass helped to reduce the price of glass to a third of its previous value. The ready availability of cheap sheet glass made it possible to have large windows, even though they were sometimes criticised for reducing the privacy of the house, thereby increasing the need for the protection provided by front gardens. Cheap glass assisted the revival of the bay window in the 1860s which was also stimulated by the desire for fresh air, particularly in seaside towns. The bay window, usually angled rather than the square more typical of the Edwardian period and often extending upwards to the first floor as well, was seen as a sign of respectability, distinguishing the house from a flat fronted working class terrace. The resulting floor plans are shown in Illus 58.

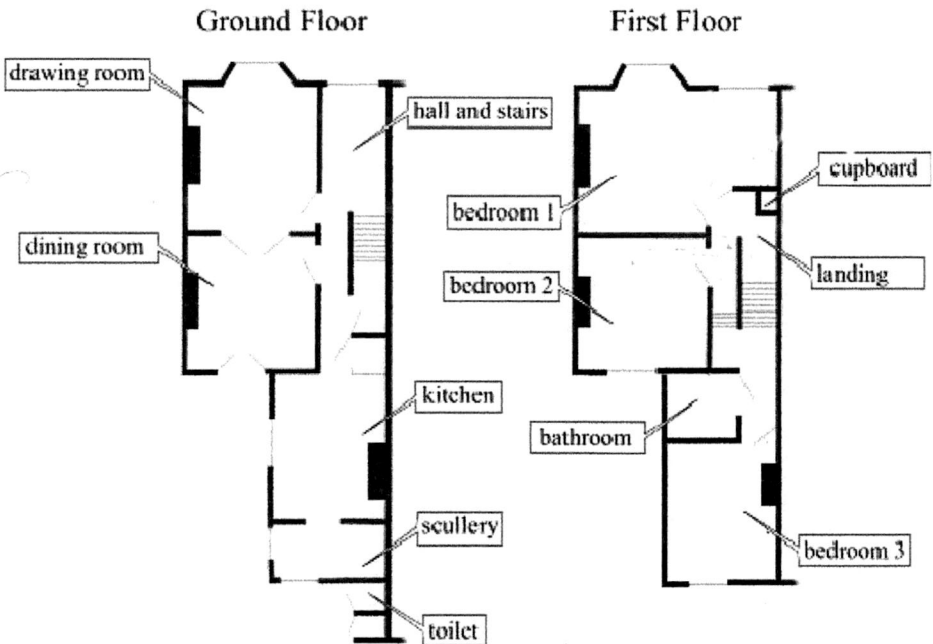

58: Floor plans

But while the bay window also introduced extra light (and fresh air) into the front rooms and made the rooms larger, John Burnett has pointed out that they provided an invitation to prying eyes and the possibility of the sunlight fading the carpets and upholstery required screening by inner curtains and floral displays. The standard designs of housing (including those in Old Park Avenue) preferred to have the top sash windows divided into four parts (lights) to create a 'cosy' look. Houses such as these, with variations, were built in South Battersea and fill the roads 'Twixt the Commons'.

There were also changes in the exterior design of terrace housing. Pevsner characterises South London housing as 'built to humdrum pattern-book recipes' as having 'their inevitable bay-window, exposed eaves, Welsh slate roofs, and fussy composition stone doorways'. Dixon and Muthesius identify such bays as characteristically having piers and capitals enriched with naturalistic leaf carving supporting lintels of stone, representing a Gothic parentage. There are many examples of this around South Battersea. Pevsner describes the houses in Honeywell Road as having characteristically elaborate brickwork and barge-boarded gables (Ill59).

59: Barge boarding in Honeywell Road

The vast majority of the earlier houses are built of stock brick or sometimes with the front faced in gault bricks, although a few have some decoration in red. By the time Old Park Avenue was being built, the cutting edge of taste had moved on considerably from the Gothic of the mid-Victorian period. Swinburne had introduced the idea of 'art for art's sake' in the early 1860s, leading to the Aesthetic Movement. William Morris and others were reacting strongly against the Gothic revival and its contention that Gothic should be the only style. Walter Pater decreed that to the aesthete, 'all periods, types, schools of taste, are in themselves equal.'

Such equality was not always easy for the less knowledgeable - or the less confident – to apply, certainly to interior decoration. As a result, there was a continuing tension between taking the freedom to pick and choose between different styles and the desire for rules that could be followed. This created the need for guides on design, if not indeed for rules. One of the first to meet this need was Charles Eastlake whose "Hints on Household Taste" began in 1864 as an article in the Cornhill Magazine, carried on as series of articles in The Queen, and was published in book form in 1868. He saw nineteenth century artistic taste as capricious and subject to constant variation, chiefly because it was based on eclecticism rather than on tradition. The introduction to his book asserted that.

> 'People are beginning to awaken to the fact, that there
> is a right and wrong notion of taste in upholstery, in
> jewellery – perhaps in millinery, too – and in many other
> fields that stand apart from a connoisseurship of what is
> commonly called 'high art'.'

Eastlake was entirely prepared to set out clear views as to what was right and wrong in design and described his intention as 'to suggest some fixed principles of taste for the popular guidance of those who are not accustomed to hear such principles defined'. The book went through many editions and was extremely influential, especially his advice that:

> 'in an age of debased taste, the simplest style will be the
> best' and 'Every article of manufacture which is capable
> of decorative treatment should indicate, by its general

*design, the purpose to which it will be applied, and should
never be allowed to convey a false notion of that purpose.'*

This celebration of simplicity made a considerable contribution
to the development of the Arts and Crafts movement. By the end
of the century 'unnecessary' decoration in the interior of the house
and heavy furniture were certainly no longer fashionable, although
naturally this took some time to filter down.

But some did move on from the strict application of rules.
Indeed one of the arbiters of style and much read writer of the
Aesthetic movement, Mrs Haweis, starting in the late 1870s, was more
concerned to promote originality and individuality than rules. She
advocated having in your home what gave you pleasure, regardless of
whether your neighbour has it, or fashion approves, or some self-styled
arbiter of taste demands it, describing originality as follows 'Originality
is like a house built of bricks taken from many places – it is the disposal
of the old bricks which makes the house an original one.'

Eastlake himself had been trained as an architect and was the
nephew of a president of the Royal Academy. However as the century
drew on interior decorating became more and more the realm of
women only. In the rest of this chapter we draw on three authors of
perhaps the most read handbooks on taste. Mary Haweis was the
daughter of the painter T M Joy and she herself painted and exhibited.
She married Hugh Haweis, a famous preacher and the incumbent of
St James Marylebone. They lived in some comfort in Cheyne Walk
where they were the centre of an intellectual, scientific and literary
and artistic circle. The second, Jane Panton, was the daughter of
William Frith, the artist who painted the famous picture 'Derby
Day'. She lived for fifteen years in Wareham, Dorset before moving to
Abbots Langley in the 1880s and then to Watford. The third author,
Mrs Alfred Praga, was the wife of the portrait painter and described
herself as a journalist. She certainly produced a large number of
books of advice, including 'How to furnish a house cheaply in
London', 'Dainty Dinner Tables and how to decorate them', 'What to
wear and how to wear it'. It seems likely that her advice, particularly
on running a household, was not based on her direct experience since,
according to the 1901 Census, she, her husband and son boarded in
Kensington rather than occupied their own house.

Queen Anne style

Matthew Arnold's "Culture and Anarchy", published in 1869, recommended the supposedly Hellenic virtues of "Sweetness and Light". These he interpreted as the creation and enjoyment of beauty (sweetness) and wisdom as the result of intellectual curiosity (light), with the result that it was no longer became necessary to adopt a single style. Sweetness and light did however lead to a more consistent treatment of external decoration in the Queen Anne Style which, despite its name had little to do with Queen Anne, except perhaps the use of red brick. It was developed from the early 1860s by architects in the circle of Rossetti, Webb, and William Morris, and was recognised publicly in 1872-3 particularly following Stevenson's building of 'The Red House' in a terrace in Bayswater Hill. In domestic housing, it reached its apotheosis in such different locations as Bedford Park and Tite Street in Chelsea. By 1878, even Charles Eastlake, himself a supporter of Gothic, felt it necessary to add a footnote to the fourth edition of his Handbook on Taste.[18]

> 'The recently revived taste for the so-called 'Queen Anne' style, or more correctly speaking for that domestic type of brick architecture which prevailed, with certain variations, from the Caroline to the Georgian period, has resulted in the erection in London of many private mansions which are very picturesque, and which reflect great credit on the architects who designed them.'

Queen Anne style (christened by Osbert Lancaster as 'Pont Street Dutch') was an eclectic collection of details where the art – and the architects did view themselves as artists – was to combine the various elements in a harmonious whole. The chief characteristics included some – and occasionally all -, of the following:

- classical but without following the principles of proportion
- hipped roofs
- lead or copper coated cupolas over turrets and oriels
- ribbed chimney stacks
- gables, either straight or Dutch
- tile- hung walls

- red brick
- Dutch or Flemish door surrounds
- brick pediments and pilasters
- white woodwork
- sash windows with small panes in upper half of casement windows or casement windows with leaded lights
- fan lights
- brick aprons below windows
- wrought iron work including on balconies
- decorative terracotta embellishments such as sunflowers

These were applied to architect-designed houses and to a variety of public buildings. As Mark Girouard put it:[19]

> ' 'Queen Anne' succeeded not because it was sensible but because it was pretty, and because by the 1870s it exactly suited the mood of the public.... In the service of enlightenment they built 'Queen Anne' schools, colleges, hospitals, libraries, and swimming-baths. All over London outbursts of red brick began to interrupt the smooth expanses of stucco. Soon the style was erupting all over the country. 'Queen Anne' had become the fashion.'

There are some examples of this architectural style in South Battersea and E R Robson's designs around Bolingbroke Grove were covered in Chapter 7. Girouard describes these as 'an agreeable group of red-brick houses with Flemish gables on the east side of Wandsworth Common'. (Ill 45) Robson was one of the important architects of the Queen Anne style and, working with his partner J J Stevenson, produced designs for the new London Board schools that captured the imagination of the public. Charles Booth described them.[20]

> 'In every quarter the eye is arrested by their distinctive architecture, as they stand, closest where the need is greatest, each one "like a tall sentinel at his post" keeping watch and ward over the interests of the generation that is about to replace our own.. Taken as

a whole, they may be said fairly to represent the high water mark of the public conscience in this country in relation to the education of the children of the people.'

One of the first four schools Robson and Stevenson designed was Winstanley Road School in Clapham, although that is more in the Gothic style. Shortly afterwards in 1876 Robson designed Belleville School (Ill 60).

60: Belleville School

It must have been schools like these that Conan Doyle contrived Sherlock Holmes to notice from a train crossing the viaduct near Clapham Junction when he said to Watson, who incidentally describes the view as 'sordid enough':[21]

'Look at those big isolated clumps of buildings rising up above the slates, like brick islands in a lead coloured sea.'

'The Board Schools.'

'Lighthouses, my boy ! Beacons of the future ! Capsules with hundreds of bright little seeds in each, out of which will spring the wiser, better, England of the future.'

What better tribute to sweetness and light !

There are also examples of genuine Queen Anne style houses in South Battersea other than those designed by Robson. We have already seen T E Collcutt worked with George Jennings on a number of buildings, starting in 1870 with 53-63 Bedford Road, before he had won the competition for Wakefield Town Hall, and moving on to 69-79 Nightingale Lane in 1879 (Ill 41). These are remarkable for their use of terracotta, pioneered by Jennings, and it is interesting to speculate whether Colcutt also had a hand in some of the other local work of Jennings, that is 81-95 Nightingale Lane in 1870 and the related houses in 2-10 and 18 Endlesham road built by Jennings in 1873. In any case, Collcutt's interest in terracotta continued, as for example in his design for the Wigmore Hall.

The style began to filter down to the more mundane speculative housing by the early 1880s as described by Mark Girouard.[22]

> 'the final great outburst as being in the 1890s, by which
> time it was thoroughly commercialised and often only
> a travesty (although sometimes an enjoyable one) of its
> origins. Inevitably, it ceased to be a style for the initiated,
> who moved on to other things.'

One example of this overuse is the sunflower motif, one of the iconic elements of the Queen Anne style. Following Morris' inclusion of sunflowers in the Oxford Union frescoes in 1857, both Rossetti and Burne-Jones started bringing sunflowers into their work, possibly as symbols of physical love and the world of the senses. By the mid 1860s they were appearing in decoration on buildings, whether potted or unpotted or even paired off with lilies. Ill 61 shows one of the sunflowers in Old Park Avenue.

Their appearance became so common it became a cliché, but nonetheless used for that. Sometimes the splendid and decorated façade at the front was accompanied with unattractive elevations to the rear, prompting the description 'Queen Anne fronts and Mary Ann backs'.

61: Sunflower from Old Park Avenue

Houses in Old Park Avenue

As in many roads in the area there are a number of different designs on Old Park Avenue. The houses built by Saker in a Queen Anne revival style comprise two detached houses and a pair of double-fronted semi-detached houses on one side of the road. On the other side he built three pairs of single-fronted semi detached, all with similar but slightly different designs and details. They include all the characteristics of the speculatively built Queen Anne style house with tile hung gables, red brick terracotta sunflowers, semi- elliptical windows and so on.

The houses built by Kettle are all semi-detached and broadly similar, except for No. 23 at the end, but again there are differences of detail. It is not clear that any of the houses was designed by an architect although Chapter 9 suggested that it was possible that N. S. Joseph and Smithem may have been involved. In any case builders usually built from pattern books or their own designs, based on previous experience or the wishes of their clients. There was a clear economic advantage in not employing an architect – Building News estimated in 1895 that 'a builder could run up a house 50% less expensively than an architect'. No other houses by Saker have been identified and of all the houses built by Kettle in South Battersea only one, 46 Hendrick Road, is known to have had an architect. However he was experienced enough to know what was likely to attract customers; he had been building the larger houses in South Battersea since 1883 and his last work prior to Old Park Avenue was to build houses on Nightingale Lane on what had been the Old Park Estate at the same time as Saker was building his houses. They all have roof crests, which had become fashionable in the 1880s and many of these still remain. (Ill 62)

62: Roof crest in Old Park Avenue

None of the houses in Old Park Avenue conform to the traditional design in the rest of South Battersea since they have no back additions. Muthesius points out that by the 1890s, 'the days of the back addition were numbered'[23]. Houses became wider and the back could then accommodate two rooms, one a kitchen often still with extension to the scullery and outside wc, and the other the dining room, now with French doors to the garden. This allowed plenty of light to both back rooms and, for the smaller houses was better adapted to a single family who no longer needed to provide separate rooms for the

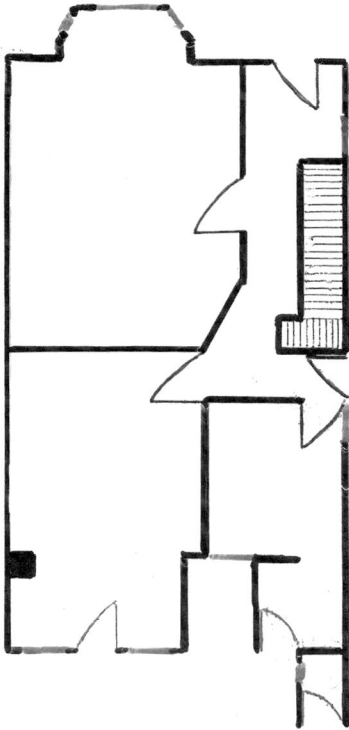

63: Floor plan for Kettle houses

servants. Muthesius says that such houses were beginning to appear by the 1890s or slightly later in the London outer suburbs, in which case the Kettle houses were an early example. By 1895 Building News could write, 'Dispense altogether with the ugly back additions'. And by 1905-10, virtually all houses followed this new model.

The ground floor room lay-out for the Kettle houses is shown in Ill 63.

There were nine rooms on three floors, a cellar under the hall, French doors at the back opening onto a raised verandah with glass roof (the suburban equivalent of a conservatory), bathroom and separate wc on the first floor, and a box room on the second floor. This is one more room than in the first houses built in Thurleigh Road and two more than in roads such as Hillier or Wroughton. To the twenty-first century eye, the rooms, with high ceilings, appear well proportioned, although no doubt they would have confirmed Mrs Haweis' worst fears of such houses[24]

> '*poorly proportioned rooms – such as we find in the majority of suburban developments, built by some dealer in brick and mortar who knows no more of design than a monkey.*'

On the basis of Muthesius' admittedly rough and ready classification, the nine-room houses of Old Park Avenue rank somewhere between the higher clerks and professionals, with most of the houses between the commons with six, seven or eight rooms in the higher clerk bracket. This can be confirmed by the choice of trees in the road, limes. As usual at that time, different trees were planted to reflect the status of the road. The well-to-do roads would have plane trees or horse-chestnuts, the working classes had none, while limes, laburnums and acacias were for the middle classes. Trees were thought to be desirable in a road because they made the environment less urban and could give additional privacy; a further reason, as stressed by Mrs Haweis[25], was that they were thought to clear the air from smuts. Most of the current residents have rebelled against the enormous lime trees and have persuaded Wandsworth Council to replace them with the much more attractive chanticleer pears.

Before moving on to the detail of the houses, it is worth drawing attention to one of the design features that it is too easy for us to take for granted but which was always the source of comment by continental Europeans. In the vast majority of these suburban houses, the rooms can only be accessed from the hall or landing and there is no interconnection between the rooms (The only exception to this is the practice in some houses, but not Old Park Avenue, of having connecting doors between the principal rooms downstairs.)

This implementation of the principle of separation of function and class and maintaining privacy, including among family members, and represented a change from eighteenth century and older houses (or apartments on the continent) where interconnections were the norm. The need for separations was frequently stressed by writers. Hooper in 1887 wrote:[26] 'The various departments of the household must be distinct, with ready communication by doorways placed wisely to increase privacy.' Robert Kerr wrote in 'The Gentleman's House.[27]

However small the establishment, the Servants Department shall be separated from the Main House, so that what passes on either side of the boundary shall be both invisible and inaudible on the other.'

Hermann Muthesius, the German architect who spent from 1898-1905 in the German Embassy in London studying the English house, noted:[28]

> 'The English room is a sort of cage, in which the inmate is entirely cut off from the next room..... The desire for privacy is only the final outcome of the feeling that has driven the English as a people instinctively to living in their own houses; the sense of being their own masters.... Communicating doors obviously rob the room of part of its special character.'

He went on to comment on the placement of doors.[29]

> 'The greatest care is exercised in choosing a position for
> the door. For one thing the draughtiness of the English
> house ensures that care will be taken to site the door
> so that parts of the room can be reserved for people to
> sit where the draught cannot reach them. The greatest
> care is also taken to see that those seated in the room
> are disturbed as little as possible by the opening of the
> door.... and this is reflected mainly in the direction
> in which the door opens. The rule known to every
> Englishman says that the door must open towards the
> main sitting area in the room, which usually means
> towards the fireplace, in a study it opens towards the
> desk, in a bedroom towards the bed. The idea is behind
> this is that the person entering the room shall not be able
> to take in the whole room at a glance as he opens the first
> crack of the door but must walk round it to enter the
> room, by which time the person seated in the room will
> have been able to prepare himself suitably for his entry.'

This approach continued long after Muthesius wrote. Gordon
Allen was still advising in 1919[30]: 'All sitting rooms doors should be
hinged to the longer length of wall which they adjoin, so as to screen
the larger half of the room including the fireplace.'

We also have some contemporary descriptions of the houses
from Stephen Potter, the author best known for "Gamesmanship"
and other mocking self-help books. Potter's father, Frank, moved
his family from 14 Estcourt (Hendrick) Road to rent No. 3 from
1895-1899 and then bought No. 36. His son Stephen, although
only born in 1900 and therefore with no direct experience of living
in the first house, described it as follows:[31] 'unshapely, flat-faced,
deeply unphotogenic, first house where Muriel was born. It had
quite a decent garden.' However he compared the second house very
unfavourably with it[32].

> 'The new desirable residence ...was in no way an
> improvement. After the disaster [Frank Potter's
> investments had gone wrong] it had to be more

economical. It was in the same road but smaller and semi-detached. Though it took me decades to realise the fact, No. 36 was really a brute of a house, though perhaps not at all worse than the rest of the ten thousand houses which were eating up the open land over this part of London at the time. Indeed it was exactly like them. Every house on this curve of the road was precisely the same. the same iron railings; the same front garden with box hedge and five dusty irises; the same shaped two rooms on every floor, with a tiny 'study' at the first half landing and a tinier 'maid's bedroom' at the second. At the back, the ground-floor drawing rooms opened on to verandahs identically covered with thick green glass to mitigate the rays of the sun. This was of some conceivable use when they backed east, as they did from 1-18; but when they backed north (20-36) this protection from non-existent sun created a kind of greenhouse of cold, preserving a perpetual dampness and a chill mould which percolated into the drawing room and attacked the very roots of the piano itself, so that there was an invalid atmosphere even about Beethoven.

And describing the building[33],

'A great word of the 'nineties was 'jerry-built'. No 36 was jerry built to its finger nails. It was not only that every water pipe was exposed to the first attack of frost and that the hot-water system worked effectively only at the moment when the gong sounded for Sunday luncheon; it was the audible transparency of the building material. The Bains who lived next door on the attached side were exposed to every evolution and convolution of Potter music. When Jack, the half-breed Irish terrier with a long heavy tail, stood in the middle of the drawing room floor and wagged his tail with his special slow, vigorous rhythm, each china piece on each little table shuddered in unison. Full chords on the piano (and

both father and myself were fond of the noble effects involved with these) caused each glass ornament, bought by my parents in Venice on their honeymoon, to ring and vibrate in sympathy, their outlines grown fuzzy. The tiles in the hall worked loose, so that each year one or more were missing. The brass door-knocker was a shade too light and a shade too mean, and the knob on which it struck was made of some kind of coloured tin, so that even the postman's bold double knock was muted to a plink-plink. The walls were so cardboard-thin that it was impossible not to know exactly in which room everyone was.'

The Potters lived in the house until 1926 when they moved out to Reigate, and it is at least possible that the memory is worse than the real experience or tinged with Potter's later contact with the good things of life, as when he says 'It was to be many, many, years before I saw the inside of a really comfortable country house.' He identifies that the term 'Edwardian' describes the well-to-do only, and then goes on to say 'there was nothing recognisably Edwardian about No. 36' However, a few pages later in his autobiography, not only does he admit that it was his roller skating inside the house that brought the tiles out of their sockets in the hall, he goes on[34] 'I should say that I took the ugliness and inconvenience of No 36 for granted. In fact I never thought of it as a bad house.'

We can have a good idea of how Old Park Avenue houses were organized internally at the start of the twentieth century from Potter's autobiography including contemporary photographs, but also from a contemporary sale notice, the auction of the leasehold of 26 Old Park Avenue in 1902. The advertisement is at (Ill 64).

Headlined 'Clapham Common', the 'Superior Modern Semi-detached Residence' is described as being

'In a good residential locality quite close to the Common, convenient for tram and omnibus routes and an easy distance from the Electric Railway Station Wandsworth Common and Clapham Junction Station.'

64: Auction sale of 26 Old Park Avenue

The accommodation is described as:

> 'Having a nice front garden and containing, Five Bedrooms, Box Room, Bath Room, Study, Drawing and Dining Rooms, convenient Domestic Offices, Tradesmen's side entrance.'

James Watts, the original occupant, was moving out and used his own skills as an auctioneer to sell the house in conjunction with the larger firm of Edwin Evans. He sold the 86 year lease for £695.

This advertisement says much about what must have been important to likely purchasers and it is certainly worth examining in more detail. It starts by stressing the good character of the neighbourhood and its closeness to transport, at a time when twenty minute walks to the station were considered nothing unusual.

The 'nice front garden' was important because it helped to isolate the house from the road and provide a degree of privacy, already emphasised by the lime trees planted at what seems now to be too small a distance apart for what are such large trees. Traditionally, front gardens would have contained a little wall with either a privet hedge or cast iron railings, together with an iron gate and tiled path up to the front door. Contemporary photographs of Old Park Avenue are not clear enough to show all the details, but walls and privet hedges, often growing over iron railings, are certainly in evidence (and still are !) and Potter's description quoted in the last chapter suggests this pattern was followed. Ill 65 shows the design of some of the railings still existing in the street.

65: Railings in Old Park Avenue

"Five bedrooms" is an indication of the size of the house, although the room on the second half-landing would usually have been, as in Potter's house, reserved for the maid. As shown by its explicit inclusion in the advertisement, the room on the first half-landing was normally a study rather than a bedroom, and was used as such by Potter's father.

On the ground floor, the names of the rooms 'Drawing room' and 'Dining Room' make clear the house is designed to attract the middle classes and this is reinforced by the reference to the 'Tradesmen's side entrance'. This was a door from the side path into the kitchen allowing the servant(s) who would be located there to enter the house without using the front door and to deal with tradesmen out of view of the whole street. The door from the hall to the kitchen was not evident when entering the front door and the plan shows that it was necessary to go through two doors at right angles to each other to reach the kitchen from the hall. The house thus avoided Robert Kerr's stricture against 'speculation villas'[35] in which 'a kitchen doorway in the Vestibule or Staircase exposes for view the dresser or the cooking range, and fills the house with unwelcome odours.'

The kitchen also had the door to the cellar and the servants would have been expected to use the outside wc. There was a coal chute from the side passage into the cellar, very necessary as the houses would probably use an average of a tonne of coal a month, all of which had to be carried by the servants. All these arrangements ensured that the master and mistress of the house could, if they chose, be insulated both from tradesmen and the servants.

Usually builders took no account of the aspect and automatically made the 'best' room the one fronting on the street (and the one with the bay window). Baillie Scott[36] commented,

> 'If you ask where the family live I cannot tell you, but, judging from the unlighted rows of front bay windows, one may conclude that they support existence somewhere at the back and reserve their front apartment to display all the evidences of advance in modern domestic furniture on which we congratulate ourselves nowadays.'

However this was not the case for the houses that Kettle built. All their dining rooms looked onto the street while the sitting room was at the back of the house. This made sense for the odd numbered houses whose back room faced south but hardly so for the even numbered houses whose best room faced north and got very little sun. The Potters obviously used their north facing back room for living in by the family and it was not reserved for 'best' which would have meant only for 'company'.

Bathrooms had been normal in middle class houses from 1880 and we can expect there to have been a bath which The Builder described as, 'happily becoming an indispensable necessity of every decent household.' The provision of a separate room for the wc was now the norm; indeed according to The Builder writing in 1899[37], 'putting [the wc] in the bathroom is a barbarism which ought to be considered out of date altogether, in any house.' but complained that occupants did not care enough about the detail of the toilet saying '…. the British Public clearly love a cheap bargain and readily accept the cheaper article regardless of its fitness or quality.' The sole bathroom, which doubled as Frank Potter's dressing room, served all the family and the maid, although jugs of cold water were kept in the bedrooms to be supplemented by 'small tin cans of hot water from the gas geyser' in the bathroom at the appropriate time.

Much of the interior decoration of the houses is obviously lost to us. There was rarely an overriding style and Mark Girouard is inclined to describe it as 'eclecticism' with clutter 'kept under control by the fastidious eye of the owner'[38]. Mrs Haweis, writing in 1881, is rather less complementary about the Queen Anne style for interior decoration, referring disparagingly to 'Annamaniacs'.[39] We do know something about the fixed elements of the interior decoration supplied by the builders because much of it remains or can be pieced together from the various houses. Generally the remaining original architectural features are remarkably similar suggesting that even those who had purchased their lease before the house was completed had little opportunity – or desire – to individualise it. We shall see that the choice of decoration, which to the modern eye at least is intended to demonstrate some degree of superiority, in fact represents taste that was out of date even at the time. With very few exceptions, the builders of Old Park Avenue had not caught up with the change away from ornamentation, described by The Builder in 1899.[40]

> 'In the reaction which is taking place against display and over-lavish ornamentation, the new school of designers appears to be losing the sense of style and the dignity of design which accompanies it, altogether. The objects

*seems to be to\make a thing as square, as plain, as devoid
of any beauty of line, as is possible and to call it art.'*

The front doors in Old Park Avenue had letter boxes and
knockers, and the postman was therefore one of the very few
tradesmen to use the front door. Muthesius spotted the postman's
etiquette, previously commented on by Potter,[41]

'The postman always uses the knocker to announce
his visit as he pushes the post through the letter-box
into the house. With a little practice one can judge
the importance of his delivery by the way on which he
knocks: for printed matter one will simply hear a curt
disdainful fall of the knocker, a loud knock will signify
a letter, and registered post and telegrams, for which
the door must be opened, will be heralded by two loud
knocks. The English door knocker is usually of the
simplest kind; it is very rarely the object of outstanding
artistic treatment.'

The front doors were originally glazed to the top with side
windows to match. Many of these are preserved and demonstrate
the glass, both leaded and etched. The doors opened onto relatively
wide halls which still retain their tessellated tiles (more expensive
houses had mosaic tiles). (Ill 66)

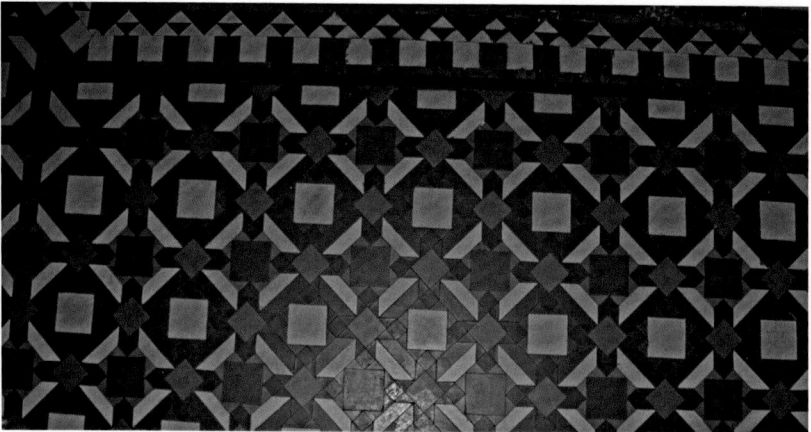

66: Hall floor tiles

There is some variety of tiles in the road and not all of which obey Eastlake's hint[42]:

> 'As a rule too many colours are introduced into them. However attractive it may appear in the shop, this kind of polychromy ought studiously to be avoided on the floor of a private house. Two tints, or – better still – two shades of the same tint (which should not be a positive colour) will be found most suitable for the purpose, and in any case there should be no attempt to indicate relief or raised ornament in the pattern.'

In the earlier standard house, the stairs started very near the front door and rose with a dog leg to take up the least space. Larger houses, particularly in the Edwardian period had a square well hole at the junction of flights with prominent newel posts. This was also adopted in Old Park Avenue with the hall newel being topped by a ball on top of an urn and the other newels with just a ball.

Like everything else at that time, the doors were carefully differentiated by room. All doors had the standard four panels, laid out in the 'correct' way, with two shorter panels below and larger ones above. There were three sizes of doors in the house;

Main rooms downstairs   36 inches by 1 ¾ inches

Main rooms on first floor   32 inches by 1 3/4"

Other rooms   30 inches by 1 3/8"

All had the same brass knob handles, another oddity that struck Muthesius[43],

> 'It is difficult to find any justification for the English habit of using a knob rather than a lever to open the door. Turning a knob is the most unsuitable way of exerting pressure on a spring, especially when, as is usually the case, it is small and   slippery. Whereas a German maid with both hands full can still press down the handle with her elbow, her English counterpart has to lay whatever she is carrying on the floor before she opens the door.'

In addition, the doors to the main rooms downstairs have 'overdoors', that is an additional pediment over the door, made in this case of wood. This had become fashionable by the late 1880s, although Fashion and Decoration could write[44]:

> 'The architectural frieze and rigid pediment of former years has long since given way to a more attractive and fanciful class of fitment. Shelves and niches for bric-a-brac are now the fashionable thing, and the more 'broken-up' in arrangement the overdoors are made, the more popular and pleasing do they seem to become.'

Needless to say, Old Park Avenue overdoors were architectural in nature (Ill 67), but this is also what was being put in similar houses in other South London suburbs

Kit Wedd in the Victorian House attributes ' an almost mythical status' to the open fire in the English home and it is still common in England to view a fireplace – and a fire – as an essential part of creating a home. This was summed up by Muthesius[45],

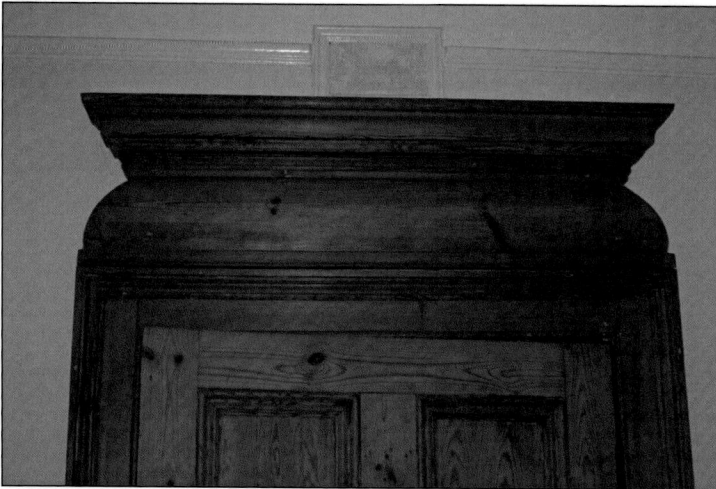

67: Overdoor

The English have never thought, and will never think of relinquishing the fire-place, however irrational it is, however much trouble it causes and however doubtful

its practical value. Out of love for the fire-place they overlook all its faults, indeed so great is their love that they are unaware of these faults. The many advantages the fire-place is deemed to possess (not least its aesthetic advantages, some of which, it must be admitted, exist entirely in the imagination) so completely convince the Englishman of its superiority to all other forms of heating that he never even remotely considers replacing it with the more efficient and more economical stove. All ideas of domestic comfort, of family happiness, of inward-looking personal life, of spiritual wellbeing centre round the fireplace. The fire as a symbol of home is to the Englishman the central idea both of the living room and of the whole house; the fire-place is the domestic altar before which, daily and hourly, he sacrifices to the domestic gods. One presumes that the mild climate is also responsible for the fact that the English have made scarcely any use at all of central heating. And even when it is installed it never replaces the open fire, for to the English a room without a fire is like a body without a soul.'

But this was – and still is – a source of some amazement to continental Europeans and Americans who cannot understand the continuing use of such an inefficient way of heating a house (Muthesius estimated that 86% of the heat from a fireplace went up the chimney) and one which also causes draughts which exacerbate the problem. Indeed he noted that the English had invented special armchairs with side pieces at the top to protect those sitting in them from the draught.(We call them wing chairs.)

The fact is that the desire for fresh air conquered the desire for warmth. Jenni Calder[46] makes clear that even for the best society it was assumed that those near the fire scorched and had to protect their skins with fire screens, while those at a distance froze. This, coupled with the deep rooted superstition that it was healthier to be cold, accounted for a great deal. As late as 1899, a manual on 'Architectural Hygiene' wrote[47] 'All heating arrangements must be subservient to the scheme of ventilation.' Mrs Haweis thought 'a sitting room over 55 °F is unhealthy and extremely likely to produce colds.'[48] Even those who recognised that the desire for fresh air could be taken to extremes were firm. Mrs Panton wrote[49]:.

> *'Without going to the outrageous lengths some lovers of fresh air consider necessary, I strongly advise everyone to sleep with some little bit of window open. I always do in summer with all that I can, in winter with one or two at the top only. I put down my singular immunity to colds to this habit of mine, and also to the open doors and windows that I always insist upon, and that for some part of the day always remain open, winter and summer, though the moment the sun goes, or rather begins to go, down, all windows, in the winter and autumn, should be rigorously closed, with the exception of about a quarter of an inch at the top.'*

Similarly, while Mrs Panton said that a room for children should never be overheated in any way; she made clear too that[50] 'No one should fall into the foolish idea that a fireless bedroom is hardening, and a fire makes people tender, for it does nothing of the sort.' Others were made of stronger stuff, giving guidance such as the following:[51]

> *'Parents should remember that children are like young plants and cannot grow to healthy maturity without light and air ... a healthy nursery diminishes the doctor's bill ... fresh air at night is almost too obvious ... in very cold weather the child must have not only warm light bedding, but also warm light clothing covering the whole body. But windows must be open.'*

Arguably, it is the continued desire for fresh air as much as anything else which has secured the role of the fireplace. This too was picked up by Muthesius.[52]

> *'The fireplace in England serves another, extremely important, purpose. I refer to ventilation. Much ventilation is needed, largely because of the high humidity of the atmosphere. Humidity is the most marked of all of all England's climatic features. It accounts for the*

*frequent fogs, for the distances in which all is veiled
in a light mist, for the luxuriant green of the plant-life,
which lasts the whole year round. As regards its effect
on people, it is responsible for that permanently chilly
feeling that so often causes visitors to catch cold. In
enclosed spaces it induces the fusty, musty, smell that
affects any room that is not thoroughly aired every day.
It necessitates extremely powerful ventilation, which,
indeed the fire-place admirably provides. At all events,
its justification in England lies in its capacity to ventilate
far more than to heat, as is demonstrated by the English
belief that every bedroom must have its fireplace, even
if the fire is rarely lit.*

*The need for adequate ventilation...... accounts, for
example, for the Englishman's fondness for sash windows,
for there is no window that can regulate the ventilation
as minutely. The large amount of ventilation is the cause
of the famous draughtiness of the English houses, which
has already provoked many a harsh word from foreigners.
But the blazing fire in the grate is solely responsible for
continuously sucking a powerful current of air through
cracks in doors and windows, towards the fire-place. The
English are more or less impervious to the draught, partly
because they are used to it, partly because they take the
precaution of wearing warm underclothing. They have a
highly developed need of fresh air. They usually sleep with
the window open, open the windows in unheated railway
compartments in winter and, in general, have nowhere
the same need of warmth as we on the continent with our
over-heated railway carriages and tropical temperatures
on our rooms.*

The relationship between sash windows, universal in most
Victorian houses, except sometimes for the top floor servant quarters,
and open fires was also picked up by a Danish architect writing in
the 1930s with a great fondness for London and its attractiveness as
a city for living in.[53]

'*Most houses are supplied with sash windows. Their frequent occurrence seems strange to a foreigner. If he be an architect he will invariably ask how it is possible to construct them so they fit. The answer is simply that they do not fit, sash windows never fit – that is why they are used. The use of sash windows and of open fireplaces, a perfectly mediaeval way of heating, may be considered as an outcome of the proverbial English conservatism. But considering the matter from the standpoint of an Englishman it may be admitted that there is a certain method in his madness. As he considers it absolutely essential that the living rooms be constantly ventilated it must be admitted that it is quite logical to use open fireplaces which can only draw when the air in the room is continually renewed; but that means that the windows must not fit closely, a quality therefore that cannot be regarded a drawback but rather a virtue in sash windows. It is worthy of notice that double windows are rarely used, not because they are too expensive, but because a draught is preferred to stuffy air. An Englishman going to America or Continental countries where the rooms are better heated and less ventilated than in England suffers terribly. He will long for his lightly constructed houses where the damp winter air whistles through the rooms accompanied by the rattle of the doors and windows.*'

Given the importance of the fireplace, there was a need for its surround to emphasise its position in the room. The standard fireplace surround in the early 1880s in middle class houses was made of marble, with its colour being used to differentiate rooms, white for the drawing room (Carrara marble for Old Park Avenue), and red or brown for the dining room, which conventional taste decreed should be a dark room. The red marble found in Old Park Avenue (Ill 68) was nicknamed "corned beef" by builders.

68: Red marble fireplace

However, by the end of that decade, fashion had moved on. Mrs Haweis regarded a white marble mantelpiece as 'a most disagreeable object', although her principal concerns were not the marble itself but the fact the machine carving is 'disgracefully coarse and inconsistent'. She covered hers at St John's Wood Road with a deep strip of blue velvet with matching fringe and set her best pieces of Chelsea china on it[54]. Mrs Panton wrote: [55]

> 'The possession of a large and hideous white marble mantelpiece and a tiled hearth to the ugly, wasteful grate says 'drawing room' too plainly for the ordinary mind to rise above the builder's dictum. Of course, some people, even in a small house, regard the possession of the marble in the light of a patent of nobility – it is so handsome (odious word), so genteel; but these belong to the hopeless class, for whom little or nothing can be done.'

Criticism gradually increased, and home manuals began to give advice on how to disguise the marble by hiding it with fabric covered board or even putting it in a wooden casing. Mrs Panton has a solution to hand,[56]

*'For, after all, a marble fireplace is to be avoided not
desired; and if you can obtain the landlord's permission,
you can soon replace it by one of Shuffery's charming
wooden mantels and overmantels; or at the worst can
even paint it the same colour as the woodwork; putting
on a plain and simple drapery which can be taken off in
a minute and shaken, and which is by far and away the
best drapery for a mantelpiece that was ever invented.'*

This criticism took some time to filter down, and marble fireplaces
were a selling point for upper middle class houses in Cardiff in the
mid 1890s and used in many areas of London suburbs, for example
Herne Hill, at the same time. What finally stopped marble being used
in mantelpieces in the modern homes was its use in smaller houses.

Virtually all Old Park Avenue houses have red marble in their
front rooms, described by Potter as dining room, and white marble
in the drawing room downstairs and the front room upstairs. Other
rooms have cast iron chimney pieces, each tailored with different
tiles to suit the room, although in one or two houses there are cast
iron fireplaces in some of the principal rooms as well. No doubt the
builders knew what their customers were likely to want and, looking
at the age and occupation of those who moved in, it is not surprising
that the fireplaces were conservative.

The arrangement of ornament in the Victorian room was
related to classical tradition for columns as well as to functionality.
The skirting board, which protected the plaster at the bottom,
corresponded to the pedestal of the column; the dado protected the
wall from being banged by chairs and marked the plinth; the picture
rail, allowing pictures to be hung (and also establishing that this
was the kind of house in which pictures would be hung) marked the
bottom of the frieze; and the cornice corresponded to the classical
cornice. Charles Eastlake wrote in 1878,[57]

*'Paperhangings should in no case be allowed to cover the
whole space of a wall from skirting to ceiling. A 'dado'
or plinth space of plain colour, should rise to a height of
three or four feet from the floor. This may be separated
from the diapered paper above by a light wood moulding*

stained or ebonized. A second space, of frieze, left just
below the ceiling, and filled with arabesque ornament
painted on a distemper background, is always effective,
but of course involves some additional expense.'

The more up-market the house, the more elaborate the mouldings would be, and there would also be differentiation between the rooms. Old Park Avenue had, as was common at the time, a dado rail only in the hall and landing, with embossed painted wallpaper below it. The main rooms on the first two floors (but not the hall) had picture rails and there is an elaborate hierarchy of both ceiling heights and skirting boards. The main rooms on the ground floor were just over 10 feet high and have 10 inch skirting board with a two inch moulding on top; the hall and stairs the same size skirting board but with a very small moulding on top, while the first floor rooms are just under 10 feet high but have a six inch board with a 1½ inch moulding. The other rooms are eight feet high with six inch skirting without any moulding.

Nowadays, we associate plaster ceiling roses and decorative cornices with the Victorian or even earlier periods, but taste was beginning to move away from these as early as the 1870s when they were described[58] as 'ugly and meaningless cornices and centre-pieces of the ceiling, looking like ornaments off a wedding cake' or 'ghastly round in the centre of the ceiling'. Old Park Avenue certainly had ceiling roses (Ill 69), although Helen Long[59] comments that roses and decorated cornices made from any material were no longer socially acceptable by the 1890s in fashionable houses.

Nevertheless, roses and cornices continued to be used in middle class houses as well as those aspiring to such status through the first decade of the twentieth century. Gordon Allen[60] was still trying to kill them off in 1919, describing them as 'expensive, dust collecting and often unsightly'.

Rooms were also differentiated by the types of cornice. The most elaborate cornice (claw and ball) was in the drawing room at the back of the house (Ill 70a), the next in the hall and front room of a dentate form which picked up one of the main decorations to the brickwork externally (Ill 70b). The plainest cornice was reserved for the three first floor rooms and landing. The top three bedrooms had no cornice. (Ill 70c)

69: Ceiling rose

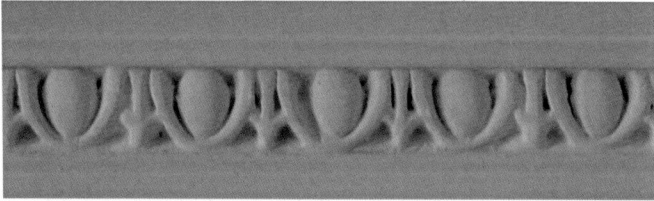

70a: Claw and ball cornice

70b: Dentate cornice.

70c: Plain cornice

The picture rails confirm that pictures were an expected part of decoration, but here as usual there was a clear etiquette for hanging pictures, which also served to differentiate rooms. Charles Eastlake gave clear advice.[61]

> 'The practice of hanging up oil and water-colour paintings, engravings and photographs in our sitting rooms, is one which I need scarcely say contributes greatly to that appearance of comfort which is the especial characteristic of an English house..... It is an old English custom to hang family portraits in the Dining Room, and it seems a reasonable custom. Generally large in size, and enclosed in massive frames, they appear well suited to an apartment which experience has led us to furnishing a more solid and substantial manner than any other in the house. Besides, the Dining Room is especially devoted to hospitality and family gatherings, and it is pleasant on such occasions to be surrounded by mementoes of those who once, perhaps, formed members of a social group which they have long since ceased to join.'

At the same time, he advised:

> 'A framed picture, however small, should never be suspended from one nail. This may seem a trifle; but, for the sake of appearance as well as of safety, it is better to depend on two points of support. The triangular space enclosed by a picture cord stretched between three points must always be inharmonious with the horizontal and vertical lines of a room.

It took an outsider, however to notice the full hierarchy of picture hanging. Muthesius observed:[62]

> 'We may also note that original paintings only are found in English rooms. Engravings and prints of all kinds, including photographic reproductions belong in English opinion to halls, passages and staircases. It is an old English idea to hang oil paintings, especially family portraits, in the dining room; the hall too, if it is large

and roomy, is a place for oil paintings. But water colours are hung in the drawing room and in the bedrooms; and original drawings, uniformly framed and hung in rows are also found in bedrooms. The habit of separating the types of wall decoration according to the character of the rooms is certainly a step forward in the process of suiting the picture to the decoration.'

When the houses were built, the kitchen would have contained a range with the chimney above and this could also have provided hot water. Washing, both of clothes and cooking or eating utensils, would have taken place in the scullery. Muthesius comments on this.[63]

'The English, however, with unshakeable obduracy, cling to their practice of wedging the kitchen stove between walls, so that every French chef who comes to England declares that he cannot possible prepare even the simplest sauce on such a mediaeval contraption. The English stove has evolved out of the fire-place... and so inseparably bound up with the English notion of an interior is it that they still want to create the impression of a fire-place in the kitchen. So all English kitchen ranges are to this very day designed to show an open fire. In every English house the cooking range is combined with a heating system that provides hot water.....The hot water system is often an abnormally heavy burden for the range and frequently results in great wastage of fuel. But thrift in the use of fuel is not the guiding principal for the English kitchen range, any more than it is for the English fire-place.'

There was clear evidence from pipes left in the wall that gas was used to light the house at some stage and Potter also refers to a geyser in the bathroom, but it is unclear whether this was incorporated when the house was built. Gas lighting was not universally popular because of the smell and the fumes. Mrs Panton wrote in 1897:[64]

'I must impress upon my readers never to have gas anywhere where they can avoid using it, and to pray heartily for that bright day to dawn when the electric

*light shall be within the reach of all...I feel consumed
with rage and anger that I was not born in a time when
the electric light will be as much a matter of course as
the present odious system of lighting by gas.'*

There was, of course, plenty of choice in the design of gas lights, Mrs
Panton preferred copper and beaten iron lamps from a shop in Bond
Street, but Charles Eastlake advised a more adventurous approach.[65]

*'Gas fittings are of comparatively recent origin and belong
to those requirements of modern life with which our
forefathers managed to dispense. There is, however, no
reason why such subjects should be of the commonplace
or stereotyped forms usually adopted in ordinary dwelling
houses. Nor, on the other hand, is it necessary that they
should assume the ecclesiastical forms generally found in
the art metal-workers catalogue.'*

Electricity would have come well after the houses were built.
St Luke's Church acquired electric lighting in 1903 as a gift of a
parishioner, which was sufficiently rare for an official electrician to
be appointed by the Parochial Church Council and for him to use
this in his advertising. (Ill 71) which also shows another use of the
descriptor 'New Wandsworth'.

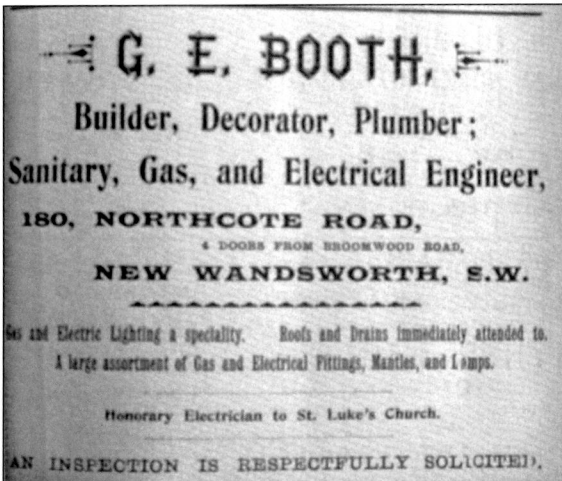

71: Advertisement for electrician

Indeed the Inland Revenue tax return in 1911 made a point of identifying 10 Old Park Avenue as having electric light, and hence increasing its value, suggesting that the others did not. The Gas Company was also advertising strongly in the Parish magazine.

It is clear that the houses in Old Park Avenue employed interior designs that were geared towards taste that was barely contemporary at the end of the 1880s. However, the builders, or at least Kettle, seem to have judged this about right, given the observation of the Bounty's surveyor that they were disposed of as quickly as they were built. Although the exteriors and internal layout of the Kettle houses are very similar, there is some small variety in the interior decoration and it may be that this was at the choice of the clients or early occupiers.

The next two chapters show how South Battersea in general and Old Park Avenue in particular developed during the twentieth century.

(Endnotes)

1. Helen Long. 1993 The Edwardian House p 147
2. Donald Olsen. 1976 The Growth of Victorian London p 216
3. Building News. 1885 quoted in Olsen Ibid
4. Robert Kerr. 1894 quoted in Olsen Ibid
5. Jenni Calder. 1977 The Victorian House p 173
6. F Maitland. Building Estates
7. Stephen Muthesius. 1982 The English Terraced House p 43-4
8. Ibid p 382
9. F Hooper quoted in Linda Osband. 1991 Victorian House Style p 16
10. Robert Kerr. 1871 The Gentleman's House
11. Hermann Muthesius. The English House 1904 English edition p 79
12. Ibid p 79
13. Gordon Allen. 1919 The Cheap Cottage and Small House p33
14. Stephen Potter. 1959 Steps to Immaturity p 26
15. Ibid p 26
16. Ibid p 27
17. Ibid p 46
18. Robert Kerr. Ibid
19. M H Baillie Scott. 1905 Houses and Gardens p141
20. The Builder. 12 August 1899
21. Mark Girouard. Ibid p 130
22. Mrs Haweis. Ibid p 199
23. Ibid
24. H Muthesius. Ibid p 190
25. Charles Eastlake. Ibid p 51
26. H Muthesius. Ibid p 189
27. Fashion and Decoration. 1891 1 December p 163

28. H Muthesius. Ibid p 104
29. Jenni Calder. Ibid p 86
30. Bannister Fletcher. 1899 Architectual Hygiene p 145
31. Mrs Haweis. Ibid p 342
32. Mrs Panton. 1896 From Kitchen to Garret Ninth Edition p 151
33. Mrs Panton. Ibid p 200
34. Quoted in Alastair Service. 1992 Edwardian Interiors p 109
35. H Muthesius. ibid 91-2
36. Steen Rasmussen. 1934 London The Unique City p 306
37. Bea Howe. 1967 Arbiter of Elegance p 144
38. Mrs Panton. Ibid p 86
39. Mrs Panton. Ibid p 10
40. Charles Eastlake. Ibid p 1123
41. Lucy Crane. 1882 Art and Foundation of Taste p 89
42. Helen Long. Ibid p 137
43. Gordon Allen. Ibid p71
44. Charles Eastlake. Ibid p 185
45. H Muthesius. Ibid p 201
46. Ibid p 96
47. Mrs Panton. Ibid p 127
48. Charles Eastlake. Ibid p 148
49. John Burnett. 1978 A Social History of Housing p 108
50. Bridget Cherry and Nikolaus Pevsner. 1983 London 2: South p 73
51. Roger Dixon and Stefan Muthesius. 1978 Victorian Architecture p 63
52. Ibid p 67
53. Walter Pater. 1873 Studies in the History of the Renaissance Preface
54. Ibid p13
55. Charles Eastlake. 1868 Hints on Household Taste Dover Edition preface
56. Jenni Calder. Ibid p 226
57. Mrs Haweis. 1882 Beautiful houses p iv
58. Mark Girouard. 1977 Sweetness and Light p 4
59. Charles Eastlake. Ibid p 25
60. Mark Girouard. Ibid p 63
61. Charles Booth. 1892 Life and Labours of the People in London Vol III p 204
62. Arthur Conan Doyle. 1894 The Naval Treaty in The Memoirs of Sherlock Holmes
63. Mark Girouard. Ibid p 90
64. S Muthesius. Ibid p 99
65. Mrs Haweis. 1881 Art of Decoration p 199

C H A P T E R 1 1

THE EARLY TWENTIETH CENTURY
1914-1945

The population movements we have seen in the nineteenth century continued into the twentieth. People were still coming to London from the rest of the country and also from abroad. There was a substantial natural net increase, reflecting the number of younger people of child bearing age coming to the city. But the overall increase in the population of London masked very substantial movements within inner London, from inner to outer London, and from both inner and outer London to outside the London area. It is often difficult to put exact numbers on these; the various census details are not always exactly compatible because the boundaries at both ward and regional level change, or because other definitions or the amount of under-recording varies. Different authors use, whether knowingly or not, slightly different definitions. Nevertheless most people accept that the population of inner London peaked just before 1911 at slightly over 4.5 million, depending on the exact definition, and then decreased steadily for 70 years before increasing again towards the end of the twentieth century. The relative balance in different parts of inner London, case defined as the LCC area, is shown below

Population of inner London (000)[i]

Year	central	inner ring	outer ring	total
1801	787	64	109	959
1921	1,364	1,186	1,933	4,483

Source: London Suburbs English Heritage 1999

i Inner ring includes Battersea, Chelsea, Islington and Lambeth
Outer ring includes Hampstead, Poplar, Wandsworth and Hammersmith

Inner London experienced a population increase of 300,000 in the 1890s[1]. However this was made up of two factors working in the opposite way. There was a net outflow of 182,000 adults but a much larger increase of births over deaths, itself of course partly a reflection of older people moving out and younger ones moving in. Similarly, although the population in 1911 was almost the same as in 1901, this reflects outward migration of 550,000 if the gain from the excess of births over deaths is taken into account.

In contrast, the population of outer London grew rapidly in the 1920s and 1930s and did not peak until 1951. We have already seen in earlier chapters that the availability of transport and consequent housing was taking people much further out of London than Clapham and South Battersea. Changes in the provision of housing and transport naturally played a part in this but while these changes accelerated in the 1920s and 1930s, many of them could be seen before the First World War. The London County Council was beginning to build housing, for example at the Totterdown estate in Tooting, built from 1903 to 1911 and this was followed by development of the 30 acre estate at Norbury in 1906 to 1910 where the land at £600 an acre was only just over half the price of Tooting. Houses were also being built outside the innermost suburbs for long term lease or sale. Wimbledon Park was developed from 1901, with three bedroom houses sold for £350 leasehold, £450 freehold, and four bedroom houses for £425 and £600 respectively. One of the most rapid areas of growth during the first ten years of the century was Merton and Malden where the population increased from 5,470 in 1901 to 14,140 in 1911, or by more than 260%.

Summing up London housing in 1914, Colin Thom[2] wrote:

> 'London's ordinary housing stock, like that of most other
> English cities, was dominated by small private houses for
> rent by the better-paid working class and middle class,
> erected by speculative builders on cheap land and sold
> in the private property market as an investment.'

However the private sector had its inevitable cycles. Although there had been a peak of house building in London in the early 1900, this faltered and the Property Owners' Journal estimated there were 90,000 empty properties in 1907. By 1909 there was more unemployment in the building industry than at any time since 1881. On top of this, the introduction of Land Values Duties in 1910, the first of many unsuccessful attempts to tax land values and whose surveys we have already used, also served to reduce the output of new houses drastically, although the extent to which it was the real cause is argued. Local taxes also increased, with Rates in Battersea doubling between 1881 and 1911.

By 1914 there was a national housing shortage; in London more rooms were destroyed than built between 1911 and 1915. This surprised the Local Government Board whose Annual Report for 1913[3] discovered 'a hitherto unsuspected need' for more and better housing. The Report was, however, clear that it was not government's role to rectify the situation, saying 'private enterprise has always been, and, so far as can be foreseen, will continue to be, the main source of the provision of houses for the working classes.' The housing shortage was exacerbated further by the war, and after the middle of 1915 there was almost no new residential building in London apart from government schemes for housing war workers at Woolwich and Kingsbury.

This reduction in activity also reflected a general decline in the housing market in the first decade of the twentieth century. Offer[4] has shown that by 1910 the volume of house sales had almost halved since 1900 and was only a third of its peak in 1897. Prices of leasehold houses had dropped by 40-0%. Rates of return were correspondingly higher, but more speculative, attracting different investors – or none at all. The Property Owners' Journal claimed in 1905[5] that 'House property will cease to be an investment into which men of moderate means will put their money, as being too uncertain in yielding a return, and too precarious in realisation when required.' Offer[6] himself puts it more starkly, 'House property after 1905 was increasingly cut off from the mainstream of investment, to become a precarious speculation on a par with Mexican mines, offering abnormal returns to hard faced men.'

The post-war housing market

The housing market changed radically after the First World War for a number of reasons, including the availability of finance, demography and the labour market, and the kind of house that people want to live in. Faced with high interest rates, a need for a large deposits, income tax at 5s in the pound running at four times its pre war level, and local Rates up still further (they doubled in Wandsworth between 1914 and 1920), only the better off middle class could afford to buy houses.

Only 1,500 private houses were built in the whole of London in 1920. Many soldiers returning from the War were forced to share accommodation and, by 1921 20% of households nationally were sharing with at least one other household, compared with 15.7% in 1911.[7] In a bid to ease the pressure, local authorities began their own building. Wandsworth Housing Committee, like many others founded in 1919 in response to a request from government, procured the building of 376 cottages on Magdalen Park, Earslfield in 1920-22 and used compulsory purchase powers to build on the Furzedown estate at the same time.

But costs had gone up. With materials and labour at a premium (bricklayers received an average wage of £5/0/7 in 1920 compared with £2/2/10 in 1914)[8], and with higher standards of amenity demanded, it cost four times as much to build a small house in 1920 as in 1914. A rent which recovered the cost of new houses was beyond the reach of those for whom the houses were designed; it was also well above the controlled rents charged for existing properties as a result of the Rents and Mortgages Act 1915 which effectively froze rents at the pre-war level for the cheaper houses. As we have seen, housing at any level was no longer an attractive investment for secure income and even the large aristocratic estates such as Berkeley Square, Millbank and Great Portland Street, began to be sold off. Investors could get a better return elsewhere, for example overseas and, as a result, deserted the housing market.

Meanwhile, the economy was creating large numbers of middle class service and administrative jobs on salaries rather than wages. These included not just teachers and senior clerks but those working in distribution and other service industries, not least finance. The number of civil servants and local government workers doubled nationally between 1891 and 1911 and the cost of the civil service, stationed mostly in London, almost trebled between 1895 and 1914. The number of middle managers in the economy increased rapidly.

The housing market changes

The proportion of national income taken by salaries (ie, monthly rather than weekly paid) reached 24% by 1938[9], having almost doubled between 1911 and 1924. Many of those earning salaries remained employed during the slump in the late twenties and early thirties, enjoying increasing purchasing power as prices fell. This was particularly true of London[10], where even though it had almost one eighth of the UK registered unemployed in 1932, its unemployment rate was 13.7 % compared with the national average of 22% and there were far fewer long term unemployed. Employment in London and the Home Counties rose by 49% between 1923 and 1937, twice the national average, with 21% of all working Londoners employed in finance or commerce. This availability of relatively well paid and secure jobs was a powerful attraction to people to come to London, in turn stimulating growth in demand for housing.

Demand grew even faster because of the increased household formation from more people marrying (42.8% of the population in 1931 compared with 34.8% in 1901)[11], often earlier than their forebears. They did not share the views of the Minister of Health who when asked in 1922 about the housing problems of newly married couples, asserted:[12]

> 'They should be so happy that they can enjoy even living in one room....Isn't the demand of the newly married for a separate house a comparatively modern development? In China and the East generally, I understand, they continue to live under the parental roof quite contentedly.'

For this and other reasons, including greater affluence and the increased tendency of the elderly to live apart from their children, the number of households increased much faster than did the population. As indeed it has done ever since.

By the end of 1922, construction wages and material prices had dropped so that the building cost per square foot dropped from £1 in 1920 to 9/4d in 1922[13] - and went on declining until 1934. Bank rate in July 1922 returned to its pre war level of 3% compared to 7% in April 1920. The cost of housing more than halved. Building Societies expanded from being small-scale and local. In 1910, 1,732 societies advanced £9.2m, financing an average of about 10-15 houses for each society; by 1938 these advances had risen to £59.7m[14]. In addition in the early 1920s the government provided subsidies for new houses in both the public and private sectors, allowing building societies to advance 90% rather than the usual 75% of the valuation for a 5% mortgage repayable over 22 years. Societies worked on the basis that outgoings including local rates should not exceed 25% of net income. By 1932 a three bedroom two reception room semi in Bexleyheath was being offered for £395 freehold and £295 leasehold, although more normal prices in the 1930s were £400-600[15]. About £1 a week bought the standard three bedroom £650 house while lower paid professionals (teachers, executive civil servants earning £300 - £500) could buy substantial semis or even detached houses of £1,000 or more.

Large-scale house building was only possible where the land was available, and that was in Outer London. Whereas the vast majority of Victorian houses were built by small builders, now was the time for larger ones and Taylor Woodrow, Costain, Wates (which started in Streatham) , Wimpey, and Laing among others, were formed at this time. These large builders produced economies of scale and were also able to reduce costs by taking on the building materials' suppliers which had operated rings to keep their prices up. The longer journeys to work required by housing in Outer London were facilitated not just by improved (or new) transport and higher earnings but also by reductions in working hours. After the First World War, office hours increasingly became 9-5 on weekdays and 9-12 or 12.30 on Saturdays, compared to the previous hours of 9-6 or 6.30 on weekdays and 9-1 or 1.30 on Saturday.[16]

A new kind of house

A new kind of house was wanted. Living-in maids were increasingly hard to get in the 1930s because of the emergence of a variety of relatively more attractive jobs. As a result, staff were much more demanding than their nineteenth century predecessors as to wages, free time, and conditions. Accordingly, the number of servants per 100 households in the London commuter belt fell from 24.1 in 1911, to 12.4 in 1921[17] and went on falling. The fact that it was very much harder to get servants meant people wanted houses that were smaller and easier to run. This was reinforced by the drop in the birth rate (from an average of 28 per 1000 in 1901-5 to 15 per 1000 in 1931-5)[18] which produced smaller families with the average number of children falling from 5.8 per family in 1871 to 3.5 in 1901 and 2.2 in the 1930s.

But it was not just convenience and household size that demanded smaller houses. As social relationships became less formal, it became less necessary to reserve a 'best' room to entertain guests. There was less reason to have large numbers of rooms in order to differentiate their use since children were admitted to the whole house and there were no servants to isolate. The house also needed to be 'modern'. People wanted a smart bathroom with plumbed hot water, an inside toilet and a modern kitchen with as much labour-saving equipment as possible to make up for the lack of servants. This called for electricity, but in 1910 only 2% of houses were wired for electricity. By 1930, domestic electricity was readily available all round London's outskirts, and during the nine years that followed, sales of electrical appliances, irons, vacuum cleaners and cookers grew rapidly. By 1939, 75% of houses had electricity and of these 30% had a vacuum cleaner and 80% an electric iron[19]. As Alan Jackson[20] pointed out, none of this was available to the housewife still living in gas-lit Edwardian and Victorian inner suburban houses, mostly rented from landlords who had no incentive to install electricity.

A number of architects had been arguing for these changes for many years. The architect Gordon Allen writing in 1919 for what was the sixth edition of his book[21] said:

> 'The clerical and other skilled workers who usually must
> reside in or near towns, were never before so conscious

(and perhaps so ashamed) of the fact that for the most part they are ridiculously and inconveniently housed. In the older and inner suburbs the "very desirable residence" of Victorian times stands supreme as the acme of discomfort and dismalism.'

He argued that houses should be designed for the family, not for guests, and that rooms should go where they were best suited, rather than automatically have the kitchen at the back. Baillie Scott, one of the Arts and Crafts architects and designer of some of the larger suburban houses, wrote in similar lines:[22]

'The average house should not be a place principally for the reception of visitors, but a dwelling for the family, and the only impression the unfortunate visitor will receive segregated amidst forbidding furniture in an unaired and obviously unused room will be mainly one of discomfort. The house should then be designed essentially for its occupants, and should consist mainly of one good sized apartment, with plenty of floor space and elbow room and with only such furniture as may be actually required.'

All this represented a considerable change in what was expected in a house. Mumford estimated that in 1800 the structure alone represented almost 90% of the value of the house and land and even at the end of the Victorian period a house did not include much in the way of amenities other than fireplaces and perhaps a conservatory. After all, it was not in the interests of tenants to invest in the structure since any improvements became the property of the landlord. By the 1930s, modern houses had much more elaborate plumbing than their precursors, electricity, as well as tiled kitchens and bathrooms. These counted for up to a third of the total cost of house and land and, with the land, to as much as half of the total.[23]

The aspiring middle classes moved out of London to the new houses that builders and building societies increasingly made available for them. Between 1921 and 1937 almost 1.4 million people moved to outer London. Electrification of Southern Railways, producing one of the largest electrified networks in the world, meant trains were easier to run and provided better services. The growth noted earlier in and around Morden continued and the table below shows the thirteen-fold increase in population between 1901 and 1939, facilitated by no fewer than seven new railway stations built in New Malden between 1920 and 1937. These stations served not just overground trains into Waterloo but the extension of the Northern Line to Morden replacing the electric trams in 1926. (An attempt to extend it further to Sutton failed.)

Merton and Malden

Year	population
1901	5,470
1911	14,140
1921	17,534
1931	41,227
1939	72,150

A policy of low fares encouraged over half a million passengers a week to use the line and the number of passengers joining at the terminal was so great that it was difficult to get on at intermediate stations. By 1936 the Northern Line was the most heavily used of all tube lines at peak hours, with 13,500 northbound passengers through Oval station between 7.30 and 8 a.m.[24] - another example in the long history of overcrowding on the Northern Line.

South west London declines

Against this background it is hardly surprising that the older areas of Clapham, Battersea and Balham became relatively unattractive after the First World War. Why should one pay £50 a year in rent, or the equivalent in mortgage, and a further £10/10/- in ground rent for an old fashioned house which was showing its age and beginning to need maintenance, when for less money one could purchase a pleasant semi-detached house with the most modern conveniences in leafy suburbs and with a rateable value a third lower? Indeed the outer suburbs provided better value for money even than the smaller four bedroom houses in the streets off Northcote Road. Even the existence from 1926 of the Northern Line underground station at Clapham South did not help.[ii] As John Burnett wrote[25]

> 'The chief beneficiaries of the mass production of speculatively built houses for sale were the expanding lower middle classes, who seized the opportunity for upgrading their housing standard by exchanging an inconvenient Victorian house in a congested part of town for a new 'labour saving' semidetached villa in the suburbs.'

72: Clapham South tube station, 1926

73: proposed sign for
Nightingale lane tube station

[ii] Ill 72 shows what it looked like before the flats were built above it in the 1930s. It was originally destined to be called 'Nightingale Lane' as the tram stop had been and Ill 73 shows what London Underground had in mind for the design. The further alternative name of Balham North had already been discarded.

And who of these could resist advertisements such as, 'Novean homes are offered to families of good breeding who want to acquire a house to be proud of at a cost of less than £1 a week.'[26]

And although Betjeman is more normally associated with the Metroland suburbs, he wrote to a writer friend who found country noises too much:

'Return, return to Ealing
Worn poet of the farm
Regain your boyhood feeling
Of uninvaded calm !'

Guides to the suburbs in the 1920s and 1930s did not include Clapham, Balham or Battersea; they concentrated on Outer London. In 1903, P G Wodehouse[27] had Psmith accepting an invitation to Clapham from the earnest left winger Mr Waller along the following somewhat unenthusiastic lines:

'The first thing to do,' said Psmith, 'is to ascertain that such a place as Clapham Common really exists. One has heard of it, of course, but has its existence ever been proved? I think not. Having accomplished that, we must then try and find out how to get to it. I should say at a venture that it would necessitate a sea voyage.'

Nor were other contemporary writers flattering. Arnold Bennett[28] wrote in 1928, 'Battersea is a different world. It is a gloomy drab street, with most repulsive tenements.' Balham and Tooting were described[29] as 'the short-pants-and-hobnails-for-holidays set' although it is not clear how this description overlapped with the creation of the active Balham Trotskyist Group expelled from the Communist Party in 1932.[30]

None of these areas were at all fashionable. The New Survey of London Life and Labour commented[31],

'To the south of St John's Hill the houses are in the main of late nineteenth century construction and are inhabited by families of the skilled working class and by middle class families, the social scale rising as the more southern areas are reached.'

They endured a period of steady decline, moving inexorably into multi-occupation and being used increasingly for lodgings. The Inland Revenue clerks Jim Callaghan and his wife to be, Audrey, had lodgings in Clapham in the 1930s, he at 36 The Chase and she at 46 North Side. Modernisation came slowly. Cars and vans were still relatively rare and horse-drawn vehicles widely used for deliveries for decades to come. Horses were still used as a means of personal transport well into the twentieth century. One long standing resident used to recall that young lads would run all the way from Morella Road to the City so that they could earn a penny by holding her father's horse's head. While it is not surprising that Percy Thornton, the conservative MP for Clapham, conducted much of his campaigning in the 1906 election from horseback, others continued to do so too. The surveyor Bertie Evans, son of Sir Edwin Evans the founder of the local estate agents and the senior partner of the firm from 1933-61, used to carry out inspections of new developments on horseback. He recalled[32] that this 'had the double advantage that it obviated the necessity for getting one's boots muddy, and both ground and first floors could be inspected without the necessity of dismounting.'

It is no surprise then that, for example, Clapham High Street was in decline by the 1920s and even described in 1929 as 'terribly derelict' by the prospective parliamentary candidate for Clapham, Roy Lowndes. The Marquess of Crewe, writing in his introduction to Dorothy Pym's book about Battersea Rise House[33] said, with all the condescension of a senior peer, 'Clapham, once a cheerful country village, is now hard put to it to maintain any identity, and any flavour of country air, amid the streets that beset it.' Tony Aldous[34] also quotes a middle class resident of Clapham as confirming Jerry White's[35] description of Clapham having a sudden loss of caste in the late 1930s:

> 'By the 1930s the place was indeed regarded as very plebeian-suburban. Miss Alice Crossthwaite, who lives in an early 18th century house with panelled interiors in North Side, remembers the response of well brought up folk in Kensington in the late 1930s when she admitted to living there. "They looked down and shuffled their feet in embarrassment; then softened it by saying 'Ah,

one of those lovely old houses on North Side!'" But Clapham was still not one of those places that 'people lived'. She remembers that, when driving over Chelsea Bridge, one had the sensation of entering a different and totally unfashionable world.'

Her grandchildren remembered her as 'not in the slightest bit conventional and totally oblivious to fashion'.

There were other examples of faded gentility. Miss Laura Ryder at Mayfield, 15 Blenkarne Road, advertised, with a telephone number:

'Lady, with nice house, offers comfortable Home to a Few Paying guests. Good Cooking. Constant Hot Water. Garden. Moderate Terms.'

She had eight tenants in 1930, but this had declined to four in 1932, and she moved on shortly afterwards.

The area still had its supporters. Noel Coward, who lived on the south side of the Common in his early years, wrote[36]. 'Clapham Common was a nice place to live'. He described 'This Happy Breed' as being set 'in a suburban middle class family between the armistices in 1918 to the humiliating years of 1938.' He responded to criticism of being condescending towards the suburbs by making clear,[37]

'.. having lived at Sutton, Battersea Park and Clapham Common during my formative years, I can confidently assert that I know a great deal more about the hearts and minds of South Londoners than they give me credit for.'

Graham Greene lived on the other side of the Common at 14 North Side and described the area to his mother in very positive terms.[38]

'The whole appearance of Clapham Common is lovely, like a wide green plateau on a hilltop above Battersea, with the common stretching out of sight in one direction, and on three sides surrounded by little country-like shops and Queen Anne houses, a pond and in the middle of the Common, the 18th century church to which the Clapham set belonged. The house was built in 1730 and was used by Macaulay's father as a school for black children.'

He used Clapham as the setting for "The End of the Affair", with the narrator 'living on the wrong – the south side of the Common'.

Patricia Hansford Johnson also had fond memories. She lived with her grandfather at 53 Battersea Rise while her father, a colonial administrator, was in the Gold Coast. Dylan Thomas came to visit her there in 1934 when he was 19, but their romance soon came to an end. Following her father's death, she and her mother moved to Broomwood Road, and she set a number of her books in the area, writing in one:[39]

> 'In those days the neighbourhood bordering between Clapham and Battersea was like a village, with all the village intimacy and cross-cutting of class. The small professional middle classes living along North and West Sides shopped along the Rise and St John's Road; sometimes, for the sake of cheapness and perhaps liveliness as well, they shopped along the stalls of Northcote Road, where bargains were to be found under the naphtha flares on Saturday night. They drank coffee at Arding and Hobbs; the young ones who were in love walked round the specimen 'furnished rooms' of that shop, pretending to be in a home of their own.'

Her affection for the area is also made clear in her descriptions of Battersea Rise in the thirties in the same book.[40]

> 'He bolted down the steps in the direction of Battersea Rise and soon disappeared into the sunset that blazed behind the minarets of St Marks and the Masonic School.'

and

> 'The Rise streamed in silver and brass down from one common to St John's Road and up towards another. The masonic minarets flashed and twinkled in the brilliant light.'

Old Park Avenue between the wars

How were these trends demonstrated in Old Park Avenue, which at the end of the war was still essentially in single family occupation, with a few servants remaining, and only one or two houses having non-family lodgers? In practice, Old Park Avenue only changed slowly. By 1930, 16 of the 30 or so heads of households in the street had been living there for more than ten years and a third for more than twenty years. These were mostly established families, some with adult children still living with them and in some cases with only one of the original couple still alive. This was reflected in the age distribution; in 1930 more than half the heads of the principal household were over 60 and a quarter over 70. Many of them were long-standing owner occupiers or had bought the long lease having been a tenant for some years first. Only 10 had a telephone during the 1920s and 1930s. The savage effects of the war were also felt in that there were at least five houses which contained groups of women only, whether sisters or living with companions. No. 23 was temporarily the 'Elvinor' Nursing Home which advertised in the St Luke's parish magazine for a short period in 1929. The matron, Miss D M Hickman, offered private rooms from 3½ guineas a week.

There is no record of any of the freeholders being asked to intervene to enforce the covenant about no business being conducted from the houses in Old Park Avenue, either in the case of the nursing home or where Mrs Elizabeth Laurie set herself up as a nurse in No. 7. This may have reflected attitudes to jobs during the Depression, which also encouraged the St Luke's parish troop of scouts to organize a taxi firm 'in order to find employment for Ex-Scouts from our Parish Troop'. The drivers were 'well trained and thoroughly reliable and smart with powerful Cars at the service of our patrons.' They charged 8/6 for a trip to a London railway terminus, but also offered 'Whole Day Country Runs of 120 miles' for 30/-.

There was a steady turnover in the lessees, recorded for each house in the files of the Governors of Queen Anne's Bounty. Robert Roberts, a Welsh banker, bought the lease of No. 28 from Uriah Hucknall's estate in 1922 and lived there with his three brothers. He moved out in 1929 to Sumburgh Road and later to Roseneath

Road, but the rest of his family stayed on with the children causing their next door neighbour Ella Robson Young to complain regularly about damage to the fences. His sister Mary lived there until June 1947.

There were increasing numbers of lodgers in the street. By 1930, seven houses appear to have contained more than one household, usually couples in their late 20s or early 30s, often renting accommodation from one of the older ladies in the street for one or two years before moving on. Evidence of this comes again from the St Luke's parish magazine which regularly contained advertisements for lodgers. Grace Haworth let the first floor of No. 19 unfurnished in 1930 and when Walter and Olive Nancarrow, her tenants of three years left, she advertised again as, 'Three rooms and bath. Electric. Re-decorated. Suit one or two adults. Attendance if required.' Gillian and Lillian Whitehead in No. 30, themselves renting from Edwin Davis, advertised in 1933 'Full or Partial Board' in a 'Comfortable Home' with 'moderate terms'. Others connected with St Luke's also found accommodation; a new young organist, Val Drewry, lived at No. 2 for three years in the early thirties and offered organ, piano and harmony lessons; while Arthur Trodd lived at No. 3 from 1935-37 and was the Honorary Secretary to the St Luke's Social Club; a new curate, Rev A J Moody lived briefly at No. 10.

The number of lodgers continued to grow in the 1930s; 13 houses had lodgers or were divided into two flats in 1935; in 1939 it was 17, or more than half the houses in the street, reflecting the fact that a number of the older more established families had either died or moved out, as part of the inexorable move to the suburbs. The Potters moved to Reigate in 1926, the Bottings to Carshalton in 1931, Frank Bodger moved with his new wife to West Wickham in 1930 and the Presburys first to Tulse Hill, and then to Esher via Worcester Park in 1935. Alice Edmonds moved to Norbury in 1927, her lease being purchased by the King sisters who moved from Brixton. This material is summarised in the following tables.

Number of households spending years at same address

Year	Years						
	10+	15+	20+	25+	30+	35	40+
1911	10						
1916	10	7					
1921	16	9	6				
1926	17	14	9	6			
1931	16	13	10	6	3		
1936	10	9	7	5	4	1	
1941	16	10	9	7	5	5	2

Source: electoral roll

Broadly speaking, about half the inhabitants stayed in the street and grew older with the houses. Their adult children often remained living with them. Houses with single women, both widows and those living with relations or companions, increasingly took in lodgers, whether to help with the rent or to provide help around the house. In some cases, houses were divided into flats, at least in practice

Age of Head of Household

Year	20s	30s	40s	50s	60s	70s	80s	Average
1901	2	4	11	8	4	1	0	46
1905	0	3	8	11	4	2	0	51
1910	0	5	13	7	3	1	0	49
1915	0	3	10	6	6	1	0	52
1920	1	1	9	9	6	3	0	53
1925	0	1	4	10	9	6	0	59
1930	0	1	2	9	8	7	1	65
1935	1	2	3	5	5	7	2	59
1939	0	3	5	3	8	3	3	61

Source: census and electoral roll

There was a continued increase in owner occupation up to 1940, reflecting established families taking opportunities to purchase the long lease or, for eight families, purchasing the lease from the previous owners and then letting rooms or subdividing the house into flats. The differences in tenure observed in the first decade of the century were largely maintained. Only one house that was owner occupied in 1901 was not owner occupied in 1930 - and the owner's son returned to live in it in 1935, and only three of them did not have their owner living there in 1939, although owner occupation did not exclude having a variety of tenants. Conversely, nine of the 15 that were rented in 1901 were still rented in 1930, and five of them still rented in 1939.

Owner Occupation

Year	% owner occupied
1896	17
1900	42
1910	43
1920	53
1930	63
1940	73

Source: electoral roll and Rate book

As a result of all these changes there were 30% more adults living in Old Park Avenue in 1939 than at the start of the century, illustrated by the table below, giving the average number on the electoral roll in Old Park Avenue.

Average number of electors

Year	Electors
1918-22	74
1923-28	74
1929-33	128
1934-39	124

Source; electoral roll

This can be compared with the number of adults (those over 21) in the 1901 Census -96 in total, made up of 62 adult family members, 22 adult servants and 12 adult children. 1911 was much the same in total with 102 adults, of whom 27 were servants and 15 were children. The apparent large increase in 1929 over previous years was almost entirely due to the inclusion of women over 21 rather than over 30, and over half the increase between 1901 and 1929 is due to the much larger number of adult children living at home (29 of whom 18 were women). It seems likely too that the number of younger children was reduced over the pre war period, reflecting in part the ageing of the households. It is difficult to know for certain how many living in servants there were, but in numerical terms servants were gradually being replaced by slightly greater numbers of lodgers. For example in 1939 three houses alone (9, 11 and 36) had between them 16 lodgers, and there may well have been children present as well. The changing demography and the more rapid movement of tenants also meant that there were only six marriages and six baptisms in St Luke's from Old Park Avenue from 1920-40 compared with 11 and 16 respectively from 1900-20.

Further commentary on the street comes from someone who lived in the road at this time. Pat was one of the children of the Hynds who lived in No. 34 as tenants of the original lessee, Eva Bayne, and with their own lodger, a secretary at the South London Hospital for Women. She describes the road as 'very middle class' and 'not the sort of road where people chatted'. She also remembers that the Hills, who had lived at No. 19 opposite since the house was built and were then in their late seventies, had a maid (definitely not called a servant) suggesting that this was no longer typical. There were still plenty of local

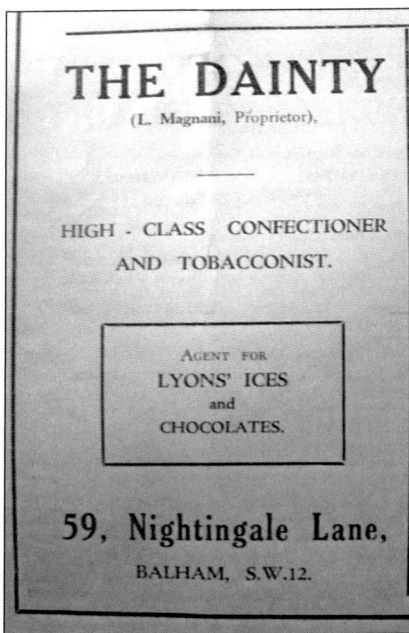

74: Dainty advertisement

75: Dainty Shop front

shops and one that sticks in her memory was called the Dainty in Nightingale Lane.[iii] John Hynds ran a small electrical wholesale business and had gradually moved to larger houses as his business grew. He had a van to help with the business, but although he had a garage in nearby Sudbrooke Road, he sometimes parked it outside the house. This was frowned upon by neighbours as 'lowering the tone of the place'. The Hynds liked the house and tried to buy it from Eva Bayne, but she was reluctant to sell because, as we have seen, it had been given to her as a wedding present by her uncle, although she did add a codicil to her will giving them first refusal when she died.

It was also clear that Old Park Avenue provided an attractive (or perhaps affordable) place to live for some who moved around between houses. Phyllis Gotto, who in the 1901 Census was 'living on own means' in Willesden had moved to 6 Old Park Avenue by 1919 staying there till 1920; in 1923 she turns up again, but this time at

---

[iii] This shop advertised in the St Luke's parish magazine.(Ill 74).

Its façade was also revealed recently when its successor was being cleaned up during its conversion to an estate agency and is shown at Ill 75.

No. 12, staying there until 1927; she lived in No. 5 in 1931 and was there when the war began. Cornelius Wernham lodged at No. 19 from 1918 to 1929 (when he was 60) but when the occupier Selina Head died, he moved to live with the two unmarried King sisters opposite at No. 30 until his death in 1942. Isabel Young was at No. 5 from 1923 to 1930 (when Phyllis Gotto replaced her); she moved next door to No. 3 and was there at the start of the war. Bertram and Ivy Fairburn rented part of No. 2 from 1928 to 1936, having their son baptized at St Luke's in 1932 and moved to part of No. 23 in 1937 to take the place of another young couple, Sidney and Rita Adams who moved out shortly after their child was baptized at St Luke's.

When the Potters moved out of 36 Old Park Avenue, the lease was bought by W Skittrall who lived in SW18. He then passed it on to the Gallier family who lived there for some years at a rent of about £60 pa, usually with one or two lodgers as well as the family. In 1936 they tried to purchase the freehold but The Governors of Queen Anne's Bounty replied rather sniffily:

> 'The Governors bought their estate at Balham as a permanent investment and are not desirous of disposing of any part of it. They are as a rule, however, willing to sell their interest to lessees, but are not in the circumstances prepared to sell it at the open market value.'

Eventually the Galliers were offered the freehold for £375 but they declined, and then moved round the corner to Thurleigh Road. The lease was then bought by a Mrs Roberts, living in Rodenhurst Road, who let it to two sisters originally from Burnley.

The Second World War

Both Clapham and Balham had been attacked occasionally by Zeppelins in the First World War but the Second World War hit Clapham and Battersea much harder. Being close to Clapham Junction, Battersea Power Station, bridges, and considerable industry, and with a large battery of anti-aircraft guns on the Common itself, they were attacked repeatedly during the Blitz. In October 1940 the Government decided that deep shelters were needed and three of the

Map 20: Second World War bombs

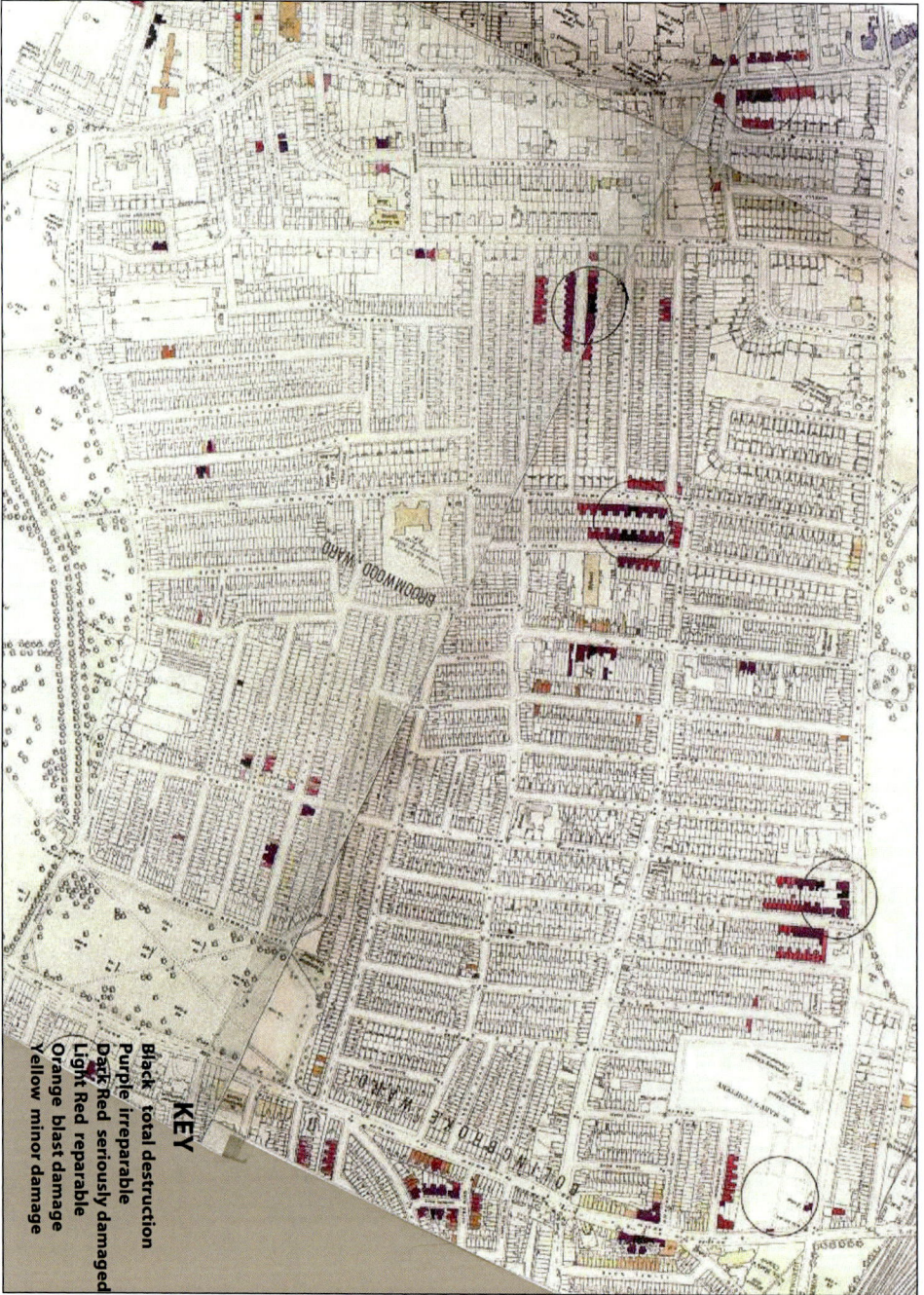

KEY

Black   total destruction
Purple   irreparable
Dark Red seriously damaged
Light Red reparable
Orange   blast damage
Yellow   minor damage

five sites selected for South London were in Clapham underneath the Northern Line with access from the underground stations. Each could accommodate up to 6,000 people between 80 and 105 feet below ground level but they were not completed until 1942, too late for the Blitz but in good time for the V1 and V2s in 1944. The Clapham South shelter became a listed building in 1998.

3,000 houses were destroyed in Battersea and almost every house there was damaged in some way as were many churches including St Luke's. 16 V1 flying bombs and two V2 rockets fell on Clapham and the V2 that fell upon Clapham Common damaged Holy Trinity so badly that steel girders had to be inserted to take the strain off the roof. Five V1s fell on South Battersea, hitting the cemetery, the Bolingbroke Grove end of Salcott and Wakehurst Roads, the Northcote Road end of Honeywell and Broomwood Roads, the Thurleigh Road end of Devereux Road, and the Rusham Road end of Nightingale Lane and Granard Road. Three more landed just outside South Battersea on the other side of Nightingale Lane. Many more bombs fell on South Battersea during the Blitz – probably more than 30 – and where the damage was worst they are marked by new post war housing or other building. There is a detailed map of all the bombs dropped in London together with the damage caused, and the part for South Battersea is shown in Map 20. The circles represent where V1 rockets fell.

Old Park Avenue received at least two direct hits, one of which created a large crater in the road and destroyed 17 and 19. They were replaced in the 1950s by police flats. One bomb fell on 38 Nightingale Lane and this caused some damage in Old Park Avenue. Both Pat Hynds and her sister in law, Mary, remember the bomb that fell in the street opposite No. 34. This was on Friday 13 September 1940, one of the first bombs in Battersea and part of a stick of three, with the second falling in Holmside Road and the third in Thurleigh Avenue. Mary herself had been bombed in London that day and had made everyone sleep in the cellar that night. The bomb blew the roof off and hit both gas and water mains. They had to get out quickly; the house was uninhabitable and they spent six months clearing it up. The incident was recorded tersely at Battersea Control.

> *'Minor bombing about 2330. H(igh) E(xplosive) and
> I(nciendiary) B(omb). Holmside Road, Old Park Avenue,
> and Morella Road. All near Nightingale Lane. Houses
> damaged. Gas main fired. 2 known casualties.'*

Eva Bayne moved back to her family in Cornwall; the war put
paid to John Hynds' business and they never bought the house.

There were regular reports to the Queen Anne's Bounty about
war damage, since sufficient damage entitled the lessee to a reduction
in the ground rent. The effect of one bomb, by no means a direct
hit, on No. 36 was described as follows by the Bounty's surveyor on
13 March 1941:

> *'front portion of the gable at second floor level is missing
> and brickwork to upper story of the front bay window
> has been seriously damaged as also has the roof slates
> and chimney stacks and there is a slight fracture to
> the bay between ground and first floors. The glazed
> verandah to the back sitting room has sustained severe
> damage. Internally the house shows signs of fractured
> walls and damaged plastering in many of the rooms, also
> some of the fireplaces are broken.'*

Some of the buildings in Battersea had a variety of other uses
during the war, and the Royal Victoria Patriotic School, possibly
because of its proximity to Wandsworth Prison was used as a
special intelligence holding centre for foreign arrivals. It was there
that Francois Mitterand was interrogated after he had left France in
November 1943.

(Endnotes)

1   Jerry White. 2001 London in the Twentieth Century
2   Colin Thom. 2005 Researching London's Houses
3   Quoted in John Burnett. 1978 A Social History of Housing 1815-1970
4   Avner Offer. 1981 Property and Politics 1870-1914 p 256
5   Property Owners Journal 1905 Sept p 1-2
6   Avner Offer. Ibid p 272
7   John Burnett. Ibid p 217
8   Alan Jackson. 1973 Semi Detached London p 91
9   John Burnett. Ibid p 257
10 Stephen Inwood. 1998 A History of London p726

11 John Burnett. Ibid p 257
12 quoted in John Burnett Ibid p222
13 Alan Jackson. Ibid p 97
14 John Burnett. Ibid p247
15 John Burnett. Ibid p 246
16 Alan Jackson. Ibid p149
17 John Burnett. Ibid p258
18 John Burnett. Ibid p 245
19 Alan Jackson. Ibid p 103
20 Alan Jackson. Ibid p 256
21 Gordon Allen. 1919 The Cheap Cottage and Small House p 4
22 M H Baillie Scott. 1906 Houses and Gardens p 40
23 Raymond McGrath. 1934 Twentieth Century Houses p 66
24 Alan Jackson. Ibid pp 237, 271
25 John Burnett. Ibid p235
26 Alan Jackson. Ibid p 169
27 P G Wodehouse. 1903 Mike
28 Arnold Bennett. 1928 Journal for 22 January
29 Jan and Cora Graham. 1938 The London Roundabout
30 Reg Groves. 1974 The Balham Group
31 New Survey of Life and Labour in London. 1934 Vol VI p 439
32 History of Edwin Evans. Wandsworth Historical Library
33 Dorothy Pym. 1934 Battersea Rise House Introduction
34 Tony Aldou.s 1980 The Illustrated London News Book of London's Villages p 58
35 Jerry White. Ibid
36 Noel Coward. 1937 Present Indicative
37 Noel Coward. 1939 Introduction to This Happy Breed
38 Quoted in Clapham in the Twentieth Century. 2002 p69
39 Pamela Hansford Johnson. 1955 An Impossible Marriage p20
40 Ibid p 55,287

CHAPTER 12

MODERN TIMES

The period since the end of the Second World War has seen further massive changes in population and housing in London. Immediately after the war, there was a pressing housing problem. 50,000 houses had been destroyed in inner London and 60,000 in outer London; 1.3 million were in need of repair.[1] Private building had come to a standstill and building skills and materials were scarce. Even in 1961 the country was reduced to just three weeks supply of bricks.[2] The population of inner London rose by 800,000 between 1945 and 1950 although it was still substantially lower than in 1939. A massive repair programme made 103,000 damaged dwellings habitable by 1947, and the London County Concil and London boroughs built 10,000 new dwellings a year for 15 years. In addition the LCC had built an additional 38,000 outside its area by 1955. As the various wartime controls on use of materials were relaxed, suburban private builders recovered and built a further 93.000 houses between 1954 and 1961, mostly in outer London.

The overall population of London only decreased slightly in this period, although this hid the continuing move from inner to outer London. The next thirty years were radically different and despite significant immigration into London, both from elsewhere in the United Kingdom and from abroad, there were very substantial net moves out of both inner and outer London, both of which lost over 20% of their population. Inner London's population stabilised in the 1980s and. since then has increased and now stands at 2.93m, 15% higher than its minimum in 1981, but still only 60% of its 1911 level. Outer London has also increased and at 4.50m is 6% above its minimum in 1991 and very near its highest ever level in 1951.[3]

London had always been a city of immigration and this was particularly true after the war. The longest standing immigrant nationality was the Irish, reinforced just before the war by the introduction of restricted immigration by the USA and, during the war by the recruitment of 100,000 Irish workers by the Ministry of Labour. In 1951 there were 112,000 Irish-born people in London and by 1981 this had grown to 350,000 first or second generation Irish, 5.3% of the population as a whole. Battersea had its share.

The next largest immigrant nationality in London was the Poles. Some had left Poland around the time of Hitler's invasion or came with General Sikorski after the fall of France; others had fought with General Anders' Polish Second Corps, or had been imprisoned or conscripted in Germany; and still more had left after the Communist takeover in 1947. About 33,000 Poles were living in London in 1951, a quarter of the total Polish migrants to the UK. One of the areas of concentration was Clapham, where a mass was regularly said in Polish at St Mary's Church in Clapham Park Road and became, according to Marzenna Michalowska-Cummins[4], almost the social high point of the week. But gradually the centre of the community moved to Balham, and funds raised in the USA were used to buy 50 Nightingale Lane, formerly Craven House, one of those built on the Old Park estate, and renamed Thomas Arciszewski House. This housed a Polish school which remained in use until 2005 when it was bought by an expanding local private school.

The deep air raid shelter at Clapham South had an unexpected use following the arrival of the SS Empire Windrush in 1948 with its 492 Jamaican immigrants. The Manchester Guardian wrote of them:[5] 'They are as heterodox a collection of humanity as one might find. Some will be good workers, some bad. Many are "serious-minded persons" anxious to succeed.' Those without connections in England were taken to the shelter as their first introduction to the country. 240 of them stayed there until they found work with a bed and three hot meals costing them 6/6d a day. They used the nearest employment exchange in Coldharbour Lane, Brixton, and within a few weeks all of them found jobs around that area. This seems the most likely reason for their settling more permanently in Brixton, although Ruth Glass attributes this to the goodwill generated by a tea party followed by a free cinema show for a representative sample of 40 of them organized by the Mayor of Lambeth at the request of the Colonial Office.[6] Accommodation proved more difficult because of the attempts by many landlords to exclude them, but many found property locally in Brixton which was, as Stephen Inwood[7] describes it, 'cheap, dilapidated, roomy and unwanted'. Many also settled in South Battersea. By 1961 there were just under 100,000 people of West Indian birth in London. Given that they had little or no access to council property and were sometimes excluded from rented accommodation, owner occupation was the only option for many, often clubbing together to support each other and taking many tenants to help pay the mortgage. Newcomers to the area in the early 1960s found that a high proportion of the houses for sale were offered by West Indians, either moving out to the suburbs or returning to Jamaica. The Wandsworth Borough News wrote in 1958:[8] 'In the eastern part of the borough in Clapham and Balham, and again in Battersea, particularly at Clapham Junction, there is a considerable coloured population, which is increasing.'[i]

As the initial thrust on repairing or replacing bomb damage eased, the next priority was slum clearance which came to the fore in the mid 1950s. The government provided substantial subsidies to encourage local authorities to replace old fashioned terrace housing with high rise flats. , and The policy of 'comprehensive development areas' meant that a large number of fit houses were demolished as well. In the late 1940s and early 1950s a large proportion of the houses locally were in multiple occupation, often as two flats, and most of the houses advertised for sale in The Borough News at that time had a sitting tenant, and were still leasehold. The prices for houses between the Commons ranged from £750 with a sitting tenant and 30 years to run on the lease up to about £2,000 for vacant possession

---

[i] The West Indians were not the first black people in the area. As mentioned by Graham Greene, Zachary Macaulay had brought back 21 boys and four girls from Sierra Leone in 1799 and started a school to prepare them to be missionaries. Unfortunately, the climate proved unsuitable, and the story had been that by 1805 all but six of them had died. In fact this was the result of some misunderstanding by Lady Knutsford in her biography of Zachary. Although a few died, most returned to Sierra Leone in 1805 leaving only six at the school. Nevertheless, there continued to be a number of black inhabitants and there was a group of Negro Minstrels in Streatham in 1900. Battersea had had the first black Mayor in the country in 1913, John Archer who ran his photographic business in Brynmaer Road. He was the agent for Shapurji Saklatvala who was elected MP for Battersea in 1924 and the third person of Indian extraction and the second member of the Communist Party to become an MP.

and freehold. The presence of the railways was still dominant. Harry Williams, writing of the area in 1949[9], observed:

> '... the dominating giant, the genius of the place, is undoubtedly Clapham Junction. This monster sprawls insolently over the heart of the town, holding it in a vice. The unfortunate inhabitants have long since forgotten that it holds them in thrall and have almost no conception of their bonds. With a weekly street market to redeem its absence of colour and life ... it is still one of the most suffocated and depressing localities in the whole of South London, a dingy wilderness of bricks and mortar.'

Meanwhile the private rented sector was given a boost by the 1957 Rent Act which removed rent controls. This helped to stimulate the use of older larger houses, but not always in attractive ways, and helped to reinforce the aggressiveapproach taken by Peter Rachman and others who did everything they could, legally or illegally, to maximise their rental income.[ii]

There was also considerable enthusiasm for commercial property redevelopment in the 1950s and 1960s. The urban geographer, Peter Hall, commented:[10] 'Ask any self respecting planner of 1963 how to renew London's outworn fabric and the answer would come straight back: bring in the bulldozers. Tear it all down. Rebuild from the ground up.' But by the mid-nineteen fifties, public opposition to high-profile developments strengthened, and a number of them were refused permission,

The worm was turning. The Civic Trust was formed in 1957 by Duncan Sandys and the Victorian Society was founded in 1958. Sandys subsequently gained the support of Lord Kennet and Richard Crossman, ministers at the Ministry of Housing and Local Government, for a Private Member's bill, the Civic Amenities Act

---

[ii] Rachman's activities in Notting Hill came to light as a result of the Profumo scandal in 1963 and included intimidation and eviction of unprofitable white tenants and replacement of then by newly arrived West Indians willing to accept gross overcrowding or, in some cases, by prostitutes such as Christine Keeler who could afford high rents.

1967, which for the first time allowed the creation of conservation areas. 250 were created in London in the first seven years after the Act. English Heritage now 'believes that all the best examples of historic suburbs should be designated conservation areas.'[11] Many round Wandsworth and Clapham Commons have indeed been so designated. More recently, English Heritage has produced two documents advising local authorities how to look after 'historic suburbs'[12].

Towards the end of the 1960s, a consensus was emerging that rehabilitation rather than new high rise blocks might be a better approach to urban social housing. This was given a great boost by the partial collapse of the tower block, Ronan Point, in Newham, after a gas explosion. The Government was gradually persuaded to change its single minded approach although it took longer to convince council housing officers. The change in approach was given effect in the Housing Act 1969 which created General Improvement Areas (GIA) whereby grants were made available for the improvement of older property. However, there was still rationing of mortgages and in the 1960s lenders restricted borrowers to loans of no more than 80% of the property and to 2½ times the main income of the family. A larger deposit was often required for older property. Even so the availability of grants stimulated increases in house prices in the areas being improved, with substantial profits going to developers and the middle class buyers rather than the original owners.

This inequity was recognised by the Government in 1973 in its White Paper 'Better Homes – The Next Priorities.' One of its proposals attempted to deal with the perceived abuse by the creation in the 1974 Housing Act of Housing Action Areas (HAA). These would be more targeted than GIAs to areas of genuine need and to keeping any benefits within the community. The Greater London Council (GLC) managed to convince the boroughs and the Government not to react solely to local pressure for the identification of HAAs but to endorse a London wide approach using objective criteria based on the 1971 census which was one of the first capable of being analysed extensively by computer.

Gentrification

The creation of the General Improvement Areas gave additional impetus to the movement of younger professionals into inner London, a process which has been given the name of gentrification. The term had been coined by Ruth Glass in 1963[13], to cover what she saw as the detrimental process of the middle class 'invading' working class areas and taking over 'shabby modest mews cottages and upgrading large Victorian lodging houses, resulting in the displacement of the original working class occupiers.'

Much academic ink has been spilt on an analysis of this process, originally with two contrasting schools of thought; the first stressed the economic arguments based on differential profit margins for developers from new build and rehabilitation and the other studied the changes in where people wanted to live. Essentially the argument is between two opposed views of life. One concentrates on changes in demand; that is, a greater inclination to move back to– or more usually stay in – the city than move to the outer suburbs. Reasons for the change included being 'fed up with the cost and fatigue of commuting from distant suburbs'[14] and 'bored with suburbia'.[15] On the other side, usually of a more Marxist disposition, are those who concentrate on the supply side, asking why houses were available for the middle class to move into.

It is now generally accepted that these are complementary processes that both contribute to gentrification, not least because the price of houses is driven by the need to balance supply and demand when the good in question is a 'positional good'[16]. These goods exist where the relative scarcity is itself attractive since it is thought desirable to possess what others cannot have or afford. Fred Hirsch[17] uses suburban living as one of the archetypal examples of a positional good. He paints a vivid picture of the probability of high inflation in house prices as a result of excess demand from the middle class who, having satisfied their general need for goods, wish to live in a socially desirable setting, by definition not available to everyone, with access to good education, low taxes and good public services. Rises in house prices merely stimulate the process further, as has been demonstrated all too well over the last 30 years.

There have been many micro-studies of gentrification, including in at least two of parts of Battersea. These tend to involve either very small samples or statistical material that is difficult, if not impossible, to disaggregate to the street level which we have been concerned with here. The analysis that follows, therefore, also draws upon the author's own experience, having been engaged in housing policy for the GLC in the early 1970s, and having lived through the gentrification process in the borough of Wandsworth for 35 years and discussed it regularly over that period.

In the 1950s, just as in the 1920s and 1930s, all the incentives encouraged those who could to move out of inner London and buy houses in the outer suburbs, but the balance began to change in the 1970s. There was some new housing, but the existence of the green belt meant that large green field sites outside London on which to build new houses were much less available. Increased demand had to be met somehow and it was cheaper to rehabilitate old buildings, including converting them into flats which were useful for the increasing number of smaller households, than to knock them down and rebuild.

However there were sufficient controls on rent increases to make it generally uneconomic for landlords to invest in improvements to their stock. Their response was either to find ways of letting dwellings to large numbers of people who had little alternative, usually immigrants, or to obtain vacant possession, a process known as 'winkling', which covered both fair means including offering large sums of money to induce tenants to leave, and foul. The result tended to be large numbers of empty or partially occupied dwellings, often in bad condition. Most people thought that the privately rented sector was in terminal decline, and many local councils did all they could to accelerate this decline, including using compulsory purchase orders to acquire empty property. For some councils, the blight had the added advantage of making it less likely that potential owner occupiers (presumed Conservative voters) would move in. However, while in the past local authorities had preferred to demolish the houses they acquired, the pressure was now to move away from demolition and redevelopment to rehabilitating existing stock. Unfortunately the government controls on the different housing accounts meant that the capacity to purchase housing exceeded the ability to plan and pay for improvements. As a result although the amount of empty property only reduced modestly, if at all, its ownership increasingly moved from the private to the public sector.

The declining privately rented sector also resulted in a decreasing amount of well appointed rental property in pleasant areas of London, and potential occupants with sufficient resources were increasingly drawn to owner occupation,. The availability of improvement grants and unlimited tax relief on mortgage interest payments[iii] made housing look like a good investment and owner occupation was increasingly seen as desirable in its own right. Demand for owner occupied housing grew rapidly, and the Barber boom in the early seventies, made mortgages freely available at relatively low interest rates, produced an explosion in land and house prices, with London leading the way. Even when this boom collapsed in 1973 and strict mortgage rationing came into play, the considerable inflation in house prices helped to convince most buyers that, at least in the medium term, owner occupation was a safe bet and that not being in the housing market was likely to lead to financial disadvantage later.

There were also considerable changes in the sources of demand for housing in London and more of them wanted to live in central London. As Jonathan Raban[18] puts it, 'From the mid 1950s, wages for young workers had risen and parental controls eased, with boys and girls in their teens migrating to the city filling bed sitters several to the room.' By the early nineteen seventies, post war baby boomers had begun to reach the age where they contemplated 'settling down',For the increased proportion of this age group which had received tertiary education, many of the new service jobs in London, including in the public sector, were well paid, enabling them to contemplate buying a house. Also, for the first time, many of these jobs were taken, and kept, by women.[iv]

---

iii The tax relief had originally been intended as an offset to the Schedule A tax on imputed rent which had previously been levied on owner occupiers.

iv It was, after all, only after the Second World War that women school teachers or civil servants were allowed to remain in work once they married. Equality legislation was only introduced in the late 1960s. Before this came into force, it was still possible – and legal - for a big city law firm to offer its male articled clerks the afternoon off to watch the Oxford/Cambridge rugby match, but not do so for their (few) female counterparts or to have two levels of gifts for those lawyers getting married, one for men and a smaller one for women which matched that given to the secretaries.

Particularly after the Robbins expansion of universities, more women were going to university and on to professional and other higher paid jobs, and most importantly, staying in them after they had children. This increased the household income and building societies slowly accepted that they should take the wife's income into account in deciding how large a mortgage to offer. Improved contraception, with the introduction of the pill, made it easier for couples to defer the birth of children.

London was swinging, and to many of the sixties generation, the outer suburbs of London seemed featureless and dull, as well as too much like where their parents lived. They also valued the social and cultural opportunities in central London, which they had already enjoyed in their first working years. Train fares after the Beeching Report were clearly going to increase at least as fast as inflation while the amount of a mortgage was fixed even if interest rates could vary. In short, commuting looked increasingly unattractive, wasting time and money, as well as making it more difficult to spend time with one's children. What could be more natural than staying in inner London, particularly if both halves of a couple were working? In response to this thinking, and the recognition that old but improved houses could indeed be resold successfully, building societies, even if reluctantly, began to look less unfavourably on lending for older houses and even converted flats, although they still tended to demand higher deposits than for suburban property.

Gillian Tindall[19] points out that there were also important changes in the environment. For many decades London endured 40-60 days a year of smog and, as people had been doing for 200 years, those who could moved out of central London to find cleaner air. The Great Smog, from 5 to 9 December 1952, which caused 4,000 deaths, finally produced change.[v] The Clean Air Act 1956 introduced smoke free zones and a number of other measures to improve air quality in Britain's cities. The replacement of coal-fired steam trains by electric ones also helped. . But the benefits were surprisingly slow in coming. In 1962 762 people died in a smog and for most of the 1960s, winter sunshine totals in the smokier parts of London

---

[v] A measure of its intrusiveness was that a performance of La Traviata at Sadlers' Wells had to be abandoned after the first act because smog filled the theatre.

were 30% less than in the rural areas around the capital. (Inrecent years there has been no measurable difference in sunshine totals.[20]) Controls were implemented at different speeds by different local authorities. Locally, Battersea had a clean air policy but Streatham did not. Since the boundary between them was down the middle of Nightingale Lane, it was inevitable that Old Park Avenue did not escape the smoke for some long time.[vi]

Much of the first phase of gentrification in London involved younger couples, often moving into their first owned house (as opposed to flat), buying in an area which a few years ago would have seemed unattractive to them. Often they saw this as an insurance against not missing a place on the housing ladder. They had a desire, expressed or implicit, to live in a 'proper' mixed community, similar to where they had lived in rented accommodation, rather than in a middle class ghetto. The first example of gentrification in London is usually thought of as Barnsbury in Islington, where younger professionals started moving in the late 1950s, although the main influx was in 1961-75. Elsewhere, the start is more often the late 1960s. Butler and Lees[21], an academic team who have studied the process, describe these 'pioneer gentrifiers' as:

> 'left leaning liberals. They were architects, planners, university lecturers, comprehensive school teachers, social workers, medical technicians, and so on; they were overwhelmingly Labour (party) voting.'

Michael Frayn caught it very well as early as 1967 in his novel 'Towards the End of the Morning'[22]

> 'They decided to find a cheap Georgian or Regency house in some down at heel district near the core. However depressed the district if it was Georgian or Regency, and reasonably central, it would soon be colonized by the middle classes. In this way they would secure an

---

[vi] This was not the only area where cooperation between the two boroughs was less than ideal. There were different designs of street lights on either side of Nightingale Lane, and in winter both boroughs insisted in gritting only their side of the road.

attractive and potentially fashionable house in the heart of London, at a price they could afford; be given credit by their friends for going to live among the working classes; acquire very shortly congenial middle class neighbours of a similarly adventurous and intellectual outlook to themselves; and see their investment undergo a satisfactory and reassuring rise in the process.'

For these couples, the architecture and interior layout of Georgian and Victorian houses was, or could be made, attractive and certainly compared favourably with inter or post war semi-detached houses. 'Original features' were much sought after. Fireplaces and pine were stripped; net curtains removed -sometimes to be replaced with blindsRooms were knocked together so that ground floors were transformed from three rooms and a kitchen to a 'through lounge' and 'kitchen-diner'. Book shelves were added; furniture came from Habitat. A good way of estimating the amount of gentrification in the street was to compare the relative number of cars being mended and those being cleaned, or to check whether skips filled or emptied overnight. England was not the only country where this happened and in the USA and Canada the process was known as 'white painting'. Michael Jager[23] described a similar process in his work on gentrification in Melbourne, Australia.

'Slums become Victoriana, and housing becomes a cultural investment with facadal display signifying social ascension. By buying into history the middle class are expressing their social distance from the classes below and constructing an identity based on consumption as a form of investment, status symbol and means of self expression.'

In the early 1980s, the process picked up speed as other new forces contributing. The leisurely habits of the City were beginning to change with work starting earlier in the morning and going on later, making it increasingly desirable to live near to work. The Conservative government also quickly implemented significant reductions in income tax on higher earners. As a result a wealthier group of professionals began to move into Islington.As the 1980s drew on, the movement spread to other parts of London. These professionals were, as perhaps would be expected, more acutely aware of the investment potential of gentrified houses, and more often bought houses in areas that were already in the course of gentrification where they could be more sure of likeminded neighbours. Since then, Butler and Lees[24] have gone on to identify a more recent phenomenon 'super-gentrification', stemming from the salaries in the global financial market now located in London, involving, for Islington,

> 'a qualitatively different group of very highly salaried 'masters of the universe' who are able to buy overpriced properties and entertain themselves in the restaurants and expensive shops of Upper Street's (p)leisure zone.'

This group buys up property which is already well gentrified and then spends large amounts of money on it, in essence, Butler and Lees argue, colonising the gentrified area in exactly the same way as the pioneer gentrifiers colonized working class areas thirty years earlier – and often receiving the same reaction. One comment quoted by Butler and Lees from Barnsbury encapsulates this,

> 'They put nothing into the fabric of the community, only money into the commercial infrastructure rather than their personalities or talents. They are making a new economy, but are absent from the community.'

Butler and Lees contrast Barnsbury with Battersea:
> 'even in Conservative Battersea, parents sent their children to the local primary school, [while] in Barnsbury a majority had withdrawn their children from the local, well performing, primary schools by the age of seven to prepare them for entry into the private sector.'

South west London after the war

How then have these trends and forces been manifested in South West London? Although Lambeth Council indulged in substantial clearance and rebuilding, its approach began to change when one of its schemes in Clapham was defeated in 1973, largely as a result of the intervention of the Clapham Society. In South Battersea, the

V1 bomb sites were all rebuilt with council housing by 1952 and individual groups of damaged houses were replaced over time, but there was only one slum clearance, the redevelopment of Chatham and Darley Roads in 1971-4. As we have seen, these had deteriorated even before the end of the nineteenth century.

There was at least one early GIA in Battersea, around Shuttleworth Road near to Battersea Park. This was studied by Munt[25] in 1985, some 10-15 years after it had started, and by which time its political colour had changed firmly away from its traditional Labour to produce a Tory ward. He confirmed that the gentrifiers had not moved back from the suburbs but had rather come 'south of the river' because prices in their originally preferred areas of Kensington, Fulham, and Chelsea were too high for them. They also fitted the pattern that we have identified earlier.

Wandsworth was Labour controlled in the early seventies and still keen on demolishing older houses for housing gain but its one attempt near to South Battersea after Darley/Chatham Roads failed. This story about the area around Louvaine Road is told in Sandra Wallman's book, 'Living in South London'[26]. These roads were built in 1860-75 and had indeed been regarded as part of 'New Wandsworth' in local directories and hence of South Battersea, with substantial houses then occupied by households keeping one, or occasionally more, servants. The railway companies contemplated building a dedicated access from St John's Hill to Clapham Junction[27] to attract the residents of these roads.[vii] However the houses were certainly too large for the smaller families of the twentieth century and although the buildings lasted reasonably well, they were rarely modernised and by 1970 had been heavily multi-occupied for 50 or more years. Although virtually all the buildings by then had a bath, kitchen, and indoor toilet, these were normally shared by the various households in each house. It was this sharing of facilities that helped it score highly in the GLC analysis of HAAs.

[vii] One such was the composer and conductor Charles Lucas who lived at No 9 Louvaine Road. He was principal of the Royal Academy of Music and composed one opera, The Regicide, and three symphonies as well as other works. The Royal Academy set up a gold medal for composition in his memory following his death in 1869.

Wandsworth Council wrote to each of the houses in the eight or nine roads in the Louvaine Road area in February 1974 asking them to offer their properties for sale to the council. There had been rumours of wholesale demolition and the residents naturally feared the worst and formed their own residents association, LARA. Complaints, petitions and lobbying of the local councillors followed and gradually the council members began to move towards rehabilitation, although they drew the line at involving the Solon Housing Association on the two principles common to Labour Councils of the time, preferring municipal enterprise and distrusting housing associations for the lack of elected representation on their boards.

Gradually the council and LARA began making the case for being made a HAA, although the officers still saw LARA as 'a group of activists, similar to squatters and other trouble makers' and often refused to collaborate in the multi-departmental initiatives which were necessary to make a HAA effective. Nevertheless, Louvaine Road was one of the first HAAs created in the country in March 1975 and progress was made over the next three years towards its rehabilitation, even if slow and laboured. The council continued in its belief that it could resolve housing problems by reducing the number of dwellings managed by absentee landlords and by 1978 had added a further 70 houses to the 65 it already owned in the HAA, 66 of which it had modernized to produce 143 dwelling units. While securing significant housing improvements, the number of empty or partially empty buildings was virtually unchanged over this period, the vast majority then being in the public sector, the rate of purchase being faster than the rate of rehabilitation, a pattern reflected over the whole borough.

The proportion of owner occupiers remained the same at 33%; council and housing association tenants grew from 15% to 41%, and private tenants decreased from 53% to 27%. This all changed after the election of the Conservative Council in May 1978. By then the number of empty properties owned by the Council in the borough as a whole was over 1,000. The Conservatives stopped the policy of 'municipalisation', the purchase of privately rented or empty property, sometimes by compulsory purchase orders, and began soon after to sell council houses, including those purchased in Louvaine Road.

Before we look at the consequences of this and other changes taking place at the time, it may be helpful to remind ourselves of what this part of South West London was like in the 1960s. There is relatively little written material on the area in the 15 years after the Second World War, although the unforgettable Peter Sellers sketch on Balham came out in 1959. It had been written earlier by Frank Muir and Dennis Norden who had come across the phrase 'Balham, Gateway to the South' in a Southern Railway promotional poster produced in the 1920s and they described Balham as lying 'four square on the Northern Line'. We can however find a number of writers to describe it as it was in the early 1960s. In his autobiography, John Walsh writes of his move in 1963 from Balham, in a house near 'the fast thoroughfare of Nightingale Lane SW12', to a house on Battersea Rise.[28]

> *'It was a very English sort of place. It had been a haven of middle-class luxury in the nineteenth century, home to well-heeled merchants and City gents who rode up to town each day in gigs and stove pipe hats......The Battersea end of Clapham Common was a dump: a service area for Clapham Junction: the busiest, noisiest, dirtiest railway junction in the country. It was a stridently working-class and immigrant neighbourhood then: a tough coarse-grained part of inner suburbia. I knew it as a tripartite ghetto, shared between the blacks, the Irish and the Poles.... It was a boring, dusty, Junction serving corridor between the smart end of Clapham and the newly proliferating suburban sprawl of Wandsworth. We weren't a village. We were barely a district. We were just an artery, a migratory conduit.'*

Another writer about London was prepared to contemplate the positive about Clapham in his 1966 guide book to London.[29]

> *'On the surface it looks irredeemable. But the bones are there, and more than anywhere else in London it is a place to sense what might and still could be. This is the perfect recipe for a neighbourhood; shops, open space, houses, a natural centre, and even a Georgian church (Holy Trinity). Now nobody cares much; it is all dog shit and bus tickets. But it could easily be marvellous.'*

This hope of better things is also noticeable in Tony Aldous'
description in 1980.[30]

> 'Three stations on the seedier, southern, end of the
> Northern Line; a large triangular Common, criss-crossed
> by traffic, and with clusters of red buses and a sad little
> Edwardian clock tower in the north east corner; the
> transport museum that local people tried (but failed)
> to keep – these are perhaps the main ingredients in the
> outsider's mental map of the place. But there is much
> more to Clapham than these. It has an illustrious past,
> and its present is lively and full of change.'

Noting that Clapham had the headquarters of at least seven trade
unions, and himself meeting a lot of civil servants there, he went on
to describe it as 'full of laundries and trade unions and civil servants.'

We have already seen how Patricia Hansford Johnson found the
Northcote Road market attractive and this is echoed by John Walsh.[31]

> 'Every Saturday, the Northcote market would move
> in and transform the bottom of our road into a multi-
> coloured souk of vegetables, meat, fish, groceries,
> American comics, old-style weighing machines, sheets
> of the Daily Sketch and the People to wrap your carrots
> in, and brawny men calling out, like so many Stanley
> Holloways playing Eliza Doolittle's dad, 'Gitcha lovely
> spuds 'ere, ahnly two bob a pahnd'

There were no supermarkets nearby and the road had as many
as thirteen butchers, three or four fishmongers and a handful of
pawnbrokers. People shopped virtually every day for food. There
is no doubt that the Northcote Road was very different from now,
although remaining popular as reported by the Financial Times in
2008[32] 'Nestled between Wandsworth and Clapham Commons,
discerning consumers have for decades flocked to south-west
London's Northcote Road in search of high quality local fare.'

In 1961, only 17% of households in inner London were owner
occupied and 64% were privately rented. Taking as best we can what

is now the borough of Wandsworth[viii], 27% were owner occupiers, 19% council tenants and 58% in privately rented accommodation. In Battersea the figures were quite different, with only 12% owner occupied and 67% privately rented. These statistics confirm significant differences between South and North Battersea with almost half of all Battersea's owner occupiers living in the four of its 16 wards most closely corresponding to 'Twixt the Commons' and Balham. About 33% of households in this area were owner occupied, twice the inner London average, and only 7% local authority. These wards voted Conservative in every election between 1900 and 1964, with the exception of 1945,[ix] and Jean Lucas[33] recounts the hard work put in by the local Conservative party in 1977 to ensure that the boundaries of the Northcote ward were redrawn to ensure that it remained strongly Conservative. North Battersea equally invariably voted Labour It is interesting too to compare the 1961 census details with John Walsh's description of the area. The census shows that approximately 4% of the population of the wards corresponding to Northcote and Balham was of Irish birth, 3.5% were from Afro Caribbean countries and 2% from other European countries. Although adding up to 10% in total, very much in line with Battersea as a whole, this is hardly the 'immigrant ghetto' described by Walsh, although in times of relatively little immigration it may well have seemed so.

Those who knew the area in the nineteen sixties all report that it remained very mixed and the relative picture had not changed very

---

[viii] Although one cannot study the individual returns from the more recent censuses, there is some statistical information available. Unfortunately it is not possible to answer all the questions that we might want. There are no tables at ward level available from the 1951 census or before and in any case questions on housing tenure were not included until 1961, and then only tabulated down to ward level. Moreover, it is difficult to create time series that are strictly comparable because of a variety of changes in detailed definitions. The local ward boundaries change between each census reflecting changes in population and this is further complicated in the case of the 1961 census because it was based on the pre GLC local authorities when Battersea and Wandsworth were separate boroughs and Wandsworth contained parts of what is now Lambeth.

[ix] The Conservative MP for South Battersea in the 1920s had been Viscount Curzon, son of the Governor General of India. The MP Between 1931 and 1945 was H R Selley a privately educated estate developer and president of the Federation of Master Builders.

much by 1971, when we have census information that is aggregated in ways that correspond more closely, although by no means exactly, to the present day boundaries. The proportion of households living in local authority housing was still four times greater in Wandsworth as a whole than in Balham or Northcote wards which had a correspondingly higher proportion of households living in owner occupied or privately rented accommodation. This is shown graphically in Figures 1-4.

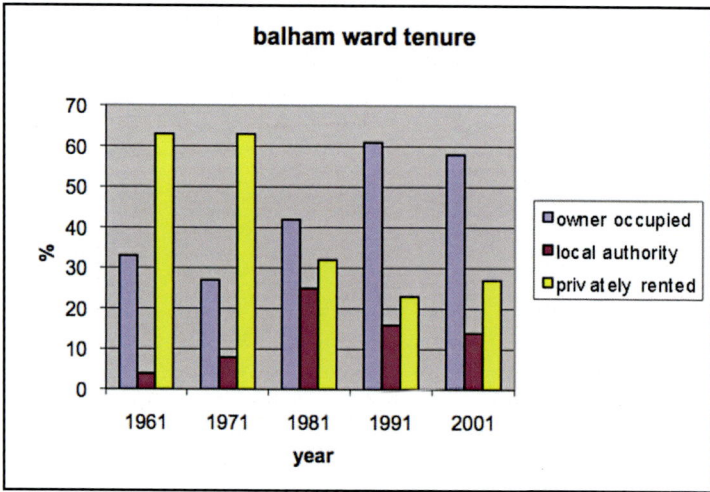

Figure 1

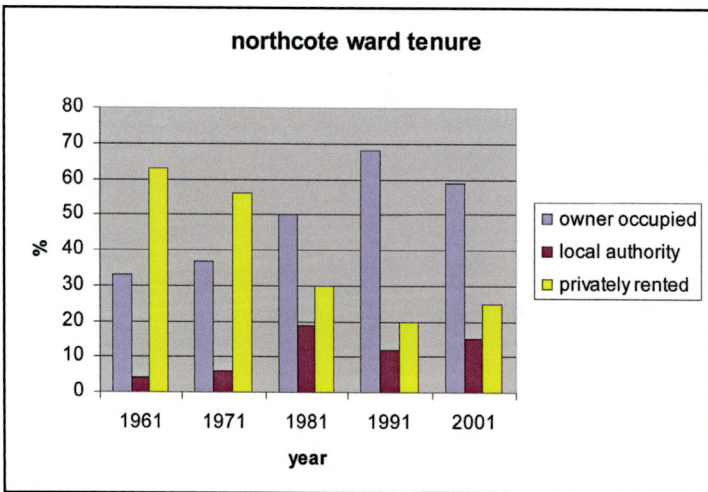

Figure 2

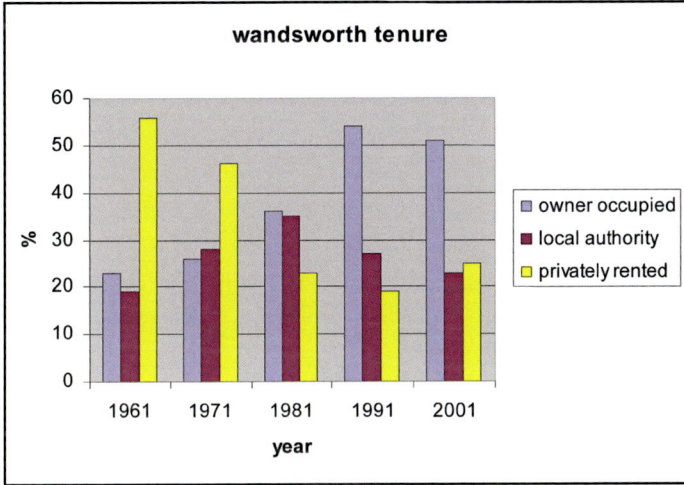

Figure 3

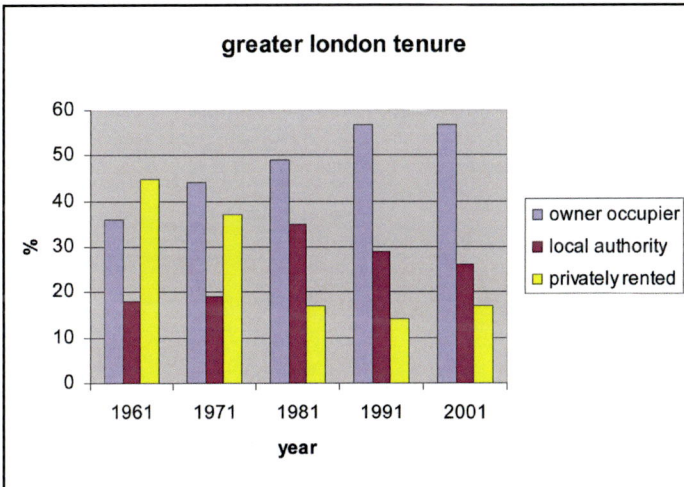

Figure 4

There was a little gentrification in Battersea as early as 1963, principally near Battersea Park, but it is clear from the figures that there was virtually none in Wandsworth then. Indeed Tom Slater[34] writes of it, with romantically rose-coloured spectacles in the early 1980s:

'At the southern end of Wandsworth Common in South London is a street called Bellevue Road. Twenty years ago, it was a quiet street lined with shops serving a long *established working class population. Local residents would greet each other in the bakery when buying warm rolls, or talk about the weather and their families whilst the butcher next door cut some luncheon meats. In the evenings there would be quiz nights in the pub, where those who worked long hours at nearby Wandsworth Prison could forget about the demands of their jobs and chat to the landlord about football, politics or a recent television documentary. Many people knew each other on a first name basis and were happy to be living so close to the open space of the Common, where their children could spend hours watching the frequent trains hurtle towards Clapham Junction, or keep out of mischief in a game of cricket or football before spending their money on a sweet assortment from the local newsagent. The entire area wasn't a space waiting to be 'discovered' – it was a place which hadn't changed for years, a home which had become inextricably entwined with each resident's identity for generations.'*

Change comes to Wandsworth

The change came at the end of the housing boom of the early seventies when young couples found themselves not just priced out of Kensington and Chelsea but also out of Hammersmith and Fulham. One person who moved in the early 1970s said 'We always longed to move north of the river. We had moved to the area because it was where we could afford to buy, but we never loved it.' When they moved out 10 years later, they sold their modernised house for ten times what they had paid for it. Nevertheless, the move to south of the river had started in earnest and John O'Farrell[35] commented later:

> *'I might have been more prepared for what was to happen in Battersea. The Sloane Rangers that had been spilling into Fulham were by now getting their passports stamped and coming south of the river as well. Alf Dubs commented 'Every skip contains a couple of Labour voters.'*

This was the time when one local magazine invented the term 'Sonies' because, it alleged, those trying to justify their move south of the river kept saying ' 'S on'y ten minutes from Peter Jones.' ''S on'y ten minutes from Chelsea.' Douglas Bartles-Smith, Vicar of St Luke's from 1975 for 10 years, says in his autobiography[36] that the area was beginning to be known as 'South Chelsea' and middle class people were moving in fast. The circumstances were very different from even a few years previously in 1968 when the then Bishop of Southwark, Mervyn Stockwood, had given a radical mission to the new vicar of St Luke's, Graham Fuller. He was told that the church was far too large and his job was to sell the current church hall for social housing and create a hall within the building of the church itself. Graham Fuller did indeed produce such a scheme but it was rejected by the parochial church council. St Luke's is now a very successful church making full use of all its buildings.

The figures also show the changes in tenure over the last 35 years, which are more significant. There were two elements to this. The first reflects the differing policies of Labour and Conservative local authorities in Wandsworth. The pressure to use houses lying empty persuaded the Conservative Government to include in their 1971 Housing Act a power for local authorities to purchase empty houses, if necessary by compulsory purchase, and provided funds for this. As we have seen, when Labour won Wandsworth in 1971, the Council made energetic use of this (describing their policy as 'a more aggressive policy of acquisition of residential property') and were purchasing 400-500 dwellings every six months. Coupled with some new build, local authority housing increased in Wandsworth as a whole from 28% in 1961 to 35% in 1971.

The policy of municipalisation was immediately reversed by the Conservatives when they won power in 1978. They sold off not just the individual houses municipalised by Labour but also large numbers of the purpose-built council houses. These policy changes by the local authority had a much greater effect in these two wards than in the borough as a whole. The comparative effect of municipalisation in Balham and Northcote wards was dramatic, with the proportion of local authority dwellings in the Labour period trebling to 25% in Balham and 19% in Northcote, although the latter will also have included the redevelopment of the Chatham Road estate. This proportion then decreased sharply over the next twenty years and, in the case of Northcote, returned to the previous very low value, well below that of Wandsworth as a whole.

In 1984 a student wrote to the Wandsworth local authority asking for their views on gentrification. The terse reply[37] - 'though gentrification has occurred in parts of the borough, the process has not been an issue that has been examined.' - was a little economical with the truth if the Tory Agent Jean Lucas' book on the Wandsworth Story is to be believed.[38] Louis de Bernieres[39] catches some of the changes in his description of Earlsfield, in Wandsworth, one train stop after Clapham Junction:

> '*A middle-class boy from rural Surrey is as much a foreigner in Earlsfield as the person who arrives from Ireland, unless he is the kind who has bought his first house, stays only a couple of years, never meets his neighbours, and then buys a bigger house nearer to somewhere 'nice'... They are a kind of ghost that flits through the lives of those who sit on the walls and chat.*'

Overlaid on this politically induced fluctuation was a continued systematic decline in the amount of privately rented accommodation and an increase in the amount of owner occupied. This was due to widespread gentrification as the young professional classes moved in and house prices soared. It is difficult to compare house prices on a consistent basis over a long period of time, because the condition of houses was variable. The Governors of Queen Anne's Bounty required their lessees to insure the houses and in the first decade of the twentieth century, the houses were insured for £500-600, or about the cost of building them. This rose gradually to £750-1,000 just after the First World War and barely changed over the next twenty years. After the Second World War, the Governors reminded their lessees that building costs had roughly doubled and the houses were then insured for £2000-2,500, with some for as much as £3000. While experience would suggest that insurance values are under-estimates, this seems compatible with one or two local sales of houses comparable with Old Park Avenue over the same period.

Advertisements in local newspapers in 1949 suggest that 3 or 4 bedroom houses between the Commons cost about £1,500-2,000. By the 1960s, one person who bought about that time reports that virtually all the houses were about £5,000, except for those which had special features such as central heating when they might cost £1,000 more. Prices then increased by leaps and bounds, doubling and more by the peak of the 1973 boom, £15,000-20,000 by the late seventies, £50,000 in the early 1980s, £200,000 or more in the early 1990s. By 2007 prices were £750,000 and upwards, with larger houses up to £1.5m - £2m.

All in all, house prices seem to have increased in the whole of Wandsworth by a factor of 30 or 40 over the last 35 years, far faster than inflation. A dramatic example is the partly modernized house the author bought for £13,000 in 1973 not far away in Earlsfield, sold ten years later for £40,000, and which was recently on the market for around £600,000. The house next door to that one was available to let for £525 a week in 2008, an annual rent approximately double the value of the house 35 years ago.

Not surprisingly, this has brought all manner of changes to the neighbourhood. Restaurants and estate agents became the most common shops as only they can afford the rising rents. The scale of this can be illustrated by another quotation from John O'Farrell[40].

> 'There had been two or three estate agents in Lavender Hill when I moved to the area (1985). Now there were twenty five. The old man who lived in the flat next to me had no bath and no central heating. When he died the flat was done up and I walked out of my door to see Cecil Parkinson viewing it with one of his daughters, A Tory Cabinet Minister thinking of buying his daughter a flat in Battersea'

The Northcote market gradually changed from its original cheap and cheerful nature to a variety of (fewer) up-market stalls. Farrow and Ball, the upmarket paint company established a Clapham branch in the road and the two star Michelin chef, Marcus Wareing, opined that 'Northcote Road in Clapham is a treasure trove [for food shopping].'[41] Private schools, at least at the primary level, boomed.

Expensive cars abounded and the 4x4s conducted the school run. Heavily engineered baby buggies were everywhere and demand from Wandsworth commuters for peak hour rail services was predicted to grow faster than in any other part of South London over the period to 2020. The area also became a haven for Financial Times journalists, if the numbers of articles about the area appearing in the paper are anything to go by.

As well as the rise in house prices, another indication of the changing population is the age distribution. This is illustrated for Wandsworth as a whole in Figure 5.

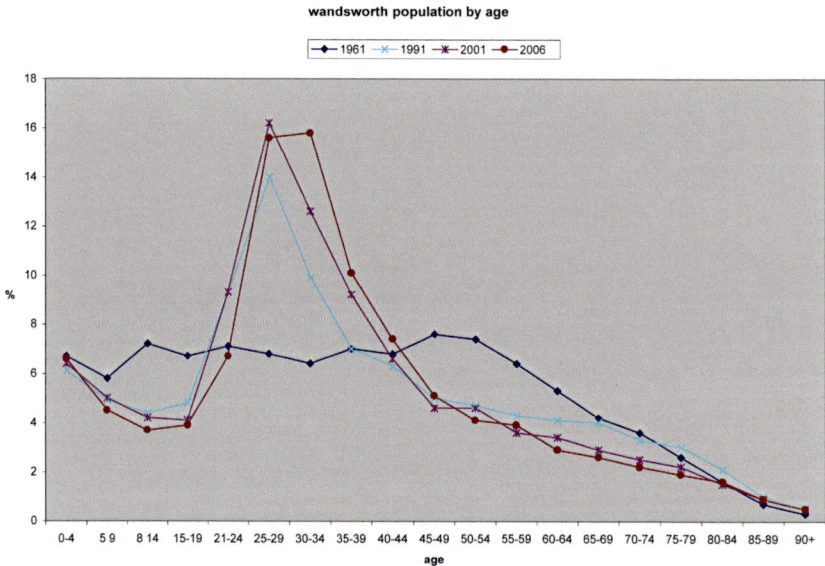

Figure 5

In 1961, the population was roughly evenly spread between the different five years age groups from 0 to 55 and then declined steadily. By 2001, there was a very marked peak at 25 to 35 with correspondingly fewer school age children and older people, although the estimated distribution for 2006 suggests a small flattening of that peak, whether because the house prices are now too high for younger people to buy or because some of those who bought are staying put.

Figure VI compares the population by age in Wandsworth in 201 with that in London as a whole and in neighbouring areas. It shows an even more marked peak for the Balham and Northcote wards where the proportion of people from 20 to 45 is 57.6% and 59.7% respectively compared with the Wandsworth average of 50%.

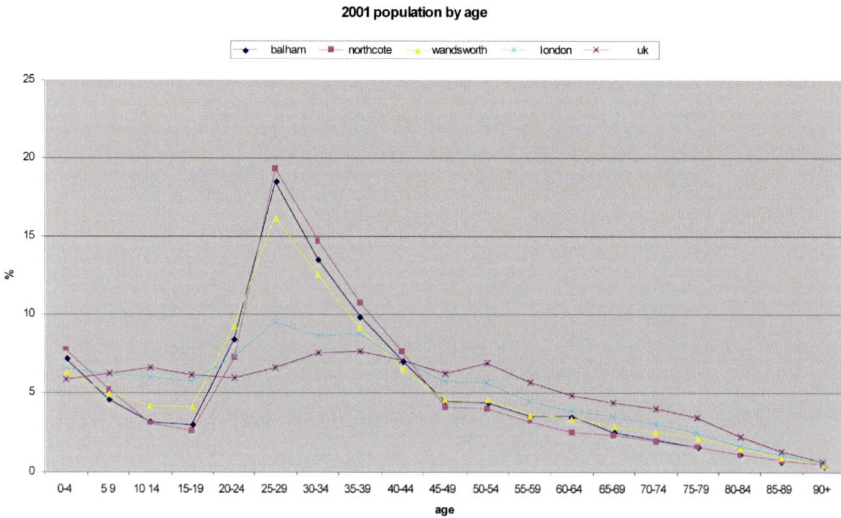

Figure 6

Battersea was the youngest constituency in the country in 2007 – as well as the fifth richest. This follows from the remarkable homogeneity of the 'Twixt the Commons' area – with almost no local authority accommodation and the terraced housing occupied almost exclusively by young professional couples with children. The area is often called Nappy Valley because of the very high proportion of small children, but this seems less borne out by the statistics where the proportion of children 0-4 is 7.2% in Northcote ward and 7.8% in Balham compared with the Wandsworth average of 6.4% and the London average of 6.7%. This is not very different from the Wandsworth average of 6.7 in 1961. Balham and Northcote wards were always a little bit higher.

Perhaps the most stunning statistic is the change in social class of the area as described by National Statistics. Wandsworth is about 70% professional and managerial compared with the national average of just under 50% and London of 58%.

Social class by year in Wandsworth

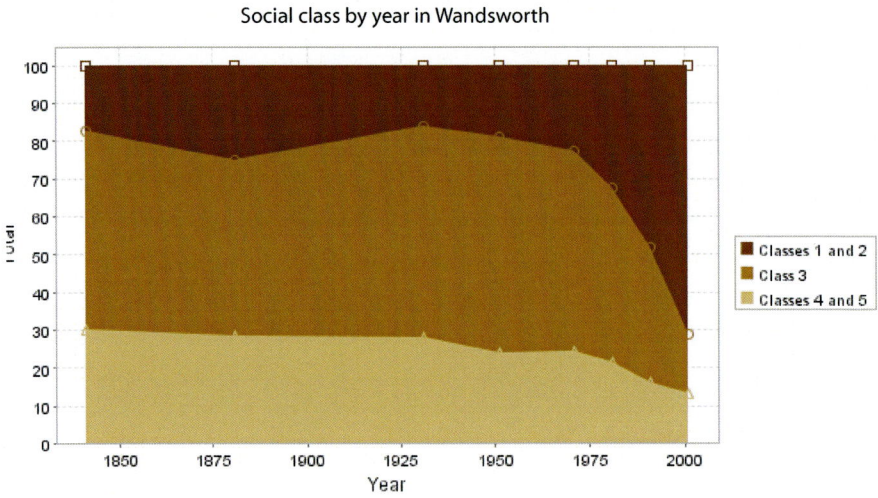

Figure 7

Classes 1 and 2 are essentially professionals and managers, class 3 are clerical and skilled workers, while classes 4 and 5 and semi and unskilled manual. The reductions in clerical and skilled manual and corresponding increases in professional and managerial appear only to have started in earnest in the 1970s. Figure VIII shows the difference from the national figure has arisen entirely since 1971, although it reflects in a more extreme form what has been happening in much of London with the effects of the explosion of jobs in financial services.

Proportion of socioeconomic classes 1 and 2 in Wandsworth

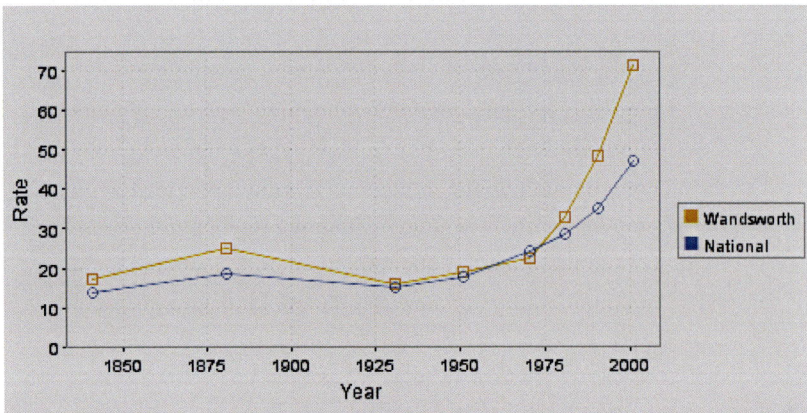

Figure 8

Wandsworth has a somewhat lower ethnic minority proportion than London as a whole (22% compared to 29%), largely accounted for by a lower proportion of Indians and Bangladeshis. Balham has the same proportion as Wandsworth as a whole but Northcote is more white at 86%. Northcote has been getting a little more white (81-86% from 1981 to 2001) while Balham has recently become more white (72%-80% over same period). Wandsworth has barely changed but this appears to conceal a combination of ethnic minorities moving in, often as immigrants and more established families moving out, particularly to Croydon and beyond. Wandsworth, together with Hackney, had the largest percentage reduction of any London borough in its Afro-Caribbean population during 1991-2001.

The population changes in Wandsworth follow the general pattern of gentrification. In the 1960s and 1970s, it was the less well off left-leaning professionals who bought property, but as the area grew more middle class and property prices soared, the richer and more affluent moved in since only they could afford the house prices. They were also encouraged by the policies of the local authority, such as low tax rates, which were designed to bring on more Conservative voters. While the level of privately rented dwellings declined steadily, the working class moved out, many taking enough money from their homes to buy in what seemed to them the more attractive outer suburbs. By the twenty first century, house prices were so high that only the very affluent could move in. Essentially this meant bankers, lawyers and others engaged in the global financial services industry; one estate agent estimated[42] that 39% of purchasers were from the City with a further 24% working in professional services. As the Financial Times put it[43], 'The Victorian terraces between Clapham and Wandsworth Commons have long been a favourite of City workers with a family and a bonus to blow.'

The age distribution table of purchasers shows 43% in their 30s and 21% in their 20s, a much younger buyer profile than seen in prime central London. 20% of purchasers are from overseas, again reflecting the influence of the city. Claims that the area is 'only 35 minutes from the South Kensington Lycee' may explain why French is regularly heard on the streets. The most exclusive estate agents moved in, eager for a share of a market that has risen by 325% in the decade to 2006, 50% more than in London as a whole.

Improvements abound, graduating from loft extensions to basements and cellars being dug out at great expense.

But the strain is beginning to tell and a recent Experian credit check revealed that Wandsworth had the fifth highest level of personal debt in the country at the end of 2008, tied largely to housing[44]. A recent article in the Financial Times[45] recorded some of the recent history. Beginning with the comment, 'Just thirty years ago, the upper middle classes tended to look down their noses at "south of the river", scorning Clapham, Wandsworth and Battersea' and quoting an upmarket estate agent that there was even a stigma 10 years ago, the author goes on to say that, 'for some reason this tiny area of Wandsworth has become intensely desirable for 30-something professional couples who can spend £700,000 on a three bedroomed house.' He found one not-quite-resident to say 'I can't afford it here; I'm from just off Lavender Hill not between the Commons, which is posh, posh, posh. To live here you have to be blonde, rich and stuck-up.'

A somewhat more scholarly piece of research, although with a sample not very much larger, was published by Butler and Robson.[46] Their view is that the 'suitability' of the area has been assiduously contrived, primarily through manipulation of markets (in education, housing and leisure) rather than spontaneous associational activity. Their sociological summing up:

> '... the social structure is more atomized here, actors motivated instrumentally by the requirements of their households and their jobs. Although the area does have a widely understood symbolic identity, the leap towards active mutuality on the basis of enlightened self interest appears not to have been made to any significant degree. It is the strength of the local markets in education, housing, leisure and consumption that satisfies the needs of the middle class residents. The cultural capital stored in the community being highly variable, the educational success of the children and the infrastructure of social interaction can ultimately be secured through the deployment of economic capital. Although there is wide scope for commercially based social activity, the connections that derive from it operate at a lower level

of interpersonal intensity and support an instrumental and relatively superficial sense of place. Battersea is, in short, less about formal participation and joining things than a community of interest based on loosely shared norms and expectations – the manifestation of which is probably eating out in the local restaurants.'

They pick out the educational aspects as one of the features that attracts people to the area, although some argue that the families move out when their children go to boarding school.[47]

'The emphasis here is on the performance and examination success rates. It is in the 'circuit of schooling' that the instrumentalist cast of the area is most apparent – the private nurseries, nannies, prep schools and flourishing primary and secondary sectors give the place a pervasive hothouse atmosphere.'

There was a relatively large number of single people living there by 2007, and it is even claimed to be the best place in London to meet an eligible bachelor forming part of what The Economist calls 'The Bridget Jones economy'.[48] This may be an explanation for the small rise in the proportion of households renting in the 15 years since 1991 as well as the ability of Northcote Road to sustain 35 restaurants. Perhaps it is this that allows Butler and Robson to write:

'The consequence of this instrumentalism is the absence of an affective dimension in people's relationships to the area. For all its prosperity and 'success', between the commons lacks an atmosphere of depth, of attachment... This can give the place a feeling of superficial homogeneity with which residents not tied in to its prevailing normative structure and institutions are often uncomfortable. The common good in Battersea is established through market based commonalities of interest based on households acting atomistically.'

However not everyone was happy. Butler and Robson commented on the amount of work related networking that goes on in these much gentrified areas, arguing that

*'the super gentrifiers actively connect global capital
flows to the neighbourhood level...which have come to
rely, to an extent, on face-to-face contacts not just in the
Square Mile, but also in the neighbourhood.'*[49]

It is this that may have led one of their interviewees, aged 32,
who had left Battersea, to tell them:

*'The dividing line between work and leisure time is
already blurred in the City without living on top of the
people you work with as well. I left Battersea because I
like to make the most of my time off. I don't like being
reminded of the work all the time. Northcote Road is a
branch of the City now.'*

These changes are not just confined to Battersea. Even though
Balham is irrevocably linked to the Peter Sellers sketch, the local MP
Martin Linton claimed, 'It has lost its joke status – it's a very nice place
to live'. Stefan Stern, writing in the New Statesman in 2000 agrees.

*'Something amazing has happened to Balham: it has
cast off the naff and embraced the new. Where there
once stood a froth-free zone - even the frothy coffee
lacked froth – now there is an espresso bar at the railway
station. The sort of properties that nurses, teachers or
even junior doctors would once have considered within
their reach are now for the bankers, the consultants and
the lawyers who have fled south in search of 'affordable'
homes. Tweedy jackets and sensible shoes are chased out
by pin-stripes and Prada. No longer just the gateway
to the south, now a highly desirable pocket of 'south
Clapham south', sucking up the not-quite-rich-enough
overspill from Battersea and Clapham (who in turn had
spilled over from Chelsea and Fulham).'*

FT.com reported more recently on Balham as another classic
London regeneration story.

*'Until relatively recently, the area was seen as something
of a nonentity, known for being Clapham's seedy relation*

and a bit too close to the prostitute haunt of Bedford Hill. One estate agent says "We now get people saying they want to be in Balham in preference to the back end of Clapham." Today the area has a well-used high street, an excellent street market and an overland train-Tube intersection. But in the mid-1980s living there was a matter of necessity rather than choice; residents socialised elsewhere and didn't walk around at night. Even in the late 1990s, says Jacqui Canham, a freelance journalist who moved to the area seven years ago, "I used to tell people I lived in South Clapham rather than Balham." Another estate agent adds "The prostitutes have been displaced by a clutch of new restaurants, bars, patisseries and coffee shops at the bottom of the hill. We even have a brand new Waitrose on the old Morrisons supermarket site - a sure sign of increasing opulence."

Old Park Avenue since the war

Old Park Avenue played its full part in all these developments. The lease of No. 24 was bought in 1936 by Mr Stanislaw, who lived in Clapham, although neither he, nor subsequently his widow, lived in the house, renting it as up to three flats. A number of other Polish families bought houses and there were Polish tenants in other houses. One of those who moved there in the early nineteen fifties is still in the same house. To judge from their names, there seem also to have been a number of families of Irish and Italian extraction.

In 1945 Josie Miller rented the ground floor of 20 Old Park Avenue which had been taken over by Battersea Council because it was empty. She found the street very friendly in those days with more children around although that may have been because they all played outside in street. Her father, whom she described as jet black and illiterate, had fled from the aftermath of slavery in Guyana, stowed away and ended up in London He worked as dogsbody and washer up for George Sanger's circus until he invented his own act with two others. In winter they lived in digs and he married his landlady's daughter, Roseanne (who was white). Josie and her brother Lance were the only black children in school in Stockwell in the 1920s. Her mother had bad arthritis and was in a wheel chair for 30 years. When Josie pushed her around in it everyone thought she was a servant, because no one could imagine a white woman having a black daughter. Josie bought a car to get her mother about and this was one of only two in the street in the1940s.

She remembered two of her neighbours who were long standing families in the street. Henry Borley lived in 18 Old Park Avenue with his daughter Edith until he died in 1951 aged 89, having been there since 1906. David Gregory in the flat above her described it as a 'Dickensian character house'. As we saw earlier, Frederick Hudson, who owned the other car in the street, had moved back to his house, 22 Old Park Avenue, to live with his son Louis and daughter-in-law Dorothy. Frederick was then in his 80s and Josie remembers that the maid had retired but continued to live as part of the family with Dorothy having to do the entire domestic work.

There was still a regular turnover of lessees but attempts to purchase the freehold were still resisted by the Church Commissioners, the successors to Queen Anne's Bounty. They replied to one request from No. 36 in the early 1950s saying:

> 'Prior to April 1948, it was considered inappropriate to dispose of the freehold of this property which formed part of a block.'

However, they did sell it for £720/10/- and later sold the freehold for No 24 for £525 to Ada Stanislaw. There was a dramatic change in policy in 1957 when there was a review of the Commissioners' residential property holding. The Commissioners accepted the recommendations of the review 'that properties on a selected estate in the North and in London should be offered to lessees or occupiers with a reasonable time limit for acceptance, followed by an auction of unsold properties'.

The electoral roll, combined with the Rate Book, demonstrate a substantial degree of multi-occupancy during the 25 years after the Second World War. The number of electors, almost certainly fewer than the number of adults, rose to a peak of 146 on a number of occasions between 1961 and 1971. Only one third of the houses at most were occupied by single families and many of them had lodgers. The vast majority were either occupied as three flats, one per floor, which may or may not have been self-contained, or let as single rooms. The Rate book for 1961 specifically records 7 and 13 as apartment houses (with 20 adults resident between them) and No. 18 as let to overseas students. It is evident from the electoral roll too that 10, 11, 13 and 28 were also let as individual rooms, since each had 10 or more adults in that period and No. 11 as many as 13 in 1967.

Table II sets out the changes.

TABLE II
Number of households spending years at same address

Years	10+	15+	20+	25+	30+	35+	40+	45+	50+	55+	60+	65+
Year												
1941	16	10	9	7	5	5	2					
1946	12	8	7	6	4	2	2					
1951	10	9	5	4	4	2	1	1				
1956	16	5	5	5	4	4	2	1	1			
1961	15	12	4	4	4	3	3	2	1	1		
1966	13	11	10	3	3	3	2	2	2	1	1	
1971	19	13	11	9	2	2	2	2	2	2	1	1
1976	17	16	10	8	7							
1981	11	11	11	7	5	5						
1986	5	4	4	4	2	2	2					
1991	5	4	3	3	3	2	2	2				
1996	12	5	4	2	2	2	1	1	1			
2001	15	11	5	4	2	2	2	1	1	1		
2006	17	14	10	4	3	2	2	2	1	1	1	

Source: Electoral Roll

There is a distinct change after the war when a relatively large number of new households moved in, often living in flats rather than the whole house, but then themselves staying for 20 years or more. In 1961, there were only four families left from before the war and those families averaged 45 years in their house. The big changes started in the early 1970s when the number of adults living in the road dropped by 20% between the end of 1972 and 1974 and then dropped by a further 20% over the next two years. This was also the time when formal planning permission was granted for conversion into flats for a number of the houses, although in one case at least, No. 20, this was no more than recognition of what had been in existence for some time. By 1971 a third of the post war households had been there for twenty or more years and two thirds for over ten years. A local boy who used to do 'Bob-a-job' in the area said the occupants were all 'very nice and always good for a shilling'[51]

In the nineteen seventies and early eighties many of those who had moved into the road after the war either died or sold up to the young professionals buying the houses in the first wave of gentrification. During this period, the last two people left from before the war died, Ella Robson Young in 1972 aged 92, having moved into No. 26 in 1905, and Mabel Howlett who died in 1975 aged 88, having moved in to No. 14 in 1915. The longest standing resident of the road, Josie Miller, stayed in her flat for over 60 years, finally moving to an old people's home in 2009.

When tenants left or died, the house would often be kept empty until a purchaser could be found, and in every case the purchasers transformed the houses back to single family occupation. Prices were rising rapidly and I well remember being pointed out at a street Christmas party in 1983 as the person who had paid an extraordinary £100,000 for one of the houses. One family had bought theirs, with a sitting tenant and entirely unmodernised for [£25,000]. By 1991, only five of the households had been in the road for more than 10 years, the lowest number ever, and that included two who had been there since 1946 and 1952 respectively. This change from multi-occupation back to single family occupation is mirrored by a dramatic reduction in the number of people on the electoral roll and an increase in the number of children, as Old Park Avenue made its contribution to Nappy Valley. The street's overall population will also have included a number of nannies and au pairs, the latter of whom would not normally have been on the electoral roll.

Table III
Average numbers on electoral roll

Years	Number
1934-39	124
1947-51	137
1952-56	133
1957-61	140
1962-66	143
1967-71	131
1972-76	123
1977-81	93
1982-86	84
1987-91	79
1996	85
2001	79

Source: electoral roll

These figures somewhat overstate the change in the 1970s since a significant part of the initial reduction came from houses being vacant, awaiting purchase and development. For example, there were between three and four houses vacant (but not always the same ones) every year from 1977-80. Nevertheless, there was a steady change from multi-occupation. In 1972, no fewer than nine houses had seven or more people on the electoral roll; in 1977 there were three, and in 1980 there was only one. On the other hand not all the houses returned to single occupancy. Apart from the block of flats built to replace the bombed 17 and 19, four houses remain as flats, now appropriately self-contained, two with at least the freeholds owned either by a housing association or the local authority. By 2006, almost half the households had been in the street for ten years or more.

What is the future for Old Park Avenue? The houses are now out of the price range of the kind of professionals who bought them 25 or 30 years ago. They now require someone with a substantial amount of capital or at least a large bonus. Only people working in the City are likely to have the funds, and they often gut the houses to produce a contemporary look rather than keep the original features. This is what Butler and Lees call super-gentrification, with the associated extensions upwards and downwards. Alternatively, as is already happening in some places, the houses will be sold for conversion into small flats such as already exist in four of the houses.

Like other parts of London, the area has been hit by the 2009 recession but seems to be weathering the storm better than many other areas as the prospect of bonuses returns[52]. Northcote Road has no higher turnover of shops than other comparable areas of London and very few estate agents have closed. Indeed, one estate agent, reported in The Times, commented that house hunters can get more for their money and still be safe in the knowledge that they are moving into an area classified as 'prime southwest London' with prices per square foot 25% cheaper than Fulham[53]. Up-market estate agent Savills says 'We are losing a surprising number of families to Wandsworth.' and another one says that 'people move to Wandsworth for the transport...the greenery, and the schools.' Honeywell School was characterised by the Financial Times[54] as one of London's desirable state primaries, describing it 'as a 'honeypot' school long beloved of the area's bankers. It is so oversubscribed that parents can't be guaranteed a place if they live even more than one street away.'

It will be interesting to see whether the newcomers have the time or the inclination to construct a local community and indeed whether they want to stay more than a few years before moving out to the country. One of the strengths of London, as for any great city, is that areas can reinvent themselves and we can expect that the less affluent but potentially active in building a community will begin to look elsewhere, whether further out from the centre or in very different parts of London, including the East End.

(Endnotes)

1   Stephen Inwood. 1998 A History of London p823
2   London Suburbs 1999 Ed Andrew Saint p 135
3   Greater London Demographic Review 2005-39
4   Clapham Society. 2002 Clapham in the Twentieth Century p134
5   The Manchester Guardian 23 June 1948

6 Ruth Glass. 1960 London's Newcomers p46
7 Stephen Inwood Ibid p855
8 The Borough News 31 January 1958
9 Harry Williams. 1949 South London p 212
10 Quoted in Roy Porter.1994 London A Social History p 358
11 London Suburbs Ibid p 169
12 English Heritage 2007 The Heritage of Historic Suburbs, Suburbs and the Historic Environment
13 Ruth Glass. 1963 Introduction to London, Aspects of change
14 Francis Sheppard.1998 London A History p 353
15 Roy Porter. 1994 London A Social History p 352
16 Fred Hirsch. 1976 Social Limits to Growth p 27
17 Fred Hirsch Ibid p 173
18 Jonathan Raban. 1974 Soft City p 53
19 Gillian Tindall. 1977 The Fields Beneath p221
20 Metereological Office website
21 Tim Butler and Loretta Lees. Trans Inst Br Geogr 2006 NS31 467
22 Michael Frayn. 1967 Towards the End of the Morning
23 Michael Jager 1986 in Gentrification of the City Eds Smith and Williams pp 79,87
24 Butler and Lees Ibid
25 Ian Munt J Econ and Planning A 1987 19 1175-97
26 Sandra Wallman et al 1982 Living in South London
27 Tim Sherwood. 1994 Change at Clapham Junction p 15
28 John Walsh 1999 Falling Angels p 51
29 Ian Nairn 1966 Nairn's London
30 Tony Aldous 1980 The Illustrated London News Book of London's Villages p 61
31 John Walsh Ibid p 54
32 Financial Times 16 February 2008
33 Jean Lucas 1990 The Wandsworth Story p 65
34 Tom Slater 2002 What is Gentrification ?
35 John O'Farrell 1998 Things can only get better p 155
36 Douglas Bartles-Smith. 2007 Fighting Fundamentalism p 45
37 Charles Brodie thesis 1985 Wandsworth Historical Library
38 Jean Lucas Ibid p 68
39 Louis de Bernieres 2001 Sunday Morning at the Centre of the World p xi
40 John O'Farrell Ibid p 191
41 The Times. The Table p 3 March 18 2010
42 taken from Knight Frank 'News Views and Reviews' 2006
43 Financial Times 30 November 2007 p3
44 Quoted by Giles Fraser in Church Times 5 December 2008
45 Financial Times 14 October 2006 p3
46 Butler and Robson 2001 Urban Studies 38 2145-62
47 Butler and Robson Ibid
48 The Economist Dec 20 2001
49 Butler and Lees ibid
50 Stefan Stern New Statesman 5 June 2000
51 Daniel Jones. Private communication
52 Financial Times 17 October 2009 p 4
53 The Times April 3 2009 Bricks and Mortar p 15
54 Financial Times 19 April 2009 Life And Arts p 1

C H A P T E R   1 3

CONCLUSIONS

This history has shown how much small areas of London can change, both becoming rich and fashionable and moving into decline. In the eighteenth century, the former rural village became the suburb of choice for bankers and merchants looking for a different life style. They wanted to protect their wives and families from the iniquities of the city but allow themselves easy access to their businesses. By the middle of the nineteenth century, the population was already very different. Most of the very rich had moved back into the centre or had taken advantage of the trains to move further out. They were succeeded by the merely well-off, living in large houses with an acre of grounds. The last part of the nineteenth century saw most of these people disappear to the outer suburbs and their villas replaced by terraced housing.

There was no great plan for the development of Clapham or South Battersea. The rich were happy to sell their land to developers as they moved, or the older generation died. The eventual terraced housing was built in a piecemeal manner, with the builders having to make the best use of the plot they had at their disposal. That is why Northcote Road stops at Broomwood Road, rather than continuing through to Nightingale Lane, why Gorst and Dents Roads were constructed as a U-bend, and why Nightingale Park Crescent was created to allow a few more houses to be built. The pattern of estates in 1836 and the timing of their disposal for development also explains why some of the east/west roads between the Commons run from Bolingbroke Grove to Clapham Common, some to Leithwaite Road and some only to Webbs Road.

With a few exceptions, semi-detached houses between the commons are found only on the original Old Park Estate. This is the one example of restrictive covenants, in this case requiring larger houses, having a lasting effect on the built environment, extending even to houses built in the late 1920s on the site of Beechholme. An attempt to maintain a similar covenant on the Dents Estate was withdrawn when the land failed to sell in the early 1880s. Nevertheless the houses on both these two estates are larger than most of those elsewhere between the Commons and the area became known as 'New Wandsworth' to avoid any suggestion that it was part of either Battersea or Balham, one of many attempts to rename the area.

The period between the wars saw yet another large population shift with an enormous building programme of modern semi-detached house in the outer suburbs of London. While many of those living in the Victorian terraced houses stayed, the younger couples moved out to enjoy houses designed for gas and electricity. Clapham and Battersea moved into multi-occupation and went down market. This process continued after the Second World War, with Irish, Polish and West Indian immigrants moving in.

Over the last sixty years, another remarkable change has taken place. South Battersea has been reborn as 'Twixt the Commons', the latest name to conceal its Battersea origins. (Many people mistakenly refer to it as being in Clapham.) It has become one of the richest parts of London, ironically populated by bankers in just the same way as in the eighteenth century, but at rather greater density. The population is also a young one, with a much higher proportion of people in their 30s and 40s, repeating the late nineteenth century trend, and with one of the highest fertility rates in Europe.

Given its history, one would have to be a brave man to suggest that there will be no further changes. The gentrification has proceeded in three stages. The first wave, starting in the late 1970s, involved young professionals looking for a different way of life from their parents. Generally they wanted to maintain as many original features of the houses as they could; they cleaned the ceiling roses, opened up the fireplaces, and took the hardboard off the Victorian doors. As house prices increased, the second phase comprised more affluent professionals; the Northcote Road market ceased to be filled with cheap and cheerful stalls, and more and more of the shops became estate agents. Private schools abounded. Those moving in during the latest phase are more inclined to strip everything out of the house and move on from extending the loft to adding a basement.

It is not obvious what will come next. There is still a rapid turnover of houses, often as families move out to the leafy suburbs or beyond or as those who want to stay look for a larger house. Any spare land is eagerly snapped up by developers for more houses, while the private schools gradually accumulate more and more of the few very large Victorian houses that are left. Many more houses are being let, perhaps evidence of financial constraints but there does not seem to be much incidence of houses being broken up into flats. It is possible that the area will gradually become filled by those (older) households who have chosen to remain but at present the age distribution does not show any dramatic change.

Perhaps the only conclusion that can be drawn is that all previous suggestions that the area will remain as it was have proved incorrect, and in 30 years time the houses will be used in a radically different way and that the demography will be correspondingly different. What perhaps will remain true are David Olsen's words quoted in the Introduction.

> 'Even the much maligned speculative building of the Victorians, when painted, cleaned, fitted with bathrooms and central heating, and manageably compact kitchens, provides as satisfactory a domestic environment as anything our architects and planners can construct for us afresh.'

BIBLIOGRAPHY

GENERAL HISTORY

G F A Bell. 1964 Temporal Pillars

John Beckett. 2007 Writing Local History

T W H Crosland. 1905 The Suburbans

H.J Dyos. 1982 Exploring the Urban Past. (Eds)David Cannadine and David Reeder

Dyos and Wolff. (Eds) 1973 The Victorian City

T H S Escott.1897 Social Transformations of the Victorian Age.

Robert Fishman. 1987 Bourgeois Utopias

Fred Hirsch. 1976 Social Limits to Growth

Pamela Horn. 1975 The Rise and fall of the Victorian Servant

Henry Lazarus. 1892 Landlordism; An illustration of the Rise and Spread of Slumland

Lewis Mumford. 1938 The Culture of Cities

Julie Myerson. 2004 Home

Hannah More. 1809 Coelebs in Search of a Wife

A Offer. Property and Politics 1870-1914

Simon Schama. 2005 Rough Crossings

Jack Simmons. 1973 The Power of the Railways in The Victorian City Ed Dyos and Wolff

Neil Smith. 1996 The New Urban Frontier

Lawrence Stone. 1977 The Family, Sex and Marriage

Lawrence Stone. 1986 An Open Elite ?

F M L Thompson. Hampstead 1974

F M L Thompson Ed 1982 The Rise of Suburbia

Davis Thorns 1973. Suburbia

Kate Tiller. 1998 English Local History: The State of the Art

Tom Slater 2002 What is Gentrification ?

NOVELS/PLAYS

Barbara Comyn. 1981 The Vet's Daughter

Arthur Conan Doyle. 1894 The Naval Treaty in The Memoirs of Sherlock Holmes

Noel Coward. 1937 Present Indicative

Noel Coward. 1939 Introduction to This Happy Breed

Louis de Bernieres. 2001 Sunday Morning at the Centre of the World

Neil Dunn.1963 Up the Junction

Michael Frayn. 1967 Towards the End of the Morning

Emily Eden. 1859 TheSemi-detached House

John Galsworthy. 1906 The Man of Property

Pamela Hansford Johnson. 1935 This Bed Thy Centre

Pamela Hansford Johnson. 1955 An Impossible Marriage

Martin Knight. 2006 Battersea Girl

W M Thackeray. 1853 The Newcombes

Robert Tressell. 1965 The Ragged Trousered Philanthropist

P G Wodehouse. 1903 Mike

SW LONDON AND NEARBY LOCAL HISTORY

History of Arding and Hobbs. 1907

Keith Bailey. 1980 Battersea New Town

Battersea Park, An Illustrated History 1996

Sir Walter Besant. South London 1907

Sir Walter Besant. 1912 London South of the Thames

J Harvey Bloom. 1926 Bygone Balham and Tooting Bec

Edward Brayley.1850 History of Surrey Vol III

J H M Burgess. 1929 Chronicles of Clapham Appendix C VII

Clapham Society. 1984 Clapham Then and Now

Clapham Society. 2002 Clapham in the Twentieth Century.

W S Clarke. 1881 Suburban Homes of London

Gillian Clegg. 1998 Clapham Past

Sean Creighton. 2005 History of Battersea

Sean Creighton. Organized Politics and Cycling in the 1890s and 1900s in Battersea

Sean Creighton. 1999 Ancient Order of Foresters in Battersea and Neighbouring Districts

H J Dyos. 1961 Victorian Suburb

History of Edwin Evans. Wandsworth Historical Library

Michael Green. 2008 Historic Clapham

Graham Gower. 1996 Balham A Brief History

J W Grover. 1886 Old Clapham

Reg Groves. 1974 The Balham Group

R J Lister. 1930 Clapham in the Eighteenth Century

Roger Logan. 1977 South Battersea The Formative Years 1851-1900

Roger Logan. 2007 Wandsworth Historical Society Wandsworth Paper 15

Patrick Loobey. 2002 Battersea Past

Jean Lucas 1990 The Wandsworth Story

Daniel Lysons. 1792 History of Battersea

Priscilla Metcalf. 1978 The Park Town Estate and the Battersea Triangle

Morgan Crucible. 1956 Battersea Works

Arthur Porritt. 1930 A Home of Fellowship

Dorothy Pym. 1934 Battersea Rise House Introduction

Percy Fitzgerald. 1893 Victorian London Vol II– The Suburbs

Janet Roebuck. 1979 Urban Development in 19th-century London

James Ruddick 2001 Death at the Priory

Tim Sherwood. 1994 Change at Clapham Junction

E F Smith. 1976 Clapham

J G Taylor. 1925 Our Lady of Batersey

Edward Walford. 1897 Old and New London – The Southern Suburbs

Sandra Wallman et al. 1982 Living in South London

John Williams. 1976 Suddenly at the Priory

AUTO/BIOGRAPHY

Anthony Anderson. 1982 The Man who was H M Bateman

Douglas Bartles-Smith. 2007 Fighting Fundamentalism

J Baker. 1819 Life of Sir Thomas Bernard Bt

Hermione Hobhouse. 1971 Thomas Cubitt

A J Berry. 1960 Henry Cavendish

Richard Church. 1955 Over the Bridge

Charles Graves. 1903 Life and Letters of Sir Charles Grove

Greville. Memoirs

Christa Jungnickel and Russell McCormmach. 1999 Cavendish

John O'Farrell. 1998 Things can only get better

Roger North. 1698 Lives of the Norths

G H Pike. 1894 Life of Spurgeon

Stephen Potter. 1959. Steps to Immaturity

William Stillman. 1901 Autobiography of Journalist

Wallace Reyburn. 1989 Flushed with Pride

Charles Spurgeon. 1881 Almanack

Charles Spurgeon. 1897 The Early Years

Helen Thomas. 1935 As it Was...World Without End

Percy Thornton. 1912 Some things we have remembered

Sam Thornton. 1891 Year recollections

John Walsh. 1999 Falling Angels

CLAPHAM SECT

Clapham Antiquarian Sciety.1927 Clapham and the Clapham Sect

E M Forster. 1956 Marianne Thornton

Michael Hennell. 1958 John Venn and the Clapham Sect

Ernest Howse. 1953 Saints in Politics

Garth Lean. 1980 God's Politician

Milton M Klein. 2004 An Amazing Grace

Stephen Tomkins. 2007 William Wilberforce

G O Trevelyan. 1876 Life and Letters of Lord Macaulay

Standish Meacham. 1964 Henry Thornton of Clapham

GUIDEBOOKS

Thomas Allen. History of Surrey 1830

Tony Aldous. 1980 The Illustrated London News Book of London's Villages 1

John Battley (Ed). 1935 Clapham Guide

R and J Dodbury London and its Environs 1761

James Edwards. 1801 Companion from London to Brighthelmston. Part I

William Gaspey. Tallis's Illiustrated Guide to London

Patricia M Jenkins. 2003 The Book of Herne Hill

Ian Nairn. 1966 Nairn's London

G F Pardon. 1862 Routledge Shilling Guidebook to London

Pigot. Guide to Surrey 1823/4

Pigot. 1834 Guide to Surrey

James Thorne. 1876 Handbook to the Environs of London

Peter Vansittart. 1992 London, A Literary Companion

LONDON HISTORY

N J Barton. 1962 The Lost Rivers of London

Mrs Arthur Bell. 1907 The Skirts of a Great City

Walter Bell. 1926 Where London Sleeps

Sir Walter Besant. London in the Nineteenth Century 1909

Charles Booth. 1900 Life and Labour of the people in London, 3d Ed

Thomas Burke. 1937 London in my time

Brian Cookson. 2006 Crossing the River

Fried and Elman. 1968 Charles Booth's London

Ruth Glass. 1960 London's Newcomers

Ruth Glass. 1963 Introduction to London, Aspects of change

Jan and Cora Graham. 1938 The London Roundabout

Chris Hamnett. 2003 Unequal City

David Knyaston. 1994 The City of London Vol I

Stephen Inwood. 1998 A History of London

Alan Jackson. 1973 Semi Detached London

Roy Porter. 1994 London A Social History

Andrew Prescott. 2002 Freemasonry in London

Jonathan Raban. 1974 Soft City

Steen Rasmussen. 1934 London The Unique City

Chris Roberts. 2005 Cross River Traffic

Ed Andrew Saint . London Suburbs 1999

Francis Sheppard.1998 London A History

John Summerson. 1945 Georgian London

Colin Thom. Researching London's Houses 2005

Peter Thorold. 1999. The London Rich

Gillian Tindall. 1977 The Fields Beneath

Edward Walford. 1878 Old and New London

Edward Walford. 1897 Old and New London – The Southern Suburbs

Jerry White. 2001 London in the Twentieth Century

Guy R Williams.1975 London in the Country

Finn Jensen. 2007 The English Semi-detached House

Alan Johnson. 2006 Understanding the Edwardian and Inter-war House

Richard Russell Lawrence. 2009 The book of the Edwardian and Inter-war House

F Maitland. Building Estates

Raymond McGrath. 1934 Twentieth Century Houses

Hermann Muthesius. 1904 The English House English edition of 1979

Stefan Muthesius. 1982 The English Terraced House

Walter Pater. 1873 Studies in the History of the Renaissance Preface

Anthony Quiney. 1986 House and Home

Richard Rodger. 1989 Housing in Urban Britain 1780-1914

M H Baillie Scott. 1906 Houses and Gardens

Michael Stratton. 1993 The Terracotta Revival

ARCHITECTURAL/ HOUSING HISTORY

Gordon Allen. 1919 The Cheap Cottage and Small House

Derek Avery. 2003 Victorian & Edwardian ArchitectureThe Buildings of Clapham. 2000 The Clapham Society

John Burnett. 1978 A Social History of Housing 1815-1970

Bridget Cherry and Niklaus Pevsner. 1983 Buildings of England London 2 South

Roger Dixon and Stefan Muthesius. 1978 Victorian Architecture

Denis Edwards and Ron Pigram. 1986 London's Underground Suburbs

Judith Flanders. 2003 The Victorian House

English Heritage. 2007 The Heritage of Historic Suburbs

Mark Girouard. 1977 Sweetness and Light

INTERIOR DESIGN

Jenni Calder. 1977 The Victorian House

Lucy Crane. 1882 Art and Foundation of Taste

Charles Eastlake. 1868 Hints on Household Taste Dover Edition preface

Judith Flanders. 2003 The Victorian House

Bannister Fletcher. 1899 Architectural Hygiene

Mrs Haweis. 1881 Art of Decoration

Mrs Haweis. 1882 Beautiful houses

Bea Howe. 1967 Arbiter of Elegance

Robert Kerr. 1871 The Gentleman's House

Helen Long. 1993 The Edwardian House

Helen Long. 2002 Victorian Houses and their details

Hilary Mandelberg. 1994 Edwardian House Style

Judith and Martin Miller. 1987 Period Details

Linda Osband. 1991 Victorian House Style

 Mrs J E Panton. 1896 From Kitchen to Garret Ninth Edition

Mrs Alfred Praga. 1899 Appearances. How to keep them up on a limited income.

Alastair Service. 1992 Edwardian Interiors

M H Baillie Scott. 1905 Houses and Gardens

Kit Wedd. 2002 The Victorian House

INDEX

Abyssinia Road 36, 136, 253

Ackerman, Isaak 40, 54, 178

Afro-Caribbeans in neighbourhood
363-4, 375, 379, 387, 391, 400

Alexandria Hotel 103

Alfriston Road 174, 248, **249**

Alleyn's estate 14

Almeric Road 142-3

Altenberg Gardens 149, 167

Amner Road 171, 248

Appleby, Charles 209-14, 216, 220

Arding and Hobbs 236, **237**, 254, 348

Arnold, Matthew 76

Ashness family 142-3, 259

Ashness Road 168, 260

asparagus 28, 38, 58

Astle, Thomas 168, 178

Atkins family 30, 34, 36, 45, 71
Henry 27

Atkins Road 72, **73, 74**

Auckland Road 130, 140, 252

Babington, Thomas 43

back addition 298, 308, 309

Bacon, George Washington 136

Bagehot, Walter 10

Baldwin, Christopher 31, 171

Balham 3, 10, 18, 23, 25, 55-57, 78-
81, 99-101, 111-116, 119, 134,
217, 188, 345, 375, 390

Balham Grove 100

Balham High Road 56, **80**, 81, 112,
113, 114

Balham Hill 56, 57, 68, 78, 80, 95,
99, 100, 112

Ballingdon Road 171, 248

bankers 7, 9, 32, 44, 45, 46, 47, 49,
93, 120

Baptists 159, 189

Barclays 37, 53, 54

Bartles-Smith, Douglas 381

Bateman, H.M. 10, 160, 293

Battersea Bridge 32, **33**, 37, 76

Battersea Borough Council 25, 85,
173, 174-5, 370

Battersea Burial Board 121-3

Battersea ferry 32

Battersea Manor 20, 27, 31

Battersea Park Road 28

Battersea Rise 9, 24, 27, 50, 75, 86,
108, 119, 126, 130, 151, 177, 178,
217, 244, 348, 375

Battersea Rise House 39, 43, 121, 224,
172-3, **173**, 245, 258, 297, 346

Bayne, Eva 284, 353, 354, 358

bay windows 299-300

Beecholme 174, 195-6, 258, 262,
284, 400

Belleville Road 144, 146, 163, 241,
268

Belleville School 162, 209, **305**

Bellevue Road 379

Bennerley Road 127, 128, 135, 136,
137, 144, 159, 168, 241, 253,
256, 268

Bentley, Charles 214, 216, 220

Berber Road 168, 260

Besant, Sir Walter 76, 105, 108, 109

Blackfriars Bridge 32, 93

Blandfield Road 256-8

Bleak Hall Farm 55, 71, 74

Blenkarne Road 209, 214, 219, 220,
297, 347

Bolingbroke Arms 126, **127**

Bolingbroke Grove 24, 55, 119, 121,
122, 124, 139, 140, 159, 169,
178, 209, 211, 214, 216, 268, 271,
304, 357, 399

Bolingbroke Grove House (Dents House) **179**, 207, 213, 216

Bolingbroke Hospital 163-6, **164, 166,** 180

Bolingbroke House **164,** 191, 192, 207

Bolingbroke Park 133, 134, 136, 143, 144, 146, 163

Bolingbroke, Viscount Henry 31, 55

Bombs in Second World War 355, **356**

Booth, Charles general 202, 235, 238, 242, 246, 247, 304
churches 11, 96, 148, 156, 159, 226, 287
Poverty **250,** 251
police walks 10, 103, 108, 119, 115, 238, 249, 251-3, 255

Booty, James Horatio 195, 261, 265

Boutflower Road 169

Bowood Road 174, 248

Bragg, William 168, 169
Henry 213-6, 218-9, 220

Bramfield Road 170, 248, 260

British Land Society 124, 135, 189, 192,

Brixton 56, 72, 97, 99, 108, 362-3

Broadlands 169

Broadoak 188

Broomfield House 20, 40, 66, 119

Broomfield Lodge 40, **41**

Broomwood House 40, 119, 163, 167, 171, 207

Broomwood Road 132, 167, 169, **170,** 171, 248, 348, 357

Broxash Road 171

Buchanan, Claudius 43

Buckmaster, John 140-2, 143

Buckmaster Road 131, 136, 142

Bullen, Thomas 195

Burland Road 168, 260

Burns, John **175**

Cairns Road 131, 136

Camberwell 1, 5, 85, 103, 139, 258, 269, 290

Canford Road 174

Carlyle, Thomas 12, 76

Cavendish, Henry 53, 71, 182

Cavendish Road 54, 95, 100

Cazenove, Philip 130, 154, 168
John 132

Cedars, The 30, 95

Chalie, Matthew 180-1

Champion, Alexander 180

Champion, Elizabeth 170, 180

Chatham Road 124-9, 131, 135, 139, 146, 156, 159, 162, 167, 168, 184, 189, 252, 253, 260, 373, 381

Chatto estate 130, 168, 260

Chatto Road 168, 174, 260

Chelsea Bridge 98, 99, 125

Child, Francis 68

Childs Bank 37, 53, 178, 183

Chivalry Road 142, 252

Church Commissioners 206, 392

Clapham Common 3, 14, 18, 25, 27, 30, **31,** 65, 98, 108, 132, 139, 235, 245, 289, 365
North Side 27, 54, 347
South Side 25, 56
West Side 24, 108, 119, 132, 169, 171, 182, 217, 248, 251

Clapham Common underground station **104**

Clapham High Street **102, 346**

Clapham House 40

Clapham Junction 25, 86-8, 128, 131, 133, 194, 210, 236, 244, 251, 305, 313, 355, 363, 364, 373 382

Clapham Manor 27, 34

Clapham Manor Street 74

Clapham North underground station 104

Clapham Park 53, 71-74, 95, 100, 238, 265, 267

Clapham Place 28, 30

Clapham Road 70, 93, 151

Clapham Sect 9, 11, 24, 29, 37, 41-4, 49, 55, 65, 66, 79, 174

Clapham Society 197, 372

Clapham South bomb shelter 355-7

Clapham South underground station 30, 244, **344**, 362

Clarence Avenue 74
    clerks 9, 103, 146, 242, 254, 258, 297, 309, 338

Cobeldick, John 167, 169, 171

Colcutt, Thomas 199, **200**, 306

Coles, James 185-6

Conservative Land Society 90, 133, 134, 135, 144, 145,146

Corsellis, Alexander 84,142, 169
    Henry 169, 170, 242

Coward, Noel 199, 347

Cowper, William 7, 37, 48

Crapper, Thomas 132
    George 132

Craven House 195, 198, 362

Crescent Grove 68

Cubitt, Thomas 53, 71-4, **73**, 86, 91, 95, 96, 98, 238, 265, 267
    William 81

Culmstock Road 171, 174, 248

Cycling **243**, 243-4

Dainty, The **353**, **354**

Darley Road 130, 167, 373

Deacon, John 66, 181

Dealtry, William 43

Death, Robert 59, **60**

Debenham and Tewson 187
    and Farmer 192, 195
    and Farmer and Bridgewater 195

Defoe, Daniel 29, 45, 49, 54

Dent family 19, 177, 181, 191

Dent, Robert 121, 178, 180-2, 191
    John 182-5

Mary 182, 191, 206, 207
    William 182-3, 191, 216
    Villiers 185-7, 192-3

Dents estate 18, 55, 111, 142, 158, 177-198, **206**, **208**, 219, 245, 253, 400

Dents Road 216, 220, 241, 242, 399

Devereux Road 168, 357

Disraeli, Benjamin 66

Dragmire Lane 54

Dudley House 195, 197

Dulka Road 168, 260

Dungate, Charles 124

Dyos, H J 1, 5, 8, 58, 240

Earlsfield 338, 382, 383

Eastlake, Charles 12, 301, 303, 319, 326, 329

Eliot, Edward James 40, 43

Elms, The 54, 167, 216

Endlesham Road 199, 206, 306

Erskine Clarke, Canon John **147**, 147-154, 167, 168, 174,195, 197, 220, 230, 237, 244, 262, 266,271-4, 289
    churches 12, 154-9, 223-32
    schools 161-3
    hospital 163-6, 178
    Charles 230, 231, 278, 290, 291, 292

Estcourt Road 48, 214, 220, 221-2221, 311
    evangelicals 29, 33, 41, 42, 44, 48

Evans, Edwin 172, 173, 174, 221, 314, 346

Evelyn, John 28

Everidge J.W. 216

Fairseat 198, 202

Falcon Brook 24, 27, 50, 119, 167, 170, 178, 207, 214, 219

Falcon Road 28, 58, 126, 236

Faunthorpe, John Pincher 170

Ferndale 190, 201-2
Five Houses Lane 55, 121
Forbes, Sir Charles 129,167, 207, 219
Forster, E.M. 35, 40, 245
Frankfort House 54
Frayn, Michael 372
Friday Grove House 74
Fuller, Graham 381
Furzedown estate 338

Galsworthy, John 207
Gauden, Denis 27-28, 30, 95
Gauden Road 95
Gayville Road 168
    gentrification 5, 366-373, 379, 387
George, William 242, 248
Gilmore House 54
Gisborne, Thomas 43
Glenelg 40, 172
Gordon, John 181
Gorst, John 111, 207-8, 216
Gorst Road 111, 132, 216, 241, 284,
    399
Granard Road 214, 241, 253-6, 357
Grandison Road 168
Grandison, Viscount 32
Grange, The 31, 171
Grant, Charles 40, 42, 66
Greater London Council (GLC) 25,
    85, 365, 367
Greene, Graham 347

Hamilton, William 40
Hampstead 6, 55, 101-2
Harrison, Benjamin 55, 79
Hawais, Mary 302, 309, 317, 321,
    325
Heathfield House 171, 182
Heaver, Alfred 136, 145, 146, 153,
    168, 214
    Edward 136

Heaver estate 113
Helensburgh 190, 198, 203
Hendrick Avenue 214, 221-2, 254-6,
    268, 308, 311
Herne Hill 14, 65, 87, 326
Hewer, William 28, 55
Higgs, William 189, 197-8, 221
High Trees House 130, 182, 191, 204
Hildeburna 27
Hillier Road 168, 171, **172**, 248,
    253-6, 284, 309
Hoare, Henry 27, 47, 95
    William 66
Hoares Bank 53
Holly Grove 100
Hollywood 55, 188
Holmside Road 174, 258, 357
Holy Trinity, Clapham parish 4, 23,
    121
    'Detached parish' 25, 55
    Church 11, 27, 34-6, 41, 42, 80,
    357, 375
Holy Trinity Brompton 156
Honeywell Road 145, 167, 241, 248,
    253-6, **300**, 357
Honeywell School 162, 167, 396
Hoper, Elizabeth 124, 139, 181
    housing finance 238, 341-2
    solicitors' role 239-41, 264-5
    housing tenure 12, 89-91, 378-80
Hucknall, Uriah 291, 351
Hughes, Henry 192, 194, 195
    William 183
Hunt, F W 158, 225
Hyde Farm 56, 74, 113

Ingram, Thomas 168, 169, 171, 213-
    6, 218-9, 220
Inland Revenue property tax 16, 278,
    332, 337
Irish in neighbourhood 361-2, 375,
    377, 391, 400
    iron church 135, 154, **223**, **224**

Jennings, George 187, 189, 190-1, 199-201, 206, 209, 306

Johnson, Patricia Hansford 244, 252, 348, 376

Keildon Road 168

Kelmscott Road 170, 241, 242, 248, 260

Kentish Town 5, 6

Kettle, David 146, 214, 216, 264, 267, 271-4, 295, 307-9

Kings Avenue 72, **73**

Knowles, James senior 74

Knowles, James junior 94-95, 96, 98

Kyrle Road 167, 169, 171, 253-6

Lambert, Charles 167, 181

Lambeth Borough Council 25, 85, 372, 373

Lavender Hill 27, 58, 76, 94, 97, 149, 151, 236, 287, 388

Leaf , William 185-6
        Walter 186

Leanach Lodge 54

Leathwaite Road 168, 399

Lindore Road 142-3

Local government 11, 25, 83-85, 339, 383

Logan, Roger 119, 124, 128

London Bridge 93, 195

London County Council (LCC)   83, 115, 172, 221, 335, 336, 361

Lord, James 124, 139, 177

Louvaine Road 373-4

Lovelace, Robert 178

Lubbock, Sir John 40

Mabel Road 142

Macaulay, Thomas 97, 106, 347

Macaulay, Zachary 42, 79, 97, 363

Magdalen Park 338

Maisonette 122, 172

Mallinson Road 127, 135, 159, 168, 241, 252, 253

Manchuria Road 171

Mansfield, Sir James 181

Martin, Thomas 37

Methodists 159

Metropolitan Board of Works 84, 124, 129, 131, 153, 192, 209, 216, 262-3

Middleton Road 131, 132, 136, 142

Milne, Thomas 57

Milner, Isaac 43

Mitterand, Francois 358

Montholme Road 168, 170

More, Hannah 43, 44, 49

Morella, Count of 181

Morella Road 181, 214, 254-6, 286, 346

Mud Lane 167

Muncaster Road 174, 248

Muthesius, Hermann 12-13, 310 et seq
         Stefan 5, 296-7, 300, 308

Nappy Valley 385, 394

National Freehold Land Society   90, 107, 124, 125, 133, 135, 211

Newmarch, William 195-7, 262

New Wandsworth 3, 18, 87, 88, 134, 135, 140, 217, 331, 400

Nightingale Lane 24, 25, 26, 55, 69, 79, 88, 112, 116, 130, 140, 170, 172, 174, 182, 187-205, **204, 205**, 214,221, 252, 280, 284, 293, 297,306, 357, 370, 375, 399

Nightingale Park Crescent 219, 399

Nightingale Pub **188**, 189

Nightingale Square 159,222

Nine Elms 78, 86, 87, 88

Northcote Road 129, 130, 135, 140, 143, 144, 159, 168, 170, 207, 219, 239, 242, 246, 253, 344, 377, 389, 390, 396, 399

Northcote Road market 253, 376, 383, 400

Northern Line 104-5, 116, 164-5, 343-4, 357, 376, 376

Oak Lodge 190, 201

Old Park 18, 19, 26, 55, 133, 181-7, **184**, **196**, 261, 267, 297
mound 186, **272**, 275

Old Park estate 18, 19, 26, 55, 133, 158, 177-198, 229, 245, 253, 261-317, 399

Old Park Avenue **2**, 3, 17-18, 21-2, 26, 146, 216, 230, 239, **268**, **271**, **279**, 300, 349-55, 391-6,
financing 240, 274-9, 295, 359, 272-298, 370, 382

Omnibuses, horse drawn 86, 88, 92, 93, 94, 102, **113**

Palmer, William 213, 216, 263-5, 271, 279, 291

Panton, Jane 106, 281-3, 302, 322, 325, 330

Pavement, The 70, 109

Peddie, Marjorie 209-211

Pelling Road 31

Pepys, Samuel 27, 28, 30

Pilditch, John 58, 162, 217, 244, 274

Pitt, Wiliam 40, 124

Playle, Abel 248

Plough Inn 58

Poles in neighbourhood 198, 362, 375, 391, 401

Potter, Frank 231-2, 292, 311-5, 317, 350, 355

Potter, Stephen 20, 148, 231, 283, 284, 285, 292, 311-5, 318, 326, 330

Praga, Mrs Alfred 282, 302

Priory, The 80, 111

Queen Anne's Bounty 178, 218, 275-7, 290, 332, 349, 355, 358, 382, 392

Queen Anne style 19, 211, 213, 221, 303-7, 317

Railways 83, 86, 88, 344-5, 371
London, Brighton and South Coast 78, 87
London, Chatham and Dover 87, 88, 93, 99
London South Western 86-87
West End of London, Crystal Palace 87, 140

Ramsden Road 101, 112, 174192, 194, 197, 226, 221, 262, 279, 286

Rectory Grove 35
refuse disposal 174-175

Robson E.R. 209-13, **210**, 216, 304-5

Rodenhurst Road 74, 355

Rolfe, Alexander 132

Roman Catholics 96, 97, 159, 222

Roseneath Road 174, 349

Roy Road 214, 219

Rusham Road 192, 197, 202, 254, 297, 357

St John, Walter 28, 31
Henry 31-2, 55, 120

St John's Hill 58, 124, 140, 149, 236, 345, 373

St John's Road 151, 236, 253, 348

St Luke's Church 132, 148, 158, 160, 167, 174, 216, 222-232, **226**, **227**, 261, 266, 270, 283, 285, 290, 331, 350, 381

St Mark's Church 131, 135, 154, **155**, 156, 157 168, 217, 223, 348

St Mark's School 154, **155**, 161

St Mary's, Battersea parish 23, 26, 84, 121, 130, 148, 154, 158, 275, 327
church 26, 36, 40, 75, 153, 225, 229, 230

St Michael's Church 156, 161, 168

Saker, Robert 267-271, 274, 278, 291-3, 307, 308

Salcott Road 135, 144, 146, 168, 241, 253, 256, 268, 357

Sellers, Peter 10, 375, 390
semi-detached houses 9, 298
covenants 267-8
servants door **145**

Sharp, Granville 42

Shelgate Road 127, 135, 136, 147, 168

Sherbrooke Lodge 195, 197, 202

Shore, John (Lord Teignmouth) 42, 66

Shrubbery, The **150**, 151, 152, 153

Simeon, Charles 43

Simpson, Henry 213, 216, 263-4
Jane 195, 261
Thomas 195, 273

Sisters, The 54

Skeldon Road 130

Smith, Sydney 42, 44
William 43

Southwark Bridge 92

Spartali, Michael 152
Marie 152

Spencer, Earl 32, 36, 45, 140-141, 148, 178

Spring well 50, **51**

Spurgeon, Charles 11, 189-190, 197, 198-9, 203
stage coaches 29, 50, 92, 93

Stephen, James 37, 42, 66

Stephen, Sir James 42

Stockwell 86, 104, 267, 392

Stonell Road **127**

Streatham 4, 23, 25, 80, 84, 85, 188, 189, 370
suburbs 6, 8, 91, 110

Sudbrooke Road 174, 192, 217, 221, 356

Sumburgh Road 171, 248, 349

sunflowers 304, 306, **307**

Swaby Road 130, 159

Synagogue 159

Teignmouth, Lord 42, 66

terracotta 199, 209, 304, 306

Tewson, Edward 194, 273

Thackeray W M 43, 67

Thomas, Edmund 145, 257-8
Helen 257-8

Thom, Colin 5, 336

Thompson, Edward 261-5

Thornton family 29, 48, 121, 177, 258,
Henry 9, 11, 29, 31, 39, 40-45, 49, 53, 66, 79, 121, 153

Henry Sykes 66
John (elder) 29, 33, 34, 37-9, 40-42, 45, 66

John (son of Samuel) 187
Marianne 40, 245
Percy 153, 244, 346
Robert (father of John) 29, 37

Robert (son of John) 39

Samuel 39, 56, 187

Thornton Road 72

Thurleigh Avenue 171, 174, 195, 220, 357

Thurleigh Road 14, 26, 167, 170, 171, 174, 192, 214, 220, 225, 241, 242, 253-6, 261, 268, 273, 280, 284, 295, 309, 355, 357

Tindall, Gillian 5, 6, 369

Tithe Map (1836) 16, 122, 178, **179**, 182, 192

Todd, Christopher 130, 131, 140

Tooting 85, 112, 115, 119, 336, 345

Totterdown Estate **115**, 338

Trams 86, 88, 93, 116, **113, 115**, 235

Twixt the Commons **2**, 3, 4, 16, 20, 24, 25, 27, 119, **123**, 169, 219, 300, 377, 385, 400

Venn, Rev Henry 33, 41, 43

Venn, Rev John 41, 43

Verdon, Rev Henry 130, 168

Wakehurst Road 144, **145**, 146, 163, 168, 174, 214, 241, 357

Wallis, Thomas 189

Wandsworth Borough Council 25, 156, 204, 220, 230, 280, 310, 367, 373

Wandsworth Common   3, 14, 18, 24, 55, 133, 140-141, 146, 178, 190, 203, 252, 258, 304, 365
North side 27

Wandsworth Common Station 87, 217

Wandsworth District board of Works 84-5, 124, 129,130, 131, 147, 189

Wandsworth Road 27

Waterloo Bridge 92, 139

Webbs family 143, 168, 185

Webbs Lane 146, 151, 168, 259

Webbs Road 143, 146, 147, 162, 167, 168, 399

Welch, Joseph 192, 194, 195

Wesley, John 56

Westerdale Road 192

Western Lane 188

Western Lodge 54

Westminster Bridge 32, 93

Wheeler, Henry 122,130, 133, 143, 144,163, 169

White, William 156, 158, 226

Wilberforce William 11, 29, 40-44, 49, 53, 66, 79, 106, 167, 172, 182
Bishop Samuel 148

Wilderness, The 37, 95

William Deacons Bank 66

Willis, William 37, 180
Henry 121-2

Willis Percival bank 37, 180

Wimperis, Thomas 211-3

Winchelsea Road 192

Winder, Reuben 216, 263-5, 271-3, 279, 291

Winfrith Road 241

Winsham Grove 171, 222, 248

Wisley road 174, 248

Wix Lane 25

Wodehouse P G 345

Wolff, George 56

women, role of 49-50

Wood, John D 145, 292

Worth, Adam 150

Wraxall, Sir Horatio 137

Wroughton Road 167,168, 169, 171, 172, 220, 253-6, 284, 309